Wakefield Press

NELLIE MELBA – THE LEGEND LIVES

Richard Davis is an internationally acclaimed writer specialising in biographies. *Melba – The Legend Lives* is the latest in a series devoted to the lives of famous Australian musicians. Previous titles include *Close to the Flame: The Life of Stuart Challender*, *Wotan's Daughter: The Life of Marjorie Lawrence*, and *A Star on her Door: The Life and Career of June Bronhill* published by Wakefield Press, and biographies of pianists Geoffrey Parsons and Eileen Joyce. These have enjoyed international critical success and earned Richard the Joan Sutherland and Richard Bonynge Award for the Arts. Richard is also the author of some lighter books including the popular *Great Australian Ghost Stories*. He also teaches creative writing.

Nellie Melba
The Legend Lives

A biography

With a foreword by Nicole Car and
a discography of Nellie Melba's recordings

RICHARD DAVIS

Wakefield Press
16 Rose Street
Mile End
South Australia 5031
www.wakefieldpress.com.au

First published 2025

Copyright © Richard Davis, 2025

All rights reserved. This book is copyright. Apart from any fair dealing for the purposes of private study, research, criticism or review, as permitted under the Copyright Act, no part may be reproduced without written permission. Enquiries should be addressed to the publisher.

Every effort has been made to identify and acknowledge the photographers of the images reproduced in this book. The publisher would appreciate advice where efforts have been unsuccessful and appropriate acknowledgement will appear in any subsequent editions.

Cover design by Stacey Zass
Edited by Penelope Curtin
Typeset by Michael Deves

ISBN 978 1 92304 213 1

A catalogue record for this book is available from the National Library of Australia

Wakefield Press thanks Coriole Vineyards for continued support

Contents

Foreword by Nicole Car — ix

Introduction — 1

Chapter 1	Nellie Mitchell	5
Chapter 2	Mrs Armstrong	24
Chapter 3	One voice in ten thousand	40
Chapter 4	Pomp and mixed circumstances	56
Chapter 5	Madame Melba	74
Chapter 6	Covent Garden	89
Chapter 7	Le cœur cède à l'amour	107
Chapter 8	The storm breaks	122
Chapter 9	Italy and America	140
Chapter 10	Rivals, old and new	155
Chapter 11	The lure of Wagner	173
Chapter 12	Campaigns	190
Chapter 13	Home, sweet home?	207
Chapter 14	The voice preserved	224
Chapter 15	Oscar and Goliath	239
Chapter 16	Sentimental journeys	252
Chapter 17	Promises	268
Chapter 18	The empress of pickpockets	283
Chapter 19	Old world, new order	297

Chapter 20	Music for the people	308
Chapter 21	Tempus fugit	321
Chapter 22	Evening star	334
Notes		353
Chronology of Melba's life and career		397
Appendix 1	Melba's repertoire	402
Appendix 2	Melba's recordings	409
Bibliography		432
Index		437

'The first rule in opera is the first rule in life:
see to everything yourself.'

Nellie Melba

Foreword

Dame Nellie Melba is often credited with putting Australia 'on the map'. She was certainly in the vanguard of the musicians, artists and writers who first demonstrated that Australians could make worthwhile contributions to European culture. She was also the first Australian whose name became a household word around the world and certain of her personality traits (good and bad) contributed to the world's view of Australia and Australians. Her fame was based on phenomenal success in the rarefied world of grand opera, achieved through a beautiful voice, the encouragement of many notable composers, determination and constant hard work.

The tradition that Australia is a wellspring of great voices also began with Melba, and perhaps her greatest legacy was the role model she provided for other Australians who followed her. In future years, and inspired by Melba, literally hundreds of singers left Australia to attempt to build careers in the great opera houses and concert halls of the world – and a remarkable number succeeded.

That tradition continues to this day and I am proud to be a part of it. I'm also proud to have had the opportunity to sing roles that Melba sang, sometimes in the opera houses in which she sang them more than a century before me.

When one is engaged for performances of opera, one is concerned with the demands of the moment, but perhaps a brief reflection on the achievements of our predecessors might offer that extra impetus to excel.

Thank you, Nellie. 'Brava!'

Nicole Car

Introduction

If sopranos were rated by the number of books written about them, then the Greek-American Maria Callas would assume first place, with no fewer than 29 volumes published and, probably, more to come. At second and third would be two Australians, both Dames of the British Empire: Nellie Melba and Joan Sutherland, all three women apparently of inexhaustible interest to the musically inclined reading public.

Fourteen books have been previously written about Melba: 12 for adults and two for children, along with two stage plays, a Hollywood film, a television documentary and a television miniseries. The first book, simply titled *Melba*, was written by the journalist Agnes Murphy, who was working as Melba's secretary at the time the book was written. It might well be classified as an autobiography, for what Murphy recorded (including an extraordinary amount of namedropping of the rich and famous) came directly from her employer. *Melba* was published in London in 1909 when the singer's career was at its peak. Sixteen years later Melba's official autobiography was released and became an overnight bestseller. For this, Melba employed the services of another accomplished journalist, the novelist, personal friend and confidante, Beverley Nichols. Nichols ghost-wrote *Melodies and Memories*, receiving, as Murphy had before him, information directly from his subject. By the time *Melodies and Memories* was written, however, Melba's career was almost over, which allowed her a little more freedom in what she revealed to Nichols. These two books then became the principal sources for the others that followed after Melba's death, most of which will be found listed in the bibliography on page 437.

Four of these later studies are of outstanding merit, with each written by an Australian. In 1967 the Melbourne journalist John Hetherington produced the first modern biography of Melba. Widely read, it provided many Australian readers with their first exposure to the life of, arguably, the most famous of all Australian women. In 1986 Thérèse Radic produced a more comprehensive biography, which set Melba's life in the context of her times. A decade later, Melba's granddaughter, Pamela Vestey, produced *Melba – A Family Memoir*, in which many personal letters and family photographs were published for the first time, and in 2008 Anne Blainey produced the entertaining *I am Melba*.

The focus of each of these eminently readable books is Melba's fascinating *life* rather than her art, and this is the justification for the present volume. As well as recounting the singer's life, my intention has been to provide more detail about Melba's voice, singing style and the musical milieu in which her career was conducted. It is my hope that this book will also persuade readers to explore Melba's legacy of recordings and that they will, like me, find endless delight in the sounds she bequeathed to us more than a century ago.

I acknowledge my indebtedness to all the previous chroniclers of Melba's life for providing information to me through their writing.

Recounting the life and career of someone as famous as Melba presents a unique set of circumstances. While biographers are often faced with a paucity of material about their subjects, in Melba's case there is a glut, due partially to the status of opera in the nineteenth century when Melba was building her career. Opera was then the ultimate form of public entertainment and attending the opera was *de rigueur* for fashionable society in most of the world's capitals. The art form's popularity also extended to provincial cities and towns and, in Australia, to remote communities, where touring opera companies met the demand.

Introduction

Opera stars like Melba and others mentioned in this book were, as a consequence, the superstars of their day, leading to a degree of interest in them, matched today only by pop stars and movie stars. Newspapers and journals reported on every detail of their lives and their careers, with the public's hunger for news of their singing idols insatiable. The amount of words devoted to Melba in the press during her lifetime is impossible to calculate, but hardly a day went by without her name appearing in several newspapers around the globe.

Inevitably, such a large body of printed material (including some of the aforementioned books) is replete with misinformation and supposition, repeated until it achieved the ring of truth. I have attempted to separate the truth and the facts from the misinformation and the supposition by referring to primary and contemporary sources where they are available. If I have inadvertently reproduced any 'fake news', I apologise and assure the reader that it has not been due to a lack of effort.

Before deciding on whether to embark on this book – considering the number of words already devoted to Melba by others – I set myself the task of determining whether more could and should be said about her. To my surprise, this assignment highlighted events in Melba's life and career and aspects of her art that had been overlooked by other writers. It is my hope, therefore, that this volume will fill in some gaps in the narrative of Melba's life and add to the historical 'portrait' of this remarkable and fascinating Australian.

Readers will see from the endnotes that I have edited many of the quotes used in the text. Most were written more than a century ago, meaning that their writing style is often convoluted and obtuse, especially when translation from languages other than English has been necessary. I have edited where necessary to make them easier to read and their meaning clearer.

I acknowledge with sincere gratitude the following individuals and organisations without whose help this book would not have been possible: Nicole Car, for contributing the splendid foreword; Patrick Togher; John Woods; Bibliothèque musée de l'Opéra and the Archives Nationales de France; Library of Congress (Washington); Metropolitan Opera Archives; National Library of Australia; Mitchell Library (Sydney); State Library of Victoria; Gold Coast City Council Libraries; and the Lilydale Historical Society. I am also indebted to Michael Bollen and his team at Wakefield Press, all of whom brought their expert skills to the production of this book.

Finally I wish to thank you, the reader, for choosing this book. Chronicling Melba's story was an exciting and enjoyable journey for me and I hope you experience the same enjoyment as you follow that journey through these pages.

Richard Davis 2023

Chapter 1
Nellie Mitchell

In her autobiography, *Melodies and Memories*, Dame Nellie Melba wrote, 'If you wish to understand me at all you must understand first and foremost that I am an Australian'.[1] It is almost possible to hear Dame Nellie speaking those words proudly and in a voice that brooked no argument. An Australian, Melba most certainly was: born and growing up in Melbourne, commencing her singing career in the eastern mainland states of Australia and returning whenever an opportunity arose once her career in Europe and America had been established. Melba also exemplified many of the characteristics attributed to Australians: common sense, bluntness in speech, distrust of pretentiousness, contempt for authority and a streak of larrikinism.

It should be noted, however, that the blood that coursed through Melba's veins was one hundred per cent Scottish. Her parents, grandparents, aunts and uncles all hailed from Forfarshire, a maritime and agricultural county now known as Angus, on the east coast of Scotland. Commingling with those 'Aussie' characteristics were several more inherited from her Scottish forebears: stubborn determination, industriousness, Presbyterian ethics and a healthy respect for money.

In *Melodies and Memories*, Melba would also write, 'Throughout my life there has always been one man who meant more than all others, one man for whose praise I thirsted, whose character I have tried to copy – my father.[2] That her father meant more to Melba than *all* other men might be challenged in the light of the events in her life, but the relationship between father and daughter was very close and Melba believed that, of her father's four daughters who grew to adulthood, she was his favourite.

David Mitchell was born on 16 February 1829, the third child of William and Anne Mitchell, tenant farmers of North Meathie in central Forfarshire.[3] The Mitchells were poor but not impoverished and their 40-acre (16-hectare) farm supported them comfortably until the family grew in number. Seven more children followed David, and by the time he reached the age of 17 the need for him to find an occupation away from the farm and to support himself had become imperative.

A fit young man with broad shoulders and strong hands, David Mitchell secured a four-year indenture to a master stonemason in Kirriemuir, a town about 16 kilometres from North Meathie. The work was hard and the wage he received was not generous, but the knowledge and skills gained would set him up for his future career as a building contractor. During the winter months, when work was restricted by bleak weather, David returned home but used his time profitably by trekking north to the town of Forfar, where he took classes in mathematics, technical drawing and construction. He was not, sadly, at home in the spring of 1849 when his father died suddenly at the age of 57.[4]

On completing his indenture, David sought work across Forfarshire, but times were hard and work scarce. This was the era of the potato famines and the Highland clearances that forced desperate families from the north to seek new lives in cities like Dundee, Forfarshire's industrial capital. Many decided that their only prospect for a better life was to emigrate to the Americas or the Antipodes – and that was the course David Mitchell chose.[5]

In March 1852 Mitchell made the decision to seek his fortune in Australia, a place where he believed his skills would be in demand. To finance his trip, David used money earned from an assortment of odd jobs, including drainage work on farms around North Meathie.

Melba later told the improbable story of her grandmother giving her father a parting gift of a purse containing 200 gold sovereigns. The equivalent in today's money would be about 35,000 Australian dollars and it is unlikely that Anne Mitchell had ever owned such an amount, but by the time Melba was spreading the story David Mitchell was no longer alive to contradict it. Farewells were said and David departed, never to see his mother again.

Ships travelling to Australia left from the English port of Liverpool almost daily. Booking a passage on the vessel *Anna*, Mitchell departed on 6 April for Melbourne, via the Cape of Good Hope. There were about 200 passengers on board, including 73 in the cheapest class ('steerage'), where David bunked down with mostly other young men, most of whom were heading for the 'diggings' in Victoria and New South Wales, where gold rush fever was at its height. David kept his savings in an improvised money belt during the day and slept on it at night.

The average time for the journey from England to Australia under sail was 15 weeks. Apart from usual dangers of travel by sea, the greatest threat to passengers was tedium, although for those on the *Anna* the frequent clashes between the officers and the crew kept them entertained. When the ship reached Adelaide, those who the press later called 'the mutineers' demanded to be put ashore to lay a complaint against the ship's captain. He responded by shackling 21 of them in irons.

With the help of several passengers (including Mitchell), the ship finally got underway, but at around midnight it was hit by a violent storm. The captain appealed to the imprisoned crew members to return to their duties. They agreed and were released, but a fight immediately broke out, the released prisoners battling the officers and those passengers who were assisting on deck. Order was eventually restored. Thoroughly drenched and nursing a few bruises after the mêlée, Mitchell discovered his physical state was the least of his worries: his savings were missing. All he had left (Melba claimed) was the single sovereign he had carried in his pocket.

While the story of the sovereigns and the theft may be apocryphal – invented by Melba to enhance her father's status as a hero – the events that overtook the *Anna* were not. The whole saga was reported in the Australian press, although no mention appears in the press reports of a theft suffered by one of the passengers. When Mitchell was safely ashore in Melbourne, he affixed his name (along with other passengers) to a letter to the editor of the *Argus*, praising the actions of the captain – an unexpected gesture from someone who had suffered a great loss and whose property had not been recovered on board the captain's ship.[6]

The city to which Mitchell arrived was just 17 years old, and a further 23 years would pass before it was famously dubbed 'Marvellous Melbourne'. The gold rush had resulted in an increase in the population, although the building boom financed by the gold had not yet begun. The streets of Melbourne were unpaved, and shanties and rickety wooden structures stood where later the elegant stone buildings that were to be the envy of other British colonies would rise. Mitchell could not have arrived at a better time. He would, by hard work and clever speculation, become one of the creators of 'Marvellous Melbourne'.

Mitchell had no difficulty finding work as a stonemason and had soon saved enough to buy a large plot of cheap land at Richmond, on the eastern outskirts of Melbourne. The land was located at the northern end of Burnley Street and stretched 500 metres down to the banks of the Yarra River.[7] Here Mitchell built his own shanty (later replaced by a mansion), with that address remaining his for the following 63 years.

With the Richmond property as his headquarters, Mitchell established his own building company, and one of his first contracts was the construction of a building on the goldfields in Bendigo. Here he recruited a team of labourers but before the job had been completed, the client declared himself bankrupt. No doubt Mitchell lost money over this venture, which may explain his decision to try his own luck on the goldfields. The erstwhile builder bought himself some mining tools and a one-pound, one-month miner's licence, but the work was backbreaking, the climate harsh and the rewards meagre. Mitchell's health quickly deteriorated and he decided mining was not for him.

Back at Richmond, Mitchell threw himself with renewed determination into developing his business. His reputation as a canny but honest and industrious builder, whose work was of the highest standard, who never failed to meet deadlines and who expected full value for the fair wages he paid, earned him a great deal of work and he prospered rapidly.

The 'old' Scots' Presbyterian Church in Collins Street was the spiritual and social hub of the large Scottish community in Melbourne. Mitchell was warmly welcomed there by, among others, James Foot Dow and his wife Jean, who also hailed from Forfarshire. James Dow had learned the engineering trade in the factories of Dundee and, when Mitchell made his acquaintance, he was manager of the machinery plant at Langland's Iron Foundry in Flinders Street, which produced castings for buildings and decorative wrought iron.

The Dows had five daughters: Isabella, Margaret, Helen, Alice and Elizabeth. The eldest, Isabella Ann, aged 19 when Mitchell met the family, was a cheerful, gentle girl with a long face and dark features, inherited, the family claimed, from a survivor of the Spanish Armada, who had washed up on the shores of Forfarshire three centuries earlier, adding an exotic strain to the family's Celtic blood. Isabella was an accomplished amateur painter and musician, playing the piano, harp and organ. Isabella's talents, combined with her personality and her physical attributes, attracted Mitchell and a courtship began. Music may well have been an interest the young couple had in common. In possession of a resonant bass voice, Mitchell had taught himself to play the violin and the harmonium.[8] No doubt the Dow family were as pleased with their daughter's choice – as David Mitchell was with his.

In 1856 Mitchell secured two major building contracts: to provide the masonry work for the rebuilding of St Patrick's Roman Catholic Cathedral in Eastern Hill and to build Melbourne's first luxury hotel, the Menzies on the corner of Bourke and William streets.[9] With the money these contracts earned him, Mitchell decided to do two things: marry Isabella and build a fine new home on his Richmond property for his bride.

On 11 June 1857[10] Isabella and David were married in the old Scots' Church and within months they were able to move into their new home: a two-storey, bow-fronted, stucco-on-brick building, with 14 rooms, along with servants' quarters and surmounted by a squat tower. If not in the same league as the great mansions that would grace Melbourne in later years, it was still impressive and a testament to David Mitchell's growing wealth and his building skills. The Mitchells chose the name 'Doonside' for their home, derived most likely from the picturesque Doonside Castle in Ayrshire.

Most of what remained of the Richmond property was used to accommodate a sprawling factory, where building bricks were formed by steam presses and baked in a giant wood-fired kiln. Melba would later recall her father saying, 'A growing city needs bricks and why should I not make those bricks?'[11] This new venture greatly increased Mitchell's income and his power in the building industry, although the noise and steam, along with the smoke pouring from the chimneys of the workers' cottages that lined Burnley Street, must have made the landscape around his home anything but idyllic.

At Doonside on 28 March 1858, Isabella gave birth to the couple's first child, a daughter, but sadly little Margaret Walker Mitchell died four days before her first birthday. A son, William James (named after his paternal grandfather), arrived on 29 July the following year, but he too died exactly one month before his first birthday. No doubt, when Isabella became pregnant again, both parents must have felt trepidation about the future of their next born.

The nineteenth of May in 1861 – a mild and serene autumn day – would prove to be an auspicious occasion in Australian musical history. As Melbournians were sitting down to their Sunday lunches, Isabella Mitchell gave birth to the future Dame Nellie Melba in the master bedroom at Doonside.[12] The names Helen and Porter were chosen for the baby, the first name probably in honour of one of her mother's sisters. The choice of the unusual middle name is a mystery, 'Porter' being a peculiarly English name applied to both males and females. 'Helen Porter' immediately became 'Nellie' and the future prima donna was happy and proud to use that name privately and professionally for the rest of her life.[13]

The local impresario William Saurin Lyster had launched his first opera season in the Theatre Royal in Bourke Street 26 days earlier, heralding what has been called 'the golden age of opera' in colonial Australia. The opera presented was Donizetti's *Lucia di Lammermoor*, with the American soprano Lucy Escott in the title role. That might be considered prophetic, for the luckless Lucia was the role Nellie sang at her Covent Garden debut 27 years later, and throughout the world for the 20 years that followed.[14]

Little Nellie was robust in body and mind, and she flourished, to the great relief of her parents. Over the next 18 years, Isabella would produce another seven children, all but one born at Doonside. There were four more daughters: Anne Fraser ('Annie'), born in 1863; Isabella Ann ('Belle'), born three years later; Dora Elizabeth Octavia, born in 1873;[15] and Vere, born in 1877, and three sons: Francis David ('Frank'), born in 1869; Charles James ('Charlie'), who arrived two years after his brother; and William Henry Ernest ('Ernie'), born in 1875.

As if the large number of siblings wasn't enough for Nellie, she would get to know and become attached to at least two of her Mitchell uncles (Andrew and William), who had followed her father to Melbourne and who then worked for him. She also came to know the entire Dow family, including her grandparents. Her large extended family provided Nellie with a stable and loving domestic environment in which to grow up and to pursue her interest in music – which was evident at an early age.

By the time she had reached the age of three or four, Nellie was in the habit of sitting under the piano in the parlour at Doonside when her mother was playing. Isabella Mitchell began teaching her daughter the rudiments of music, but that role was soon taken over by Isabella's sister Alice, who was passionately fond of her niece. Aunt Alice taught Nellie musical theory, piano and singing, making her the future diva's first singing teacher.

Melba also told her first biographer, Agnes Murphy, that she often sat on her father's knee while he amused himself at the family's harmonium on a Sunday afternoon: 'He would blow the bellows and sing a bass accompaniment to a hymn which I picked out on the keyboard with one finger'. Melba also told Murphy how at the age of about eight she felt impelled one night (long after the household had retired) to go downstairs to the parlour piano and play the opening of Beethoven's 'Moonlight' sonata. When David Mitchell went to investigate, the sight of his daughter in her white nightgown engrossed in her playing touched him deeply. Instead of chastising her for waking the house, he swept Nellie up in his arms and carried her back to her bed.[16]

Alice Dow and another of Nellie's unmarried aunts, Lizzie, took responsibility for their niece's general education until Nellie commenced school, allowing Nellie's mother to devote her time to caring for her younger children. Both aunts remained dear to Nellie until their deaths, and she was happy to acknowledge the contribution they had made to her development.

When Nellie was aged six, her aunts organised a small evening concert in aid of the local Presbyterian Sunday school. Held in a hall in Richmond, the concert provided Nellie with the opportunity to make her public debut as a juvenile singer,[17] with the young debutante preparing the popular song 'Shells of the ocean' by

John Cherry, and – in the hope of being asked for an encore – the traditional Scottish song 'Comin' thro the rye', one of her three favourite songs at the time, the words of which her grandmother Dow taught her to pronounce with the right Scottish accent.[18]

The concert was a great success and Nellie was the acknowledged star. She sang both of her songs sitting on a high stool, receiving encouraging applause for each. In a state of high excitement, Nellie was unable to sleep after being put to bed and next morning she rushed to the house of a girl friend who lived further down Burnley Street and who had attended the concert. To Nellie's frustration, her friend said nothing about the previous night until Nellie lost patience and demanded: 'But what about the concert?' Nellie then received one of the most disconcerting critiques of her entire career: 'Nellie Mitchell, I could see your drawers!'[19]

In October and December of the following year Nellie had two more opportunities to display her precocious musical talents. In October, after a concert in the Richmond Lecture Hall to raise money to build a Presbyterian church in what was then the growing suburb of Richmond, she received her first press notice. The local newspaper reported: 'Miss Mitchell both sang and played the piano and is a perfect little wonder'.[20] In December she took part in the first concert held in the original Richmond Town Hall, also to raise money for the church building fund. To an appreciative audience of 600, Nellie sang the sea shanty 'Can't you dance the polka?', the slightly ribald words no doubt sanitised for the occasion, and the second of her favourite songs, Samuel Lover's ballad 'Barney O'Hea'.[21] The local newspaper again trumpeted Nellie's success and made a prescient prediction: 'The incomparable Miss Mitchell will make crowded houses wherever she is announced'.[22]

Nellie's piano playing would respond in later years to professional tuition (as would her singing), but the organ was the first instrument for which she took professional lessons, beginning at the age of 11. This may have been prompted by the contract her father won in the same year to build a new Scots' Church on the site of the previous building and the prospect of the second largest pipe organ in Australia at the time being installed in its interior.[23]

Nellie's first organ teacher was Joseph Summers, organist at St Peter's Anglican Church at Eastern Hill, where she presented herself every Tuesday and Friday for a one-hour lesson. Thomas Harbottle Guenett took over the lessons when Nellie enrolled at her first school[24] and he in turn was replaced by Otto Vogt, a former pupil of Summers and organist at St Mark's Anglican Church in Fitzroy.

Each of these professional organists contributed to Nellie's growing skill and her ambition at the time to become a church or civic organist. David Mitchell encouraged his daughter to follow this path, playing the organ in the service of God being a more acceptable occupation than being a concert pianist or, doing the unthinkable and becoming a singer on the stage. That encouragement took practical form when the new Scots' Church organ was installed and Mitchell arranged for Nellie to be allowed to practise on it. Mitchell also offered to buy Nellie a gold watch if she could learn 12 new organ pieces in 12 days. The sharp mind and good memory that would serve Nellie her entire life ensured that she succeeded and the prize was duly won. Unfortunately, a few weeks later Nellie lost the watch in a Melbourne Street. It was found by a policeman, who was able to identify the owner by an inscription on the case and returned it to Doonside – dial shattered, movement smashed and case crushed. Half a century later Nellie could still recall: 'I shall never forget the look of disapproval on Daddy's face when he saw the ruins of the watch in my hand. "You will never get another from me", he said. And I never did, but I keep the old watch to this day in one of the drawers reserved for happy memories.'[25] Nellie would eventually become a sufficiently competent organist to occasionally play for services at Scots' Church and, on 10 November 1877, to play in the Melbourne Town Hall during a concert to raise funds for famine relief in India.

While studying the organ, Nellie also resumed piano lessons, this time with Julius Buddee, one of Melbourne's fashionable teachers, whose fame rested on his having once been the accompanist of the legendary soprano Jenny Lind. Nellie's musical education was well in hand, but the need for her to have equivalent skills in non-musical subjects became urgent as she approached her teenage years. Her parents decided to send her to Leigh House Ladies College, a boarding school in Bridge Road, Richmond. Why a boarding school only a few blocks from Doonside was chosen is unclear: perhaps the school did not accept day pupils or, more likely, David and Isabella Mitchell believed the discipline of a boarding school would benefit their irrepressible daughter.

It certainly didn't suit Nellie, who resisted being sent to Leigh House, got into trouble with the school's staff and complained about having to remain there. Melba later described the regimen at Leigh House as spartan and recalled how she overcame the discomfort of cold showers at 6 am daily by taking an umbrella into the shower until she caused a flood and was punished.

Probably the only bright spots in Nellie's time at Leigh House were the weekly lessons Guenett gave her on the school's harmonium. Murphy describes Nellie's miserable state the rest of the time:

> From the upstairs windows of the school she could see the tower of Doonside. This intensified her grief and for hours at a time she would stand at the window screaming piteously to be taken home. When Mr Mitchell heard of this, he made a point of passing Leigh House whenever he went in or out of the city, so that she might be consoled by seeing him. But the sight of her father only made matters worse and when she espied him in a buggy or on top of an omnibus she cried even more.[26]

The Mitchells finally relented and Nellie was withdrawn from Leigh House just a few months after she had arrived. Throughout her life Melba was adroit at getting exactly what she wanted, a strategy that began at an early age. It was also symptomatic of the strong personality she was developing.

From this time onwards and until she grew to adulthood, numerous anecdotes about Nellie's behaviour accumulated – some true and some not – the choicest of which throw light on her character. It is also significant that the words 'Come on. Let's have some fun!' were those that young Nellie's contemporaries recalled hearing most often from her.

Nellie Mitchell's character displayed a strong tomboy element, if not through her appearance or manner, then certainly through her actions. From an early age she dismissed dolls and other feminine toys as trivial and unworthy of a girl who was going to make her mark on the world.

Nellie also preferred the company of boys, with Otto Vogt claiming that his pupil (who terrified him, he said) would dash off after her lessons in Fitzroy to swim naked in the Yarra with boys. One of those boys, the story goes, kept a lookout in case David Mitchell appeared, warning her: 'Look out, Nellie, your old man's coming!' in time for Nellie to bolt for home. In support of this story, one of Nellie's swimming companions can be identified. This was Billy Neilson, who would go on to have a modest career as a tenor in Australia. Unfortunately, the future Mr William Neilson never let on about what actually happened on the banks of the Yarra. That Nellie should have swum with boys is consistent with her character, but that she should have done so naked seems highly unlikely, even for a girl with abundant self-esteem and confidence.[27]

In an effort to encourage her older children to appreciate good music, Isabella Mitchell sometimes took them to concerts and even the occasional theatrical performance – carefully avoiding any event where the program was questionable or the performers tainted by scandal. Prime examples of the latter would have been the concerts given by the celebrated Croatian soprano Ilma di Murska in Melbourne in 1875. Di Murska had sung many of the operatic roles Nellie would later sing and Nellie might have benefited from hearing her, but the singer's bohemian lifestyle disqualified her from Isabella's list of suitable attractions. At the opposite end of the scale was the English pianist Arabella Goddard, a fine musician and a pillar of respectability, whose concerts the family did attend. Nellie was on her best behaviour in the Melbourne Town Hall for Goddard's performances and expressed her admiration for the pianist in whispers, but on other occasions when she disapproved of what she saw or heard, Nellie would cause embarrassment by criticising them in a loud voice.

Not all of Nellie's escapades occurred away from home, one instance being a visit from her uncles William and John to play whist with her father. Nellie surreptitiously crawled under the table with a set of bellows from the fireplace, and placed the nozzle of the bellows up a leg of one uncle's trousers, pumping as hard as she could. The mayhem that followed can be imagined, but, as both uncles were devoted to her, it is doubtful whether Nellie received more than a mild rebuke. On another occasion, when a pair of nuns were collecting for charity in Burnley Street, Nellie cobbled together a make-believe nun's costume and beat them to Doonside's front door. When a servant answered her ring, Nellie asked for an audience with the master of the house. David Mitchell appeared and was taken in by the disguise, giving the 'nun' a sovereign.

As David Mitchell's building empire grew, he turned his attention to other potentially profitable fields: cattle and sheep farming, quarrying and winemaking. To pursue these new interests he bought several parcels of rural land across Victoria. The closest to Melbourne were two dairy farms and cattle-breeding properties in the Yarra Valley, one at Steele's Flat and the other at Dalry, and both were close to Coldstream, where Melba would one day build her retirement home. William Mitchell was put in charge of both properties and the Steele's Flat farm became the Mitchells' regular retreat during holidays. The idyllic surroundings appealed to Nellie and also offered a stage for further escapades.

On the last leg of the journey from Melbourne in a wagonette, Nellie would always insist on sitting up front with the driver, loudly commenting on the beauty of the landscape and scaring her younger siblings by pretending to spot snakes. Once there, Nellie would spend her time riding and fishing, sometimes in the company of the men who worked on the property. The farm workers liked Nellie and she liked them. It has been suggested that these companions (or even the youthful swimmers in the Yarra in Melbourne) were responsible for the colourful language she had learned and used unashamedly throughout her adult life.[28] The freedom of country life appealed to Nellie and it's not hard to imagine her being downcast each time she had to return to the social order of Melbourne.[29]

Anecdotes such as these about her behaviour as a child and later as an adult, continued to surface throughout Melba's life. She gave credibility to some by repeating them in interviews and in her writings, and none was ever denied. If questioned about a particular incident, Melba would say, 'They say what they say. Let them say.' The obvious explanation for this policy of Melba's lies in the adage 'any publicity is good publicity'. It has been noted by other writers that when she began her career in the United States the image of a free-spirited daughter of pioneers was more acceptable to Americans than that of an 'English' rose.

In the year that David Mitchell completed the new Scots' Church, he also built the impressive Presbyterian Ladies College in Albert Street, East Melbourne.[30] Opening in February 1875, the school soon gained a reputation as a progressive institution. In October of that year David and Isabella Mitchell enrolled Nellie and her sister Annie as day students at what is still universally called 'PLC'. No doubt their hope was that the school would convert Nellie from 'a free-spirited daughter of pioneers' into more of a 'rose', albeit a *Scottish* rather than an English one.[31]

The headmaster at PLC, Professor Charles Henry Pearson, was an enlightened educator, and the curriculum he set was based on what male students at England's great public schools were being taught, a radical move at the time, when the education of females was considered to be of secondary importance. Pearson also encouraged the study of music as something more than a social accomplishment. Although Nellie did not do well in scientific subjects, she excelled in English, drawing and painting. In later years several of Nellie's teachers at PLC came forward to share their recollections of their former (and by then famous) student, with the consensus of opinion being that she had been occasionally rebellious and mischievous, but hardworking and diligent in her studies. Several also commented on Nellie's habit of constantly whistling or humming, which they had found annoying but admitted may have contributed to her development as a singer.[32]

Although she would soon direct all her efforts into learning to sing, when Nellie entered PLC she was still intent on becoming an organist, but a shift of focus onto the piano coincided with the arrival of a new member of the faculty in 1878. Alice Charbonnet was an American-born Frenchwoman, just three years older than Nellie but already established as a concert pianist and budding composer. The two young women got on well and for a time the Frenchwomen inspired Nellie to follow in her footsteps. Whatever refinements as a pianist Melba retained after she became a singer should be credited to Charbonnet.[33]

Nellie also received her first professional singing lessons at PLC. These were provided by a Canadian contralto, Mary Ellen Christian, who had a successful career in England before ill health drove her to seek a warmer climate in Australia.[34] Mary Ellen Christian had studied in London with Manuel Garcia the younger, who was arguably the most successful voice teacher of the mid-nineteenth century and she remained a disciple of the 'Garcia Method' of singing all her life. That Nellie was taught the Garcia method from the start of her serious singing studies is significant, for when she later studied in Paris with her most famous teacher, Mathilde Marchesi, it was the same method Marchesi advocated. Just what Melba gained from Mary Ellen Christian's teaching is hard to quantify or qualify. In later years Melba dismissed her first professional singing teacher's efforts as 'not a matter for serious attention'.[35] Christian herself was more forthcoming. In an interview when she was almost 80, she revealed:

> I had Nellie Mitchell under my care for about two years at which time her youthful voice boasted a sweetness in the lower register that resembled the lower tones of a violin. As Melba she lost that peculiar timbre under the training necessary to acquire the top notes characteristic of the coloratura repertoire.[36]

In 1880 Nellie left the Presbyterian Ladies College and her studies with Christian ceased.[37] It appears she continued her piano lessons with Charbonnet privately, for she was always proud to relate how in March the following year she appeared at a soirée given by Charbonnet's students at Melbourne's Government House. According to Nellie, the Marchioness of Normanby, wife of the governor, took her aside after the soirée and told her: 'Child, you play brilliantly, but you sing better. Some day you will give up the piano for singing, and then you will become famous.'[38] One suspects that Nellie had already reached that conclusion before she played and sang at Government House, for she had begun taking singing lessons from Pietro Cecchi, a retired Italian operatic tenor, who taught from his home in Drummond Street, Fitzroy.

The influence Cecchi and his teaching had on the development of the future Melba has been the subject of passionate debate over the years, prompted initially by Melba dismissing his influence, just as she would that of Mary Ellen Christian. There can be no doubt however that in the six years Cecchi taught her, the Italian laid the foundations of Melba's singing technique, and the refinement and style that was added later was absent only because of Cecchi's limitations. Early biographers of Melba dismissed Cecchi as a colonial charlatan but his musical credentials were sound. He was born in Rome in 1825 and aspired to be a singer at an early age, but his father insisted he also pursue a more practical career as a draughtsman. In that capacity he became a citizen of the Papal States and worked in the service of Pope Pius IX. He had also studied singing with the composer Pietro Romani, also the teacher of Guiditta Pasta, Giovanni Mario and William Saurin Lyster's prima donna, Lucy Escott. Cecchi made his debut in Rome, subsequently singing principal tenor roles in opera in Milan, Naples and Turin. His later association with Garibaldi and the Italian nationalist movement fighting against French and Austrian occupation and against Papal rule made him *persona non grata* at the Vatican. Cecchi was forced to leave Italy but continued his career and was engaged by the American soprano Agatha States for the small opera company she brought to Australia in 1871.

Reviews of Cecchi's singing in Australia were not glowing and suggest his voice was in decline. Perhaps for that reason, he decided to settle in Melbourne and to return to his old profession as a draughtsman. For a while he worked for Reed & Barnes and was given responsibility for drawing the elevations for the classical portico that was added to the front of the Melbourne Public Library. He continued to appear occasionally in opera or in concerts but from 1875 he concentrated on teaching.

Christian had focused her efforts on the mid-range of Nellie's voice, believing her to be a mezzo-soprano, but Cecchi immediately recognised her potential as a higher-voiced soprano. Cecchi envisaged his student one day singing the great coloratura soprano roles of Donizetti, Bellini, Rossini and Verdi on stage and for these she would need what is called a 'bel canto' technique, the sound produced smoothly on the breath over an extended vocal range and with an armoury of technical devices to be utilised for effect.[39]

Cecchi set about training his student to achieve the great future he envisaged for her and, no doubt, Nellie embraced her new teacher's exciting plans, although it is unlikely that David Mitchell shared their enthusiasm. Preparations for Nellie to have a career as a professional opera singer were probably not revealed at Doonside for some time and non-musical matters were dominating the Mitchell family's life.

In 1878, David Mitchell had purchased Cave Hill Farm at Lilydale, located on a vast limestone deposit, and immediately began quarrying the stone and using it to manufacture cement. The enterprise itself was most unattractive, with Nellie herself describing the gaping chasm it created in the pleasant green landscape as 'mess, muck and money'.[40] Not having to rely on others to supply his concrete strengthened Mitchell's grasp on the building trade and when the civic authorities decided the city should show off its transformation to 'Marvellous Melbourne' by hosting an international trade exhibition in a purpose-built building, he was one of the first to be asked to serve on the organising committee. The site chosen for what would be named the Royal Exhibition Building was a plot of land in the Carlton Gardens on the northern edge of the CBD. Reed & Barnes designed the monumental structure and Mitchell secured the contract to build it.[41] Mitchell was among the VIP guests at the grand opening ceremony on 1 October 1880 and Nellie partnered him, for by then Isabella Mitchell was terminally ill.

In 1877, at the age of 44 Isabella had given birth to the couple's last child. An impressive list of names was given to the little girl – Victoria Florence Maude Vere – but she was always known by her last name. Soon after Vere's birth, Isabella contracted chronic hepatitis, with recurring bouts of the illness robbing her of her strength. By the time of the opening of the Royal Exhibition Building, Isabella had withdrawn from society and a year later, on 21 October 1881, she died at Doonside.[42] Hours before her death, Isabella Mitchell had summoned her children, one by one, to her bedside and charged each of them with a task to perform after her death. Nellie's task was to be a mother to three-year-old Vere.

Following the end of the first phase of mourning, Nellie resumed her lessons with Cecchi and did not abandon her dream of becoming a singer, but she did assume the management of her father's house for a time and had Vere's cot moved into her own bedroom as part of her promise to her mother. On 19 January the following year, Vere developed a sore throat and a fever. Nellie built up the fire in their room and watched over her little sister through the night. Nellie later claimed that the spirit of her mother appeared to her while she dozed and made a sweeping gesture towards Vere's cot and then disappeared. Next morning the child's fever had intensified and Nellie asked her father's permission to summon a doctor. David Mitchell considered the request to be an over-reaction and said that he would see how the child was when he returned from his day's business. At around four that afternoon, little Vere's throat became so swollen that she could not breathe and she died in Nellie's arms.

Chapter 2

Mrs Armstrong

Deep sorrow once again consumed the Mitchell household and none would have felt it more than Nellie, who bore the added burden of believing that she had failed in her promise to her mother. As the months passed and the despondency that he and his eldest daughter were feeling showed no sign of abating, David Mitchell decided that a change of scenery and some new faces would benefit him and Nellie. Typically, however, Mitchell decided to combine business with recuperation.

A few days after Nellie's twenty-first birthday in May, the press announced the formation of a syndicate called the Queensland Central Sugar Factory Company, along with plans to build a sugar mill at Marian, 24 kilometres west of Mackay on the central Queensland coast.[1] Mitchell tendered to build the mill and by the end of July the contract was his. The prospect of accompanying her father to Queensland and experiencing the exotic tropical north of Australia must have heartened Nellie, even if it meant missing lessons with Signor Cecchi. The prospect of making a substantial profit did the same for her father.

On 12 August David Mitchell and Nellie embarked from Port Melbourne on the first leg of their 2800-kilometre journey to Mackay.[2] Two changes of ship (in Sydney and Brisbane) brought them to Flat Top Island, near the mouth of the Pioneer River. Here a small craft transferred them to shore and they had their first glimpse of the burgeoning town that was then called Port Mackay.

Travelling on the same ship from Brisbane was George Smith,

a member of the syndicate. Smith, his wife Jane and his daughter Leila made the Mitchells welcome in Mackay and Smith introduced Mitchell to Alexander McKenzie, the engineer responsible for establishing the processing plant in the new mill. When Mitchell and McKenzie travelled to Marian to commence work, Nellie stayed on in Mackay as a guest of the Smiths.

At that time Mackay had a population of about 2000 'Europeans', with an equal number living in the surrounding area, along with a displaced Indigenous population, which was never counted. It was typical of many towns in coastal Queensland: profiting from the booming sugar industry and sourcing labour for the cane fields from islands in the Pacific by blackbirding. If Nellie or her father had any opinions about this human trade, they never expressed them. Mitchell was fully occupied sourcing materials and recruiting workers in Marian while Nellie was busy impressing the local society, proudly introduced into their midst by Jane and Leila Smith, both of whom were keen amateur musicians.

The ladies of Mackay were thrilled when Nellie offered to accompany a local amateur soprano at the piano during an afternoon tea party – cannily keeping her own vocal accomplishments in reserve for another, more public, occasion, which was not long in coming.

On 15 September, Nellie wrote to Cecchi:

My dear Signor Cecchi,

I suppose you will be astonished to hear from me, but I want to tell you that although I am nearly 2,000 miles from Melbourne I am not forgetting my practising, for I manage to get a little every day. I am going to sing at two concerts, one on Monday and the other on Saturday. I hope I shall be successful.

Will you please send me six or seven nice *English* songs up, as the people here do not understand Italian. I daresay you will be able to find some pretty ones, send them as soon as possible.

> I shall not be home for two or three months yet. I intend taking a long holiday, as I am enjoying myself so well. I go out either riding, driving or yachting every day. Will you kindly remember me to Mr Nobili, also to Mr Bracchi if he is in Town. Hoping you are well.
> Believe me, your affectionate pupil,
> Nellie Mitchell[3]

The first of the two concerts Nellie referred to was held in the Mackay School of Arts on 18 September and the second in the Mackay Presbyterian Church a week later, both in aid of charities. The distinction therefore goes to Mackay as the place where Nellie sang in public for the first time as an adult, although what she sang was hardly representative of her future repertoire: three popular songs of the day with little to commend them other than providing a vehicle to display Nellie's voice and its superiority to the regular fare at Mackay concerts.

After the first concert the local newspaper reported that the whole audience listened intently to 'the well-trained voice of the fair songstress' and after the second it commented: 'Miss Mitchell fully maintained the excellent impression she had made on the previous occasion. Her vocalisation was perfect and artistic.'[4]

While little store can be placed in the musical judgement of these local critics, their words indicate that, within a month of her arrival, Nellie had catapulted herself to the top of the town's small cultural coterie. After the second concert Nellie wrote proudly to Cecchi:

> I had great *success* at the two concerts I sang at, so much so that all the ladies up here are jealous of me. I was encored *twice* for each song, and they hurrahed me and threw me no end of bouquets. Everyone asks me who my master is, and when I say Signor Cecchi, they all say 'When I go to Melbourne he shall be my master too'.[5]

Competition was about to arrive, however, but in the end it only served to consolidate Nellie's position. A small touring opera company, grandiloquently styled 'The Royal English

Opera Company', arrived in Mackay in October and gave single performances of seven different popular operas, all sung in English. The singers were third-rate, the pianist who provided the accompaniment was barely competent, and the costumes and sets were tawdry. One can imagine Nellie sitting in the audience with her new friends and knowing that, given the opportunity, she could have outsung any of the females then strutting on the stage of the School of Arts.

Nellie may well have persuaded her father to accompany her to one of these performances for David Mitchell was back in Mackay temporarily to appear at a sitting of the Queensland Land Court. Always on the lookout for any opportunity to add to his wealth, Mitchell applied for and was granted two large parcels of land at Plane Creek, where the town of Sarina now stands, 1280 acres (518 hectares) in his name and a like amount in Nellie's. That land would eventually become a bone of contention between Nellie and the man she would soon marry and to whom she was introduced in Mackay shortly after the grants were made.

Just how Nellie and Charles Armstrong ('Kangaroo Charlie' to his mates) met is unclear, although it was probably at a social function in the home of one of her new friends. From the time of his arrival in Mackay, the 24-year-old, tall and handsome son of an Irish baronet, with his bright-blue eyes and gift of the blarney, had become popular in Mackay. He had also become the target of many marriageable-age girls and their ambitious mothers. No doubt Nellie was attracted to Charlie Armstrong when they first met and probably thought she had found a kindred spirit when she learned about his adventurous life to that time.

Charles Nesbitt Frederick Armstrong was the son of Sir Andrew Armstrong, of Gallen Priory, Kings County, Ireland.[6] His father was 73 at the time of Charlie's birth and already had five other sons and seven daughters, so the prospect of Charlie ever succeeding to the baronetcy or benefiting from his father's estate was extremely remote. Showing the independent spirit that would mark him throughout his life, Charlie set out at the age of 15 to make his own way in the world, first taking up an apprenticeship as a seaman, but discovering that life at sea was not to his liking. On returning to Ireland, he drifted about, unable to find an occupation that suited him and earning a few pounds in prizes as an amateur boxer.

A year after Charlie's birth his father had died and his eldest brother succeeded to the title. Charlie either chose (or was instructed by his eldest brother) to travel to Australia and work for John Alexander Bell, whose wife Frances was one of his sisters. Bell owned several pastoral properties in Queensland and work was found for Charlie as a jackaroo.[7] His skill as a boxer and his horsemanship earned him the respect of other employees on Bell's properties, but his pugnacious character led to a physical altercation with one of Bell's managers and Charlie's dismissal. Charlie headed for Sydney, where he refined his boxing skills at the bareknuckle champion Larry Foley's boxing school and earned income as a horse dealer. Droving a herd of horses to Queensland had brought Charlie to Mackay some months before Nellie and he had stayed on.[8]

No doubt Charlie Armstrong was also attracted to Nellie. Photos of her taken at this time show a shapely young woman with attractive features and (for the camera at least) a rather serious mien. Her apparel reflects her father's wealth and the superior style of Melbourne couturiers, but the sex appeal that would be revealed in photographs taken in Europe a few years later is concealed by modest necklines, curly hair and an absence of make-up.

Compared with many of the other young women Armstrong encountered, Nellie shone with vitality – and with the glitter of her father's money. He also probably admired Nellie's wild spirit, believing that if a relationship between them developed, he would be able to restrain and mould it to his will, as he had done with so many mares. Time would prove that belief to be horribly misguided.

As the weeks passed, a romance developed between Nellie and

Charlie, based, one must assume, largely on physical attraction and the similarities in their personalities, for the couple had very little else in common. Charlie's interest in music, by way of example of their differences, began and ended with roistering music hall songs and the catchy tunes of Gilbert and Sullivan.

Nellie continued to appear in concerts in Mackay, the undisputed star among local musicians, demonstrating her skills as a pianist and as a singer. Occasionally she sang duets with Amy Davidson, the wife of the leader of the local sugar industry, and among her solos were two songs that would remain in her repertoire for as long as she remained in Australia: 'The Angel at the Window' by Frank Tours and Paolo Tosti's 'Bid me good-bye'.[9] No doubt Charlie escorted Nellie to these concerts and sat in the audience, clapping dutifully after each piece, but secretly determining that her desire for such public displays would have to be curbed if they married.

Charlie proposed to Nellie, but before accepting Nellie went to her father. David Mitchel liked Armstrong but was initially opposed to their marriage on the grounds that the couple had known one another for such a short time. By the end of November Nellie had secured her father's consent, probably because Mitchell had convinced himself that marriage was the way to put an end to his daughter's ambition to become an opera singer, an ambition finally revealed to him before they left Melbourne. That was another understanding that time would prove wrong.

As work on the Marian mill no longer required Mitchell's presence, it was decided that he, Nellie and Charlie would travel to Melbourne, stopping along the way in Brisbane for the marriage to take place. Annie Mitchell was given time to travel up from Melbourne to be her sister's maid-of-honour. Just why it was decided to hold the wedding in Brisbane rather than in Scots' Church in Melbourne has always puzzled chroniclers of Melba's life. The official reason given was that the Mitchells were still in mourning for Isabella and that a society wedding in Melbourne would have been inappropriate. In fact, the first anniversary of Isabella Mitchell's death had passed while Mitchell and Nellie were in Mackay and, as one year was considered the appropriate time for a family to emerge from mourning, that explanation does not carry much weight. The most likely explanation was simply impatience on Nellie's part.

The wedding took place on a hot Monday afternoon, 22 December, not in a church but in the study of the manse next door to St Anne's Presbyterian Church, abutting King George Square. The ceremony was conducted by the minister of St Anne's, Reverend Charles Ogg. A Brisbane solicitor named Arthur Feez, whom Charlie had met on the steamer transporting them from Mackay, was best man. David Mitchell, Feez and Reverend Ogg's daughter, Margaret, acted as witnesses. Margaret Ogg took note of Nellie's wedding dress and later described it to the press as 'a close-fitting, white dress buttoned to the waist with large pearl buttons and a bonnet tied under the chin with a large bow'.[10]

After Nellie had become famous, Feez was persuaded to describe his part in the proceedings, hinting that he had not warmed to Nellie when they first met. Feez also claimed that Charlie had come to him the night before the wedding, distraught, and claiming that he had discovered that Nellie had a lover in Melbourne. Feez recalled that he had convinced Charlie to go ahead with the wedding because the rumour was probably exaggerated and because of the social disgrace that would be attached to Nellie if it was called off.[11] Time would prove that it might have been better for all parties if the ceremony *had* been called off.

Nellie and Charlie honeymooned in Brisbane for a week and then the party set out for Melbourne, Nellie no doubt impatient again, this time to show off her new, handsome and aristocratic husband to all her Melbourne friends.

Charlie spent the first few weeks of 1883 at Doonside with Nellie and the rest of the Mitchell family. As he had no income, he tried unsuccessfully to drum up some business for himself in his old trade of horse dealing and was away from Melbourne for days at a time. In her husband's absence Nellie resumed her lessons with Cecchi. David Mitchell also tried unsuccessfully to find permanent employment for his new son-in-law. He could, of course, have employed Charlie at one of his own enterprises but chose not to, probably believing that Nellie's husband should stand on his own feet.

Nellie was still receiving an allowance from her father and Charlie demanded that she hand it straight over to him. Laws had recently been enacted allowing wives to own money of their own, but the tradition that a husband had a right to everything his wife owned was still widely observed. Nellie's refusal caused one of the many arguments between the couple that resounded through Doonside long into the night and which, Melba later claimed, resulted in her frustrated husband striking her.[12]

Within weeks of their marriage, both Nellie and Charlie must have begun to realise the error they had made. Nellie was not prepared to abandon her ambitions or to become an obedient and submissive wife, who stayed at home cooking her husband's meals, washing his clothes and bearing his children. And as those were the expectations Charlie had of her and he was not prepared to compromise, conflict was inevitable. It is easy to take Nellie's side in the situation, but it should be remembered that in the Victorian era, the law, society and tradition had rules for marriage very different from those that apply today, and a wife was effectively her husband's property, to deal with as he saw fit.

An eventful year would pass before Nellie and Charlie would separate for the first time, and the only thing that seems to have bound them together during those turbulent weeks at Doonside was their continuing physical attraction for one another. What was probably 'making up' after an argument resulted in Nellie conceiving a child.

When the sugar mill at Marian was almost completed, the syndicate advertised for a manager and Charlie applied. Although he had only scant knowledge of the sugar industry and none of managing a complex business with a sizable workforce, his popularity in Mackay (and possibly some influence from David Mitchell) secured him the position. He departed for Mackay in early March, leaving strict instructions for Nellie to follow as soon as an outbreak of dysentery in the Mackay region had subsided. Charlie made a lengthy stopover in Sydney en route to Queensland and Nellie was instructed by letter to join him there. The reason for the stopover was unclear but when Nellie arrived in Sydney she found her husband was not there. Two more weeks passed before Charlie showed up and they were able to proceed to Mackay.

In the meantime Nellie made the most of her imposed stay in the New South Wales capital and wrote to Cecchi:

My dear Signor Cecchi,

I might have stayed a week or two longer in dear old Melbourne, for when I arrived here I found that my husband could not meet me for some time, and I have been quite miserable here, just thinking how many lessons I have missed. I start for Port Mackay and I expect to arrive there on Monday week, so I shall soon be in the tropical regions again. I met a German gentleman here that you know. His name is Mr Ampt. He thought a great deal of my singing, as indeed everyone does, for they all call me the 'Australian Nightingale'. I have had four musical parties given me since I have been in Sydney. I was asked to sing at a concert, but of course I had not time; I have promised to sing for them next time I am here.

The Italian opera season commences here tonight. I hope they will have more success here than they had in Melbourne. I intend going to hear them on Monday night. I wish Alice Rees were going to sing, for I would like to hear her very much. I shall now stop, hoping to hear from you soon.

Believe me, always your affectionate pupil,
Nellie Armstrong[13]

When Charlie finally turned up at the end of April, he and Nellie embarked for Mackay, via Brisbane, where they visited Arthur Feez. 'They seemed happy enough', Feez later reported.[14] Nellie was sick on the final leg of the journey, probably suffering from morning sickness, compounded by the motion of the ship.

The manager's house being built next to the mill at Marian was not finished when Nellie and Charlie arrived in Mackay, so they lodged in a Mackay boarding house until the work was completed. Nellie wrote again to Cecchi from their temporary lodgings.

> My dear Signor Cecchi,
>
> I am once more in Mackay and 2000 miles away from dear Melbourne and all my dear friends there. I arrived here last Tuesday week after a most dreadful trip, for I was seasick the whole way. It has been raining in torrents ever since I have been here. I have just come in nicely for the end of the wet season, and it is really most dreary and miserable. We are not in our own house yet. We do not expect to get into it for six weeks. The Montague-Turner Company are expected to arrive here in a week or two. I sincerely hope they will do well, for they have been very unfortunate lately. How is my sister [Annie] getting along with her singing? I hope she goes regularly and practises well. Will you kindly send me up the low copy of a song called 'Ehren on the Rhine'? I hope to be able to get down to Melbourne early next year, so it will not be so very long before I see you all again. I shall now stop as there is no news to tell you, except that my voice is in very good order, and I practise every day. My husband wishes to be kindly remembered to you. Hoping you are quite well.
>
> Believe me, your affect. pupil,
> Nellie Armstrong[15]

If Nellie was approached to sing or play the piano at any concerts in Mackay during these weeks (or in the months that followed), she declined, either at the behest of her husband or so as not to displease him. She did, however, insist on practising her singing in private each day.

There were other pleasures to be enjoyed, one of which almost ended in disaster. One morning Charlie took Nellie and Leila Smith out in a small sailing boat but unfortunately they got into difficulties as they crossed the bar at the mouth of the Pioneer River. A squall struck the small craft and it capsized, throwing the three occupants into the sea, although they managed to cling to the overturned hull until help arrived. The lookout at the port's pilot station had witnessed the accident and sent a vessel to the rescue. Years later Melba told Agnes Murphy that such was the heat and the monotony of her life at the time that she almost welcomed the accident as a break in the dull routine, but, as she was about four months pregnant when the accident happened, it must have seemed anything but welcome at the time.[16]

Nellie celebrated her twenty-second birthday with friends in Mackay and a month later she and Charlie moved into their new house at Marian. That house still stands, but in a different location and is now a Melba museum. It was a typical, medium-sized, single-storey 'Queenslander', built of timber on raised stumps (to allow air to flow beneath the floor) and roofed in corrugated iron. Wide verandahs on three sides protected it from the heat, while doors in every room provided access to the verandahs. Melba's claim that it was constantly hot and airless may be attributable to her having grown up in cool, temperate Melbourne.

The house was originally located directly beside the Marian sugar mill, backing onto the Pioneer River, where it would have been subjected to dust, smoke, steam and the overpowering smell of molasses. Melba later described the house (and other writers accepted her description) as being surrounded by oppressive jungle, but contemporary photographs show it fenced off from rough land, which had been cleared during the construction of both the mill and the house. The thick tropical bushland that Melba described as 'jungle' began, however, not far beyond the house's yard.

What Melba did not exaggerate in her recollections of Marian was the humidity and the rain, which arrived with the next wet season. In *Melodies and Memories* she wrote:

> Soon after we arrived in that desolate lonely place, with no other company than that of birds and reptiles, it began to rain; and rain in Queensland is rain indeed. It rained for six weeks. My piano, which had been sent up from Melbourne, was mildewed, my clothes were damp, the furniture fell to pieces, spiders, ticks and other obnoxious insects penetrated into the house, to say nothing of snakes, which had a habit of appearing underneath one's bed at the most inopportune moments. It rained and rained, a perpetual tattoo on the roof and as the days passed by, and the weeks, I felt I should go mad unless I escaped. My only recreation was to sit on the verandah and to watch the luxurious tropical vegetation, burdened with water. Sometimes I would try to bathe, but as I walked, hot and disconsolate, towards the river, I would see green tree snakes hanging from the branches, and even in the water itself there would be leeches that fastened with painful precision to one's hands, arms and legs. Nor did I forget the tales which I had heard of a giant crocodile only a hundred yards upstream.[17]

While this passage sounds like an extract from a novel by Somerset Maugham, there is no reason to doubt its veracity – in all but one detail. Marian was not as lonely as Melba described. Weather and her pregnant state permitting, she could drive (or be driven) in the mill manager's buggy to visit friends. Pre-eminent among these were Amy Davidson and her influential husband John Ewen Davidson, as well as Charles and Winifred Rawson, who owned a grazing property called 'The Hollow' about 10 kilometres upstream from Marian at Mirani.[18]

A major diversion from 'the dull routine' of Nellie's life was provided by the arrival of the Montague-Turner Opera Company, mentioned in Nellie's April letter to Cecchi. Compared with the company that had visited Mackay the previous year, this group, led by soprano Annis Montague and her tenor husband Charles Turner, was superior in all departments. Montague and Turner, both Americans, both had fine voices and established reputations and brought with them a chorus of 12, a small orchestra, and a distinguished musical director, John Albert Delany. Among the other five principals in the company was the 21-year-old soprano Frances Saville, who would go on to have a celebrated career at Covent Garden, the Metropolitan Opera in New York and the Hofoper in Vienna, sometimes in competition with Nellie.

The company offered a season of five nights in the Mackay School of Arts, with a different opera performed each night and season tickets available. Persuaded by Nellie, Charlie bought season tickets for them both. Nellie was enthralled by the opening night performance of Balfe's *The Bohemian Girl* and wrote in an ebullient mood to Cecchi.[19]

> The Montague-Turner Company are up here now. I called on Mrs Turner and like her very much indeed. This afternoon Mr Armstrong and I are going to take them for a drive and show them some of the sugar plantations. They are having very good houses, I am happy to say, and I think will do very good business. They charge six shillings for dress-circle seats, and it is well filled every night, so they ought to be satisfied. I have quite recovered from my small illness, and feel very jolly and happy. My voice, I think, is better than ever, although I am afraid I do not practise as I ought. Mackay is very gay just now. Any amount of dances and balls.
>
> I hope we shall be able to get to Melbourne in January. Of course I shall go on with my singing when we do come. I wrote to Mr Nobili the other day asking him to get me a comic song that my husband is very anxious to get. I hope he didn't think me very rude

for asking him, but I knew he was the most likely person to be able to procure it for me.

We are having the most lovely weather. Very cold mornings and evenings and warm in the middle of the day. Very like spring in Melbourne. We have not had any fires yet. I suppose you have them burning all day long in Melbourne. I have exhausted my small stock of news, so I shall stop.

Believe me, your affect. pupil,
Nellie Armstrong[20]

As the weeks passed, the time for the birth of Nellie's baby drew closer. In the early hours of 16 October Nellie went into labour and Dr Robert McBurney, surgeon-general of the Mackay District Hospital, was summoned to Marian to assist with the birth. A few hours later, Nellie gave birth to a healthy baby boy. The names chosen for him were George and Nesbitt, the latter after his father. No doubt Charlie was delighted to have an heir bearing his illustrious family name, and Nellie happy to be a mother and to have survived the ordeal of childbirth.

A local nurse, a Mrs Manfin, came to live in the house and to care for young George. Charlie took a dislike to Mrs Manfin and to her husband, who shared the nurse's room. Mr Manfin and Charlie came to blows a few weeks after George's birth and nurse and husband departed, leaving Nellie to care for her child alone while suffering, it is believed, a bout of post-natal depression.

The arguments between Nellie and Charlie that had begun in Melbourne had continued since their arrival in Marian, but now became more frequent and more volatile. One topic that was guaranteed to cause disagreement was how little George should be brought up. Nellie wanted him to enjoy a solid education when he reached the right age and to develop an appreciation of the arts and the finer things in life; Charlie wanted to turn his son into a replica of himself.

Nellie claimed that Charlie threw a heavy clock at her during one of these arguments and one afternoon when they were out driving in the buggy, Charlie became annoyed with the horse and took the whip to it. Nellie objected, calling him cruel, so Charlie turned the whip on her, giving her a clip on the cheek which, apparently, left no permanent mark. Nellie claimed that she came to live in fear of her husband's temper, fearing also for the safety of little George. In desperation she took the child and sought refuge with the Rawsons at The Hollow.[21] There Nellie seems to have made the decision that it was time to resume her dream of becoming a singer. From The Hollow she wrote again to Cecchi, carefully avoiding mention of the true situation and reporting concessions on Charlie's part that may or may not have been given.

> My husband is quite agreeable for me to adopt *music* as a profession. I do not mind telling you that times are very bad here, and we are as *poor* as it is possible for anyone to be. We have both come to the conclusion that it is no use letting my voice go to waste up here, for the pianos up here are all so bad it is impossible to sing in tune to them. Not only that, the heat is so intense that I feel my voice is getting weaker every day. So you will understand that I am anxious to leave Queensland as soon as possible. I must make some money. Could you not form a small company and let us go touring through the Colonies, for of course I should like to study for the Opera, but would have to be earning money at the same time. My husband will accompany me, and my baby will be quite big enough to leave in Melbourne with my sisters. Madame Elmblad would join us, I am sure. Do you think we could make money? I shall wait anxiously for a letter from you, for I am very unhappy here. We spoke of August next year; let it be much earlier than that if you can possibly arrange it, for I believe I should be <u>dead</u> by then. Remember, whenever you are ready for me I can come at once, for there is nothing to detain me here now.
>
> Believe me, your affect. pupil,
>
> Nellie Armstrong[22]

Cecchi replied immediately by telegram: 'Come to Melbourne at once', adding a statement about how he would help her and look after her best interests. Nellie showed the telegram to Charlie. His reaction was to shrug and tell his wife that he couldn't give a damn what she did and he would be staying on at the sugar mill until it became clear what the future held for them both. As little George was only three months old, it was agreed that he should stay with his mother at least for the time being.[23]

Nellie took a room in Mackay for herself and George and before departing for Melbourne, took part in a concert at the School of Arts. She first played a piano solo based on Stephen Foster's minstrel song 'Massa's in the cold, cold ground', following which she sang Bishop's 'Lo, here the gentle lark' (with flute obbligato[24]) and, appropriately, Tosti's 'Bid me good-bye'. Four days later, Nellie, baby George and a new nurse embarked from Mackay on the steamship *Wentworth*, bound for Melbourne, via Sydney. Marriage had been an experiment that Nellie believed had failed and the warmth, comfort and support of Doonside beckoned.

Chapter 3

One voice in ten thousand

Nellie's return to her family relieved her of the burden of having to earn immediate money, although when she visited Cecchi she found that his promise to look after her interests had not included organising the touring concert party she had requested. Cecchi advised her to resume her lessons and to wait patiently for an opportunity to sing in a prestigious event in Melbourne.

That opportunity eventuated 11 weeks after Nellie's homecoming. A concert was organised by the Melbourne Liedertafel, to take place in the Melbourne Town Hall on the evening of Saturday 17 May.[1] The concert was a benefit for a local musician, Carl Gottlieb Elsassar, who had suffered a stroke, which had caused paralysis and loss of speech and left his family in dire straits. Cecchi proposed Nellie as a volunteer to sing one item at the concert and David Mitchell likely added his support to the proposal since he did business with members of the society.[2]

Elsasser was a popular figure in the cultural life of Melbourne and 2000 people filled the Melbourne Town Hall that night to pay tribute to him with their purses. Nellie herself contributed one guinea to the fund. The other soloists appearing at the concert were all professionals and included Australia's leading tenor Armes Beaumont (blind as the result of a shooting accident), soprano Fannie Simonsen (prima donna of her own opera company), Nellie's former teacher at PLC, Mary Ellen Christian, and a talented young flautist, John Lemmoné, also making his first appearance. Almost every item on the program had a different conductor, with these including another four of Nellie's former teachers: Joseph Summers, Julius Buddee, Thomas Guenett and Otto Vogt.

Cecchi persuaded Nellie to choose as her offering the great *scena* that ends the first act of Verdi's *La Traviata* ('Ah! fors' è lui ... Follia, follia! ... Sempre libera!'), in which the courtesan Violetta first ponders on whether her depression is due to falling in love with one man, and then dismisses love as folly and swears to remain free and devote herself to pleasure. This is a long solo and offers the singer an opportunity to display her voice in a range of tempos and dynamics, as well as her capacity to sing wide intervals and her trill and scale work, and finishing with a climactic top note, guaranteed, if sung well, to rouse an audience.[3]

On the morning of the concert Nellie woke with a sore throat, a condition she suffered before important performances throughout her career and caused by nerves. And she may well have been nervous on this occasion, for it was the first time she would be singing with an orchestra and the first time since her childhood that she would be singing in Melbourne, where audiences and the critics were more knowledgeable and discerning than those in Mackay. Appearing on the same program with some of the best singers in the country (where direct comparisons could be made) would also have been a challenge.

Nellie dressed carefully in a new gown made of gold satin, white satin slippers and long white evening gloves and carried a small posy of flowers, which she would carry onto the platform. David Mitchell drove Nellie in the family buggy to the town hall and deposited her at the artists' entrance just as the strains of 'God Save the Queen' echoed through the building, marking the arrival of the vice-regal party, comprised of the Acting Governor of Victoria, the Governor of Fiji, their ladies and their entourages.

Half a dozen items were scheduled to be performed before it was Nellie's turn to appear. When the applause for two Italian singers who had sung a duet from Verdi's *Rigoletto* subsided, Nellie took a deep breath and strode out onto the platform. She was greeted by polite applause, following which the conductor of her piece raised his baton and launched the woodwind section of the orchestra into the delicate notes that introduce the first part of the *scena*.

Nerves troubled her for the first few bars and then, rising to the occasion – as she would on so many more watershed moments in her career – Nellie let her voice soar out freely over the vast assembly and, as each vocal challenge arose, she overcame it in masterly style. As the last note died away, the audience rewarded her with thunderous applause. Because the program was long, encores had been banned, but the audience demanded Nellie return to the platform twice to receive their acclamation and to accept several floral tributes, passed up to her.[4]

Every major newspaper in the city reviewed the concert, with most opening their remarks with an enthusiastic assessment of Nellie's performance. When Melba wrote *Melodies and Memories* 40 years later, she chose to quote the most glowing of all these reviews, written by the distinguished critic James Nield in the *Australasian*:

> Mrs Armstrong whom her friends have long known as Nellie Mitchell, had previously confined her performances to private circles, but consented to appear in public last Saturday night in the cause of charity. If therefore her success had been but moderate, she would have merited the warmest recognition, but when it is said that she sings like one picked out of ten thousand the obligations due to her are all the greater. The Elsasser concert will never be forgotten on account of the delightful surprise afforded by Mrs Armstrong's singing, and everybody who heard her will desire to hear her again and everybody who did not hear her is at this moment consumed with regrets at not having been present.[5]

Others also remembered that concert, including John Lemmoné, who wrote in 1946: 'Nellie Melba and I made our debuts together in Melbourne. It was the beginning of a long association and a life-long friendship that lasted until the final curtain on 23 February 1931, when I was at the great diva's bedside when she died.'[6]

Nellie and Lemmoné were contemporaries, he born in Ballarat of a Greek father and an English mother, one month after Nellie. At the time of the Elsasser concert, Lemmoné was described as tallish, olive-skinned, with prominent blue-green eyes and a full-lipped mouth. Melba would later describe him (with a lack of cultural sensitivity) to her friend, the Australian pianist Una Bourne as 'the finest, whitest man I've ever known and I'd trust him with my life'. Nellie always had a penchant for attractive men, but after Lemmoné re-entered her life some years later – and contrary to rumour – they did not become lovers. He would instead become Melba's manager, confidante and principal adviser on her career. His wisdom and loyalty would be rewarded with many generous gifts over the years, culminating in the gift of a brand new Rolls-Royce in the early 1920s.

Nellie's success at the Elsasser benefit concert opened doors for her, and the public's desire to hear more of her, predicted by James Nield, resulted in invitations to appear in other concerts in Melbourne. At the first of these – one of the regular concerts mounted by the Metropolitan Liedertafel, the rival group to the Melbourne Liedertafel – Nellie received a small fee, marking her first 'professional' engagement. Armes Beaumont and Maggie Elmblad were the other soloists and Nellie sang Benedict's variations on 'The Carnival of Venice'. She also sang in a soirée at Allan's music warehouse and at a benefit for the 13-year-old prodigy pianist Ernest Hutcheson, who would go on to have a long and distinguished career in America. At both of these concerts Nellie sang pieces from Donizetti's opera *Lucia di Lammermoor*: the Mad Scene at the first and a duet with Beaumont in the second.

Just as momentum in Nellie's career began to build, she received news that Charlie's pugnacious character had, once more, got him into trouble. After a fist fight with one of the employees at the Marian mill, Charlie had either been sacked or been obliged to resign as mill manager. Compensation had to be paid to the employee, leaving Charlie broke. He had then moved into a cheap room in Wills Hotel in Mackay, but continued to attract trouble. In the billiards room of the hotel, he provoked a fight with a man named Michael Ready, with whom he had 'history', after which, Charlie claimed when appearing before the Mackay Police Court, Ready and some of his mates had set upon him in the street. A request for protection against Ready and his gang was denied by the sitting magistrate and the hearing ended with the public gallery erupting into laughter.

Just why Nellie decided to travel to Mackay (with little George and a maid) upon receiving the news that Charlie was unemployed is unclear. It would be gratifying to speculate that she did so to help her husband, but it's doubtful she felt any obligation to him after the events of recent months. More likely is that she reasoned that, while her husband's fortunes were at low ebb, she might be able to persuade him to become the amenable husband she had always hoped for and someone who would assist in building her career.

Nellie stayed in Mackay for six weeks, not in the same hotel as Charlie but probably with friends. Charlie's appearance in the Police Magistrate's Court took place some time after Nellie had arrived in Mackay and it may well have been, for her, the last straw. She immediately booked her passage back to Melbourne. On the night before she left, 20 October, Nellie agreed to sing at a concert to raise funds for Dr McBurney's hospital and when the concert had finished, she, George and the maid boarded the SS *Fitzroy*, bound for Melbourne, leaving her husband behind in Mackay.

A few days after Nellie's departure, Charlie sold off all his possessions, including the furniture and Nellie's piano from the house in Marian. With the money raised by the auction, he was able to stay on in Mackay for a few more weeks and then headed south to 'parts unknown'. He and Nellie kept in touch through infrequent and often explosive letters, but there is no record of them meeting again until March 1886 – 17 months later.

Nellie resumed her concert appearances in Melbourne, including a farewell concert for Julius Buddee, who was moving to Sydney; a charity concert in the seaside resort of Sorrento (organised by the doyen of Australian theatre, George Coppin, who was developing the resort); and more appearances with both the Melbourne and Metropolitan Liedertafel.[7] She also appeared as a supporting artist to the long-forgotten Italian pianist–composer Eduardo Fittipaldi in concerts in the Western District and in Ballarat. Sitting in the audience for the concert in Ballarat was a young man whose name has sadly been lost – his initials were 'R.M'. So taken was he with Nellie that he travelled to Melbourne and offered her an extravagant fee of 20 pounds to appear as a soloist with the Ballarat Liedertafel, of which he was a member. Her success in Ballarat led to two more engagements there and with the fees she earned in the gold-rich city she bought herself a new concert gown, of cream silk and lace, trimmed with ostrich feathers and amber beads.

Increasingly, Nellie reduced the number of songs she sang in concerts and replaced them with operatic arias, although the prospect of appearing in staged opera remained beyond her reach. While opera was performed regularly in Melbourne, Nellie understood that if she auditioned to join an opera company she would incur the wrath of her father and probably bring her husband storming into town forbidding her to shame them both (and their son) by appearing on the stage.[8]

An offer to be the soprano soloist in a performance of Alfred Plumpton's *Mass in G* at St Francis's Roman Catholic church on the corner of Lonsdale and Elizabeth streets, where Plumpton was director of music and his wife was organist, drew only mild rebuke from David Mitchell about 'singing with Papists'. The performance took place on Whitsunday and Nellie's performance was so well received that she was invited to return three weeks later to perform in Haydn's *Nelson Mass*.⁹ This in turn led to Plumpton offering Nellie the paid position of soprano soloist at his church, where the quality of the solo and choral singing already there had placed St Francis's at the forefront of the city's church music-making.¹⁰

During her time at St Frances's Nellie would also feature as a soloist in Weber's Mass in G, Opus 76, and in Gounod's *Messe Solennelle*. On occasions she was also called upon to sing a solo during the offertory. Her singing of the 'Inflammatus' from Rossini's *Stabat Mater* or Gounod's *Ave Maria* as coins were dropped into collection boxes might have tempted the congregation to applaud, but such displays were forbidden in church.

But not everything was quite so pious. Annie Mitchell was responsible for a story that Nellie was talking to her neighbour in the choir stalls during mass one Sunday and a senior male choir member leant over and chastised her in an angry whisper: 'How would you like to be reprimanded from the pulpit, Mrs Armstrong?' Nellie replied cheekily, 'Yes, *please*.'¹¹

Nellie's position at St Francis's was not formalised with a contract until the following October, which may have been because Nellie had received another offer, one that would keep her absent from Melbourne for a time. George Musgrove (on behalf of the powerful theatrical entrepreneurs Williamson, Garner and Musgrove) offered Nellie an engagement to appear as the leading supporting artist to one of the instrumentalists who had appeared at the Ernest Hutcheson benefit concert and who was about to embark on a major concert tour encompassing Melbourne, Sydney and rural Victoria.

The instrumentalist was the 26-year-old violinist Johann Kruse, on a visit back to his homeland after achieving rapid and phenomenal success in Europe. He currently held the post of leader of the Berlin Philharmonic Orchestra and was assistant to his former teacher, the great violinist Joseph Joachim, at the Berlin Hochschule für Musik. Kruse's father ran a pharmacy in Richmond and Nellie had known the charismatic young violinist since childhood. Nellie leapt at the offer. Not only were the concerts being promoted as high-profile events and the 20 pounds per week fee Musgrove had offered her generous, but there was also the added bonus of spending time with someone she liked and admired.

Kruse had an air of 'the conquering hero', but to Nellie he was friendly, kind and solicitous. Over the weeks that followed, their friendship deepened and Nellie confided in Kruse about her troubled marriage and her own aspirations for conquering the world. A young tenor, Frank Boyle, who was making a name for himself in Gilbert and Sullivan, and an even younger French pianist, Cyril de Valmency, who acted as accompanist, made up the rest of the talented and youthful party.

Their first concert took place in the Melbourne Town Hall on 25 June. Nellie sang her *La Traviata* scena and a duet with Boyle. James Nield reported: 'Mrs Armstrong went quite beyond anything she has hitherto done, and caused quite a tumult of applause. All her remarkable attributes were strikingly illustrated on this occasion and it is not too much to say that Mrs Armstrong shared with Herr Kruse the honours of the evening.'[12]

Another two concerts in Melbourne and two in Bendigo followed, before the party travelled by train to Sydney, with Annie Mitchell joining Nellie for the trip to Sydney. The full houses that had marked their concerts in Melbourne and Bendigo were not repeated in the nine they gave in Sydney's Theatre Royal. The first of these, on 4 July, was Nellie's public debut in that city. The Sydney press (including the *Sydney Morning Herald*) were generous in their praise of her voice and her singing but not, in Nellie's estimation, generous enough. From the Metropolitan Hotel, she wrote to Cecchi:

My dear Signor Cecchi,

Although I have had great success as regards public taste, my critique in the *Sydney Morning Herald*, although not bad, was not good. Mrs Fisher writes for that paper, and as she is a great friend of Alice Rees, I can understand why she is afraid to praise me too much. In one of the evening papers, it was said that I was the best singer that had ever visited Sydney. We have all been run down, even Kruse in two papers yesterday, and we all wish we were back in Melbourne. I cannot think what the people want here. I feel too disgusted to write any more.

Believe me, your affect. pupil,
Nellie Armstrong[13]

The Sydney concerts provided some light moments. One night an over-enthusiastic admirer threw a bouquet to Nellie while she was singing. Hitting de Valmency in the head, it disintegrated, showering the stage with flowers. The audience laughed – as did Nellie, who was forced to abandon the song she was singing.

When not performing, Kruse, Nellie, Annie and de Valmency spent a great deal of time together and the young pianist developed a crush on Nellie's sister. Annie was flattered but told a friend that, while she liked the young man (three years her junior), the notion of a romance with 'a child' did not appeal to her.[14] Nellie also made two new friends in Sydney: Sylvester Arthur Hilliger, the 29-year-old secretary of the German Club, just a few doors from the Metropolitan Hotel, and who preferred to be called Arthur, and Hilliger's friend, Jack Moore. As with Kruse, Nellie felt that Arthur Hilliger was a person in whom she could confide, and both she and Annie continued to write to him after their return to Melbourne.[15] Moore had organised a beach picnic for the concert party at Narrabeen on the Northern Beaches and received a copy of a photograph of Nellie taken in Ballarat earlier in the year, inscribed 'with kindest regards from Nellie Armstrong'.[16]

In mid-July the party returned to Melbourne for two more concerts in the Melbourne Town Hall and one in Ballarat, the last marking the end of the tour. Kruse and Nellie appeared together again in a benefit concert in August before the violinist returned to Berlin. Sadly, for her singing in that concert Nellie received her first bad press notice. The critic of the *Argus* praised her singing extravagantly and compared her favourably to Ilma di Murska.[17] That seems to have riled the critic of *Table Talk*, who dismissed the comparison as ludicrous and accused Nellie of having a tremolo (a wide, fluctuating beat) in her voice, which would, the critic prophesied, ruin her voice if she didn't overcome it.[18] It is doubtful whether Nellie or Cecchi took much notice of that. No critic over the next 40 years would make a similar accusation.

Nellie felt despondent when Kruse departed for Europe and she wrote to an unidentified friend:

> I would give ten years of my life to be able to get to Europe to be able to have a real trial. I feel certain I would have some success. I do not want to boast, dear, but since I have been singing with Kruse I have made a great name for myself. All the papers say that I am the *first* concert singer in Australia and the *Argus* the other day likened me to Di Murska. Kruse thought a great deal of me; he says he never met anyone more musical than I am. He says I ought to have been Home [United Kingdom] four years ago. The more I think of it the more desperate I get, I feel every day I stay here is another day wasted. There is no one that can teach me anything here. Cecchi is very good for Italian music, but after that he is no good.

Later in her letter Nellie reveals that she has been pleading with her father to allow her to go to Europe and to fund the trip: 'I cannot understand my father being so pigheaded, especially as I have had such great success in Melbourne. Oh God, if I only had a few hundred pounds, but I suppose it is not to be.'[19] In fact the circumstances that would fulfil Nellie's desire would soon arise.

At the time when Nellie was contending with snakes and childbirth in Mackay in 1884, the British Government was making the decision to stage an exhibition of industry and culture in London. To be held in 1886, it was modelled on the Great Exhibition of 1851 and with the Prince of Wales (the future King Edward VII) nominally in charge. It was to be called the Indian and Colonial Exhibition and all member nations of the British Empire were invited to exhibit. Over the following months purpose-built exhibition halls were constructed at South Kensington, many in 'Indian' style.[20]

As the creation of the Commonwealth of Australia was still 17 years away, each of the Australian colonies was invited to exhibit independently. The Government of Victoria appointed a group of 'commissioners' under the leadership of politician Joseph Bosisto, a former mayor of Richmond. He may have been responsible for David Mitchell being invited to be a commissioner, given Mitchell's experience with the Melbourne Exhibition of 1880. Mitchell accepted and joined the other Victorian commissioners in choosing the exhibits and arranging their transportation to London. A further aspect of the commissioners' role was to attend the exhibition and remain in London for a few months as advocates of Victoria's potential for trade and foreign investment.

Mitchell's initial plan was to travel to London alone and to install his family at one of his rural properties to ensure they were removed from the temptations of Melbourne during his absence, a plan that triggered a revolt at Doonside. Nellie, Annie and Belle were aged 25, 23 and 20 respectively and, of the younger children, only Ernie had yet to reach teen age. Not unreasonably, most of them objected to the plan. For Nellie it would have meant a cessation of her lessons with Cecchi and a halt to her career.

Succumbing to pressure, Mitchell invited Nellie, Annie, Belle and baby George to accompany him to London, although Annie was no happier with that plan than she had been with the first. She wrote to Arthur Hilliger: 'Father is too Scotty and would be very strict, so after due consideration I think I prefer my liberty at home'.[21] Eventually Annie was persuaded to go. Nellie needed no persuasion. She saw the trip as a stroke of good fortune. She was not so pleased, however, with her father's plan: when they arrived in London, the Mitchell family would present a picture of unity and total respectability, and therefore Nellie was to write to her husband and invite him to join them.

With great reluctance, Nellie obeyed her father. Perhaps as a trade-off, Mitchell agreed to allow Nellie to audition for some of London's leading singing teachers while they were there, and to finance her stay in Europe and her lessons for one year if any of them accepted her as a pupil. What was probably not discussed between daughter and father was what would happen at the end of the year. Mitchell assumed Nellie would return to Australia, but she had a different idea. If she was accepted by a noted teacher and thereafter invited to sing in Europe, returning to Australia would be indefinitely deferred.

In the meantime Nellie continued her concert career in Melbourne, Ballarat and Bendigo, hoping to accumulate enough funds of her own to prolong her stay in Europe. After Johann Kruse had departed, engagements came more sporadically and fees did not come in as regularly as Nellie would have wished. She wrote to Cyril de Valmency, who had remained in Australia, suggesting they collaborate for a concert tour of Tasmania, although this never eventuated. She also wrote to Hilliger to enquire whether he believed more concerts in Sydney might be profitable.

An opportunity for Nellie to sing for the first time in Adelaide presented itself just before Christmas 1885 when Professor Joshua Ives of Adelaide University came to Melbourne to recruit soloists for a performance of Handel's *Messiah*. Professor Ives auditioned Nellie and, to her dismay, rejected her as 'too operatic for oratorio'. For the rest of his long career Ives would joke about his own temerity in rejecting the future Melba. Nellie did get to sing in *Messiah* that Christmas – but in Sydney, not Adelaide. The Sydney Philharmonic Society had been delighted to engage her for their performance of the Handel oratorio and while in Sydney, Nellie sang twice for the Sydney Liedertafel. *Messiah* was performed in the city's Exhibition

Building, with a choir of 230 voices, an orchestra of 55 and organ. The Sydney press did not find Nellie 'too operatic' and her singing was extravagantly praised.[22]

Nellie then travelled to the mid-north coast town of Grafton for a series of concerts organised by the organist who had played in the *Messiah* performance – Charles Heunerbein – but the concerts were so poorly patronised they had to be abandoned. The ship returning the concert party to Sydney hit a sand bank; Nellie was drenched with seawater and thrown against a steel bulkhead. She was so bruised she could not appear in public for two weeks. Similar concerts in Bathurst after Nellie had recovered were no more successful than those held in Grafton.

The only bright spot in this excursion into New South Wales – apart from *Messiah* – was a farewell benefit concert given by Nellie in Sydney before her return to Melbourne. The Governor of New South Wales patronised the concert and Nellie was presented with one of those mementoes of which Victorians were so fond: a gilt medal in the shape of a star suspended from a blue silk ribbon. The money the benefit raised probably pleased Nellie even more.

Back in Melbourne Nellie embarked upon a round of farewell appearances as the time for the Mitchell family's departure for London approached.[23] However, two events – the first true and the other possibly an invention of Nellie's – almost put paid to her accompanying her father.

Nellie recounted the first of these in *Melodies and Memories*:

> One night I went to the theatre with an old friend and his sister. When we came out our carriage for some reason or other was delayed, and so my friend suggested that we three should fill in twenty minutes by going to a little adjoining restaurant for supper. We went; we ate some oysters, and then we departed. It happened that a certain Frenchman, whose wife (I thought) was a friend of mine, was in the restaurant at the same time. He went straight home and he lied to his wife by saying that he had seen me with a

strange man, alone, late at night, in an oyster saloon. She repeated this to my father. I knew nothing of this, but the next morning my father said to me: 'I am very sorry, Nellie, but I have made up my mind not to take you to England.'

Nellie was both distraught and mystified. It was not until sometime later that the Frenchman's wife discovered her husband had lied and explained the situation to David Mitchell. 'A few minutes afterwards my father came to see me. "I'm sorry, lassie", he said. And then he bent down and kissed me. I was to go to England after all.'[24]

The other event involved Pietro Cecchi.

For both Agnes Murphy's account of her life and her own *Melodies and Memories*, ghost-written by Beverley Nichols, Melba gave her version of a disagreement she had with Cecchi as she was preparing to travel to London. The cause, according to Melba, was 80 guineas in unpaid fees for singing lessons. *Melodies and Melodies* contains these graphic passages, in which her Melbourne teacher is depicted as some kind of monster:

> I heard rumours that Signor Cecchi was threatening to seize my trunks if I did not pay his bill before I left. I was overcome with astonishment that Cecchi, who had said that he was teaching me for love, would behave in this manner. It seemed utterly impossible. I went to see him, and I shall never forget his small, dark, swarthy figure and the bright avaricious eyes that examined me coldly as he remarked: 'You owe me eighty guineas. That money must be paid before you leave.' I was in despair. I had given a farewell concert at which the takings had been £67 4s 8d. Most of that had already gone to pay bills. I did not dare ask my Daddy, because he had already paid my passage. Had it not been for a dear old uncle and a friend, I might never have gone to England; but at last I raised the eighty guineas and stuffing them into my purse, I went to Cecchi and threw the money, purse and all, onto his table.

'Here', I said, 'is the money you say I owe you. We had been friends for so many years that I thought you knew me better than you evidently do; for surely you must have known that if I made a success I would repay you tenfold.' He shrugged his shoulders and put the money into his pocket. 'That is not all', I said, 'If I ever do have a success, I shall never mention your name as having been a teacher of mine. I shall never refer to you in any way whatever. So good-bye, Signor Cecchi, and may this gain bring you happiness.'[25]

Melba goes on to say that she never did mention Cecchi's name again and that she believed he died of apoplexy speaking of her and of her ingratitude. On the same pages she dismisses both Cecchi and Mary Ellen Christian as bad teachers, describing how she had to unlearn all they had taught her when she studied under her last teacher, Mathilde Marchesi, in Paris.

There is very little evidence in support of Melba's story. Cecchi may well have had need of the 80 guineas and suspected he would never see any of it after Nellie departed. He would also have been aware of the number of engagements Nellie had fulfilled since returning to live in Melbourne and the fees she had received, estimated at a total of about 700 pounds, despite the lean period following Kruse's departure. The only other tiny piece of evidence that *might* lend credibility to Nellie and Cecchi having some kind of falling-out concerned her farewell concert in the Melbourne Town Hall. Cecchi, although he had not sung in public for years, volunteered to sing the tenor's three lines when Nellie sang the 'Traviata' scena, but withdrew at the last moment. The press was given the standard excuse when singers fail to appear: 'indisposition'.

Even if we concede that Cecchi may have asked for payment of his unpaid fees, the scenario that Melba described is refuted by much evidence. In Murphy, she states the confrontation she had with Cecchi occurred the day following the benefit concert; in *Melodies and Memories* she places it many weeks earlier. But the decisive piece of evidence that discredits Melba's story can be found among her surviving letters. After two hectic months in London, Nellie wrote a long and affectionate letter to Cecchi describing the concerts she had attended, how she herself had sung in London, how her father had been ill, how she had been plagued with toothache and how little George was flourishing. It ends with 'love to all enquiring friends' and could never be mistaken for a missal to an avaricious enemy.

If we accept that Nellie invented her disagreement with Cecchi, that raises the question of her motive. Other writers who share my belief that it was invented have offered various theories. One suggested that it might have been done on Mathilde Marchesi's instructions and as a condition of her being accepted by her, Nellie's next teacher. More likely is that it was a convenient means for Nellie to justify her dismissal of a colonial teacher and to encourage people to believe she was the product of Paris and not of Fitzroy.

Cecchi did not die of apoplexy with Nellie's name on his lips, dying from long-term heart disease in 1897. At the time of his death it was revealed that he had been deeply upset for years about seeing no mention of his name in local and foreign press articles about Nellie's early life. Colleagues sometimes leapt to his defence with letters to the press – Fanny Simonsen took the trouble to write from Milan in 1891[26] – but to little avail. Nellie's words held sway. Fortunately, Cecchi was not around to read her version of events in Agnes Murphy's *Melba* or the melodramatic version in *Melodies and Memories*, quoted earlier.

This episode does not reflect well on Nellie and it would not be the only evidence of her disregard for other people's feelings or their reputations and of a streak of self-serving arrogance in her character, which would cast a long shadow over her own reputation and which lingers to this day.

Chapter 4

Pomp and mixed circumstances

In preparation for auditioning in London, Nellie sought letters of introduction from various prominent people in Melbourne. She sang for Alfred Cellier, the English composer of the hit light opera *Dorothy*, who had arrived in Melbourne just a week earlier, and he was sufficiently impressed to provide her with two letters. One commended her to Sir Arthur Sullivan (composer from the Gilbert & Sullivan team) and the other to Wilhelm Ganz, a fashionable singing teacher in London, whose song 'Sing, sweet bird' Nellie had sung many times in concerts. Other letters were written to composer–teachers Hubert Parry and Alberto Randegger and the piano manufacturer John Brinsmead.[1]

What would prove to be the most useful letter was provided by Madame Elise Wiedermann-Pinschof, wife of the Austro-Hungarian consul in Melbourne, a great patron of the arts and a friend of the Mitchells. Wiedermann-Pinschof was a former opera singer who had enjoyed a successful career in Europe before being obliged to retire when she married a member of the diplomatic corps. The letter recommended that Nellie be given a hearing in Paris by Wiedermann-Pinschof's own former teacher, the celebrated Mathilde Marchesi.

With these precious letters stored carefully in her luggage, and along with her husband, her son, her father and her sisters Annie and Belle, Nellie boarded the Royal Mail Steamer *Bengal* at Port Melbourne, bound for London via Colombo, Aden, Suez, Malta, Gibraltar and Plymouth. The press reporting on the day described the scene on the pier on which 2000 people had gathered as 'a sea of waving handkerchiefs and parasols'.[2]

Also travelling on the *Bengal* was James Moorhouse, the Sheffield-born Anglican Bishop of Melbourne, who was returning to England to become Bishop of Manchester. Moorhouse and his wife had attended some of Nellie's concerts in Melbourne and admired her singing. The bishop insisted Nellie join the small choir he formed for Sunday services on board.

After her arrival in London, Nellie wrote a letter to the tenor Rudolph Himmer, who had sung at her Melbourne Town Hall farewell concert. In that letter she described life at sea:

> We had lots of fun on the *Bengal*, there were many musical people so we had six concerts, four balls and one fancy dress tableau-dramatic, entertainments, sports, cricket etc. Have you ever been to Colombo? Are not the curries there delicious and I have dreamt about them ever since.[3]

Curries were not the only delights experienced by the first class passengers in Colombo. They were all driven to the Grand Oriental Hotel, where hot baths and expansive beds were provided to restore their spirits after 13 days at sea.

Confined to their cabin every night during those 13 days with two-and-a-half year old George to care for had not, as might have been expected, provoked arguments between Nellie and Charlie. Perhaps the excitement of shipboard life had occupied them, but when the *Bengal* left Colombo on the next leg of its voyage and the heat became intense in the Red Sea, tempers flared. Nellie claimed that Charlie had struck her, causing temporary deafness in one ear and she sought refuge in the cabin her sisters shared, taking George with her.[4]

When the *Bengal* reached Valetta, the port capital of Malta, the Mitchells and the Armstrongs toured the city, during which another conflict erupted, this time in public. Inside the busy Co-Cathedral of St John, Nellie and Charlie argued over whether George's cap should be removed. The cap ended up skidding across the marble floor and Nellie's face received a glancing blow from the back of Charlie's hand.[5]

By the time the *Bengal* had reached Plymouth a week later, Nellie was probably desperate for the journey to end, but bad weather forced the ship to stand off for another six days, finally docking at Tilbury on 1 May. From there the Mitchells and the Armstrongs travelled by train to London. Melba recorded her impressions of the capital on arrival:

> We had come through Tilbury and the sight of the grey skies, the dirty wharves, the millions of grimy chimney pots, had struck a chill to my heart. How can I sing in such gloom? I had thought to myself. But Tilbury passed and the rest of London with its gay hansom cabs, its vast shops, its crowds of people and, more than anything, its crimson and yellow tulips in Hyde Park, struck me with a sense of incredible adventure.[6]

Nellie was also impressed by the elegant, furnished house her father had leased for their stay: No. 89 Sloane Street, Belgravia, overlooking Cadogan Gardens. On crossing the threshold, Nellie sang an exultant trill – the first occasion her voice was heard in London.

The party's arrival coincided with the beginning of the 1886 social and musical season in the city. The newspapers were filled with advertisements for concerts and opera, but before Nellie could begin to sample these or present any of her letters, a family matter arose. A letter had awaited Charlie at Sloane Street, informing him that his mother, Lady Frances Armstrong, was seriously ill. He and Nellie travelled by train to Littlehampton on the coast of West Sussex and on to the nearby village of Rustington, where Lady Armstrong's home, Seconfield House, was located.

They found Charlie's mother (then in her 60s) slightly improved and delighted to see her son for what was probably their first meeting in 18 years. Frances Armstrong was equally delighted to meet her new daughter-in-law and to welcome Nellie into the Armstrong family. Whether Charlie acquainted his mother with the stormy nature of their marriage is unknown, but if he did, it made no difference to her. She and other members of the Armstrong family took an instant liking to Nellie. Satisfied that Lady Armstrong was recovering, Nellie and Charlie returned to London to attend the opening of the Indian and Colonial Exhibition on 4 May.

As a commissioner, David Mitchell was provided with a number of tickets for the opening ceremony in the Royal Albert Hall. Whether Nellie witnessed the various other festivities marking that day is unclear, but Londoners turned out in their thousands, determined not to miss one exciting moment. The queen – short, stout and dressed from head to toe in black – travelled from Windsor Castle by train. From Paddington Station she progressed in bright sunshine past the tulips in Hyde Park, escorted by troops of the Life Guards. At the main entrance to the exhibition she was met by the Prince of Wales and led through the exhibition before moving on to the Royal Albert Hall.

For Nellie, the opening ceremony was much more than a spectacle – it was a musical milestone. The Royal Albert Hall Choral Society opened with the 'Hallelujah Chorus' from *Messiah*. An exhibition ode written for the occasion by Sir Arthur Sullivan with words by Tennyson was performed next. The composer conducted and the solo part was sung by the great Canadian soprano Emma Albani, Queen Victoria's favourite singer and one whom Nellie would eventually replace in the public's esteem. Albani then sang Henry Bishop's 'Home, sweet home', before the queen departed to the strains of 'Rule Britannia'. In her letter to Rudolph Himmer, Nellie described the whole ceremony as very grand, with Albani's singing as going straight to her heart.[7]

While her father attended to his duties at the exhibition, Nellie set about using the letters of introduction she had brought from Melbourne. Firstly, she wrote to Marchesi, mentioning the recommendation she carried from Elise Wiedermann-Pinschof. It is known that Marchesi respected Wiedermann-Pinschof's judgement and a reply was sent inviting Nellie to present herself at Marchesi's Paris studio in two months time.[8]

Despite there being no record of the exact order in which Nellie visited the others for whom she carried letters, the responses she received are clearly documented. When she tried to make an appointment to see Hubert Parry at the Royal College of Music, she was informed that he had received so many requests from aspiring singers in recent months that he was seeing none. Sir Arthur Sullivan at least agreed to see her and when she presented herself at his flat in Westminster she found the composer at the piano, absentmindedly picking out a tune.[9] Barely concealing his boredom, Sullivan asked what Nellie would sing for him. When she asked what *he* would like her to sing, he replied 'Oh, it's all the same to me'. Nellie sang the *La Traviata* scena, presumably accompanying herself on Sullivan's piano. When she finished, Sullivan was silent for a moment and then said, 'Yes, that's alright, Mrs Armstrong'. Nellie was disappointed and even more so when the composer told her that there were currently no vacancies in the ranks of singers performing his comic operas, but if she studied for another year, he might find her a small part in *The Mikado*.

Nellie called on Alberto Randegger, the esteemed pianist, conductor and composer at the Royal Academy of Music, and was received graciously and when she sang for him he praised her voice, but disappointed her by explaining that he had no time to teach her in the foreseeable future.[10] At the Brinsmead piano showroom she was received by either John Brinsmead or one of his sons. The verdict delivered was: 'The tone of your voice, Mrs Armstrong, is reminiscent of our pianos'; Nellie was unsure of whether to take that as a compliment or otherwise.

Nellie had more luck when she called on Wilhelm Ganz at his home in Harley Street. After reading Cellier's letter, Ganz asked

Nellie what she wished to sing for him; again she chose the *La Traviata* piece. Nellie knew that Ganz had accompanied both Jenny Lind (as Julius Buddee had) and the reigning 'Queen of Song', Adelina Patti, during his career, so when she finished singing and Ganz praised her lavishly she knew his words carried weight. He did not, however, agree to take Nellie on as a student explaining that, in his opinion, she needed no further instruction.

When Ganz wrote his memoirs in 1913 he devoted many paragraphs to Nellie:

> Madame Melba came to me soon after she arrived from Australia. She sang for me the grand aria 'Ah, fors' è lui' from *La Traviata*. I was delighted. It could not have been better sung; the vocalisation was perfect and she warbled her runs and shakes without any effort. When I asked her to sing me something else she pleased me very much with her rendering of my song 'Sing, sweet bird'.[11]

Between these forays to present her letters, Nellie attended concerts and plays, anxious to hear the great singers, instrumentalists and actors who were appearing in London. On the afternoon of 8 May she returned to the Royal Albert Hall to witness a concert at which Albani sang once again, as did the Swedish soprano Christine Nilsson, Edward Lloyd (the leading British tenor of the time) and the baritone Charles Santley – for whom Gounod added the aria 'Even bravest heart' to his opera *Faust*. She had also heard the pianist Vladimir de Pachmann and had seen the actors Lily Langtry and Sarah Bernhardt, but she had to wait another three weeks before hearing the singer she most desired to hear: Adelina Patti.

When writing to Himmer, she gave her verdict on all of these artists: 'Albani has a truly beautiful voice, but Nilsson was very disappointing. She sang like a schoolgirl. The others all have beautiful voices, and Pachmann played as I have never heard before in my life. It was so beautiful.'[12]

After hearing Patti singing the Mad Scene from *Lucia di Lammermoor* and five other pieces at the diva's first concert in London for the season, Nellie summed up her impressions of the three leading sopranos. Of Nilsson she said, 'I think I can do better than that'. Of Albani she said, 'I think I can do as well as that' and after hearing Patti, she conceded, 'I shall try to do as well as that'.[13]

In the meantime, Wilhelm Ganz was creating opportunities for Nellie to sing in London, arranging for her to participate in three minor concerts in London on 1, 2 and 21 June. He also arranged for Nellie to audition for Carl Rosa, impresario of the Royal Carl Rosa Opera Company, which occasionally appeared in London, but spent most of its time touring the provinces. Ganz invited Rosa to hear Nellie at Ganz's house and the impresario scribbled the date on one of his shirt cuffs. When the day came, Nellie turned up, but Rosa did not. His shirt had gone to the laundry and he had forgotten the engagement. True to her character, Nellie was furious and swore she would never sing for Carl Rosa. As time proved, it was well she did not join Carl Rosa's company or her career might never have reached the heights it did.

Nellie made her London debut at the concert on 1 June, as one of three supporting artists to a 10-year-old piano prodigy named Pauline Ellice. The concert took place in Prince's Hall near Piccadilly Circus, a venue that no longer exists. Nellie sang the same pieces she had sung for Ganz at his home and he conducted a small orchestra. London was blanketed by fog that evening and the hall was sparsely filled. Apart from the significance of the occasion in Nellie's career, the only other feature of note was that the composer Paolo Tosti appeared, accompanying a baritone in one of his songs.[14]

The daily newspapers did not review the concert, but the journal the *Musical World* did, briefly. Nellie's performances earned one complimentary sentence: 'Mrs Armstrong from Melbourne made her first appearance in Europe and produced a very favourable impression in an aria from *La Traviata* and

Ganz's song 'Sing Sweet Bird', the latter of which was encored.'[15]

When Herman Klein, the distinguished critic of *The Sunday Times* and himself a pupil of Manuel Garcia, the younger, came to write his recollections of musical life in London, he revealed that he had been present at the concert. Klein also recalled his less favourable impression of Nellie on that occasion: 'Beyond admitting the quality of her voice, I was not much impressed by her efforts'.[16]

The second 'concert' was not a public event. It was the musical entertainment at the 41st annual dinner of the Royal Theatrical Fund, held in the Freemasons' Tavern. The great and the good of London's theatre world met to discuss their fund, and then enjoyed a sumptuous dinner, after which six singers, one violin virtuoso and a small orchestra conducted by Ganz entertained them. The dinner was chaired by Augustus Harris, who had managed an opera company at Drury Lane Theatre that year and who would take over Covent Garden in 1888.[17] Nellie sang Ganz's song again and Gounod's *Ave Maria*, with the violinist Anna Lang providing an obbligato. Harris was apparently much taken by the Gounod song, which he had not heard before. It is a pity he was not *as* taken with the singer.

The young and still virtually unknown Henry Wood, future conductor of the Proms, claimed to have heard Nellie at this time and the most likely occasion would have been at the Royal Theatrical Fund dinner. In his autobiography, Wood remembered:

> I was deeply impressed by the beauty of her voice but her name meant nothing to me at the time. I certainly did not dream that she was to become the great Melba or that she would one day give a concert with the Queen's Hall Orchestra and me.[18]

The *Musical World* applauded Nellie again in another article in the same issue, while Nellie, not to be outdone, praised herself fulsomely in her letter to Pietro Cecchi (referred to in the last chapter):

You will be pleased to hear that I have already sung twice in London and had the greatest success, splendid critiques, and everyone predicts a great future for me. Herr Ganz, the man who wrote 'Sing Sweet Bird' has taken a wonderful fancy to me, and declares my voice is more like Patti's than any voice he has ever heard. Antoinette Sterling was singing at one concert where I sang [the Royal Theatrical Fund dinner] and she was in a fearful rage because I got a bigger reception than she did. At the first concert I had the biggest [sic] orchestra in London to sing to.'[19]

Charlie was preoccupied with other matters. Four days before Nellie's first concert he received a commission as a lieutenant in a reserve militia unit: the 3rd Battalion, Prince of Wales's Leinster Regiment.[20] He may or may not have attended that concert, but according to Nellie, he 'accidently' tipped a jug of water over her as she was about to leave for either the Prince's Hall concert or the Royal Theatrical Fund dinner.[21]

Sometime after his immediate duties at the exhibition had been discharged, David Mitchell travelled to Scotland, presumably to visit those of his family still living in Forfarshire and any friends from his youth who might still have been around. As Nellie reported in her letter to Cecchi, while there Mitchell became ill and took a couple of weeks to recover. Although there is some doubt about whether Nellie accompanied her father on this trip, she did write to Ganz at this time, apologising for not having come to see him before she departed temporarily from London for some undisclosed destination. In the same letter Nellie asks Ganz, very optimistically, if it might be possible for him to arrange for her to sing at one of Patti's concerts.[22] Ganz was not able to achieve that but did secure her third concert engagement – to sing again at Prince's Hall, on 21 June. On this occasion the concert was a benefit for the widow of a recently deceased professor from the Guildhall School of Music, meaning that Nellie was not paid a fee. The other artists participating in the concert were no more distinguished than those at Nellie's first, but at least more interesting. They included the future musical superstar Marie Tempest, the Carl Rosa soprano Rose Hersée, who had sung with Lyster's company in Australia, the pianist Isidore de Lara and the future aunt and uncle of Noel Coward. In such company it is not surprising that Nellie didn't rate a mention in the press reports or reviews.[23]

A week after this concert Charlie left for Ireland, where his unit was stationed for one month. Nellie felt obliged to accompany him – or he insisted she did so. They stayed with Charlie's brother, Reverend Sir Edmund Frederick Armstrong, the current baronet, but Nellie didn't remain there for long. She returned to London to prepare for her trip to Paris to sing for Mathilde Marchesi.

Serious discussions with her family preceded Nellie's departure for the French capital. Little George was consigned to the temporary care of his aunts. David Mitchell agreed to pay for a second-class ticket on the boat train to Paris and for a room in a modest hotel in Paris for as long as it took Marchesi to decide whether she would take Nellie on as a student. Mitchell also imposed an ultimatum on Nellie before she departed. Having failed to be accepted by any of the other teachers she had approached, he insisted that if Marchesi rejected her, she would return to Australia when his duties at the exhibition were done and there settle down as a wife and mother and confine her singing to charity events. Nellie was so desperate that she agreed, but it is doubtful that she viewed her father's ultimatum as permanent or binding.

The Paris to which Nellie journeyed was a city enjoying the period in France's history now known as La Belle Époque. After 100 years of revolution and war, stability had brought a flowering of science, commerce and the arts and the emergence of a new social class – *les nouveau-riches* – to patronise the pleasures captured on canvas by Renoir and Toulouse-Lautrec. In the world of music, the *vieille guarde* was represented by César Franck, Charles Gounod and

Ambroise Thomas; the *avant-garde* by Camille Saint-Saëns, Léo Delibes and Jules Massenet, with Claude Debussy just beginning to make his mark. In the midst of the city's musical life, Mathilde Marchesi presided over her own singing school, which enjoyed the patronage of most of the composers just mentioned and to which would-be opera stars flocked from all over the world.

Mathilde Marchesi, born Lisette Sophie Jeannette Mathilde Graumann in Frankfurt am Main in 1821, had an impressive musical pedigree. Her aunt, Dorothea von Ertmann had been a favourite piano pupil of Beethoven, and Mathilde was initially taught singing by Felice Ronconi (brother of the famous baritone Giorgio Ronconi) and by the composer Otto Nicolai.

Mathilde had made her concert debut as a mezzo-soprano in 1844 and that same year she was befriended by Mendelssohn, who taught her how to sing some of his songs. In 1845 she moved to Paris and began studying with Garcia the younger, whose principles she embraced and which later formed the basis of her own teaching. While singing in London, she met the Sicilian baritone Salvatore Marchesi. His real name was Salvatore Castrone della Rajata and he too had been a pupil of Garcia.[24] They married in 1852. Two years later, Mathilde began teaching, first in Vienna and later in Paris. Her successful students before Nellie arrived had included Ilma di Murska, Antoinette Sterling and Elise Wiedermann-Pinschof.[25]

The day following her arrival in Paris, Nellie presented herself at Marchesi's apartment and studio at 88 Rue Jouffroy.[26] In *Melodies and Memories* Nellie recounted how she rang the doorbell and her ring was answered by a liveried footman. After she explained to the footman her purpose in coming and handed him Wiedermann-Pinschof's letter, he disappeared inside, leaving her standing on the doorstep. The footman returned a few minutes later with the message that 'Madame' would see Nellie at ten o'clock the following morning. What transpired that following morning became the stuff of legend, but like most legends, the details are questionable. Nellie herself launched the legend in 1898 with remarks she made during an interview for the December edition of the New York journal the *Musical Age*:

> I had a letter of introduction to Madame Marchesi and I lost no time in going to Paris. She heard me sing and from the first gave me the most generous encouragement. After my second song she rushed excitedly out of the drawing room and, calling to her husband, she said: 'Salvatore, j'ai enfin une étoile!'[27]

Later versions, which appeared in other interviews, had Marchesi *running* upstairs to her husband, bursting into his study, snatching a newspaper from his hands and announcing what was now translated as 'Salvatore, I have found a star!' It is likely that Marchesi would have wanted to share her discovery with her husband, but less likely that, at the age of 65, she would have done much 'bursting' or run anywhere, least of all up a flight of stairs.

When Melba provided accounts of her first meeting with Marchesi for Murphy in 1909 and Beverley Nichols in 1925, she added much detail, most of which sounds factual. From those a version of the event can be described, one that is probably as accurate as possible at this distance in time.

Upon returning to Marchesi's house 20 minutes before 10 am the following day Nellie was shown into a large room containing gilded furniture and a magnificent chandelier. The walls were lined with portraits of famous singers, with a grand piano and a small, raised platform standing at one end. A dozen other young woman were already in the room, most of them established students waiting for their lessons, along with two or three other nervous aspirants seeking a first hearing from 'Madame'.

Although Nellie described herself as terror-struck when Marchesi first entered the room, she subsequently painted a detailed picture of her first meeting with the great teacher:

> She seemed to me a mixture of alarm and attraction, standing very upright in the middle of the room, dressed all in black, a small

grey-haired figure, but one which it was impossible to overlook. And then she smiled and her whole face with its long upper lip and its intelligent eyes, seemed to be transformed.[28]

Marchesi had, apparently, studied Wiedermann-Pinschof's letter, for she approached Nellie first and questioned her (in what Nellie described as a business-like manner) about what her former pupil had written. Marchesi then told Nellie to sit and wait her turn. A couple of the other aspirants were invited to sing and Nellie's confidence soared as she listened to voices inferior to her own.

When Nellie's turn came, Marchesi asked what she wished to sing and Nellie nominated the first part of the 'Traviata' scena – the aria 'Ah! fors' è lui'. Nellie mounted the platform, Marchesi waved her young studio pianist, Fritzi Stradewitz, away and sat at the keyboard herself. Marchesi played and Nellie sang. When, near the end of the aria, she commenced a rapid downwards scale on a bold top 'B', Marchesi stopped playing. She swung around on the piano stool and demanded to know why Nellie 'screeched' her top notes and was she incapable of singing them *piano*? Without waiting for an answer, Marchesi struck the note 'B' and Nellie sang it as softly as she could. 'Higher!' Marchesi demanded. From the piano came a top C and then D and E, and Nellie's voice followed the instrument up the scale into the territory that is the exclusive province of the coloratura soprano, singing confidently – and softly.

It was at that point that Marchesi left the room to deliver her news to her husband. Nellie reported that in Marchesi's absence the other young women in the room began to chatter and she assumed they were voicing their contempt at her efforts. When Marchesi returned she made Nellie repeat the last part of the aria and then took her by the arm and led her into an adjoining room. The conversation that followed as the two women faced one another in private went something like this.

'Mrs Armstrong, are you serious?'

'Yes', Nellie replied firmly.

'Alors', Marchesi continued. 'If you are serious, and if you can study with me for one year, I will make something *extraordinary* of you', the word extraordinary pronounced as two words to emphasise its meaning. Undoubtedly, Nellie replied with profuse thanks and expressed her eagerness to begin as soon as arrangements could be made in London.[29]

Nellie returned to London the day after being accepted by Marchesi to break the news to Charlie and her father. As Nellie remembered it, Charlie threatened to attack her with his military sword.[30] David Mitchell received it more calmly and arranged for Nellie and George to travel back to Paris and booked a respectable *pension* for them. He also deposited a sum of money into her account, which would enable Nellie to pay Marchesi's fees, pay for George's care while Nellie was studying, and live frugally for one year, in accordance with the promise he had made in Melbourne.

The location of the *pension* is not known, but within a month of commencing her studies with Marchesi, Nellie and George left the *pension* and Nellie rented a small, sparsely furnished apartment on the fifth floor of a building in one of the less fashionable parts of Paris – 12 Avenue Carnot. The apartment was on the top floor of five flights of stairs, but it was within walking distance of Rue Jouffroy. Marchesi's studio pianist lived in the same building and had probably helped Nellie to find the apartment. Stradewitz also assisted Nellie with employing a young Parisian girl to care for George, while two elderly Irish sisters, the Misses Hyland, who lived nearby, befriended Nellie and helped her out with food and the occasional loan when money ran short.[31]

Nellie quickly fitted into the routine at the École Marchesi, which began at nine with a morning assembly of all the students currently studying with 'Madame' – averaging about a dozen. Marchesi led the assembly through vocal exercises, sung in unison, and then singing lessons for individuals accounted for the remainder of the morning. In the afternoon, classes in musical theory, languages and stagecraft were presented. Some of these were given by Marchesi and others by the specialist teachers she employed.[32]

Nellie followed this routine for the first month and then Marchesi promoted her to what she referred to as the 'Opera Class', where basic instruction in singing was replaced by preparation for a debut and a career in opera. As the weeks passed and convinced more than ever that Nellie was destined for stardom, Marchesi pushed her hard. Their relationship has been described as 'diamond rubbing against diamond', but Nellie was wise enough to defer to 'Madame' on most occasions when conflict seemed imminent. On one memorable morning, however, Nellie found it impossible to contain her emotions. Marchesi was guiding Nellie through the Mad Scene from *Lucia di Lammermoor* and was driving her relentlessly and shouting demands at her with such vehemence that Nellie burst into tears and ran from the room, vowing that she would not attend another lesson. Marchesi (according to Murphy) followed Nellie, threw her arms around her and soothed her with the words: 'Nellie, Nellie! You know I love you. If I bother you it is because I know you will be great. Come back and sing as I wish.'[33]

Marchesi's love for Nellie was genuine. Knowing that Nellie's real mother was dead, Marchesi began referring to herself as 'your mother' and occasionally 'your loving old mother'. Nellie was happy to return the compliment by referring to herself as 'your loving daughter'. This did not go down well with Marchesi's three daughters, who lived at Rue Jouffroy, particularly wounding Blanche Marchesi, who acted as her mother's assistant and aspired to a career as a singer herself. The affront was exacerbated when Blanche realised that Nellie's voice was immeasurably superior to her own and that her mother was focusing all her energy on forging a career for her star pupil and not for her daughter. In years to come Blanche Marchesi would concede the quality of Melba's voice, but accuse her of sabotaging her career. The recordings Blanche made some years later confirm the real reason for her pedestrian career.

It is timely, at this point to consider what Marchesi taught Nellie in relation to that she had already learned from Pietro Cecchi, as touched on in chapter 1. If we accept Marchesi's accusation that Nellie was 'screeching' her top notes at that first audition and we discount nerves as the cause, perhaps this is evidence of Cecchi having taught Nellie a more vehement style of singing than Marchesi advocated. The comparison may be taken a stage further. When Nellie wrote that Cecchi was 'only good for Italian opera', she may have been referring to the fact that he was a typical 'Italian' tenor, who was prepared to sacrifice vocal continence for dramatic effect. The fact remains, however, that the sound Nellie was producing when she first sang in London (as confirmed by those who heard her) was true to the nature of her voice. What Marchesi had to work with, therefore, was a secure instrument with an unblemished tone and which needed only the addition of those qualities Cecchi had not been able to impart – sophistication, an added sheen and an extension to Nellie's vocal virtuosity.

What is perhaps the most revealing testimony on this topic comes from another of Marchesi's students: 'Madame had a wonderful gift for training voices already placed, but she was not so fortunate in her way with the underdeveloped voice, although anyone would have incurred her undying enmity by saying so'. Speaking of Melba (but not naming her), the same student wrote: 'Therefore her pride made Madame conceal with private lessons the fact that this brilliant new soprano had little to learn and in truth was well along the road to vocal sophistication before Madame ever saw her'.

These words were written by the strikingly beautiful American Emma Eames, four years younger than Nellie and also possessed of an exceptionally fine soprano voice, similar in sound and colour to Nellie's.[34] It is possible (even probable) that Eames was among the students in attendance when Nellie auditioned for Marchesi, for she had been at the École Marchesi for almost a year when

Nellie arrived. The American considered herself, up until then, the 'star' among the current batch of students, but either on that day or soon after, Eames discovered her position had been usurped by Nellie. Bitter rivalry quickly developed between them, expressed with more vitriol by the American than by the Australian. Although Eames never had a kind word to say about Melba, there is no reason to question the remarks she made about Marchesi and untrained voices.

We have only the opinions of others by which to judge how Nellie sounded before she came under Marchesi's influence, but the recordings she began to make in 1904 demonstrate what became known as the 'Marchesi Method'. Its hallmarks were brilliant top notes; clean, fresh tone supported on the breath; steady emission of sound; an absence of vibrato ('beat') in the voice; and accurate and precise intonation. These commendable qualities were accompanied by a tendency to sing notes up to the middle of the treble stave using the chest register rather than the head register, which does not equate well with contemporary taste and perhaps explains why listeners today will sometimes accuse Melba and other singers of her generation of 'hooting'.[35]

These characteristics can be found in varying degrees in the recordings of all Marchesi's students, but the method did not suit every student. In some instances it resulted in the loss of top notes in mid-career, Evelyn Scotney being an example of this phenomenon. When Eames suffered the complete loss of her singing voice and was forced into retirement at the relatively early age of 44, she blamed Marchesi; however, singing roles too heavy for her voice may have done more damage than 'Madame' ever did. Some students who enrolled at the École Marchesi did not stay long. The Scottish soprano Mary Garden, for example, left after just three weeks, rebelling at having her voice drilled into a style of singing that did not suit it or her. The method suited lower-voiced female singers less well than sopranos, with very few contraltos among Marchesi's long list of successful students.[36] Males are entirely absent from the list.

Marchesi's method was ideal for Nellie's voice and her desire to give credit to her 'loving old mother' is entirely understandable. What is sad is that she was not prepared to share that credit with Mary Ellen Christian and, more importantly, Pietro Cecchi.

As 1886 drew towards its close, David Mitchell's duties at the exhibition ended and in September he and Belle returned to Australia. Annie Mitchell stayed on in London and eventually joined Nellie in Paris. Her sister's presence in Paris was a comfort to Nellie and no doubt young George was delighted to have one of his aunts living with them. While Nellie pursued her studies, Annie took George on excursions all over Paris.

Annie would also have been intrigued and pleased when Nellie returned to the apartment one afternoon with the news that she had a new name. Madame Marchesi had initiated a discussion with Nellie about the unsuitability of the names 'Nellie Armstrong' or 'Nellie Mitchell' for a future diva. 'Such names are too *ordinaire*', Madame had advised, adding, 'a prima donna needs a more exotic name, preferably something that sounds vaguely Italian and something that will lodge in people's memories'.

After much discussion it was decided that 'Nellie Melba' would suit perfectly. The new name met all the criteria: it paid tribute to Nellie's home town and it meant that she would not be saddled with Charlie's name when she became famous. On 30 December that year Nellie sang at Marchesi's annual end-of-year musical soirée using the name that was to become a household word around the globe within a few years. 'Melba' was born.

Chapter 5

Madame Melba

Marchesi held concerts, styled 'musical soirées', at least twice each year, usually in her studio but sometimes in a concert hall. They served two purposes: to showcase the talents of her students and to enhance the prestige of her school. The latter was achieved not only by the singing of the students, but also by the distinction of the guests who attended. The leading French composers of the day – most of whom Marchesi could claim as friends – were often present, while opera company directors, concert managers, artists' agents and music critics were also included on the invitation list. It was hoped that these influential people would help to launch the careers of those students who were ready to embark upon their professional lives – and they often did.

At the soirée in which Nellie (now 'Madame Melba') made her first appearance, the guests included Ambroise Thomas, the composer of two operas remembered today: *Mignon* and *Hamlet*. In honour of Thomas, Nellie sang Ophélie's Mad Scene from *Hamlet*. The 75-year-old composer was impressed and when Nellie had finished, congratulated her. In the not-too-distant future, Thomas would prove to be a loyal supporter and help Nellie prepare to sing the role of Ophélie in stage performances of *Hamlet*, but for the moment she would have been content to receive his praise in front of the audience and in front of her fellow students.[1]

Also present at the soirée was Henri Heugel, editor of the influential Paris music and theatre journal *Le Ménestrel*. In the next edition of his journal, Heugel reported: 'Madame Melba revealed a lyric soprano voice of a rare timbre seldom heard these days, remarkable technique and accurate intonation'.[2]

At this time, Nellie was also heard by the concert and opera impresario Maurice Strakosch.[3] Although he may have been present at the December soirée, the occasion was some weeks into the New Year, when Nellie was having a lesson and Strakosch was visiting Salvatore Marchesi – according to the information Nellie gave Murphy.[4] That version has Strakosch enjoying a cigar in Marchesi's study when the strains of Nellie singing 'Caro nome' in the studio below floated upstairs. Strakosch was reported as exclaiming: 'I must have that voice!'

Presumably with Mathilde Marchesi's approval, Strakosch persuaded Nellie to sign a contract on the spot, making him her manager for five years and giving him exclusive rights to present her in public.[5] The terms of the contract included a payment to Nellie of 1000 French francs per month for the first year, with the amount doubling in each subsequent year. Nellie would soon regret signing that contract, but at the time she thought it a great advancement. She wrote to Arthur Hilliger, explaining proudly that Strakosch had told her she would have great success under his guidance and that she would eventually succeed Adelina Patti as the most famous soprano in the world.[6]

Strakosch seems to have done nothing to promote Nellie until some months later when he discovered she was about to break their contract. In the meantime, Nellie suffered an unexpected, short and fiery visit from her husband and a failed audition at the Paris Opéra. Nellie chose to forget both these events when she recounted her story to Murphy and Nichols.

The audition was arranged by Madame Marchesi and took place in an anteroom at the magnificent Opéra, known locally as the 'Palais Garnier' in honour of its architect. Nellie sang two arias, probably accompanied at the piano by Fritzi Stradewitz. No other details have survived, although it seems likely that it was Pedro

Gailhard, co-director of the Opéra and a former singer himself, who auditioned her. Gailhard did not offer Nellie a contract, but based on subsequent events, it seems he did not forget her and set her name aside for future consideration.[7]

Nellie continued her studies with Marchesi and her appearances at Marchesi's soirées. At Rue Jouffroy Nellie made the acquaintance of composers Charles Gounod, Léo Delibes and Jules Massenet. Like Ambroise Thomas, Gounod and Delibes pledged their support for her. Two of these soirées were public events and were held in the concert hall in the Erard piano and harp manufacturer's building – the famous Sallé Erard. The first, on 24 March 1887, was a benefit for the widows and children of deceased musicians and attracted a full house. Nellie sang the Mad Scene from *Lucia di Lammermoor*, interpolating a cadenza Marchesi had written for the occasion and which Nellie continued to use whenever she sang 'Lucia' in the future.[8] The second, on 11 June, was a benefit for victims of a catastrophic fire that had recently destroyed Paris's second opera house, the Opéra-Comique, claiming 87 lives.

In the audience for Nellie's first appearance in Marchesi's soirées (back in December) had been a Belgian music lover and patron of the arts, named Elkin. He immediately wrote to Joseph Dupont and Alexandre Lapissida, joint directors of the Théâtre de la Monnaie, the opera house in Brussels, suggesting that on their next visit to Paris they should hear Madame Melba, whom he described as just the sort of singer that would appeal to Brussels audiences. Dupont and Lapissida took Elkin's advice and travelled to Paris to attend the first of the concerts in the Sallé Erard. There they listened and marvelled at Nellie's singing and resolved to engage her.

Then, as now, most directors of opera houses in Europe keep abreast of their competitors' activities, and Lapissida had heard that Gailhard was interested in Nellie for the Opéra, so before contacting Nellie, he called on Gailhard in the director's palatial office at the Palais Garnier. Lapissida then employed a cunning trick to ensure his and Dupont's bid for Nellie's services would not be thwarted by Gailhard. The meeting was, ostensibly, just a courtesy call, but towards the end of their conversation Lapissida casually dropped Madame Melba's name into the conversation. He then added that he had heard rumours that Gailhard was interested in her and followed up with something like: 'Well, if that is the case, Monsieur, *you* go ahead and engage her. I've heard her French is *atrocious* and she sings with a horrible Australian accent! Our audiences in Brussels would not accept that, but of course yours here in Paris are probably less discriminating.' As soon as Lapissida had left, Gailhard searched the clutter on his desk, found a note he had kept about Nellie's audition and threw it in his wastepaper basket.[9]

Next day a message arrived for Marchesi from the two Belgian directors, requesting they call at Rue Jouffroy and audition 'Madame Melba' with a view to engaging her for their theatre. The audition was arranged, Nellie sang for the visitors and they offered her a contract to join their company for their forthcoming season, commencing in September and ending the following May – and another for the season after.

Nellie was offered five principal roles in her first season: Gilda in *Rigoletto*, Violetta in *La Traviata*, the title roles in *Lucia di Lammermoor* and Delibes's *Lakmé*, and finally, towards the end of the season, Ophélie in *Hamlet*. All costumes would be provided by the theatre and Nellie would receive 3000 francs per month from October until the end of the first season. A higher fee was offered for the second season.

As Marchesi pointed out to Nellie, it was a remarkably generous offer, especially in regard to the period it covered. Opera companies generally offered debutantes very short contracts until *after* they had proved themselves. To offer an untried singer contracts for two full seasons was almost unknown. Marchesi also identified other advantages for Nellie in making her stage debut with the Monnaie company: the theatre was not too large, the number of principals was relatively few (so there would be less competition from within the company) and Brussels audiences were traditionally kinder to newcomers than those in Paris. Additionally Marchesi promised that her friend Félix Gevaert, director of the Brussels Conservatoire of Music, and his wife would be on hand to look after Nellie.[10]

Nellie pointed out that she was already under contract to Maurice Strakosch, but Marchesi dismissed that with a wave of her fingers. Strakosch was a friend she said, and she and Salvatore would put things right with him. With that reassurance, Nellie signed, and a date for her debut in opera was agreed. She was to sing Gilda in *Rigoletto* on 13 October; her career would be launched and the next stage in her dream fulfilled.[11]

Whether Marchesi had been coaching Nellie in complete opera roles cannot be determined from the information available – and if so which roles. It is likely she had, but much learning and much preparation still needed to be accomplished in the months that followed and before Nellie departed for Brussels.

Work was interrupted one morning a few weeks later when (according to Nellie) Maurice Strakosch arrived uninvited at her apartment, demanding to know whether the rumour he had heard about her signing a contract with the Monnaie was true. When Nellie admitted it was, the impresario flew into a rage and denounced her and Marchesi. What, if any, actions that had been taken to appease him had obviously failed. The prospect of actions the impresario *himself* might take as a result hung over Nellie like a Damoclean sword.

When the École Marchesi closed for its summer break, Nellie returned to England, taking George with her. They stayed for three weeks with Lady Armstrong at Rustington. Charlie was trying his hand at farming and horse breeding at nearby Littlehampton. This provided an opportunity for little George to experience the English countryside, dogs and horses in the company of his father. Charlie informed Nellie that he was about to resign his commission from the militia after serving only 15 months and regaled his son with details of an adventure he had recently had, although whether George was old enough to appreciate it as fully as Charlie hoped is doubtful.

Buffalo Bill's American Wild West show had been touring England as part of the festivities for Queen Victoria's Golden Jubilee. In each city they visited it had been advertised that Buffalo Bill would pay 50 pounds to any member of the public who could ride the show's prize buckjumper. Many had tried; none had succeeded. When Charlie had visited the show, he had taken up the challenge and Buffalo Bill (taking Charlie for an English fop) had agreed to let him try. When the horse was brought in, Charlie nimbly leapt onto its back. The horse bucked like fury, but Charlie had had its measure and after a few minutes the battle was won. Charlie had cantered the horse around the show ring, dismounted and collected his prize. Mother and son returned to Paris and Nellie wrote again to Arthur Hilliger: 'My husband is frightfully jealous of the success I've been having and I have not had a very easy time with him'.[12]

Nellie and George moved to Brussels a few weeks before she was scheduled to make her debut at the Monnaie. She took a small apartment at 3 Rue du Bailly and engaged a maid.[13] They were joined by Annie and also by Charlie, who had come to see his wife succeed – or fail. His presence did not help Nellie's nerves and she would later say he threatened her with a razor in the Brussels apartment.[14]

Back in Paris, *Le Ménestrel* reported:

> One of Madame Marchesi's most brilliant pupils, Madame Melba, has departed for the Théâtre de la Monnaie in Brussels where she will appear in performances of *Rigoletto* in Italian. These will mark Madame Melba's debut in the theatre and we predict that she will create a sensation; her voice is charming and the singer's art is developing.[15]

The announcement that Nellie would sing her role in Italian would have surprised readers of *Le Ménestrel*, for it was the practice in Brussels (as it was in Paris) to sing all operas in French. The decision to allow Nellie to sing in Italian had been made after careful consideration and probably with a degree of reluctance by Dupont and Lapissida. Nellie had learned to communicate in French since her arrival in Paris and French was the language spoken at the École Marchesi, but she had yet to perfect her accent. It was not 'atrocious' as Lapissida had told Gailhard, but it was not good enough to be exhibited on the stage of the Monnaie. Accent issues would plague Nellie throughout her career in Brussels and if we listen to her recordings of French music made in later years it would seem she never quite perfected her French accent.

The company Nellie joined in Brussels was comprised of just 24 principals, only about half a dozen of whom had reputations outside Belgium and France. Among the sopranos, only two would provide competition for Nellie – Rose Caron who sang both lyric and dramatic roles and a newcomer, Lise Landouzy, the possessor of a hard little voice who specialised in soubrette roles. Also in the company were the great dramatic soprano Félia Litvinne, the distinguished contralto Blanche Deschamps and the young Maurice Renaud, who would go on to become one of the great baritones of his time and sing often with Nellie in Paris, London and New York.

Dupont was to conduct *Rigoletto*, and the cast he and Lapissida had assembled included Arthur Henri Séguin in the title role and François Pierre-Émile Engel as the Duke of Mantua. The other principals were asked to respond in Italian when Nellie sang to them in Italian and otherwise to stick to French when she was not singing.[16]

Rehearsals began as soon as Nellie arrived in Brussels but on the morning of the first, that Damoclean sword fell. As Nellie was alighting from a carriage at the stage door of the Monnaie, a strange man stepped in front of her and handed her a blue document – a legal order restraining her from performing at the Monnaie because she lacked the consent of Maurice Strakosch. Nellie (possibly in tears, but more likely furious) rushed into the theatre and straight to Lapissida's office. The co-director took the document and thus began a heated exchange of telegrams and letters between him and Strakosch. In the hope that Strakosch would relent, the rehearsals continued, but Strakosch held his ground. As the days passed, it appeared increasingly unlikely that Nellie would sing. Her name was removed from the billboards and another soprano (probably Caron) was asked to be prepared to take over the role of Gilda if necessary. Nellie became increasingly stressed and had difficulty sleeping.

The final dress rehearsal for *Rigoletto* was scheduled for the morning of 10 October. As Nellie was dressing in her apartment, Lapissida arrived and ran upstairs shouting: 'Strakosch est mort! Il est mort hier au soir, dans un cirque, et je vous attends au Théâtre à onze heures!' ('Strakosch is dead! He died last night at the circus and I await you at the theatre at eleven o'clock.')[17] Nellie's name was reinstated on the billboards in, she claimed, even larger letters than before, which added to her anxious state.

The morning before Nellie was to make her evening debut, Thursday 13 October 1887, dawned dull and rainy. Nellie may have experienced one of those nervous sore throats that plagued her at key moments throughout her career, but if she did, she chose to ignore it in the many accounts she gave of her stage debut. Mathilde and Salvatore Marchesi, who had come to Brussels to witness the event, arrived in the late morning to offer support. Nellie left for the theatre at around six. After being dressed in Gilda's first act costume, she sat patiently in her dressing room as a makeup artist did her makeup, but refused to wear the blonde wig that was traditionally worn for the role of Gilda, wearing her own hair in two plaits instead. It is likely that Lapissida and Dupont called on her to wish her good luck, before Dupont descended to the pit to take up his baton and start the performance. Seated with the Gevaerts in their box and nervously anticipating the rise of the curtain were Mathilde and Salvatore, Annie and Charlie.

Gilda does not appear in the first scene of the opera, entering in the second. She would have listened to Seguin intoning Rigoletto's great soliloquy 'Pari siamo' (or 'Nous nous valons!' on this occasion) and then stepped out onto the stage to greet him, not with 'Mon père' but with 'Mio padre.'

Nellie's account of her reception by the audience, given to both Murphy and Nichols, was unrestrained by modesty, but undoubtedly accurate.

> From the first note I sang, there was a hush that hardly seemed human, a hush in which I heard my voice floating out into the distance as though it was the voice of someone other than myself. Nor shall I forget the thunder of applause which broke in after the end of the act. I said to myself 'This cannot be for me. They are clapping and cheering for somebody else.'[18]

The enthusiastic appreciation continued to the end of the opera and Nellie gloried in the audience's ovation, taking numerous curtain calls and receiving a great number of floral tributes. The only sour note came at a supper party after the performance, at which Marchesi challenged Nellie for missing two notes in the third act quartet. Melba replied that she had hoped her teacher would not have noticed. Dupont broke in with: 'Don't bother her, Madame, she has had the most marvellous success. Why don't you think only of that?'[19]

Next morning the Brussels press clamoured to outdo one another in praise of the new star. The *Étoile Belge* claimed that she had the profile of an empress, that her singing had been a revelation and that she was the equal of Patti and Nilsson.[20] *Indépendence Belge* not only praised her voice and every aspect of her singing but also her acting – the one stage skill for which Nellie would in years to come be criticised.[21] *La Patriote* summed up its laudatory review with the prediction that 'within two years Madame Melba will be known as "La Melba"'.[22]

The Brussels correspondent of *Le Ménestrel* spoke with Nellie soon after her debut and reported to Paris:

> Madame Melba is from an excellent family, and it is passion for music alone that drives her. Here is a new star, and a real one, just arisen, and I think we will be talking about it very soon in Paris. She has everything needed in the high register – the éclat and the sweetness. Her vocalization is of the first order; she has an incomparable trill and she combines all this with a dramatic instinct which is quite remarkable. The Monnaie management were very smart to take advantage of this wonderful windfall.[23]

Nellie's success was also reported in London. An anonymous correspondent for *The Times*, described as a member of the British aristocracy, recounted Nellie's triumph and added 'She will appear next season in London'. It is very possible that the correspondent was Lady de Grey, Marchioness of Ripon, who would soon become a friend of Nellie's and her mentor in Britain. While it might seem unlikely that a pillar of British high society should be a correspondent for a newspaper, Gladys (pronounced *Glay-dis*) de Grey was a keen supporter of the arts and had been present at Nellie's debut in Brussels. The most persuasive evidence about the identity of the writer, however, can be found in the correspondent's final remark – about Nellie singing in London the following year. It was Gladys de Grey who had persuaded Augustus Harris to take over Covent Garden and while that comment may well have been wishful thinking, no one could exert more influence to ensure that it became a reality than she.[24]

With several more performances of *Rigoletto*, Nellie well and truly earned the exclusive right to sing the role during the season. Queen Marie Henriette, the unhappily married wife of King Leopold II of Belgium, attended the second and Nellie was summoned to the private salon adjoining the royal box in the interval between acts two and three and was there presented to the queen by Joseph

Dupont. That was Nellie's first encounter with a monarch, and it would not be her last. The element of snobbery that would develop in Nellie's character as her fame and power grew would thrive on such encounters, with each listed in detail in Murphy's and Nichols's books. Recounting this first meeting to Nichols, she said: 'My first Queen! How gentle and sweet she was with her grey hair and her diamonds and the soft voice in which she told me "You are wonderful" and I believe that then I did begin to realise something of the triumph I had enjoyed'.[25]

Despite the praise she had received for her acting as Gilda in *Rigoletto*, it was this aspect of her performance that brought Nellie close to failure in her second role: Violetta in *La Traviata*. Conceivably, having sung Violetta's great act one *scena* so successfully in concert for so long, Nellie might have become complacent about performing the rest of the role. If so, then she had underestimated its histrionic demands. Compared with the innocent Gilda, Violetta is a complex, multi-layered and very 'human' character. All of this is reflected in Verdi's score, but to portray the character convincingly on stage requires mature acting skills and experience, neither of which Nellie as yet possessed.

Nellie sang Violetta for the first time on 9 November, again supported by Engel and Seguin and with Dupont in the pit. She sang in Italian; the others in French. She had no difficulty singing the music and did so spectacularly – if not particularly movingly. She also had no problems projecting the tender moments in her part; but when high drama was required the best she had to offer were virginal notes, a few stock poses and passé expressions.

On the following day, the critics praised her singing and, generously, attributed her disappointing acting to inexperience. While the audience applauded the technical accomplishment of her singing, the more discerning audience members lamented her dramatic deficiencies.

Nellie was devastated by her own failure, telling Murphy that she cried for a week, which sounds singularly uncharacteristic of her. What she probably did do was work on a more convincing portrayal of Violetta and by the second performance the criticism of her acting was barely mentioned in the press.

With a few days gap in her performance schedule, Nellie travelled to Paris to consult with Marchesi on the next role she was to sing: the title role in *Lucia di Lammermoor*, determined not to repeat her error,[26] returning to Brussels in time to celebrate Christmas with George and Annie, as well as Charlie, who had stayed on as a less-than-welcome guest. The arguments between husband and wife showed no sign of abating and as Charlie watched his wife's career blossoming his frustration probably made them more frequent. To relieve his frustration he became a temporary member of an exclusive sports club in Rue Dupont, where he was able to defuse some of his anger through boxing and fencing.

His attempts at farming in Littlehampton had met with only modest success and when he became aware that David Mitchell and Nellie still held land at Sarina in Queensland he resolved that it should be transferred to him, enabling him to return to Australia to establish a cattle and horse breeding run. That proved to be another subject for argument, but eventually Charlie would get his wish. His underlying agenda of taking his son to live in Queensland with him, however, was never fulfilled.

In due course Charlie departed for Littlehampton, but returned again a few months later, arriving unannounced one afternoon when Nellie and Annie were having their portraits drawn in pastel by the fashionable artist Emile Wauters. Charlie leapt to the wrong conclusion and accused Nellie of having an affair with the handsome young artist. Nellie finally placated him with a gift of 200 pounds.[27]

Lucia di Lammermoor, which opened on 4 January, completely restored Nellie to the favour of Brussels audiences, although the opera itself did not please them. In the last quarter of the nineteenth and the first half of the twentieth centuries, in locations outside the Latin countries, the operas of Donizetti, Bellini and Rossini, composed in the 1820s and 1830s (Rossini's 'The Barber of Seville' excepted), were considered old-fashioned and only worth reviving as vehicles for elite singers.[28] Nellie qualified as an elite singer and the critics could find nothing in her performance to criticise in their reviews.

More performances of *Lucia di Lammermoor* and *Rigoletto* followed and in the interim Nellie attempted to improve her French accent in preparation for the next two roles she was to sing, both written by French composers using French texts. Félix Gevaert arranged for her to have lessons with Jeanne Tordeus, professor of elocution at the Brussels Conservatoire. Nellie also returned again to Paris, where Delibes coached her through the title role in his opera *Lakmé*, and Thomas did the same for the role of Ophélie in *Hamlet*.

Delibes came to Brussels to witness Nellie's debut in *Lakmé* and when asked by the press about her accent, he is reported to have said: 'She will sing *Lakmé* with a small accent, but it doesn't matter what the accent is, as long as she sings it!'[29]

Melba sang *Lakmé* for the first time on 8 March – in French. The role of Lakmé's father, the priest Nilakantha, was sung by Maurice Renaud, marking the beginning of a long and illustrious association between the two singers. The critics praised Nellie's singing, especially of the famous 'Bell Song' in the second act. They also noted that her accent was still irregular, but as she was singing the part of a Brahmin in an opera set in India, it hardly mattered.

A month later rehearsals began for *Hamlet* and, at what must have been an uncomfortable meeting, Lapissida and Dupont informed Nellie that, despite her preparation and her efforts to improve her accent, they wished her to sing her role of Ophélie in Italian, while the rest of the cast sang in French. It was, they explained, the safest option. Nellie had no choice but to comply. Thomas came to Brussels to supervise the final rehearsals, as did Jules Barbier, who had crafted the libretto from Shakespeare's tragedy. Seguin sang the title role, with the important role of Gertrude sung by Félia Litvinne.[30] Dupont conducted. On the first night both Nellie and Thomas were summoned to the royal salon to receive congratulations from Queen Marie Henriette and the following morning the press praised Nellie's performance extravagantly, with very little comment on language issues.[31]

On 9 May, the Monnaie season ended with a final triumphant performance of *Hamlet*.[32] As six months separated the close of the 1887–88 season and the opening of the 1888–89 season at the Monnaie, Nellie prepared for her departure from Brussels. In *Melodies and Memories* she shared two endearing vignettes relating to this time. On the day following the season's end, Lapissida visited her in her dressing room as she was packing the costumes she had worn as Gilda, Violetta, Lucia, Lakmé and Ophélie. To his question of why she was packing the costumes, she replied that she believed that they now belonged to her. When Lapissida reminded her that the costumes were the theatre's property, Melba expressed such disappointment that eventually Lapissida relented and told her she could have them. The second anecdote concerns Nellie's last day in Brussels; Lapissida presented her with a leather box which, he said, might be useful when she next sang Violetta. When she opened the box, Nellie found that it contained a magnificent set of paste 'diamonds' – necklace, earrings and a large brooch.

Nellie's success in Brussels had been regularly reported in Paris and the press had railed against Pedro Gailhard and his co-director at the Opéra, Eugène Ritt, for failing to engage her for the Opéra and for allowing their rivals in Brussels to secure her services for two seasons. Gailhard had attended a performance of *Lucia di Lammermoor* in Brussels and after the performance he had invited Nellie to appear as a guest artist at the Opéra during the break between her first and second season at the Monnaie. Nellie declined the offer. According to the Paris press, her refusal was due to the paltry fee offered by Gailhard, but there was another more important reason.

In London Gladys de Grey had persuaded Augustus Harris to engage Nellie and by the time Gailhard had made his offer, Nellie had a contract to appear in the 1888 spring season at Covent Garden. If indeed it had been Lady de Grey who had said in 1887 that Nellie would sing in London the following year, she had accomplished that.

Parisians would soon hear Nellie singing at the Opéra, but before that, she would sing for the first time in the opera house that would become her 'artistic home' and where she would reign as *prima donna assoluta* and a force to be reckoned with behind the scenes for the next 38 years.

Chapter 6

Covent Garden

Nellie's first season at Covent Garden was not the unqualified success she had hoped for, but nor was it the complete failure portrayed by some other writers.

It was also Augustus Harris's first season as manager of the Royal Italian Opera, an institution that had existed in Covent Garden since 1732 and which had survived two theatres being destroyed by fire, numerous name changes and a long and colourful list of managers.[1] Harris had inherited many of the soprano stars who had occupied the stage under his predecessors, including Emma Albani and the American Lillian Nordica. This season several debutantes had been promised, with Nellie being the most anticipated.

The Times made this telling pronouncement:

> Prima donnas from over the seas are by no means a rarity on the Royal Italian Opera's stage, which has drawn many successful singers from America. But so far, our Australian colonies have not taken any prominent part in this international race for musical honours. Madame Melba therefore stands in the position of a pioneer, whose success may induce others to follow in her wake.[2]

In the exchange of letters between Nellie and Harris that had resulted in her engagement, Nellie had requested she make her debut as Gilda in *Rigoletto*. Harris had refused that request, insisting she make her debut in *Lucia di Lammermoor* and explaining that Albani felt she had the right to sing Gilda, at least for the season's first performance of *Rigoletto*. Knowing that London audiences shared the same view as those in Brussels about 'old-fashioned' operas, Nellie became concerned that the choice of opera might jeopardise her prospect of success. Information that the stage production had updated the action from around 1700 to the late-Georgian period was little comfort to her.

It had been announced in the press some weeks before the season began that *Lucia di Lammermoor* with 'Madame Melba' in the title role would open the season on the evening of 15 May, but Nellie's arrival in London was delayed for some now-forgotten reason. Another opera had to be substituted for the first night. Nellie's debut finally took place on 24 May (Queen Victoria's birthday), four days after she had arrived and settled into lodgings in Bayswater.[3]

Harris had assembled a strong cast to support Nellie, almost all Italians. Her Edgardo (Lucia's lover) was assigned to Luigi Ravelli, an experienced tenor and a favourite in London, and Enrico (Lucia's scheming brother) to Antonio Cotogni, a veteran baritone who would later have the distinction of being the earliest-born opera singer to ever make a recording. One of the most famous opera conductors of the nineteenth century, Luigi Mancinelli, was to lead the performance, and this time there would be no language issues. Italian opera was performed in Italian in London, but if that sounds like wisdom prevailing, it should be remembered that German opera, French opera and Russian opera were also performed in Italian in English-speaking London.

The audience at Nellie's debut were generous in their acclaim of her. The great sextet in the second act had to be repeated and after Nellie had finished the Mad Scene, she had to pick herself up off the stage (where Lucia swoons) and repeat the second half before the audience would allow the performance to continue. Five solo curtain calls followed.

The press reviews all carried derogatory remarks about Donizetti's opera, describing it as hackneyed, tedious, conventional, commonplace and uninteresting, with this selection of negative adjectives appearing in just *one* review.⁴ About Nellie, the critics were more generous, but most qualified their remarks rather than committing themselves to unconditional praise until they had seen and heard her in a more 'acceptable' opera. Herman Klein, writing in *The Sunday Times*, was the least reserved:

> Madame Melba has made enormous improvement since she sang here – more or less as an amateur and under her own name as Mrs Armstrong – just two years ago. Thanks to hard study and the excellent tuition of Madame Marchesi, she has developed her gifts to a degree that must astonish at least one good judge who then advised her to refrain altogether from entering the profession. But there can be no doubt as to the character of the success won in 'Lucia' by Madame Melba on Thursday with a critical Covent Garden audience. She managed to rouse first their admiration and then their enthusiasm.⁵

On the 29 May 'Lucia' was performed again and on 11 June Nellie sang at a concert in St James' Hall, featuring members of the Covent Garden company. The following evening she finally sang in *Rigoletto*, with the Portuguese baritone Francesco d'Andrade in the title role. Before the curtain rose on that performance, it was announced to the audience that Nellie was suffering from hoarseness, although little trace of it was evident in her singing. Once again the audience were generous in their praise and the critics reserved in theirs.

Unfortunately, manager Augustus Harris took more notice of the critics' reaction than the public's. The next part he offered Nellie was the trouser role of the page, Oscar, in Verdi's *Un Ballo in Maschera*. Oscar is a secondary role in Verdi's opera and although leading sopranos sometimes sing it, Nellie decided it was not worthy of her talents.⁶ Even the alluring prospect of singing with Jean de Reszke, the era's greatest tenor, who was to star in the opera, was not sufficient to tempt Nellie to accept the role. She requested to be released from her contract and Harris made no objection. Nellie packed up the costumes she had brought with her from Brussels and returned to the Belgian capital, where she believed she was better appreciated.

Another who was disappointed by Nellie's reception at Covent Garden was Gladys de Grey and believing that her protégée, and now personal friend, had not been treated fairly in London immediately set about arranging a return engagement for the following year and under more auspicious conditions.

Nellie's second season at the Monnaie in Brussels was even more successful than her first, the 'full house' sign appearing every time she sang.[7] Nellie made her return in the second week of the season singing Gilda. Lucien Solvay, *Le Ménestrel*'s Brussels correspondent, complained that she was still singing the role in Italian in a French-sung performance, but admitted:

> From Madame Melba, everything is accepted, and if she sang in Chinese no one in the audience would think to complain, provided that she was heard throwing off in the second act of *Rigoletto*, the famous trill that has sealed her reputation.[8]

Nellie repeated each of the other roles she had sung in her first season and when she sang Violetta in *La Traviata* the critics commented on how much her acting in the part had improved. She also added a new role, a role that would be viewed as one of her most successful: Juliette in Gounod's *Roméo et Juliette*, based on Shakespeare's tragedy.[9] Nellie sang Juliette in French and Gounod had offered to come to Brussels to conduct the opening night, but unfortunately illness prevented him making the journey.[10] Neither circumstance affected Nellie's triumph. The public responded on the first and on subsequent nights with frenzied applause, while the press congratulated Nellie for basing her interpretation of Juliette on that of Adelina Patti and commended her for being almost as successful as her model.

What the critics probably did not know was that Nellie had

actually seen Patti singing the role only a few weeks before she sang it herself. It had been announced in the Brussels press that the Paris Opéra was reviving *Roméo et Juliette* (with some 'improvements' to the score by the composer) as a vehicle for Patti and Jean de Reszke. From the time she first heard Patti in concert in London, two years earlier, and remarking that she hoped she would one day be able to sing as well as Patti, Nellie had longed to see her idol in opera. The opening night of the revival coincided with a few days in which she had no commitments in Brussels, so Nellie enlisted Marchesi's help in securing a scarce ticket and made a rushed journey to Paris to attend. She was not disappointed, particularly when she was told later that it was the first occasion on which Patti had sung in opera in two years and the first time she had sung the role in French, being accustomed to singing it in Italian.[11]

During her second season in Brussels Nellie also appeared in concerts at the Monnaie and at the Brussels Conservatoire, including three performances of the oratorio *Saint Francis* by the young Belgian composer and pupil of Félix Gevaert, Edgar Tinel, and one of Handel's *Ode for Saint Cecilia's Day*.[12] She also sang at least one performance of *Hamlet* in Antwerp, and concerts there and in Liege. Taking part in the concert in Antwerp was Joseph Joachim – Johann Kruse's teacher. A close friendship developed between Nellie and the 57-year-old violinist, which lasted until his death in 1907. Joachim, it was rumoured, was besotted with his young Australian friend and tried to persuade her to tour Germany with him as his supporting artist. When Nellie consulted Marchesi about the offer, Marchesi adamantly opposed it. Fear that the influential Joachim would replace her as Nellie's mentor and guide may well have prompted Marchesi's response. Nellie accepted her teacher's advice, but Blainey, in her biography of Melba, suggests that this marked the arrival of a sense of being 'controlled' by Marchesi which Nellie began to resent. Although that well may have been the case, no serious rift between the two women ever appeared.

Offers to sing in opera at the Kroll Theatre in Berlin, at the Teatro Real in Madrid and the Mariinsky Theatre in St Petersburg arrived while Nellie was singing in Brussels, but by then she had secured a second contract to sing at Covent Garden – and a contract to sing a number of guest performances at the Paris Opéra.

Pedro Gailhard and Eugène Ritt had reopened discussions with Nellie when she was in Paris to hear Patti. Believing their negotiations were complete and all that was required was an exchange of signatures on a contract, Nellie travelled to Paris in January 1889. When reviewing the contract in Gailhard's office, she discovered that her fee was given as 3000 francs per month, while the figure she believed Ritt had earlier offered her was 4000. Ritt denied this and Nellie stormed out of the Palais Garnier to catch the next train back to Brussels. The negotiations continued by letter for many more weeks before the situation was resolved – probably in Nellie's favour. She then returned to sign the final contract, but the delay meant that there would only be time for her to sing four performances of *Hamlet* in May before she was due in London to commence rehearsals for her second season at Covent Garden.[13]

Nellie arrived in Paris on 2 May and she and George settled into a suite in the fashionable Hotel Scribe, just 100 metres from the Opéra. Three days after Nellie arrived, the 1889 Paris International Exposition, celebrating the centenary of the storming of the Bastille, was officially opened and the city was abuzz with excitement. The exposition was located on the Champs de Mars, with the newly constructed Eiffel Tower – then the tallest structure in the world – as its centrepiece.

Nellie's sister Belle travelled from Melbourne to join her and Annie and to witness Nellie's debut at the Opéra. She also stayed in the suite at the Hotel Scribe and, along with Annie, took young George to the exposition when Nellie attended rehearsals. He (now almost six) showed his aunts around other sites in Paris, with which he was more familiar than they, including a visit to an art exhibition, where a portrait of his mother painted by Anna Chalot (mother of the noted painter Jean Chalot) was on show.[14]

Piano rehearsals for *Hamlet* commenced on the day Nellie arrived in Paris, but there was no time for an orchestral rehearsal or a dress rehearsal on the stage. Then the first night, scheduled for 6 May, had to be postponed twice because of the illness of the singer assigned the role of Gertrude – Helene Richard – allowing Nellie the time to appear at a gala concert at the Comédie Française.

On 8 May the great night finally arrived. Richard had recovered sufficiently to sing her role, but two of the other principals were forced to withdraw at the eleventh hour because of illness – the great baritone Jean Lassalle, who was to sing the title role, and the noble-voiced Pol Plançon, who could sing a trill in the bass register with the same facility as Nellie in the soprano register and who was cast as the king. Two competent but much less famous singers had to step into their roles at short notice.

Although these delays and disruptions must have added to Nellie's nerves, none of them affected her triumph. With her sisters and Mathilde and Salvatore Marchesi observing her from a box, Nellie had the audience enthralled from the moment she stepped on stage, with a sea of flowers and demands for solo curtain calls marking the end of the opera. The Paris press employed their most flattering adjectives to describe her performance, with no hint of criticism in any of the seven long reviews that appeared in the newspapers. August Vitu, writing in *Le Figaro*, ended his review by quoting Voltaire: 'Each society has its turn in history to reign' and added, 'Australia's time has arrived'.[15]

On the morning after her debut Nellie agreed to be interviewed in her hotel suite by Robert Sherard, a reporter from London's *Pall Mall Gazette* and a future biographer of Oscar Wilde. In-depth interviews with celebrities were rare in Victorian times and the *Pall Mall Gazette* was a pioneer in this field. The interview resulted in a lengthy article in the 23 May issue of the journal, under the heading

'A morning chat with the Australian prima donna' and illustrated with a line drawing of Nellie. Sherard's words indicate that Nellie had not yet recovered from the previous night's excitement, but was already adept at handling the media.

> All the flowers overflowing from her sitting room, which made the antechamber fragrant, were evidence of the Melbourne girl's triumph. One could have sat there for a long time, but Madame does not keep one waiting, and, in a blue peignoir, trimmed with white lace, makes a pleasant apparition among the roses and lilac – tall, elegant, with an expressive face and more than noticeable eyes. 'You have been very successful?' I asked. 'Yes', she replied, 'it was a perfect triumph, and after the fourth act I was recalled four times, a compliment which, they say, has not been paid to a singer here for thirty years'. I asked if she was happy. 'Oh, intensely', cried Madame Melba, and I think that but for the dignity that does hedge in a prima donna, she would, girl-like, have clapped her hands.

Asked about her early life, Nellie confirmed the success she had in Australia as a singer, pianist and organist, and added:

> But ever since I was a baby I longed to go on the stage. I dreamt of it and desired it all those years. I suppose I am a flower which can blossom only in the warmth of the footlights. I do not exaggerate when I say that I must be on the stage or I must die.

Melba then discussed arriving in Europe, studying with Marchesi and making her debut on the Continent at one of Marchesi's soirées, where she earned the support of Gounod. She drew Sherard's attention to a silver-framed photograph of Gounod on the mantelpiece. She then recounted being engaged by Dupont and Lapissida for the Monnaie and how Gailhard and Ritt had wanted her for the Opéra 'for so long'.

> Some months ago the directors of the Opéra here asked me to come and sing Ophélie in Thomas' *Hamlet*. I came and I know I

conquered because after the fall of the curtain, Monsieur Ritt, otherwise a silent and reserved gentleman, nearly wrung my hand off in enthusiasm and prophesied great glories in the future. Is it not jolly?

After further questions about her future, Sherard asked if Nellie ever read the newspaper reviews and reported that she showed no affectation when she answered:

Oh, indeed I do, and I am very unhappy when they are unkind. Most are good to me, but those that are disposed to be unkind can only find against me that I am a foreigner – that I am an Australian girl of which I am proud. This morning, though, I have no reason to be unhappy.

Sherard completes his article by regretting that Nellie's wonderful voice cannot be 'registered' on some 'machine', but can only be described with a pen. History would soon change that.

The other three performances of *Hamlet* mirrored the success of the first, and Gailhard and Ritt were now desperate to re-engage Nellie and to put an end to the continuing criticism of them emanating from the press and their subscribers for their past failures. Since the expiry of her second contract with the Monnaie, Nellie no longer had the security of a permanent engagement with any opera house, but in all other respects she held the trump cards. No doubt Gailhard and Ritt had to show due respect to Nellie and open their purses (to the tune of 6000 francs per month) to ensure her signature on a contract.[16] They succeeded and it was announced in the press that Madame Melba would be joining the permanent company at the Opéra's next season, following her appearances in London.

While in Paris Nellie appeared at two soirées. One was Marchesi's annual 'showcase', where she sang the 'Bell Song' from *Lakmé*, accompanied at the piano by Delibes, and the 'Waltz Song' ('O légère hirondelle') from Gounod's *Mireille*, accompanied by Gounod. The other was organised by Maria Pavlovna Benardaky, wife of a Russian state counsellor and an accomplished amateur singer and a friend of Tchaikovsky. For this event, Melba and Delibes repeated the 'Bell Song' and Nellie sang a duet with her hostess. The architect who had redesigned and reconstructed central Paris in the 1850s, Baron Haussmann, was an honoured guest at both soirées.

Nellie also sang at a fashionable 'fete' at the home of Paul Veron, editor-in-chief of the illustrated journal *Le Charivari*, an event giving rise to memories that Nellie would treasure for the remainder of her life. Sarah Bernhardt recited a piece from one of her famous roles, Paderewski played pieces by his compatriot Chopin, and Jean de Reszke and his brother Edouard (a celebrated bass) both sang. Nellie sang 'Caro nome' and the duet 'Doute de la lumière' from act one of *Hamlet.* Her aged partner in the duet was the most famous French baritone of the previous generation, Jean-Baptiste Faure, who had created the role of Hamlet in 1868 and also the role of Rodrigo in the world premiere of Verdi's *Don Carlo* in Paris in 1869.

If Nellie's reception at Covent Garden had raised fears that she might never be accepted outside Brussels, that month in Paris dispelled them forever. It also provided confirmation that she had reached the top echelon of practitioners in her chosen profession.

The contract Augustus Harris sent Nellie for her return to Covent Garden had been accompanied by an encouraging letter from Gladys de Grey, in which she promised Nellie a better reception than she had received the previous year. It also mentioned that among those who wished for her return was the Princess of Wales – the future Queen Alexandra. It ended with, 'I shall see that you do not lack for friends or hospitality'.

On her arrival in London on this occasion, instead of lodgings in Bayswater, Melba took a suite in the Grand Hotel, facing Trafalgar Square. Young George was entrusted to the care of his grandmother at Rustington and given permission to spend time with his father at Littlehampton. Gladys de Grey was as good as her word and invitations to be a guest at high society events from her and her friends arrived for Nellie. Recognising their importance to her success, Nellie accepted those she could, meeting the Prince and Princess of Wales socially several times during the season. The prince took a liking to Nellie: she was exactly the sort of woman he admired – intelligent, forthright and handsome. Despite his deserved reputation for philandering, there was never any question of romance between them, but the pair became friends, and when he showed his pleasure in her company by behaving like a schoolboy Nellie had to remind herself that he was the future king.

The soprano contingent in the company Harris had assembled for his second season at Covent Garden was, once again, led by Albani and Nordica, but as the season progressed Nellie would match Albani's popularity and exceed Nordica's. This time, Nellie gained the concession she had been denied the previous year and was permitted to make her debut as Gilda in *Rigoletto*, while the title role was sung by her colleague from Paris, Jean Lassalle. The conductor was none other than Alberto Randegger, who three years earlier had been too busy to accept her as a pupil. No doubt some colourful exchanges between soprano and conductor ensued when they were introduced at the first rehearsal.

Although undoubtedly engineered by Lady de Grey, when Nellie first appeared on stage she was greeted with a welcoming round of applause from the sparse audience that had braved a thunderstorm to attend. Her singing of 'Caro nome' elicited a chorus of 'bravos', but the greatest acclamation came when Nellie and Lassalle sang the great 'father-daughter' duets, with the final scene reaching a height of dramatic intensity that would have surprised those who had seen Nellie in the same role the previous year. A touch of absurdity accompanied the moments after the opera ended. As the curtains parted to reveal Nellie and Lassalle still 'in character', a cascade of flowers descended onto the stage. Nellie extracted herself from the sack in which Gilda had 'died' to take her bows with Lassalle, subsequently stumbling over the sack as she left the stage, loaded with bouquets.

The following day the critics commented on how much Nellie's singing and acting had improved. Herman Klein's revue in *The Sunday Times* was typical:

> The Australian artist has profited by her experience and her companions; she can now boast something beyond a beautiful voice, a faultless method and agility of the most dazzling order. She has learnt to put heart into her singing and to act with something like real dramatic grip. All that was previously wanting to bring Madame Melba into the foremost rank of lyric artists, has been acquired.[17]

Nellie's next role – Juliette in *Roméo et Juliette* – confirmed her star status at Covent Garden. The cast Harris assembled was also stellar. Jean de Reszke sang Roméo with an elegance no other tenor of his generation could match, and acted the role like the matinee idol he was. Edouard de Reszke sang Friar Lawrence and Nellie's frequent partner in Brussels, Arthur Seguin, sang Capulet. Making Nellie feel even more 'at home', the opera was staged by Lapissida. Mancinelli conducted. The press must have struggled to find superlatives they had not exhausted earlier in their reviews of *Rigoletto*, but succeeded.

In his review of *Rigoletto* Klein perceptively observed that Nellie had benefited from her fellow performers. Singing in Paris with Jean Lassalle and Pol Plançon, both of whom were superb actors as well as great singers, had undoubtedly assisted her to improve her own dramatic skills; being able to rehearse and perform with Jean de Reszke in London had a lasting impact on Nellie as a stage performer. For Nellie, the Polish-born, Italian-trained, French-adopted tenor was the 'beau idéal' of what a male opera singer should be – handsome and elegant in appearance, blessed with a beautiful voice and furnished with a patrician style of both singing and acting. Among other tenors Nellie encountered in her long career, only Enrico Caruso would match 'Cher Jean' in voice and none matched him, in her estimation, as an actor.

Sold-out performances of *Roméo et Juliette* followed in quick succession and Nellie was invited to sing at a concert at Buckingham Palace, commanded by the Prince of Wales, but on that day she was ill and had to send her abject apologies. On 2 July Nellie participated in a royal gala concert at Covent Garden to honour Nasar-al-din, Shah Qajar of Persia, who was visiting London.[18] The sixth and final performance of *Roméo et Juliette* was also a gala event, celebrating the marriage of the Prince and Princess of Wales's daughter, Princess Louise, to the Duke of Fyfe. The press commented that they had never seen so many 'royals' at Covent Garden. Nellie would have relished the opportunity to be presented to all of them at both galas.

During the season Nellie sang one more performance of *Rigoletto* and one performance of a role she had studied with Marchesi but not sung before, that of Marguerite in Gounod's *Faust*. Jean de Reszke took the title role, Lassalle sang Valentine and the Méphistphélès was Edouard de Reszke. The performance was marked by an incident that might have ended in tragedy. Nellie was waiting in the wings to make her first appearance as a 'vision' of Marguerite in Faust's study. Without warning, a piece of scenery was ignited by a candle and a sheet of flame leapt up in full view of the audience. While firemen (who are always on hand in theatres) doused the flame, Nellie stepped out onto the apron of the stage and reassured the audience that the situation was under control. She probably did not realise it at the time, but *Faust* would prove to be one of the two operas Nellie would sing most often during her career.[19]

At the end of the Covent Garden season, Nellie had a period of about seven weeks before she was due in Paris for her first full season at the Opéra.[20] She planned to take George, Annie and Belle for a holiday in a hotel on the shore of Lake Geneva. When she went to Rustington to collect George, Charlie was there and, anxious to spend more time with his son, asked if he might accompany them. Melba reluctantly agreed.

Before leaving Rustington Melba also agreed to a request from her mother-in-law that her grandson be baptised. A ceremony was hastily arranged at a local church. Among those present were Charles and Winifred Rawson, Melba's friends from Mackay, who had left Australia to live in London. Melba had asked Winifred Rawson to be George's godmother and she had agreed – probably one of the few decisions made by his wife of which Charlie approved. At the end of the ceremony, as the water was being drained from the baptismal font through an outlet pipe it made a loud gurgling noise. George shouted out in French: 'Là, c'est le diable qui part!' ('There, that's the devil leaving!')

On the journey to Switzerland, the holiday party stopped at the Hotel Buckingham in Paris and there, true to form, Nellie and Charlie had a violent argument. According to Nellie, Charlie had accused her of mislaying a pearl-set tie pin of which he was particularly fond. Nellie denied his accusation and the situation quickly escalated. Charlie picked up his razor and slashed his hat, telling Nellie it should have been her head. Nellie rushed to her sisters' room to escape.

The party reached Lake Geneva and stayed at the Beau Rivage Palace Hotel, a five-star establishment near Lausanne, and there hostilities resumed. Seeing how his son had flourished in the West Sussex countryside, Charlie was determined to rescue him from pampered world his mother was creating for him and to take him back to Australia. To that end, he encouraged George to defy his mother whenever the opportunity arose. On one occasion as the group strolled along the lake shore, Charlie encouraged his son to throw stones at his mother and his aunts.

Charlie himself (according to Melba) threw a heavy candlestick at her in their suite in the Beau Rivage Palace and again demanded a share of his wife's earnings, which, he said, he needed to develop the property at Sarina.[21] Melba gave him another £200 on condition he departed immediately, but the fear that eventually she would lose custody of her son and that Charlie would take him to live in Australia lingered on.

At the end of the holiday, both Belle and Annie returned to Australia.[22] George returned to England to commence his education at a boarding school at Worthing and Nellie set herself up in a comfortable apartment at 9 Rue de Prony near Parc Monceau, Paris, along with a number of servants. Her neighbours included Gounod and Sarah Bernhardt, and Rue Jouffroy was close by. The location suited Nellie and it also suited George when he came to stay with his mother during school term breaks; he delighted in strolling in the Parc Monceau with his mother and visiting the Bois de Boulogne to ride in the goat carts and on the carousel.

Nellie returned to the Opéra with a performance of *Hamlet* on 9 October, continuing to sing her other customary roles with uniform success – and the occasional mishap. At one performance of *Lucia di Lammermoor*, the tenor Emile Cossira, singing Edgardo, lost his voice and for as long as she could, Nellie tried to save the situation by singing his part as well as her own. When both characters had to sing simultaneously, she abandoned her strategy and the performance ground to a halt. Fortuitously, Nellie remembered that she had given a ticket to François Engel, her Edgardo in Brussels. Engel had been in Paris trying to gain an audition with Gailhard and Ritt, and good-spiritedly agreed to change out of his evening clothes into Edgardo's costume and join Nellie on stage to complete the performance.[23]

On another occasion, Emma Eames came down with illness before a performance of *Roméo et Juliette*, and Nellie volunteered to take her place – and sang like an angel. Eames was furious. Sarah Bernhardt was in the audience for that performance and during an intermission strode into Nellie's dressing room and announced: 'Bah, you make up your face like a schoolgirl. You have no idea how to do these things. You are too innocent. Take a lesson from me, the wicked one.' The most famous female actor in the world then took Nellie's face in her hands and deftly applied touches of rouge, blue pencil, powder and lipstick – and Nellie was forbidden to check the mirror until Bernhardt had finished, at which point Bernhardt threw out her hands and said: 'Voila! Now you may look my pretty.' Nellie looked and was amazed at the transformation.[24]

One of the other roles Nellie was asked to sing was Marguerite in *Faust*, sung by her just once before – the 'fiery' performance in London. On that occasion she had not felt happy about how she had sung or acted. Nellie enlisted Gounod's help to improve her understanding of the music and through the auspices of Marchesi, called upon Bernhardt to teach her the finer dramatic points of the role.

In Murphy's *Melba*, Nellie offers an intimate account of the sessions she had with the 71-year-old composer, describing how Gounod always wore a velvet smoking cap and sang or hummed all the other parts in the score himself as they worked together on the opera, occasionally making a joke and displaying his delight as Nellie's 'Marguerite' developed.[25]

Nellie always remembered the day that she and Marchesi spent in the company of Bernhardt. They were ushered into the actor's sitting room and told that 'Madame' was still dressing, giving Nellie time to study the extraordinary room. In *Melodies and Memories* she described it:

> It was an immense room that gave the impression at first sight more of a circus than a salon. There were heavy stuffs hanging over the ceiling, drooping down and catching the dust. There were the skins of animals on the floor, the heads of animals on the walls, the horns of animals on the mantelpiece – there were stuffed tigers, stuffed bears, even a stuffed snake. And side by side with this extraordinary menagerie were busts of Sarah herself, busts of mythological persons, easels, pieces of tapestry, dying plants and an endless collection of bric-a-brac.

Melba describes how the 'Divine Sarah' came running in and leapt upon a large box, which stood in the corner of the room. Shaking her legs like a schoolgirl, Bernhardt bombarded Melba with questions and then stepped down, took Melba's hand and said 'You sing like an angel. I want to teach you to act like an angel too!'

Together the singer and the actor worked through the score of *Faust*, Bernhardt offering numerous suggestions about the facial expressions and gestures Marguerite should adopt at critical moments in the opera. When, for example, Marguerite's brother, Valentine, curses his sister and tells her that her hands will never be worthy of spinning again, Bernhardt instructed Nellie to thrust her hands behind her back as if she was ashamed of them and wanted them removed from her sight. Nellie would later say that every time she sang Marguerite and was cursed by Valentine, she remembered the expression of utter torture in Bernhardt's eyes as she demonstrated that reaction.[26]

On 30 October, Nellie was one of a group of famous singers, instrumentalists and actors who took part in a mammoth concert to mark the closure of the Paris International Exposition. She and Léo Delibes once again performed the 'Bell Song' from *Lakmé*. That morning the composer had been rewarded for his services to French music with the Legion d'Honneur. Nellie rewarded herself for her success at the Opéra (and her contract to remain a member of the company until May 1891) with the purchase of a lease on a spacious apartment at 97 Avenue des Champs-Élysées, to serve as a base from which to manage her career in Europe.[27] Securing a luxurious permanent home for herself and George, Melba reasoned, would also strengthen her case for custody of her son if and when Charlie challenged that in court. Both mother and son loved Paris, but Melba made sure that her son, like she, also never lost his love of Australia – but preferably from afar.

In the autumn of 1889, Léon Jehin, who had graduated from conducting in Brussels to the same role in Paris, was appointed musical director of the Opéra de Monte Carlo in the Principality of Monaco. Jehin immediately suggested to the director of the Monte Carlo company that he engage Nellie as a guest artist for their forthcoming winter season. Nellie obtained a *congé* (short period of leave) from the Paris Opéra and travelled to Monaco at the end of January 1890 to sing two performances each of *Roméo et Juliette* and *Hamlet*.[28]

Nellie made her Monte Carlo debut as Juliette on 5 February with the tenor Étienne Dereims as her Roméo, and her old colleague from Brussels, Jacques Isnardon, as Friar Lawrence. A week later *Hamlet* was performed – but in a version different from the one with which Nellie was familiar. At the request of several notable tenors, Ambroise Thomas had rewritten the title role in the tenor register and so, instead of a baritone partner, Nellie sang Ophélie to the Hamlet of Dereims. Another colleague from Brussels, Blanche Deschamps (now married to Jehin) sang Gertrude.

Nellie was acclaimed in both roles by the rich and famous who flocked to Monte Carlo to enjoy the winter sun. The Princess of Monaco – Alice Haine, an American, recently married to Prince Albert I – befriended Nellie and declared to the press that her new friend was also 'the new Adelina Patti'.

Chapter 7

Le cœur cède à l'amour

Similar claims were being made in London when Nellie arrived in May for her third season at Covent Garden. Although Adelina Patti would be persuaded to return to Covent Garden in 1895, for one more season, her long and triumphant stage career was nearing its end. Her dominance over international opera and her crown as 'Queen of Song' were now available to any soprano bold enough to wrest them from her. Nellie was the leading contender and stepped into Patti's place willingly, triumphantly and without ever losing her respect for her predecessor. Patti, as far as we know, never acknowledged Nellie as her successor. If she had, she might have complimented Nellie on her voice and her singing and added some remark about their different temperaments. Patti was (like Sarah Bernhardt) a creature of the theatre and, if contemporary reports are to be believed, threw herself into her stage impersonations with an intensity of which Nellie would never be capable.

Nellie sang 17 performances during the 1890 season at Covent Garden, repeating her regular roles and adding two new ones. After her first appearance – in *Roméo et Juliette* with Jean and Edouard de Reszke – Herman Klein in *The Sunday Times* reported his astonishment at the progress she had made in recent times:

> This artist once again returns to us bearing with her evidence of unrelaxing study, fresh ideas and extended vocal resources. To see and hear her now, and compare her with the Madame Melba who made her debut here in 'Lucia' two years ago makes it difficult to recognise the same artist. The voice has grown wonderfully in

volume and richness; its higher tones are employed with infinitely greater ease and certainty of effect and the clever vocalist has developed into a brilliant and finished mistress of her art.[1]

Being the honest critic that he was, Klein felt obliged to add a caveat at the end of this review: 'Melba's Juliet is a woman of full age who falls in love as a matter of course and maintains her composure with easy self-control'.[2] Such remarks (and others less subtle) would occur repeatedly in reviews for the rest of Nellie's career and although her acting would improve in the next few years, she would have to content herself with unqualified praise for her singing and the adjective 'cold' frequently being applied to her acting. One could imagine the future Dame Nellie reacting to that with a remark like: 'I'm the greatest soprano *singer* in the world! What more do they bloody want?'[3]

Of the two new roles Nellie sang at Covent Garden that year, one was in an enduring masterpiece, remaining in her repertoire for some years, while the other belonged in an opera now justifiably forgotten. The music dramas of Richard Wagner represented the most radical development in nineteenth-century opera and the public had an insatiable appetite to hear them performed. Consequently, singers, even those trained to sing the Italian and French repertoire, aspired to perform Wagner, in some cases risking their voices by trying to produce the more robust sounds the German composer's scores demanded. For lighter-voiced sopranos like Nellie, the roles of Elsa in *Lohengrin* and Elisabeth in *Tannhäuser* represented the least perilous paths by which to show the public they could sing Wagner, and it was Elsa that Nellie essayed for the first time at Covent Garden on 10 June – sung in Italian and without, it is claimed, an orchestral rehearsal. Jean and Edouard de Reszke had both previously taken on roles in Wagner's operas with success and it was they who supported Nellie in her first venture into Wagner's tumultuous sound world.

Nellie was only partially successful. The critic of *The Times* reported: 'Madame Melba sang in very fine style, although much of the music lies rather too low for her voice. If she cannot be regarded at present as an ideal Elsa, her performance shows that she may claim to be a more than capable one.'[4]

Some of the critics commented on Nellie's elegant appearance in the role and in particular on the magnificent cloak she wore in the wedding scene. It had been commissioned by Nellie from the House of Worth in Paris, the couturiers who had begun to make most of her street clothes, and probably cost her more than she earned from the two performances of *Lohengrin* in which she sang.[5]

The second new part Nellie assumed was the title role in an opera by the English composer Arthur Goring Thomas, based on Victor Hugo's novel *The Hunchback of Notre-Dame*. *Esmeralda*, as it was called, had been performed by the Carl Rosa company in 1883, but this was its first production at Covent Garden. To satisfy the growing fashion for French opera in London, the English libretto was translated into French and the happy ending of the original changed into tragedy with sufficient carnage to satisfy another current fashion. The singers who took the major roles – Nellie, Jean de Reszke and Jean Lassalle – were all supportive of the composer and did their best to make the production a success, but the result was less than successful. Goring Thomas's music lacked originality, while the lyrical inspiration of the music of his teachers, Gounod and Massenet, was sadly lacking. After the first night, on 12 July, the performers received generous praise from the critics, but the composer did not. Despite telling the press that she was delighted with this new role,[6] after two more performances Nellie let Esmeralda slip quietly out of her repertoire without, one imagines, much regret.[7]

During this stay in London, Nellie also sang at several concerts and soirées, including one at Buckingham Palace by command of the Prince of Wales, and another at Windsor Castle. The Windsor concert, on the afternoon of 4 July, was commanded by the queen as entertainment for her eldest daughter, Victoria, widow of Frederick III, Emperor of Germany and mother of Wilhelm II ('Kaiser Bill'), who was on a visit to England. Nellie never forgot the first time she sang before Queen Victoria, but not all the memories were pleasurable. She, the de Reszke brothers, Jean Lassalle and Luigi Mancinelli, who was to act as accompanist, travelled from London by train but on their arrival at Windsor station found no vehicle waiting to convey them to the Castle.[8] Cabs had to be found to transport them to the Castle, where on their arrival the party was asked to wait in an anteroom until summoned. The concert was scheduled to begin at four and to finish in time for Nellie and Mancinelli to return to London, where she was to sing and he conduct an evening performance of *Rigoletto* at Covent Garden. No summons came and at 4.30 pm a senior Castle servant explained that the delay was due to the absence of the German empress; she, it was explained, had gone for a drive and not yet returned. The Queen, the servant added, wished the concert to commence without her daughter, and the party was conducted into a grand salon. In *Melodies and Memories*, Nellie described the events that followed:

> As we entered the room a tiny figure in black, attended by her ladies-in-waiting, took a step towards us. She shook hands with us one by one, looking us straight in the eye as she did so. I had a dim sense of a picture come to life, so like was she to her portraits: the smooth silvery hair, the heavy eyelids.[9]

Nellie sang 'Caro nome' from *Rigoletto*, the duet 'Parigi, o cara' from *La Traviata* with Jean de Reszke, and the final act of *Faust* with both of the de Reszkes. Halfway through the concert the German Empress arrived, expressed her apologies and sat down beside her mother. The queen then requested the artists repeat the part of the concert her daughter had missed.

Nellie and Mancinelli were now desperate to depart. In a whisper, Nellie explained the situation to one of the Queen's

Le cœur cède à l'amour

ladies-in-waiting. The message was conveyed to the queen and the party was finally dismissed, each bearing a gift from the queen – for Nellie a small brooch of rubies and pearls.[10]

By the time Nellie and Mancinelli reached Covent Garden, the curtain had gone up on the first scene of *Rigoletto*, with a substitute conductor in the pit, Nellie's understudy costumed and waiting to go on for the next scene and Augustus Harris in a panic. After a rather longer delay than usual between scenes, Mancinelli took over the baton and Nellie entered on cue as a rather frazzled and hungry Gilda.

A more serious problem also plagued Nellie during these months in London. As the season progressed, she experienced increasing difficulty in singing her top notes and had to resort to the vocally unhealthy practice called *coup de glotte*, where the singer attacks notes with a sudden, explosive expulsion of breath. On mornings after a performance Nellie also found her voice sounding husky. One of the first to observe this was Jean de Reszke. Using the affectionate name by which he always addressed her – 'Melbie' – the great tenor explained to her that if she continued to sing in this way she would ruin her voice. De Reszke recommended she consult a doctor. Nellie went to Felix Semon, a noted laryngologist who cared for the voices of many famous singers. Semon detected a callous-like nodule about the size of a pinhead on Nellie's left vocal cord and prescribed complete rest for six to eight weeks.

That diagnosis must have terrified Nellie. Nodules on the vocal cords, caused by overuse or unwise use of the voice, prevent the vocal cords from vibrating evenly. They usually require surgery to remove them and one slip of the surgeon's scalpel can seriously impair or destroy a singer's voice. Several famous singers before, during and after Nellie's time, have had their careers cut short by nodules on their vocal cords.

At the time she consulted Dr Semon, Nellie was scheduled to sing one final performance at Covent Garden – and in a third new role. To round off his season with a performance from a stellar cast, Augustus Harris had asked Nellie to sing the secondary female part of Micaëla in Bizet's *Carmen*. The title role was to be sung by the Brooklyn-born mezzo-soprano Zelie de Lussan, but what had probably persuaded Nellie to agree was the importance of the occasion to the other two principals: Jean de Reszke would be singing Don José and Jean Lassalle the toreador Escamillo, both for the first time in their careers. After receiving the laryngologist's diagnosis, Nellie reluctantly withdrew.

Nellie also had commitments in France. Some she could not break; others were cancelled. She began the period of enforced silence Semon had recommended by heading to Rustington. Nellie knew her husband's relatives would welcome her, but one was missing. Charlie's mother had died the previous March and Nellie found Seconfield House depressing and 'empty' after the departure of its chatelaine. Nellie didn't stay long. Taking her brother Ernie, who was now 15 and attending the same boarding school as George, with her, she crossed the channel and headed for the fashionable spa resort of Aix-les-Bains in the southeast of France. Here she sang two performances (one each of *Hamlet* and *Lucia di Lammermoor*) in the local opera house, after which they stayed at the Beauséjour Hotel at Ouchy on Lake Geneva. From nearby Lausanne Ernie was put on a train to begin his journey back to England and Nellie moved to a secluded villa in the Swiss town of Les Avants, where she remained for several weeks.[11]

In late September Nellie moved back to the Beau Rivage Palace Hotel, her summer holiday destination near Lausanne with her sisters, her husband and her son in the summer of 1889. While there, she consulted a Geneva laryngologist, who gave her the good news that the nodule was shrinking and that surgery would not be necessary. By year's end the nodule had completely disappeared.

Overjoyed, Nellie returned to her apartment in Paris and her duties at the Opéra. On 11 December she sang for the only time in her career at Paris's 'other' opera house, the Opéra-Comique, rebuilt after the disastrous fire of three years earlier. Her role was the one she had been scheduled to sing on the last night of the Covent Garden season: Micaëla in Bizet's *Carmen*. This time Nellie agreed because the single gala performance of the opera was to raise funds to erect a statue of the composer in Paris, and it also gave her the opportunity to appear on stage with the legendary Celestine Galli-Marie, who had created the role of Carmen at the opera's premiere in 1875. Another reason may well have been a desire to show off the 'Micaëla' costume she had commissioned from the House of Worth for the London performance and which had sat, unworn, in its box.[12]

Jean de Reszke and Lassalle reprised the roles they had sung in London. Galli-Marie was suffering from a cold and the wear and tear on her voice of a 30-year career. Nellie stole the show. *Le Ménestrel* reported: 'One cannot dream of a Micaëla more exquisite than Madame Melba. But how she must shiver to run through the mountains with bare shoulders and in such a short skirt!'[13]

That performance brought Nellie's working year to an end. It had been both a rewarding and a difficult year, but Nellie had received strong support through the good times and the bad – the support of a devoted lover, whose love she returned with equal devotion. In Juliette's 'Waltz Song' from *Roméo et Juliette*, which Nellie had sung countless times, comes the line 'Le cœur cède à l'amour' – 'the heart succumbs to love'. Nellie's heart had 'succumbed' during this year in a way she had never experienced before and never would again.

The first mention of the name of Prince Louis Philippe Robert, Duc d'Orléans, in connection with Nellie, appeared in *Le Figaro* on 19 June 1889 in a review of a performance of *Roméo et Juliette* at Covent Garden. The review praised the performance and added: 'The Count and Countess of Paris and the Duc d'Orléans, who attended the performance, were not the last to applaud the charming diva.' A year later (almost to the day) the Duke attended another performance of the same opera at Covent Garden, this time in the company of the Prince and Princess of Wales. Two weeks later, when Nellie sang at a concert in St James's Hall, he reappeared and after the concert visited Nellie in the artists' room. Exactly what transpired at that first meeting is unknown, but it seems to have marked the beginning of a love affair. The Duke became a regular flower-and-gift-bearing caller at Nellie's suite in the Metropole Hotel and there, the pair became lovers.

Nellie Mitchell, builder's daughter from colonial Melbourne, could not have been other than flattered to have attracted the attention of a prince, especially one who was rated as one of the most eligible bachelors in Europe. 'Philippe', as his friends called him, was the son of the Comte de Paris and great-grandson of Louis Philippe I, the last king of France, who had been deposed in 1848 and been forced to seek sanctuary in England. At the time, royalists in France still hoped to restore the French monarchy and so Philippe would, upon the death of his father, become the 'pretender' to the throne of France and, perhaps, one day, king.

Sponsored by Queen Victoria, Philippe had trained as a soldier at the Royal Military College, Sandhurst, and upon graduation, was assigned the rank of sub-lieutenant in the King's Royal Rifle Corps. In the two years prior to his meeting Nellie, Philippe had served with the 'Rifles' in India, explored the Himalayas, fathered an illegitimate son in Switzerland, become engaged to his cousin, Princess Marguerite d'Orléans, smuggled himself back into France and served a brief term as a privileged prisoner in Paris's Conciergerie prison.

Philippe was what might be called today 'a fit catch'. Eight years younger than Nellie, he was tall, athletic and handsome, with thick, light-coloured hair and bright-blue eyes. A similarity in physical appearance between him and Charlie Armstrong did not escape those who knew both men, but their characters could not have been more different. Philippe was a gentleman to his fingertips, and while he would have had no qualms about engaging in mutually agreeable and satisfying love affairs, he would never have abused a woman in the way Nellie claimed Charlie had abused her. In acknowledgment of Philippe's youth and in private, Nellie called her lover 'Tipon', an infantile contraction of his name.

By the time they became lovers, Nellie had acquired the elegant appearance and sex appeal that had been missing in her youth. She was never beautiful in the conventional sense, but care with her appearance, the grace of movement she had acquired on stage, strength of character and an aura of stardom drew the Duke to her like a magnet. Both parties realised that their relationship could never progress beyond a clandestine love affair because Philippe's family was devoutly Catholic and, as pretender to the throne of France, his marrying a Protestant commoner would have been out of the question. Delight in each other's company and passionate sex were rewards enough for both of them for the time being.

Nellie was now sufficiently well established in London and Paris society for her liaison with the Duke to be accepted by her aristocratic friends, who themselves were often engaged in affairs, but the rules of society demanded absolute discretion.[14] As both Nellie and Philippe were readily recognisable public figures, that proved difficult for them and later, when they began to take risks, scandal would erupt and destroy their relationship.

Philippe was on hand to comfort Nellie after she received the diagnosis about the nodule on her vocal chords, and when she and Ernie travelled to Aix-les-Bains, he accompanied them. They remained together at the Beauséjour Hotel in Ouchy (where the Duke registered as Monsieur Revelle), at the villa in Les Avants and at the Beau Rivage Palace Hotel when Nellie received the good news about her condition. An instruction from the Duke's father to accompany him on a trip to the United States and Canada, which arrived a few days later, then separated the lovers for two months, and while the Duke and his father toured the battlefield sites of the American Civil War, Nellie embarked on a new and exciting extension to her career.

In 1889 Nellie had declined the first offer to sing at the Mariinsky Theatre in St Petersburg, opting to concentrate on making her Paris Opéra debut and her second foray into Covent Garden. Another offer for St Petersburg arrived in 1890 and on this occasion Nellie readily accepted – appearing at the Imperial Opera in St Petersburg was a prize coveted by all singers. Some of the best singers in the world sang there each winter, receiving astronomical fees and extravagant gifts from the city's affluent society.

Le Ménestrel announced that Nellie and the de Reszke brothers were among those engaged to perform in St Petersburg in the New Year, also informing readers that Nellie had been given another congé by Gailhard and Ritt to travel to Russia.[15] The same journal reported that Nellie's contract with the Paris Opéra had been extended until the end of 1891, no doubt with, as conditions stipulated by Nellie, a substantial rise in salary and permission to accept the Russian offer and to appear in another season at Covent Garden.

Nellie travelled to St Petersburg by train, stopping over in Vienna, where she was joined by Philippe, who had returned from America and was eager to be with her again. They stayed in the Hotel Sacher for three nights, registered under the assumed names of 'Mrs Anderson' and 'Comte de Nevers'. On the evening of 18 January the couple took a calculated risk by attending a performance of Gluck's opera *Armide* at the Wiener Hofoper. The attraction may have been the opera itself, dating from 1777 and which Nellie probably had not seen before, or perhaps the opportunity hear the Hofoper's leading soprano, Amelia Materna, in the title role.[16]

Unfortunately, the elegantly attired couple, sitting in a private box, were recognised by a local journalist, who realised he had a potential scoop on his hands. After the performance the journalist sought out Blanche Marchesi, who was then living in Vienna, asking if she could confirm the couple's identity.

As recounted earlier, there was no love lost between Madame Marchesi's daughter and her mother's star pupil, but, probably to save her *mother* embarrassment rather than Nellie, Blanche implored the journalist not to reveal what he had discovered. She then visited Nellie at the Hotel Sacher to warn her about the situation, but Blanche's pleas had fallen on deaf ears, with the journalist publishing his scoop. A short piece in the next issue of his newspaper informed the Viennese public that there was a prince and a prima donna 'incognito' in their midst. Nellie and Philippe beat a hasty retreat from the Hotel Sacher and by the time the newspaper hit the streets they were on a train bound for St Petersburg.[17]

At the Russian border in the early hours of 21 January, the train was stopped by customs officials who insisted on removing all of Nellie's trunks from the luggage car and searching them. When Nellie spotted her *Lohengrin* cloak dragged out beside the track and tossed in the snow she stormed from the carriage, rescued the prized garment and berated the officials soundly, no doubt venting the pent-up anger she had carried since the incident in Vienna.

On arriving in St Petersburg, Nellie and Philippe took up residence in the Hôtel de France, where the de Reszke brothers were already installed. Nellie described her first impression of the city in *Melodies and Memories*: 'It seemed a city of ineffable sadness, given over to a strange silence, broken only by the cold, monotonous jingle of sleigh bells. I felt melancholy.'[18] But the melancholy didn't last; the next day the three singers were invited to the palace of Grand Duke Alexei (a brother of the Tzar). After being shown over the palace by the Grand Duke, they were invited for an informal dinner. Nellie ate enthusiastically from the trays of food that first appeared, without realising that these were the hors d'oeuvres preceding the five-course meal that followed, eaten off gold plate in a magnificent dining room. The three singers willingly sang for the Grand Duke and his guests. The next morning a casket was delivered to Nellie at her hotel. Containing a gift from the Grand Duke – a sapphire and diamond bracelet – it was the first of many gifts she would receive in the coming weeks.

On 24 January (11 January on the Russian calendar) Nellie made her debut at the Imperial Opera in the Mariinsky Theatre as Juliette in *Roméo et Juliette,* conducted by the Imperial Opera's musical director, Eduard Nápravník, and with the de Reszke brothers in their accustomed roles. Tsar Alexander III and the Tsarina Maria Feodorovna (the former Princess Dagmar of Denmark and sister of the future Queen Alexandra) attended. Nellie achieved another triumph, with the international press reporting that she took 30 calls.[19]

In the month that followed Nellie sang more performances of *Roméo et Juliette*, Elsa in *Lohengrin* and Marguerite in *Faust*.[20] In the middle of the month, the de Reszke brothers received news that their sister Joséphine, also a singer, had died, prompting them to withdraw from the season. Nellie remained, with local singers and other guest singers taking the roles the de Reszkes had been scheduled to sing. She also sang privately for the Russian pianist, composer and conductor Anton Rubinstein, who had sent her a note explaining that he was too ill to attend the theatre and asking if she would visit him. Nellie agreed and Rubinstein accompanied her as she sang several pieces for him. The composer inscribed a card for Nellie as a souvenir.

Nellie also sang privately for the Tsar and Tsarina at another dinner organised by Grand Duke Alexei, this time at the Winter Palace. Nellie boasted for years to come about how the Tsar himself had taken her on a tour of the great state rooms of the Winter Palace and led her into dinner. After the meal Nellie sang for the other guests and the next day a gift from the Tsar arrived, this time a bracelet of engraved diamond cubes and pearls strung on gold and platinum. While in St Petersburg Nellie also received an exquisite Fabergé parasol handle from the Tsarina, a turquoise and diamond brooch from Grand Duchess Paul (wife of the Tsar's brother Grand Duke Paul) and a tortoiseshell writing box (with her name inlayed on it in gold) from Count Leo Tolstoy.[21]

On 28 February, Nellie delivered her farewell performance at the Imperial Opera. As she left the theatre a crowd of young men removed their cloaks and covered the footpath so she would not have to tread in the snow. One admirer thrust an autograph book and a pencil into Nellie's hands and after she had signed her name, he bit the pencil into several pieces and distributed them among his friends. Caught up in the moment, Nellie removed her gloves and threw them to the crowd, who scrambled like children to catch one.

While Nellie was travelling back to Paris (and Philippe to London), the press announced that she had been in negotiations with Maurice Grau, director of the Metropolitan Opera in New York, to appear with his company the following winter, but the negotiations broke down and no deal was struck. Nellie would sing at the Met, but not for another three years, during which New York's leading opera house would be reduced to a hollow shell by fire, with its interior subsequently rebuilt.

Any arrangements that Nellie and Philippe had made to spend time together during the months before she was due back in London for her next season at Covent Garden is unrecorded, but his presence was noted at one concert Nellie gave on Good Friday at the Paris Conservatoire. The press observed Philippe publicly congratulating Nellie on her singing after the concert and it was reported in London: 'Madame Melba, for whom the Duke professes great admiration, will not open her heart on the subject, only acknowledge that the Duke of Orléans did pay her a complimentary visit after the concert'.[22] The same article reported that Philippe had been passing through Paris on his way to Tiflis (Tbilisi, the capital of Georgia) to hunt, and that upon reaching that city he had telegraphed Arthur Meyer, the editor of the royalist-supporting Paris newspaper *Le Gaulois*, denying all the rumours that had been circulating since the Vienna article had been published in January. Ominous clouds were gathering, but it would be another six months before the storm broke.

Nellie resumed her performances at the Opéra and her appearances at concerts and soirées in Paris. One concert Nellie missed was a memorial for Léo Delibes, who had died while she was in Vienna. She had volunteered to sing the 'Bell Song' from his *Lakmé*, but came down with a heavy cold and, reluctantly had to withdraw. Nine days before Nellie's 30th birthday, the British Ambassador to France, Lord Lytton, and Lady Lytton organised a grand dinner party to honour her. Among the guests was 'Colonel' Mapleson, who after the meal offered Nellie 30,000 pounds to tour America under his management. Nellie told the impresario she would consider the offer, but in the end rejected it.

Nellie arrived in London on 1 June to commence her next season at Covent Garden, making her first appearance the following night in *Roméo et Juliette*. Three nights later she sang Gilda in *Rigoletto*. For the first time Nellie had the most celebrated singing actor of his time, Victor Maurel, as her stage father. Maurel had sung the role of Iago in the world premiere of Verdi's *Otello* at La Scala in Milan in 1887, and in 1893 he would be the first to sing Verdi's *Falstaff*. Rigoletto was one of Maurel's greatest roles and his presence on stage encouraged the rest of the cast to deliver their best performances.

Nellie also sang Elsa in *Lohengrin* (with the de Reszkes and Maurel), *Lucia di Lammermoor* and one performance as Micaëla in *Carmen*. Emma Albani returned to the company that season and Emma Eames made her Covent Garden debut, complaining later that she believed her engagement had been delayed several years by Nellie's malignant influence over Augustus Harris. Eames shared the roles of Juliette and Elsa with Nellie and the critics were generous to her without quite conceding she was equal to Nellie.

Two of Nellie's performances in *Roméo et Juliette* this season were marked by comical mishaps. In one, her hair extension fell off in full view of the audience. Jean de Reszke artfully captured it with one of his satin slippers and then kicked it into the wings. The incident was mentioned a few days later at Gladys de Grey's home and the Princess of Wales commiserated with Nellie: 'And they were *such* nice curls too, my dear'. On the other occasion, before the curtain rose on act five, Jean de Reszke went on stage to speak to Nellie, who was already lying on her tomb. The curtain rose while they were still in conversation, meaning that the audience saw 'Roméo' on stage several minutes *before* he was supposed to arrive, chatting to the 'dead' Juliette. Showing quick intelligence, de Reszke altered the text to justify his early presence, while 'Juliette' and 'Friar Lawrence' (Edouard de Reszke) struggled to hide their amusement.

The grandest event of the London season was staged at Covent Garden on 8 July. The German Kaiser was on a visit to Britain and a gala evening, comprising scenes from four different operas – *Lohengrin, Roméo et Juliette*, Gluck's *Orfeo ed Euridice* and Meyerbeer's *Les Huguenots* – was organised by Harris to entertain Wilhelm II.[23] As the silk program presented to the dignitaries who attended noted, the event was 'By command of Her Most Gracious Majesty the Queen'. The Kaiser (moustache oiled into bat-wing spikes) and his wife, Empress Augusta Victoria, were joined by most of their British royal relatives, but not the Queen, who was in residence at Buckingham Palace and probably spent the evening with her aged feet up.

The pageantry inside and outside Covent Garden, the glittering uniforms, the gowns, the diamonds and the profusion of flowers (including rare orchids) with which the auditorium was decorated must have almost outshone the performances. Nellie and de Reszke contributed the balcony scene from *Roméo et Juliette*, after which the Kaiser applauded vigorously. Nellie was angry when only Harris was summoned to the royal box to be presented to the Kaiser after the performance. Some compensation might have come in the knowledge that Eames (who had sung Elsa in the *Lohengrin* scene) was not presented either.

Chapter 8

The storm breaks

At a morning rehearsal at Covent Garden during the recent season, Nellie had received an unexpected visit from one of Charlie's brothers; which one is unclear, but it was most likely Montague Armstrong. During a break in the rehearsal he told Nellie that he had overheard a salacious conversation at his London club in which Nellie was named as being the mistress of the Duke of Orléans. He had come to ask her if it was true. Nellie denied the accusation vehemently, telling her brother-in-law that the Duke was an infatuated boy who followed her about compulsively, without encouragement from her, an explanation that might have been accepted had the brother-in-law not spotted Philippe lounging in one of the boxes close to the stage as he passed through the darkened auditorium.

Charlie was at Sarina at this time and his brother wrote to inform him that he was being cuckolded. This was not news to Charlie. He had already seen rumours of the affair reported in Australian newspapers, including the *Mackay Mercury and South Kennedy Advertiser*. His brother's letter confirmed his suspicions. Charlie wrote to Nellie to say he was embarking for Europe immediately and would be coming to Paris to 'sort out' this 'duke fellow', but fate intervened and Charlie was unable to embark for Europe for some time. After settling at Sarina he had joined the volunteer Mackay Mounted Infantry, with the rank of captain. When Queensland became embroiled in a statewide stand-off between striking shearers and their grazier employers, Charlie found himself in

Rockhampton – instead of Paris – seconded, along with his troop, to maintain order at the trial of a group of belligerent shearers.

Nellie must have felt that she had been granted a temporary reprieve and she continued to see Philippe, but fate seemed to be conspiring against her as well. A fire broke out at 97 Avenue de Champs-Élysées, and Nellie (in her nightdress and clutching her jewel case) had to be rescued by a fireman. The building was so badly damaged it could not be reoccupied for many months, prompting Nellie to seek refuge with Mathilde and Salvatore Marchesi at Rue Jouffroy. Since her apartment had not been directly affected by the fire, she arranged to have her stage costumes retrieved and cleaned.

Nellie also succumbed to a virulent dose of influenza and struggled to fulfil her commitments at the Opéra and to the Monnaie in Brussels where she had agreed to a return engagement. She had promised to sing two performances of *Lakmé* and then one each of *Rigoletto* and *Lucia di Lammermoor*. After travelling to Brussels, Nellie was forced to cancel the performances of *Lakmé*. She tried valiantly to sing in *Rigoletto*, but had to withdraw at the end of the second act when her voice gave out. The performance of 'Lucia' was cancelled and Nellie returned to Paris and to the care of Madame Marchesi.

News arrived soon after that Charlie had embarked from Australia and Nellie's reprieve would soon end. She did not fear her husband suing her for divorce – never imagining he would have the effrontery to name Philippe as co-respondent if he did – but she was concerned that Charlie would use the affair as a way of proving she was an unfit mother for George. To avoid that possibility, she consulted Earl de Grey, Charles Rawson (her old friend from Mackay) and a law firm called Wadeson and Malleson. Their advice was to apply for George to be declared a Ward in Chancery. His welfare would then become the responsibility of the British Court of Chancery. In support of this application, Nellie set up a financial trust with de Grey and Rawson as trustees, to cover George's maintenance until he reached his 21st birthday. The application was granted and although Charlie defied it a few years later, George was, effectively removed from his father's grasp at least while he was in the United Kingdom.

Nellie also applied to the British High Court for a legal separation from Charlie. Accompanying the application was a sworn statement detailing all the physical and psychological abuse she claimed Charlie had subjected her to since their marriage. Nellie signed the application for separation at the office of the British Consul in Paris on 12 September 1891.

Charlie arrived in Paris soon after and confronted Nellie. As a last-ditch attempt to deter him from taking any action, Nellie repeated the denial she had fabricated for his brother and added that professional jealousy had provoked Emma Eames into spreading the rumours. Charlie did not believe any of it and as he was leaving the venue, a reporter spotted Nellie and approached her. He also mistook Charlie for Philippe and addressed him as 'Monsieur le duc'. The fat was in the fire.

Back in London, Charlie engaged a legal team of his own and a team of detectives to gather any information they could about the couple's relationship. On 27 October he filed for divorce from Nellie on the grounds of her having committed adultery, naming the Duke of Orléans as co-respondent. At the same time he initiated a law suit against Philippe, claiming 200,000 pounds in damages, and applied for custody of his son. All this was reported in the British, European and Australian press.

On 31 October a summons was served on Nellie at Rue Jouffroy requiring her to appear in court in London at a yet-to-be-determined date to answer the charge made against her. The Paris press converged on Rue Jouffroy and a visibly distressed Nellie stated that her husband's claims were false, that she had had no warning of his intention to file for divorce, that she deeply regretted the Duc d'Orléans being unjustly dragged into the affair and that she had already filed for legal separation from 'Mr Armstrong'.[1]

Through his lawyers, Philippe issued a statement denying the claims. A summons was also prepared for him but he managed to avoid it being served for several months while travelling about Europe. An agent appointed by Charlie's legal team finally caught up with him on the platform of Vienna's North Railway Station. The agent had tried to deliver the summons at the estate of the financier Baron Maurice de Hirsch in the Tyrol, where Philippe had been hunting, but Philippe's entourage had blocked his access. When Philippe stepped off a train at the Vienna station, the agent slipped past Philippe's companions and thrust the document into his hands.

In the coming months Charlie's lawyers built up their case against Nellie and Philippe by interviewing staff of the Metropole Hotel in London, the Beau Rivage Palace Hotel in Lausanne and the Hotel Sacher in Vienna. The staff of the latter were the most forthcoming and their evidence the most damning, although their statements were vague. Charlie or his legal team released their findings to the press as they came to hand and readers avidly devoured the details, along with their morning toast or croissants.

In December Charlie told the press that, regardless of the court's determination in the case, he planned to challenge Philippe to a duel and as the aggrieved party he would be choosing pistols as their weapons. Duelling was illegal in the United Kingdom and as Philippe's father, the Comte de Paris, pointed out, his son's rank (and Charlie's lack of it) meant that if such a challenge were made, Philippe would be entitled to ignore it without reflection on his character.

That bold and true-to-type threat of violence from Charlie seemed to turn the tide against him. What sympathy there had been for him in the British press began to wane and the French press treated the threat as a joke. Both Nellie's and Philippe's lawyers had also been assembling a raft of reasons why the case could not proceed, principal among them being that Charlie was not a permanent resident of the United Kingdom and, therefore, the suit should have been lodged in Australia, and that Philippe's nationality protected him from judgement by any British court.

Gladys de Grey collected the signatures of several of London's leading society matrons on a letter testifying to Nellie's innocence, while the Irish-born journalist Agnes Murphy (who would one day become Nellie's secretary) took up her cause in Australia, defending Nellie but blaming the situation on Philippe.

Eventually the divorce case and Nellie's application for legal separation were heard together in London. The magistrate ruled that the evidence of the staff of the Hotel Sacher in Vienna was inadmissible. Charlie's lawyers appealed that decision but were overruled. The case was adjourned, resuming in August the following year. By then Charlie's lawyers were advising him to withdraw his suit and his claim for damages, but he pressed on. On 8 August the court dismissed both Charlie's divorce suit and Nellie's bid for legal separation. Nellie would remain Mrs Charles Armstrong for another eight years, but all communication between them ceased until Charlie abducted George from his school in 1894. Charlie took his son, now aged 13, to live with him in America, where the British Court of Chancery had no jurisdiction. In a Texas court in 1900 Charlie successfully sued Nellie for divorce on the grounds of desertion and Nellie did not contest the case.[2]

The affair had lasting repercussions for Philippe. Conservative elements among the French royalists demanded his father keep him under tighter control. Philippe's engagement to Princess Marguerite d'Orléans had been broken off, but in 1896 he married a Hungarian archduchess and two years later he became the target of a planned assassination, but the assassin lost track of him on the streets of Geneva and fatally stabbed the Empress Elisabeth of Austria instead.[3]

Just as he represented Nellie's greatest love, she represented Philippe's and he never forgot her. In 1975 Lady Maie Casey published an essay about Nellie and included in it a letter written by Philippe from the Ritz Hotel in London on the evening after he and Nellie had met and on the eve of a second meeting, almost 30 years after the scandal and the legal battles.[4] Dated 1919, the letter, translated from French, reads:

> My dear Nellie,
>
> What can I tell you of the tender emotion that I felt again after so many years? It seemed to me that it was yesterday that I said *au revoir* to you and I found myself feeling the same as I had thirty years ago. I was so happy to find you, in spite of your moral and physical sufferings, the same Nellie who has never changed and who remains in my sometimes sad life the only constant and faithful friend to whom – even in the delirium of death that I so closely escaped – my soul and heart reached across space. For you know me and understand me! In spite of all the world has done to separate the one from the other, I am satisfied because the confidence you gave me is my recompense. Thank you for the few moments in which you have really made me happy in evoking the past years of my youth that I have relived through you and with you. I count the minutes that separate me from the moment when I will see you tomorrow evening. I hope for longer than this evening? I have so many things to say to you that I cannot write. But tomorrow evening the words will come of themselves from my lips when I am near to you. I hope that you will give me time to tell you all that I have in my heart. Meanwhile, my dear Nellie, I kiss most affectionately your pretty hands and am always your old
>
> Tipon

At the time this letter was written Philippe was 50 and Nellie 58.

Prince Louis Philippe Robert, Duc d'Orléans died of pneumonia at the Orléans palace in Palermo, Italy, on 28 March 1926, while Nellie was planning her farewell performance at Covent Garden.[5] Sadly, but understandably, when Nellie came to provide information to Murphy for *Melba* and to Nichols for *Melodies and Memories*, she felt obliged to omit any mention of Philippe. To have done so at those times would have invited further trouble, but to have been forced to expunge Philippe from her life story must have exacted its own toll on Nellie's heart.

In future years Nellie's name would be linked with other men, including John Lemmoné, the Australian playwright Haddon Chambers, the American novelist Francis Marion Crawford and the sculptor Bertram Mackennal, but she had learned discretion and no details of her love life ever leaked out again. In his biography of Nellie, the Czech-American journalist, Joseph Wechsberg, quoted a friend who had known her as saying that Nellie's friends would always be curious about her love life, but never dared to question her about it. The friend also relates how Nellie had a clever way of dismissing other guests when she was expecting someone they were not supposed to know about. The question, asked purposefully, 'What are you doing tonight?' was their cue to depart.[6]

Throughout these turbulent months Nellie attempted to get her life back in order. She surrendered the lease on the apartment in the fire-damaged building in the Champs-Élysées and returned to her old address at Rue de Prony. She also tried to sustain her career, ever mindful of the potential the scandal had to damage her professionally. She remembered how in 1886 Patti had been hissed at the Opéra following her divorce from a marquis to marry a tenor. Nellie feared she might receive the same treatment when she returned to the Opéra as Juliette on 6 November 1891, the date on which Philippe's encounter with the official serving the summons at the railway station was reported in *Le Figaro*. She need not have worried. When she appeared on stage, the audience encouraged her with generous applause. Nellie was so touched by this support that she cried and the more tears she shed the more the audience clapped, adding cheers and throwing her a couple of bouquets – before she had sung a note. At the end of the opera she was recalled to tumultuous acclaim. No hissing or any other demonstration of censure marred the evening.

Around this time it was announced in the Paris press that Eugène Bertrand, who had taken over from Eugène Ritt as co-director of the Opéra, had secured Nellie's services for a further year. Also foreshadowed for the next season was the new management team's plan to mount Massenet's *Hérodiade* and a new opera, *Stratonice*, by a pupil of Delibes, Émile Fournier, and that Nellie would be offered the leading roles in both operas. Although ultimately Nellie did not sing either of these roles, she could comfort herself with the knowledge that her position was secure with both the management of the Opéra and the Paris public.

The following year – 1892 – would prove a tumultuous year for Nellie, and not only because of the continuing public exposure of her affair and the legal battles, with these not resolved until August. The first three months were spent in Italy and the south of France. In June she would return to Covent Garden and, just before Christmas, she was to make her debut at the Metropolitan Opera in New York.

In the summer of the previous year, Carlo di Giorgi, the impresario of Palermo's Teatro Politeama, had offered Nellie 30,000 French francs to sing six performances at his theatre during a national exposition being staged in the Sicilian capital. The opera agreed upon was *La Traviata*. Nellie had been keen to restore the role of Violetta to her regular repertoire ever since her unsuccessful first attempt in Brussels, and a city remote from Paris and London seemed the ideal location for her second attempt.

Since the time of her studies with Marchesi, it had always been assumed that one day Nellie would perform in the great operatic centres of Italy – Rome, Milan and Naples – and the less prominent Palermo also seemed an ideal place for her to test the reaction of Italian audiences to her voice and her singing. Marchesi approved of the plan and Salvatore wrote to Giuseppe Verdi, telling the

78-year-old composer that his wife's star pupil would be visiting Italy and asking if the 'maestro' would allow her to visit him and coach her through the role of Desdemona in his *Otello*, which Nellie was preparing to add to her repertoire. Verdi declined, explaining he was too old to coach singers.

It was, therefore, with mixed feelings and some trepidation that Nellie, along with her secretary Louise ('Louie') Bennett from Melbourne and a maid, set out from Paris to travel by train to Naples and from there to Palermo by ship. The last leg of the journey was a trial, with bad weather whipping up the Tyrrhenian Sea. Nellie was exhausted when she reached her Palermo hotel at five in the morning and took to her bed, leaving instructions she was not to be disturbed.

A few minutes after she fell asleep, Nellie was awakened by the sound of a cello being played in the room next to hers. The mystery cellist was playing a piece Nellie knew and had often sung in Australia – 'Angel's Serenade' by Gaetano Braga. Nellie joined in, singing the words of the piece and the cellist accompanied her expertly to the end. An aged male voice then came through the wall: 'Chi è la?'

Nellie returned the same question (Who are you?) and the answer came back: 'Sono Braga'.

Nellie responded with: 'Sono Melba'.

Nellie's neighbour was the composer of the piece and was giving concerts in Palermo during the exposition. Braga demanded to be admitted to Nellie's room immediately, but recent events had taught Nellie discretion. She told Braga she would permit him to visit her at two that afternoon. The 62-year-old composer arrived with a bunch of flowers, and singer and cellist performed 'Angel's Serenade' again, this time without a wall between them and to an audience of two: Nellie's secretary and her maid.

Nellie made her Italian debut, singing Violetta, at the Teatro Politeama on 21 January 1892. Foreign stars of Nellie's magnitude were seldom heard in Palermo, so audiences were welcoming and not hyper-critical. The numbers were also swollen by international visitors attending the exposition, so the audiences Nellie faced in the Teatro Politeama were hardly representative of those she would later encounter in other Italian cities. The opera critic of the *Giornale di Sicilia*, acknowledged the beauty of Nellie's voice and 'la perfezione della sua tecnica di canto', but made no comment on her portrayal of Violetta.[7] Carlo di Giorgi was happy with his imported prima donna and, after the final performance, presented Nellie with a solid gold visiting card case inscribed with her name and a message of appreciation.

A more comfortable voyage took Nellie to her next engagement at the Grand-Théâtre de Marseille, where the triumphs she had become accustomed to on French soil were repeated. Nellie sang performances of *Hamlet*, *Lucia di Lammermoor* and *Rigoletto* before moving on to Nice, where the carnival season was in full swing. In addition to singing three performances of *Lucia di Lammermoor*, Nellie entered a decorated carriage competition! Her effort (giant Lohengrin-swan's wings affixed to each side of the vehicle, the interior loaded with carnations and roses) featured in the grand parade and won first prize.[8]

From the south of France Nellie travelled to Rome to fulfil a contract she had with the prestigious Teatro Argentina. She stayed at the historic Hotel Quirinale and was given just one rehearsal before making her debut as *Lucia di Lammermoor* on 4 March. This occasion was an evening and a performance Nellie would always remember with lingering dread and when she came to provide information to Murphy and Nichols for their respective accounts of her life she omitted this trip to Rome from her story.

On the night of her debut, Nellie was beset by one of the worst cases of nerves she had ever suffered, and so severe was the condition that it badly affected her voice. From the moment Nellie appeared beside the fountain in the second scene of 'Lucia' and sang Lucia's first few lines, she knew she was in trouble. Her voice was unresponsive and sounded underpowered in the giant theatre and she was well aware that she was not providing what a Roman audience demanded – passion and power – while the audience itself made no effort to hide their disappointment. At the end of the second act substantial numbers of the audience departed, complaining that they had been duped by the advance publicity proclaiming Nellie as the new Patti.

The Mad Scene, in act three, remained as the only opportunity for Nellie to redeem herself. Determined to control her nerves and to address the bitter self-disappointment she was feeling, she gave her utmost to the scene. She was finally rewarded with genuine applause and a couple of shouts of 'brava'. One solitary tribute of flowers was passed up to her, flowers that had been ordered by telegram and carried on their card the name 'Tipon'.

Newspapers across Italy the following day reported on 'un fiasco strepitoso' ('a resounding failure'). Even the old complaint about her accent was revived. The kindest of the critics wrote:

> Last night at the 'Argentina' was the first performance of the famous Melba as 'Lucia', but success eluded this artist. While she was much admired as a beautiful and elegant lady, her voice was found to be not very extensive and weak. Her performance was rather cold and awkward; its only highlight being the Mad Scene, which was interpreted with a certain animation, but not such as to challenge the memory of other, better artists.[9]

Nellie's partial success in Palermo, her failure in Rome (and her later appearances in other Italian cities) highlight the fundamental problem Nellie had with Italian audiences and they with her. Taste in singing was rapidly changing in Latin countries. The 'verismo' school of composers was emerging; those writing their operas about ordinary people in 'real life' (often low-life) situations and requiring a full-blooded type of singing, which Nellie was incapable of delivering. To Italians, her style of singing, with its focus on producing a smooth and graceful vocal line, a lack of 'beat' in the voice and technical virtuosity, was anachronistic. Fortunately for her, that preference was not yet shared by audiences in the United Kingdom, France or America.

Nellie returned to Covent Garden as Juliette on 4 June, relieved to be back in the company of regular collaborators (the de Reszke brothers and Pol Plançon) and unreservedly acclaimed by a London audience and the critics. Her reception there was also a relief to Nellie because there had been rumours that the queen was 'not amused' by Nellie's affair with one of her protégées.[10] Victoria may well have been displeased with Nellie, but for once her subjects had not followed her example. The Prince of Wales didn't obey his mother's embargo either, commanding Nellie to appear at a gala concert for the King of Rumania at Buckingham Palace on 1 July.

In the 1892 season at Covent Garden Nellie found herself in a more competitive milieu than she had encountered previously. Augustus Harris had added nine new operas and a clutch of new and up-and-coming singers to his season's offerings. Wagner's *Ring Cycle* was to be mounted at Covent Garden for the first time, conducted by Gustav Mahler and featuring some of the leading Wagner singers from the Continent, while two operas by the foremost 'verismo' composer, Pietro Mascagni, were to be staged. To these were added three new operas – by Polish, English and French composers – the latter featuring Nellie in the title role.

Among the new singers was another former pupil of Marchesi's, Emma Calvé, whose voice was not unlike Nellie's but whose acting ability rivalled Bernhardt and whose repertoire embraced dramatic soprano roles. Calvé was to become the most famous Carmen of all time and in time assume a legendary status similar to Nellie's. During this season she sang the leading roles in the two Mascagni operas (*Cavalleria Rusticana* and *L'Amico Fritz*) and triumphed in both. Emma Calvé represented a level of competition Nellie could not ignore, although there seems to have been no explicit rivalry between the singers.[11] To add to the competition, Emma Eames was scheduled to share three of Nellie's roles.

Elaine, the new French opera in which Nellie appeared was based on the epic poem 'Lancelot and Elaine' from Alfred Lord Tennyson's Arthurian collection, *Idylls of the King.* The libretto was crafted by French playwright Paul Ferrier and the music composed by a young friend of Nellie's from Paris, Herman Bemberg.

The son of an Argentine banker and a former opera singer, Bemberg was generously endowed with charm, good looks, enough money to ensure he could pursue his musical ambitions – and a passion for practical jokes. On several occasions Nellie had been the victim of Bemberg's practical jokes, most notably when he and his friend, the Comte de Mornay, surprised her one April Fool's Day by sending her twenty proposals of marriage from fictitious noblemen, a live rabbit, a dead turkey and a mountain of exotic cakes. The following April Fool's Day Nellie retaliated by paying an ironmonger to deliver a dozen enamel baths to Bemberg's apartment. From her comments about him, Nellie clearly adored this charming practical joker, but only platonically, for it was well known in society that Bemberg was homosexual.

Herman Bemberg also had considerable musical talent, which he developed by studying with several of France's leading composers, including Bizet, Gounod and Massenet. That talent produced a number of charming songs (five of which Nellie would later make recordings) and the opera *Elaine*, written for and dedicated to Nellie and Jean de Reszke. When the time came to sign their contracts for the 1892 season, the dedicatees had 'persuaded' Harris to give the world premiere of Bemberg's opera at Covent Garden, although 'foisting it upon him' might better describe their approach to the impresario.

Nellie and de Reszke claimed to be charmed by the music of *Elaine*, but after the opening night, the majority of the critics disagreed with them, claiming that the *succés d'estime* it had achieved could be attributed to the cast, rather than the composer. About Nellie – in the role of the innocent Elaine, who is deceived by Lancelot – the critics were unanimous in their praise. Perhaps the most startling review of *Elaine* was penned by George Bernard Shaw, the incorruptible and sometimes caustic music critic of the *World*. Shaw's words must have delighted Nellie and been a balm to her wounded self-esteem – from her unfortunate experience in Rome – as well as the competition she was facing from Emma Calvé:

> I am obliged to *Elaine* for one thing in particular: it reconciled me to Madame Melba, who is to all intents and purposes a new artist this year. I do not mind confessing now that I used not to like her. While realising the perfection of her merely musical faculty, I thought her hard, shallow, self-sufficient, and altogether unsympathetic. This year, however, I find Madame Melba transfigured, awakened, no longer to be identified by the old descriptions – in sum, with her heart which before acted only on her circulation, now acting on her singing and giving it a charm which it never had before. The change has completely altered her position from being merely a brilliant singer, she has become a 'dramatic' soprano of whom the best class of work may be expected.[12]

All the critics (including Shaw) complained that the opera was too long and for the subsequent four performances it was dramatically reduced.[13] At the end of the run, Bemberg withdrew the work and set about revising it for its second production – in Paris.[14]

The only other significant events in Nellie's sojourn in London in the summer of 1892 were a performance of *Faust* at Covent Garden on 23 June and an emotion-filled concert in St James's Hall. The title role in *Faust* was sung by Ernest van Dyck, the tenor who had, allegedly, revealed Nellie and Philippe's presence in Vienna to the press. That Nellie was prepared to sing with van Dyck 18 months later suggests that his involvement in the affair *was* invented – or that Nellie was unaware of it. The aim of the concert was to raise funds for a scholarship in memory of Arthur Goring Thomas (the composer of *Esmeralda*), who had committed suicide by throwing himself in front of a train earlier in the year.

Nellie returned to Paris in August, where she heard about the fire at the Metropolitan Opera in New York and the cancellation of the forthcoming season. With an existing contract, Nellie would have been entitled to claim the fees due to her had she performed there. However, to ensure that she would be re-engaged when the opera house reopened, Nellie advised Maurice Grau and his co-director, Henry Abbey, that she would waive any fees due to her.

The cancellation of the season at the Metropolitan Opera prompted Augustus Harris to invite Nellie to appear at Covent Garden again that year, during his 'winter season'. Not patronised by high society, the winter seasons offered opera at cheaper ticket prices, usually without the stars of the summer seasons. Nellie's acceptance of his offer was considered a coup for the impresario and her status as 'prima donna' of the 1892–93 winter season went unchallenged.

Nellie repeated her familiar roles in *Rigoletto*, *Faust* and *Lohengrin* and took the opportunity to sing two new roles: the title role in Verdi's *Aida* and Desdemona in *Otello*. Calvé's success during the summer season and the recent accolades she had received about her acting may well have motivated Nellie to attempt to show that she too could sing 'modern' Italian dramatic roles. She was also encouraged by the knowledge that Adelina Patti had sung Aida in her heyday.

Mathilde Marchesi was not in favour of Nellie tackling Aida, believing the role to be too heavy for Nellie's voice; rather than seeking 'Madame's' help, Nellie turned to Paolo Tosti to coach her through the role. With Tosti at the piano, Nellie enjoyed learning the role, and delighted in singing the sustained legato phrases inserted by Verdi into the music sung by Aida, but she did not warm to the character she represented. After the romantic 'damsels' she was accustomed to playing, the role of an enslaved Ethiopian did not appeal to her. Neither did the costume she was obliged to wear: a pale green shift with a brown shawl, a noisy array of heavy 'tribal' jewellery and a wig that resembled black rope. Most distasteful was the requirement to darken the skin of her face, arms, ankles and bare feet with greasepaint.[15]

At the final rehearsals, with Tosti's piano now replaced by a large orchestra and an army of choristers, it must have been obvious to Nellie that she had misjudged her capacity to sing this role as it should be sung and that she was taking an enormous risk by proceeding. To compound the situation, most of the other cast members were robust-voiced Italians, who sang in the new 'full-blooded' manner.

After the first night the critic of *The Times* echoed the sentiments of most of his colleagues:

> Some interest attached to the performance of *Aida*, since it was the first occasion on which Madame Melba had essayed the principal part. So many light sopranos have appeared in it that the fact has been forgotten that it requires a voice of dramatic calibre to do it full justice. In the triumphal scene and through the whole of the scena 'Ritorna vincitor' much of the effect of Madame Melba's beautiful singing was lost. Madame Melba endeavoured to realise the dramatic side of the part; but her histrionics compared unfavourably with the Amneris of Signorina Giulia Ravogli, one of that great artist's finest impersonations.[16]

The evening was also marred by a farcical incident when the artists took their bows. A large arrangement of chrysanthemums, orchids and lilies was placed on the stage and Nellie assumed they were for her and she reached for them; Ravogli made the same assumption, also reaching for them. An argument ensued in full view of the audience. Nellie wrestled the flowers from Ravogli and next morning the fiery mezzo-soprano told Harris she would never again sing with 'that Melba'. And she did not – at least for a couple of years. Amneris was sung at the second (and last) performance of *Aida* by a much less 'great' artist. Nellie would return to the role of Aida in Philadelphia in 1898, but for the time being her score of *Aida* was, wisely, shelved.

Unlike Aida, the second new role Nellie took on this season, Desdemona in Verdi's *Otello*, which she also studied with Tosti, suited her voice to perfection. Desdemona belonged to the romantic world of Juliette and Ophélie, and the music Verdi had composed for the gentle bride of the Moor might have been (but was not) written with Melba in mind. Nellie sang Desdemona for the first time on 22 November and triumphed, despite losing her place and skipping several bars in one scene.

Herman Klein in *The Sunday Times* pronounced Nellie the best interpreter of Desdemona ever heard and seen in London; and as those interpreters included Emma Albani and Emma Eames, Nellie was more than delighted.[17] The praise, however, was not enough to allay Nellie's nerves and at the second performance of *Otello*, she barely avoided fainting and had to take several days off to recover. Desdemona would become one of Nellie's greatest roles, but for the time being she wisely set it aside.

In the midst of the winter season at Covent Garden, Nellie made a special trip back to Paris to participate in a concert that gave her another opportunity to link her name with a legendary singer of the past. This time it was the great contralto Marietta Alboni, who was celebrating the 50th anniversary of her stage debut. Now in retirement and obese (Rossini called her 'the elephant who swallowed a nightingale'), Alboni was still a venerated figure in the world of opera and, at 66, this one-time pupil of Rossini could still startle auditors by the preservation of her voice. Alboni sang 'Una voce poco fa' from her former master's *Il Barbiere di Siviglia* and an aria from Nicola Vaccai's version of *Giulietta e Romeo* at the concert. Nellie contributed two arias from *Elaine*.

A few days later a letter from Alboni arrived at Nellie's apartment in Rue de Prony:

> I write to you, my dear Madame Melba, to thank you for having been so graciously amiable on the occasion of my 'artistic' golden anniversary. I am very keen not only to thank you, but also to tell you how admirable you are as a virtuoso singer, and as a dramatic singer; I was perfectly happy, my dear Madame Melba, to hear you, and I am very keen for you to know this. I kiss your pretty face. Your affectionate ex-contralto, Marie Zieger-Alboni.[18]

For Nellie, that letter was the perfect Christmas gift.

Chapter 9

Italy and America

Four days before she sang in the 1892 winter season at Covent Garden, Nellie had accepted an offer from a local impresario to give a concert in Manchester – her first appearance in the English provinces. The fee was generous, the hall packed and the audience enthusiastic. This success prompted Nellie to take advantage of the hiatus the cancellation of her trip to America had caused with a concert tour of England, Scotland and Ireland. Her London agent, Daniel Mayer, was instructed to make the arrangements and six supporting artists were engaged, including the young Australian contralto Helen Mearns, who had just completed her studies with Marchesi.[1]

The tour began with a return to Manchester, followed by concerts in Liverpool, Birmingham, Bradford, Hull, Newcastle, Brighton, Edinburgh, Glasgow, Dublin, Cork and Belfast and occupied most of January and February. The success Nellie had enjoyed in Manchester the previous year was not replicated in every city and, at the end of the tour when all the expenses were paid, Nellie was left with a deficit of 315 pounds. In future years, extended concert tours would become an important part of Nellie's career, but for the time being she considered the experience to be a salutary lesson and returned to opera.

Nellie's attention was now entirely focused on fulfilling a commitment she had made in the previous October: to make her debut at Milan's Teatro alla Scala, arguably the world's most famous opera house. After her experience in Rome, the prospect of facing more Italian audiences must have alarmed Nellie, but Marchesi encouraged her to accept the offer, pointing out that Milan was one of the citadels every opera singer had to conquer before claiming their career was truly international and their status pre-eminent. The musical director of La Scala, Franco Faccio, had invited Nellie to select the operas in which she wished to appear and after much consultation with 'Madame', *Lucia di Lammermoor* and *Rigoletto* were proposed and accepted.

In the first week of March, Nellie, Louie and a maid arrived in Milan. Not unreasonably, Nellie expected some of the city's leading musicians to call on her to wish her '*in bocca al lupo*' (literally 'in the wolf's mouth' meaning 'good luck') but only one did – the composer Arrigo Boito, who was also the librettist of Verdi's *Otello* and *Falstaff*. Probably from Boito, Nellie learned of recent triumphs at La Scala (Patti singing there in January and the premiere of *Falstaff* in February) and that Milanese audiences were a little exhausted by the largesse they had recently been offered. The conditions were not ideal for the arrival of *un soprano australiano*, no matter how much she might be admired in Paris and London.

Within a day or two of her arrival Nellie began to receive letters threatening that she would be poisoned, stabbed or suffer a fatal accident in her hotel lift if she did not withdraw from the performances at La Scala and leave Milan. In Murphy and Nichols, the only explanation for the letters Nellie offers is public animosity, but, as they were all written in the same spidery handwriting, a more likely explanation is that they were penned by the 'chef de claque' of La Scala. Every opera house in Italy had its claque – a group of individuals who would guarantee success for a singer (by their applause and cheers) for a suitable fee, and who would sabotage a singer's success if they were not paid.

That Nellie would have been approached by the claque on her arrival in Milan is certain, and if she had refused to comply with their demands, their campaign against her might well have been begun with threatening letters. Equally likely is that the claque would have been responsible for the rumours that then began to spread about Melba being a singer unworthy of the hallowed stage of La Scala. Nellie was terrified by the threats and seriously considered leaving Milan without singing, but Louie Bennett, on whom Nellie had come to rely heavily for advice, talked her into going ahead with the performances, and this proved to be wise counsel.

On 16 March, when the curtain rose on the second scene in *Lucia di Lammermoor*, Nellie got her first glimpse of the audience, and what she saw (or thought she saw) was not encouraging. In *Melodies and Memories* she recounted:

> It seemed to me that the occupants of the boxes were turned away from me, so that I could only see their backs. So startling was this that I almost forgot the phrase I was singing. And then the beauty of the music caught me by the heart and I sang the opening melody as I had rarely sung it before. And as I was singing I saw the audience turning, gradually, in my direction. I had forgotten that the boxes at La Scala are so built that many of the seats are actually turned away from the stage.[2]

By the time Nellie had finished that scene, with the scintillating aria 'Quando, rapito in estasi', the audience's attention was entirely focused on her, with thunderous applause and spontaneous shouts of 'Brava! Brava!' echoing through the vast auditorium. The scenes that followed were received with similar enthusiastic approval and following the Mad Scene Nellie was recalled for 11 solo curtain calls. No doubt, Nellie herself was 'in ecstasy' at her triumph over adversity and the prestige that would arise from conquering 'the citadel' of La Scala.

Next day the Milan newspapers echoed the audience's approval. Aldo Noseda of the *Corriere della Sera* wrote what must have been one of the longest and most colourful critiques Nellie ever received. It began with:

It was a true and genuine success. Who expected it? No one, or almost no one. The public this year is not in an optimistic mood. To nibble now and then at a bit of a soprano, to take a mouthful of tenor, is its regular function. The betting might have been ten to one that almost all the spectators went to La Scala last evening with a certain fear, mingled with ill-concealed self-flattery that they were about to preside over the holocaust of the diva Melba, the complete annihilation of 'Lucia' and the said annihilation to terminate with the sanguinary sacrifice of the diva herself. When, at the end of the first act, the public realised that its gloomy expectations had melted away in the warm light of reality, it seemed as stupid as an elephant before a corkscrew.[3]

While in Milan Nellie was introduced to Italy's up-and-coming man of opera, Giacomo Puccini, and to a young composer named Ruggiero Leoncavallo, who had just scored his first success with his opera *Pagliacci*.[4] The meeting with Puccini was brief, but Nellie spent considerable time with Leoncavallo. They were introduced at a dinner given to honour Nellie by Victor Maurel and the following day Leoncavallo called on Nellie and played through the score of his opera for her. He also obtained a promise from her that when the opera was produced at Covent Garden later in the year she would sing the principal soprano role – on the proviso that Augustus Harris agreed.

Success at La Scala led to an influx of offers to sing in other Italian opera houses, but Nellie only had time to accept two before she quit Italy. She sang performances of *Lucia di Lammermoor* at the Teatro Paglioni (now the Teatro Verdi) in Florence and the Teatro Carlo Felice in Genoa with members of the La Scala company.[5]

After leaving Italy, and on her way to London for her next season at Covent Garden, Nellie appeared for the first time at one of the prestigious 'Concerts Lamoureux' in Paris. With the Orchestre Lamoureux, conducted by its founder, Charles Lamoureux, Nellie sang Elsa's arias from *Lohengrin*. The press hailed her return to Paris and bemoaned the fact that she was no longer a member of the regular company at the Opéra. Despite entreaties and offers from Eugène Bertrand, Nellie had decided not to renew her Paris contract. She maintained her apartment in Rue de Prony, along with her love for the French capital and her French friends, but had decided that the central focus of her career would, henceforth, be London, where her popularity and influence at Covent Garden were growing year by year.

As evidence of her popularity, Nellie was given the honour of opening the 1893 summer season at Covent Garden in *Lohengrin*. Jean de Reszke had suffered an injury to his leg, which delayed his arrival in London, so the title role was sung by the clarion-voiced Spanish tenor, Francesco Vignas. Such was her influence at Covent Garden that Augustus Harris allowed her to sing the role of Nedda in the first production in the United Kingdom of Leoncavallo's *Pagliacci*.

Nellie worked hard to be worthy of this important assignment. She engaged Henry Wood as a repetiteur and spent long hours mastering the role of Nedda, guided by what the composer had revealed to her in Milan. She also devoted herself to the histrionics of her first verismo role, recognising that she would not only be expected to sing the part well, but to act it convincingly.

The opera we know today as a one-act work was to be given in two acts and Harris had assembled a strong cast. Fernando de Lucia was to sing the tragic clown Canio, Mario Ancona was to sing Tonio (both were established stars in London), and the young English baritone Richard Green would take the role of Silvio, with whom Nedda sings a long and passionate duet. Henry Wood remembered Nellie taking 'infinite pains' over rehearsing that duet with her young colleague.[6]

Leoncavallo came to London to attend the stage rehearsals and all her careful preparations were rewarded with complete success.

The first performance was on Nellie's thirty-second birthday and London's elite turned out to see and hear the new opera. The audience gasped and applauded when Nellie made her entrance leading a donkey and her first attempts at 'stage comedy' drew genuine laughter. Of the final dramatically charged scene, where Canio kills Nedda, Herman Klein in *The Sunday Times* reported: 'both Madame Melba and Signor de Lucia rose magnificently to the occasion'.7 At the end of the opera, Nellie led the composer on stage to share the cast's triumph.

Pagliacci with Nellie would prove to be the hit of the 1893 Covent Garden season, as *Cavalleria Rusticana* with Calvé had been during the previous one. Nine performances were mounted during the season, including two on consecutive nights when Calvé was too ill to perform in Boito's *Mefistofele*, and one performance in the giant Drury Lane Theatre, which Harris also managed.

Two-and-a-half weeks later, Nellie undertook another new role, her second in a verismo opera. This was one of the many operas Pietro Mascagni would write over the next 40 years, trying unsuccessfully to repeat the success of *Cavalleria Rusticana*. Like *Pagliacci*, *I Rantzau* had not been performed in the United Kingdom before. The same team of Nellie, de Lucia and Ancona led the cast and Mascagni himself conducted. The four-act opera contains some impressive music and, in the character of Luisa, Nellie had a splendid aria to sing in the first act, but the work had nothing like the impact of Leoncavallo's opera. The first performance, on 7 July, was also the last.

Nellie liked the young and handsome Mascagni and he was impressed with her. He presented Nellie with a photograph showing himself with Puccini. It was inscribed: 'To Nellie Melba. So good. Your friend Pietro Mascagni.'

During her break at the end of the Covent Garden season, Nellie visited Mascagni at his home on the Tuscan coast and there the composer showed her an opera he was working on called *Romana*.

Nellie left with another signed photograph, this time inscribed: 'To Melba, who I hope will create the part of Romana. Pietro Mascagni, Livorno, August 1893.' Sadly, *Romana* never reached production. The composer either did not complete the score or destroyed it, since no trace of it appears to survive today.

When Jean de Reszke arrived to join the company, he and Nellie returned to their familiar partnership in *Roméo et Juliette*, a combination of opera and cast of which the public seemed never to tire. One performance was a state occasion to celebrate the impending marriage of the eldest son of the Prince of Wales to Princess May of Teck – the future King George V and Queen Mary. On that occasion the tomb scene was omitted on the grounds that it was too sad for such a happy occasion! Among the royalty and celebrities in the audience that night were Mascagni sitting in Lady de Grey's box, and Philippe, his attention, no doubt focused on Juliette.

Upon her return to Paris from Livorno, Nellie expected to depart immediately for the United States, where she was to sing with the Metropolitan Opera company at the Chicago World's Fair, but a message arrived saying that Abbey and Grau had pulled out of that commitment and Nellie would not be required in America until the Met's New York season began at the end of November. Nellie now had another hiatus in her engagement diary. To fill in one idle day, she joined Mathilde and Salvatore on a visit to Chantilly to attend the races, where a horse named in Nellie's honour was racing. The three set out mid-morning in the Marchesis' light carriage for the 40-kilometre journey, but got no further than the intersection of Rue Jouffroy and Rue de Rome, where the carriage was struck by an omnibus and one of its lanterns shattered. The occupants of the carriage were showered by glass and, although Nellie had raised her arms to protect her face, one shard of glass gashed her ear. Mathilde and Salvatore were unharmed but Nellie's ear bled copiously and the trip was abandoned.

A name from a grim period in Nellie's past re-emerged at this time: Strakosch. Karl Strakosch, nephew of Maurice Strakosch, had followed in his uncle's footsteps as an entrepreneur and had been offering engagements to Nellie, which she had declined. Setting aside any resentment she may still have had towards his family, Nellie contacted Strakosch and agreed to sing under his management in the weeks before she sailed for America. She would appear first at the Grand-Théâtre in Lille in *Roméo et Juliette* and *Faust* and then in Stockholm and Copenhagen. Evidence that the past had not been forgotten, however, is demonstrated by a clause inserted in their agreement, one on which Nellie had never insisted before: Strakosch was to pay her in cash on the afternoon before each performance, or there would be no performance.

After the appearances in Lille, Nellie, her entourage and Strakosch travelled to Stockholm. Advance publicity ensured that, when Nellie made her Scandinavian debut in Stockholm on 31 October as Juliette, the public and the press were primed to give her an ardent welcome.[8] Sold-out performances of *Lohengrin* and *Faust* followed and a composite program of scenes from *Lucia di Lammermoor* and *Hamlet* completed the short season. Most of the Stockholm press hailed Nellie, with only one dissenting. A writer calling himself (or herself) 'Black Domino' expressed the opinion that Nellie's performance during the 'Lucia' Mad Scene resembled a small dog who had fallen in the water and was rushing about trying to dry itself.[9] Strakosch leapt to Nellie's defence, complaining to the relevant newspaper that his star had never before been treated in such a disrespectful manner.

Nellie was about to leave Stockholm when a message arrived for her from Oscar II, King of Sweden and Norway. The king had been in Oslo during the past weeks and expressed his disappointment at not having heard Nellie sing. Would she, the king asked, delay her departure for a few days, and sing an extra performance for him upon his return to his capital. A royal request such as that could not be refused and neither Nellie nor Strakosch would have wished to, because Oscar II was known to be a great supporter of the arts in his own kingdom and abroad. Nellie replied that she would be honoured to comply with the request and asked the king to select the program. Nellie might well have regretted that last concession, for when the king's choice was conveyed to her she was taken aback to find it comprised the whole of act two of *Lohengrin*, the balcony scene from *Roméo et Juliette*, the Mad Scene from *Lucia di Lammermoor* and the complete last act of *Faust*.

Nellie managed the mammoth program and several times the king stood up in his box and led the applause. At the end of the performance Nellie received a note requesting she call on the king at the Royal Palace at 11 am the following day. There Oscar addressed Nellie in Italian and she pointed out that she was Australian. 'Then we shall speak Australian!' the king said and the rest of the conversation was accomplished in English.

The king presented Nellie with the Swedish decoration 'Litteras et Artibus', but when he came to pin the gold medal with its blue ribbon on her he found it had no pin. He asked if Nellie had one, but she had only a long hat pin. A groom provided a pin, and the king pinned the decoration on Nellie's bodice, at the time explaining to her that borrowing a pin was supposed to bring bad luck, but that he knew how to avert that. Leaning close, the bewhiskered king kissed Nellie on both cheeks.[10]

Nellie claims that 5000 people turned up to farewell her at Stockholm railway station when she departed for Copenhagen. In the Danish capital Nellie gave concerts before returning to Paris, with two more countries now added to her list of conquests. In Paris Nellie donated 300 francs to a fund that had been set up to raise a memorial to Charles Gounod, who had died a few weeks earlier, after which she, her maid and Louie Bennett embarked from Le Havre for New York.

Opening in 1883, the Metropolitan Opera House on Broadway that year offered a mix of Italian and French operas, with Christine Nilsson and Marcella Sembrich as its leading ladies. The following year it became a German-style opera house with all performances sung in German by mostly German artists, maintaining this approach for the next eight years. In the season preceding the fire and under the directorship of Abbey and Grau, it had reverted to a more eclectic repertoire, with Patti and Albani, the de Reszkes and Lassalle leading 'international' casts.

Because of the delay in Stockholm and a rough Atlantic crossing, Nellie did not arrive in New York until the end of the first week of the Metropolitan season. During that week Emma Eames had sung Marguerite in *Faust*, Lillian Nordica had sung Elsa in *Lohengrin* and Calvé had made a spectacular Met debut in *Cavalleria Rusticana*, soon to be followed by her unrivalled Carmen. Both Eames and Nordica enjoyed enormous popularity among their countrymen. Nordica and Nellie appeared to display no professional rivalry and enjoyed a casual friendship, but Eames, Nellie knew, would not hesitate to mobilise her fan base to sabotage Nellie's attempts to win over Americans. To add to Eames's rancour, Nellie's contract stipulated a fee of 1250 American dollars for each of her performances, the highest fee paid to any female artist on the roster, while Eames received only 900.

The choice of *Lucia di Lammermoor* as her debut role at the Met had been negotiated between Nellie, the co-directors and Mancinelli, who was to conduct. It seemed (as it had at other opera houses) to be an ideal vehicle for Nellie to display her voice and her virtuoso technique, but in the United States it was considered not only old-fashioned opera, but a 'Patti' role, sung by that idol of the American public at the Met in the season prior to the fire.

To support Nellie, Vignas had been cast as Edgardo and a baritone she had sung with frequently in Europe, Eugène Dufriche, was scheduled to sing Enrico, but on the morning of the performance Dufriche became afflicted with laryngitis. For a while it seemed that the performance would have to be cancelled as none of the company's other leading baritones was available to take Dufriche's place. Jean de Reszke, who was also engaged for the season, suggested his former pupil, Victor de Gromzeski should be given the opportunity to move up from the minor roles he had been contracted to sing to a major role, forcing Nellie to sing a large part of the opera with a nervous and under-rehearsed singer.

With Nellie attired in one of her exquisite Worth costumes, her appearance appealed to the less-than-capacity audience, but they took a long time to warm to her singing. It was not until she had sung the Mad Scene that the audience abandoned its reservations and gave her the ovation she deserved. For once, the critics were more enthusiastic than the public, with W.J. Henderson, the perspicacious critic of the *New York Times* writing: 'Mme Melba is a soprano whom this public will very speedily learn to admire'.

Henderson continued by crediting Nellie with complete command of every aspect of the art of singing and concluded with: 'It should be added that her style is less cold than reports from abroad had led us to expect'.[11] Henry Krehbiel in the *New York Tribune* agreed with his colleague: 'Last night, Madame Melba revealed herself to be the finest soprano heard on the local stage since Madame Sembrich made her American debut ten years ago and no exception need be made, even in favour of Madame Patti'.[12]

Perhaps influenced by what they had read in the newspapers, the denizens of the 'Golden Horseshoe' (the holders of the most expensive private boxes in the house) decided that Nellie was worthy of their support at the opera – and socially. Henceforth Nellie's performances were sold out and a few invitations to private functions arrived at the New York Savoy, although, as Nellie discovered, most of the upper crust of New York society were decades behind Europe in their moral attitude towards 'theatre folk'.

Two nights after her debut, Nellie sang Ophélie in the season's only performance of *Hamlet*, followed by the Metropolitan premiere of *Pagliacci*, with the same trio of principals who had sung the opera at Covent Garden – Nellie, de Lucia and Ancona. It was now Henderson's turn to display reservations. The role of Nedda, the critic argued, should have been assigned to a singer who was a great actress and possessed a dramatic soprano voice. Acknowledging how superb Nellie's accomplishments in other areas were, he pointed out that she possessed neither of those attributes.[13]

With Eugène Dufriche restored to the role of Enrico, the Met cast of *Lucia di Lammermoor* then gave performances of the opera in Philadelphia and Brooklyn, while three nights before Christmas *Pagliacci* was performed again at the Met, on this occasion presented in a single act and in a double bill with *Cavalleria Rusticana*, the coupling we are familiar with today.[14] Nellie was unwell and in poor voice and Calvé triumphed in the Mascagni opera. It was not a night Nellie wished to remember.

Nellie's self-esteem was restored when a new production of *Rigoletto* opened on 29 December with de Lucia as the Duke and Ancona as Rigoletto. The opera was repeated in Philadelphia on 9 January, and a stage mishap that evening almost caused Nellie serious injury or, possibly, her life. The scenery had been transported from New York but, unknown to Nellie, a part of it was missing. Singing the last phrases of 'Caro nome' and in sight of the enraptured audience, Nellie climbed the stairs leading to Gilda's bedroom. She passed through a door, anticipating more stairs by which she could descend to the back stage area, but the stairs were missing. The trill Nellie was singing came to an abrupt end as she lurched back just in time to prevent herself falling several metres to the stage below.

Three nights later and back in New York, Nellie sang a role she had not sung previously: the title role in Rossini's *Semiramide*. The role of the Babylonian queen who murders her husband and falls in love with a man who turns out to be her son is one of the pinnacles of the bel canto repertoire and only the most accomplished sopranos attempt it. With the great Italian contralto Sofia Scalchi singing the trouser role of her son, Nellie's attempt was successful and, again, flattering comparisons with Patti were made. Six further performances of *Semiramide* were given during the season (three in New York and one each in Boston, Philadelphia and Chicago), Nellie earning praise from everyone, including Scalchi.

At the end of January Nellie sang another role for the first time, her second in an opera by Richard Wagner. The 'Paris' version of *Tannhäuser*, sung in Italian, opened on 29 January with Nellie as Elisabeth, Vignas in the title role, Ancona as Wolfram and Pol Plançon as the Landgrave. Wearing a costume made by Worth for her and which was reputed to have cost her several hundred pounds, Nellie enjoyed a qualified success. Elisabeth made even greater vocal demands on her than Elsa in *Lohengrin*, but, if the critics are to be believed, Nellie surmounted them in her own 'lyrical' way on this and three more occasions during the season.[15]

Nellie herself believed that the performances which finally earned her unqualified acceptance from audiences in New York and the approval of Abbey and Grau were her more familiar roles: Ophélie, Juliette (with Jean de Reszke as her Roméo), Gilda, and Marguerite in *Faust*, which she sang on the last night of the New York season. The Met company then went on its annual tour, with Nellie singing in Boston, Chicago and St Louis, before returning for a supplementary season in New York.

Nellie also appeared in five Sunday night concerts at the Met, two galas where single acts from different operas were combined and a charity concert in Carnegie Hall. She also returned to Boston after the Met had closed to perform as a soloist in a concert with the Boston Symphony Orchestra, describing that orchestra as 'the greatest in the world'.

Nellie had spent five months in the United States and travelled thousands of kilometres. She had established herself at the Met with

48 performances of nine roles, earned the approval of American audiences and enjoyed working with familiar colleagues, but she had been lonely, with only Louie Bennett to share her triumphs and occasional disappointments. She had made a few new friends in the United States, including Francis Marion Crawford, but missed her French and English friends and the network of support they provided her. She had also held a vague hope that she might see George during her travels, but that hope had not been fulfilled. Her son and her husband's last known address was a post office box in Cherokee, North Carolina, and their current whereabouts was a frustrating mystery. Once, when she stepped off a train in Chicago she spied a boy selling newspapers who reminded her so much of George that she approached the boy and asked how long he was required to stand in the snow. 'Until I've sold me 50 papers, ma'am', the boy replied. Nellie fetched a note out of her purse and bought the lot.

Nellie returned to Europe aboard the French liner *La Touraine*, docking at Le Havre, after which she, her maid and Louie began the long train journey to Milan, where Nellie had been invited to sing again in the 1894 season at La Scala. Nellie sang to full houses and after one performance she received a distinguished visitor in her dressing room. In *Melodies and Memories*, she recounted:

> One night after I had been singing in *Rigoletto*, I learnt that the Maestro, Giuseppe Verdi, had been in the house, and that he was now outside my dressing room waiting to see me. I bounded to the door and said, 'Maestro, what an honour! They didn't tell me that you were here.' He bowed, slowly, almost sternly. It was like a tree trying to bend. That was the impression he gave one, of some gnarled, old, wonderful tree. There was an impenetrable reserve about him which made conversation with him slightly stilted. And yet, he had bright eyes, like a boy's, and eager restless hands.
>
> Greatly daring I ventured on a suggestion. 'Maestro, I have a favour to ask of you.' (I felt rather as though I was appealing to a judge.)

'Yes', said Verdi.

'I want to sing to you your opera *Otello*.'

Then very slowly he smiled. 'That, Madame, is not a favour', he said. And straight away we arranged that on the following day I should go round to his house and sing to him.

I shall always remember that lesson – the long, cool room, with the sun streaming through the windows, and Verdi sitting at the piano, and playing and playing until we had finished the whole opera. He was an inspiring master. He made one feel his phrases as he himself felt them, and he gave to each phrase an added loveliness.

When at last we finished and I had sung the few, halting high notes which mark the passing of poor Desdemona, he leant back, looked up at me with one of his rare smiles, and said: 'Tell me – with whom have you studied this role?'

'With Tosti', I told him.

'Ah!' He nodded. '*Caro* Tosti! I wondered. He is the only man who would have taught you to sing my opera like that.'

We parted firm friends (I hugging a precious photograph) and his last words to me were that one day he would listen to me singing his opera in public. But alas! I never did that, for not long afterwards, he died. It was a terrible disappointment to me, but I feel that I may console myself by remembering that I sang his music as he himself told me it should be sung.[16]

After returning to the role, Desdemona would remain in Nellie's repertoire for the remainder of her career, one act from the opera featuring in her farewell performance at Covent Garden 32 years later. Nellie also recorded both the 'Willow Song' and the 'Ave Maria' from the opera twice in America in 1909 and 1910, the first in particular demonstrating how ravishingly she sang Desdemona's music and how much drama can be achieved simply by singing the notes as written. No doubt a share in that success belongs to the music's composer.

Chapter 10

Rivals, old and new

At the end of May 1894, Nellie returned to London and what had become her home-away-from-home in the English capital: the Savoy Hotel. On 2 June she began her eighth season at Covent Garden, the opera house that had become her artistic home. Calvé and Eames were there to provide soprano competition, along with Nellie's regular male collaborators. There had been discussions about reviving Ambroise Thomas's opera *Mignon*, with Nellie and Calvé in the two leading soprano roles, but that had not progressed beyond the planning stage, probably because Harris believed it extravagant to offer his two leading ladies together for the price of one ticket – or perhaps because one of them objected to sharing the stage with the other. As it transpired, Nellie did not sing any new roles during this season, only repeating her familiar roles.

On the 27 June Nellie also appeared at the five-day Triennial Handel Festival at the Crystal Palace, competing with a raft of popular British singers, including Albani and a young English contralto of Amazonian physique and with a voice to match: Clara Butt. Nellie sang on what was called 'Selection Day', the occasion on which excerpts rather than complete works by Handel were performed. She offered 'Let the bright seraphim' from *Samson* and the aria 'Sweet bird that shunst the noise of folly' from the ode *L'Allegro, il Penseroso ed il Moderato.* Nellie had added the latter piece to her repertoire for concerts in Paris and it had been her *pièce de résistance* in the Sunday night concerts at the Met. She would continue to sing this taxing showpiece for as long as she could and made three recordings of it. The third (recorded in 1910 in America) has John Lemmoné playing the obbligato.

While Nellie was in London for this Covent Garden season, Lemmoné wrote to her, reminding her of their first meeting and indicating that he had recently arrived in London. Nellie had not seen the handsome young flautist since the Elsassar concert in Melbourne in 1884, but she remembered him and invited him to call on her at the Savoy. At their meeting, Nellie asked Lemmoné about friends and old colleagues in Melbourne and the state of musical life in Australia, also thoughtfully providing him with letters of introduction to Daniel Mayer and to Tosti. In his memoirs, published in serial form in an American journal, Lemmoné wrote: 'The welcome I received from Melba was so warm and genuine that I felt I had a friend – a real one – in this great (and to me) mysterious London'.[1] The renewed friendship lasted for the rest of Nellie's life.

Nellie also received a request for an audition from another Australian artist at this time. The young Gippsland-born contralto Ada Crossley turned up at the Savoy carrying letters of introduction from Nellie's sisters Annie and Belle. Crossley sang for Nellie in Nellie's suite and left us this recollection of the encounter:

> When I began she was sitting close to me on my right, but soon she walked about restlessly, and then stood in front of me until I had finished. When I turned to her there were tears in her eyes, and she said, 'Oh, what a glorious voice. I've heard nothing like it for years. The world wants a voice like that.'[2]

Nellie sent Crossley off to Paris and Madame Marchesi. She would become one of the few successful contraltos ever taught by Marchesi, going on to have a highly successful career as Clara Butt's rival in oratorio and concerts.[3]

The Savoy Hotel also features in another story belonging to this year. To reward the hotel's celebrated chef, Auguste Escoffier, for the meals he was preparing for her, Nellie gave him two tickets to a performance of *Lohengrin*. To show his gratitude, the chef created a special dessert for her: what we know today as 'Peach Melba'. It comprised ripe, peeled white peaches poached in a sugar syrup infused with vanilla and topped with a purée of ripe strawberries served on a base of vanilla ice cream.

When Escoffier first served the dish to Nellie and a group of friends being entertained by her, it was presented on a block of ice carved in the shape of Lohengrin's swan and announced as 'Pêches au Cygne'. The name was changed soon after to 'Pêches Melba', while some time later the strawberry purée was replaced by a purée of raspberries. To this day, the dish features on the menu at the London Savoy and in restaurants worldwide.[4]

After a well-deserved holiday in the south of France, Nellie headed back to the United States for her second season at the Met. She arrived in October to allow her to participate (as the top-billed soprano) in a dozen concerts of operatic excerpts being presented by the Met company in New York, Philadelphia, Boston, Albany, Buffalo and New Haven before the regular opera season in New York opened. The season began on 19 November with the ever-popular *Roméo et Juliette*, featuring Nellie, the de Reszkes and Plançon.

The novelty of the season was the Met debut of the Italian tenor Francesco Tamagno in eight roles, including Verdi's *Otello*, the part he had created at the opera's premiere at La Scala in 1887. Victor Maurel was also on hand to sing his now famous Iago. Nellie had hoped that she might have been given the opportunity to display her recently acquired insights into the role of Desdemona with this historic cast and was disappointed and angry when it was assigned to Eames.

Nellie did sing once with Tamagno: she as Lucia di Lammermoor and he as her Edgardo and the partnership was rated a success, but it is not difficult to imagine why there were no further collaborations. Francesco Tamagno possessed a voice of such power that it was claimed it could set the great chandelier at Covent Garden rattling.

After that one 'Lucia', Nellie probably decided she preferred to pit her voice against the more temperate tones of 'dear Jean'.5

Nellie's encounter with Tamagno this season also gave rise to one of the most famous anecdotes in operatic history and one which, one suspects, Nellie enjoyed recounting to her friends back in London and Paris. The subject was the tenor's extreme parsimony. Nellie, Jean de Reszke and Tamagno were among the guests at a dinner in the home of a New York socialite and at the end of the meal they watched in amazement as Tamagno filled his pockets with bon-bons and carried off a display of orchids that had been the centrepiece at the dinner table. A few days later he repeated the episode at a luncheon, wrapping the left-over lamb cutlets in a napkin and pocketing them, explaining that they were to be a treat for his dog. Next day Mancinelli had cause to call on Tamagno in his hotel suite and found the tenor and his daughter (but no dog) lunching on cold lamb cutlets.6

A week before Christmas the Met gave the American premiere of Bemberg's *Elaine*, engineered no doubt by Nellie and Jean de Reszke. Bemberg came to New York for the opening night and his presence distracted and amused Nellie. It was rumored that Pol Plançon also enjoyed Bemberg's company and that the two were found in *flagrante delicto* in Plançon's dressing room. The American public enjoyed the opera's spectacle (the tournament scene had been restored) but like their counterparts in London, the New York critics found the music of *Elaine* too derivative. The anonymous critic of the *Sun*, who had perhaps heard the rumour about the composer and the bass, pronounced it 'decidedly effeminate'.7

Emma Calvé was absent from the company this season, with Zelie de Lussan assigned the unenviable task of replacing her as Carmen. At Abbey and Grau's request, Nellie agreed to bolster the appeal of these performances by singing Micaëla, as she had done in London in 1891, but the highlight of the season was a series of spectacular performances of Meyerbeer's *Les Huguenots*. In what was billed as 'A night of seven stars', Abbey and Grau threw caution to the wind and put seven of their biggest stars on stage together to perform on the same nights – and ramped up ticket prices accordingly.

Les Huguenots is a great rambling work in five acts, which, if the audience demands encores, can stretch to an evening lasting up to four hours, and it is one of those works that requires first-class singers in top form if it is to succeed. The Met that year offered Nellie as Marguerite de Valois, Lillian Nordica as Valentine, Sofia Scalchi as Urbain, Jean de Reszke as Raoul, Victor Maurel as Comte de Nevers, Pol Plançon as Comte de St Bris, and Edouard de Reszke as Marcel. The work had probably never been performed by such a stellar cast in the half-century since Meyerbeer had composed it. New Yorkers revelled in the opportunity to see so many of their favourite singers together on stage. The opera was performed a record 15 times, first in New York and then on tour in Philadelphia, Boston, Chicago and St Louis.[8]

Reginald de Koven, reviewing the opening night of *Les Huguenots* in the *New World*, was clearly smitten by Nellie's Marguerite de Valois: 'Madame Melba was dazzling in appearance, and acted with much grace and spirit, while her vocalisation was like some fabric of richest lace – so delicate, so dainty, so fairy-like and finished was it. This usually secondary part was glorified and made much of last night.'[9]

The last performance of the season was a matinee of *Faust* on 27 April 1895. The *New York Times* reported:

> And as soon as the curtain went down on the trio of the last act, the mass of enthusiasts surged toward the stage and settled down to the business of calling out Messrs. De Reszke and Madame Melba. Again and again the tired but smiling artists went to the footlights, and still the cheers and applause continued. On the tenth recall the three artists, to the intense delight of their admirers, sang without accompaniment the trio from *Robert le Diable*. Seven more

recalls followed, and flowers rained on the stage. Madame Melba picked up the flowers and pelted the audience with them. Finally she leaned forward and shook hands with the woman nearest the stage. Of course, her associates had to do the same thing. At length the lights were turned off and the ushers gently but firmly induced the audience to depart.[10]

Including concerts, Nellie had sung a remarkable 69 performances for the Met this season. She had worked hard, filling the Met's coffers, but did not believe she had been treated by Abbey and Grau with the consideration her labours and popularity entitled her to, the casting of *Otello* being at the top of Nellie's list of grievances. At the end of the season (and with the tour of Australia abandoned), she contemplated forming an opera company of her own and taking fully staged opera across the United States. In the end that plan was also shelved as being too risky and because Nellie feared that the Met would not re-engage her if she went into competition with them.[11]

When Nellie returned to London for the 1895 season at Covent Garden, nine years had passed since she had made her European debut in that city and eight since her debut in opera in Brussels. Based on the critiques and comments that appeared in the press, it would seem that Nellie reached her vocal prime at around this time. Critics began to talk about a new warmth, power and richness in her voice, gained without the loss of any of its other estimable attributes. Another sure sign that Nellie was carving a place for herself in the pantheon of legendary singers was the proliferation of arguments about her voice and her singing that began to appear in print, most (but not all) writers citing Nellie as a paragon in every aspect of the singing art. But what none of these writers could predict was that Nellie's 'prime' did not (as it does with most singers) herald a decline. Nellie's 'prime' was maintained for a remarkable number of years and some of those 'estimable attributes' remained with her until she retired more than 30 years later.

It would be another nine years before Nellie's voice was preserved by recordings, allowing us to make our own judgements about it, but based on contemporary printed sources it is possible to construct a fairly reliable description of what those lucky enough to hear her sing in the 1890s would have experienced.

Nellie's voice covered just over two octaves from 'middle C' to 'top E', although, unlike many coloratura sopranos of her time, she did not interpolate stratospheric notes simply for effect and seldom sang above 'top D' unless a score demanded it. The most remarkable thing about her range was the consistent quality of the notes, from the highest to the lowest. In search of metaphors, critics often described Nellie's voice as being like a string of perfectly matched pearls. She never entirely abandoned the practice of taking her voice up too high in the chest register, which tended to destroy the illusion of being matchless, but the power of her notes from the top to the bottom of her range was almost uniquely equalised.

A further aspect of Nellie's singing that the critics and the discerning public found remarkable was the 'attack' and accuracy of her intonation. Compared with most singers, Nellie didn't actually have an attack. She simply inhaled smoothly, opened her mouth and the note 'appeared'. Of her intonation, George Bernhard Shaw observed: 'You never realize how wide a gap there is between the ordinary singer who simply avoids the fault of singing obviously out of tune and the singer who sings really and truly in tune, except when Melba is singing'.[12] The necessity for accuracy of intonation was essential for Nellie's style of singing. Singers who sing with a wide vibrato ('beat') in their voices can give the impression of being in tune by 'circling' around the correct note, but for singers like Nellie who have almost no vibrato in their voices, each note has to be pitched and sustained perfectly or the sound becomes excruciating.

As Nellie's voice matured, her command of all the technical devices her repertoire demanded also strengthened. She could manage wide intervals between consecutive notes with apparent ease and without being forced to slide up or down to reach any note. She also had the ability to deliberately use a sliding effect (portamento) with great refinement when she considered it appropriate. She could sing ascending or descending chromatic scales with the precision of an instrumentalist, becoming louder (crescendo) or softer (decrescendo) at will. Singing a perfect trill on notes in any part of her upper range was one of Nellie's hallmarks – and hers was a trill, not just a shake as so often passes for a trill with singers who have less control over their voices. Both Joseph Joachim and Jules Massenet made a comparison with an instrumentalist when they independently described Nellie as 'Madame Stradivarius'.[13]

The actual sound that Nellie produced (before recordings arrived) is more difficult to describe, but unlike many singers of later generations, Nellie's prime objective was to make beautiful sounds and she succeeded most of the time. Jean de Reszke described her voice as the most beautiful of its time and even her friendly rival Calvé described it as 'divine'.[14] Critics agreed that the sound was 'silvery' in timbre and sometimes reminded them of a boy soprano, but that last metaphor should not be taken too literally, for Nellie's voice was not sexless. It was the voice of a woman with strong character.

One quality on which all agree is that her singing had enormous vibrancy and energy. Even when pitted against larger voices like Tamagno's, the sound was always bold and brilliant and carried to the extremities of the largest auditoriums. Perhaps the best description of that brilliance was provided by fellow soprano Mary Garden, who heard Nellie singing Mimi in Puccini's *La Bohème* in 1903. Garden described how Nellie sang Mimi's last note at the end of the first act:

> The way that Melba sang that high C was the strangest and weirdest thing I have ever experienced in my life. The note came floating out

over the auditorium at Covent Garden: it left Melba's throat, it left Melba's body, it left everything, and came over like a star and passed us in our box, and went out into the infinite. I have never heard anything like it in my life, not from any other singer, ever. That note was like a ball of light. It wasn't attached to anything at all – it was *out* of everything.[15]

Nellie needed to muster all her talent when she returned to Covent Garden in May, for Augustus Harris had assembled a remarkable squad of sopranos for his 1895 season. Firstly, he had persuaded Adelina Patti to return to Covent Garden after an absence of 10 years, offering her whatever roles she chose. The now 51-year-old soprano nominated roles she had been famous for at the height of her career: Violetta in *La Traviata*, Rosina in *Il Barbiere di Siviglia* and Zerlina in Mozart's *Don Giovanni*, agreeing to sing two performances of each. Albani was also back, after skipping a year, and had laid claim to the roles of Elsa in *Lohengrin*, Elisabeth in *Tannhäuser* and Desdemona in *Otello*, agreeing to share them, not with Nellie, but with Eames, who was less competition to the 48-year-old Canadian.

Marcella Sembrich was also persuaded to join the company and take over the role of Violetta following Patti's two performances. The most famous Italian soprano of the time and a great favourite of Verdi's, Gemma Bellincioni, also made her Covent Garden debut that season and Calvé joined the company mid-season.

Nellie had to content herself with her familiar roles in *Lucia di Lammermoor*, *Rigoletto*, *Faust*, *Roméo et Juliette* and *Carmen* and one performance of *Les Huguenots*, by which Harris hoped to emulate Abbey and Grau's hit in New York. On this occasion Albani sang Valentine and, with Jean de Reszke absent from the company this season, the tenor lead was assigned to Tamagno.[16]

In the hope of making a return to Desdemona, Nellie requested she be allotted one performance of *Otello*. That was advertised for

18 June (with Tamagno and Maurel) but within hours Nellie's name had been withdrawn. In both Murphy's *Melba* and in *Melodies and Memories*, Nellie states simply that she was 'indisposed', but it seems more probable that Albani had persuaded Harris to change the cast.

Albert Alvarez, with whom Nellie had sung in Paris, and Vignas were on hand to partner Nellie, but the absence of Jean de Reszke meant that she had to sing with at least one unfamiliar tenor – Charles Bonnard (from the Opéra-Comique in Paris).[17] Bonnard proved eminently forgettable in the title role of *Faust*, but one performance of that opera turned out to be unforgettable for a non-musical reason and reminiscent of another performance of the same opera in 1889. Pol Plançon, playing Méphistophélès, made his entrance in act one, while a 'fire machine' at the rear of the stage provided red flickering light. Plançon faced the audience and began to sing: 'Me voici! D'où vient ta surprise?' ('Here I am! So, I surprise you?') but the audience got more of a surprise than they expected! The fire machine had set a piece of scenery ablaze. Neither Plançon nor Bonnard could see what was happening, but Nellie in the wings could. The stage manager lowered the curtain and there were sounds of alarm from the audience. As firemen doused the flames, Nellie (no doubt, with memories of the 1889 stage fire during the same scene) stepped out in front of the curtain and reassured the audience that the situation was under control. Panic subsided and after a short break the performance resumed – without the piece of damaged scenery.[18]

Adelina Patti came and sang and then retreated to the castle in Wales in which she lived. Audiences were ecstatic about her performances, but the critics felt obliged to point out that time had taken its toll on her voice and that where she had once sung with abandon, she was now obliged to sing cautiously, using her voice economically; similar comments were made about Albani. Sembrich was accused of poor acting and Bellinciona's voice was dismissed as 'not to English taste'. In the end it was only Calvé who threatened

Nellie's supremacy and such was the relationship between them that Nellie was happy to sing Micaëla four times opposite Calvé's Carmen. The honour of closing the season was given to Nellie; she, Alvarez and Plançon sang the last of six sold-out performances of *Roméo et Juliette*, after which Harris invited Nellie to present a jewel-encrusted baton to Mancinelli.

Apart from the great maestros of opera (like Mancinelli), Nellie seldom had the opportunity to sing with leading conductors, but London was awash with famous conductors that season and Daniel Mayer arranged for her to be the soloist at the first of a series of concerts conducted by Arthur Nikisch in Queen's Hall. Nikisch was chief conductor of the Berlin Philharmonic Orchestra and when the concert was first advertised Nellie was listed to sing Elisabeth's greeting from *Tannhäuser*. By the time the concert took place on 15 June Wagner had been replaced by Thomas. Nellie sang the Mad Scene from *Hamlet* and Handel's 'Sweet bird', with John Lemmoné providing the flute obbligato.

As well as occupying a suite at the Savoy this season, Nellie also leased a comfortable house called 'The Lodge', 50 kilometres west of London in the Thames Valley, near the town of Maidenhead. Here she was able to relax when time between performances permitted and to entertain her friends. Among the visitors at the Lodge was Agnes Murphy, the journalist who had supported Nellie in the Melbourne press during her affair with Philippe. Murphy had returned to Europe after many years in Australia and was working for the *Pall Mall Gazette*. Murphy would, one day, accept employment from Nellie as her secretary.[19]

Another encounter during this season in London that would have a long-term effect on Nellie's career occurred during a performance of *Faust*: Nellie noticed a young man with saucer-shaped eyes gazing at her from the wings as she performed and when he followed her towards her dressing room after the curtain had fallen, she demanded to know who he was.

The young man explained that his name was Landon Ronald and that he was one of the company's repetiteurs, one, presumably, Nellie had not encountered before. He was also, Nellie later discovered, the illegitimate son of Henry Russell, a well-known musician of an earlier generation famous for his song 'A life on the ocean wave', and his brother was Henry Russell Jnr, a singing teacher and later a successful opera entrepreneur.

Nellie was then beginning to study the title role in Massenet's *Manon*, so asked if Ronald knew the opera. He said he did, so Nellie invited him to call on her at the Savoy at noon the next day for an audition to be her assistant in learning the role. Ronald had, in fact, not been entirely truthful. He did not know the Massenet opera, but hastily found a score and sat up most of the night learning it. Next day he played so well that Nellie engaged him. That was the beginning of another professional relationship and a friendship that lasted until Nellie's death, Ronald becoming her regular accompanist at concerts and, later, for recordings.

Having memorised Manon's words and notes, Nellie returned to Paris and an intense period of study on interpretation of the role with its composer. From the couturier Jacques Doucet, she also ordered a spectacular costume for the third act of the opera, where Manon is living in luxury as the mistress of an aged nobleman. Nellie was eagerly anticipating her debut in that role at the Metropolitan in the forthcoming season.

Nellie's plan to form her own opera company in the US had never been entirely abandoned and in the months since it had been shelved she had been planning its resurrection, but in a more modest form. The new plan was to take a small company of singers and a medium-sized orchestra around the Unites States and southern Canada and to offer arias and songs in the first half of each program, followed by a semi-staged act from one opera in the second half. For this venture Nellie went into partnership with Charles Ellis, manager of the Boston Symphony Orchestra, who did most of the groundwork before Nellie arrived in New York in September. With Nellie's approval, Ellis engaged Mathilde Bauermeister, a singer of supporting roles with whom Melba had performed numerous times at Covent Garden and at the Met, the contralto Sofia Scalchi and the baritone Giuseppe Campanari, a principal at the Met. Finding a tenor of equal calibre proved the biggest problem and Nellie had to accept the best Ellis could come up with: one Thomas Lloyd Dabney from New York who, as Lloyd D'Aubigne, had sung David in *Die Meistersinger* and Tybalt in *Roméo et Juliette* at the Met the previous season.

So impressed had Nellie been with Landon Ronald that she invited him to join her in America as the company's musical director and conductor. The itinerary comprised 46 concerts in about two dozen locations, opening in Montreal at the beginning of October. Audiences in places Nellie had never visited before flocked to hear her and the only incident marring the success of the tour was an article published in the *Chicago Times* when the party were in that city. The article asserted that Nellie had been 'entertaining' (an obvious euphemism for having sex with) certain 'gentlemen' of Chicago. Nellie sued the newspaper for libel, claiming 120,000 dollars in damages. As there seems to be no public record of a legal hearing, the case was likely settled out of court.[20]

At the end of the tour Nellie settled into the New York Savoy to prepare for her next season at the Met and to celebrate the Christmas of 1895 – and a memorable Christmas it proved to be. At Nellie's invitation her sister Annie and her brother Ernie joined her from Australia. Annie was now 32 and unmarried. Ernie was 20 and possessed a fine lyric tenor voice. He had been studying with George Marshall-Hall, professor of music at Melbourne University, and over the next few months Nellie tried to persuade him to continue his studies in Paris. She hoped her brother would have a career in opera as successful as her own, but that was not to be. Ernie would later say that one prima donna in the family was quite enough.

Keeping it a secret from her trusted secretary and companion, Nellie also invited Louie's fiancé Kenyon Mason, a clerk at the London Stock Exchange, to join them. He arrived four days before Christmas and when Nellie saw how devoted the couple were she volunteered to organise and pay for their wedding. On 14 January, Louise Bennett became Louise Mason in a ceremony conducted by Michael Corrigan, Roman Catholic Archbishop of New York, in the drawing room of the archbishop's palace, next door to St Patrick's Cathedral. Annie Mitchell served as Louie's maid-of-honour. Nellie arranged a sumptuous wedding breakfast at the hotel and among the guests were Calvé, Nordica, the de Reszkes, Maurel, Plançon and Henry Abbey. Nellie (it was reported in the social columns of the press) made a grand entrance at the wedding breakfast on the arm of the archbishop, splendidly attired in mauve to complement the archbishop's purple. Nellie also gave the young couple 1000 dollars and paid for their honeymoon – a luxury trip back to England. How Louie might have felt about having her marriage turned into an 'operatic' production by her boss is a matter for speculation, but if she had any negative feelings she had ample time to get over them as she began a new life in England with her new husband. Nellie must have felt bereft at the prospect of no longer having the faithful Louie at her side; and one also wonders if the invitation to Annie was a ploy to provide a replacement for Louie, at least for the short term.[21]

As well as Calvé and Nordica, Nellie encountered a new rival when the 1895–96 season at the Met commenced. This was the Californian-born, Melbourne-raised Frances Saville, last encountered by Nellie in Mackay with the Montague-Turner company in 1883. Like Nellie, Saville had studied with Marchesi and made her debut at the Monnaie in Brussels. She had then sung with success in St Petersburg, London, Monte Carlo, Paris and Warsaw before being engaged by Abbey and Grau for New York. Nellie had no objection to sharing the roles of Juliette, Marguerite in *Faust* and Micaëla with her Australian compatriot because, accomplished singer though Saville was, her voice presented no real threat to Nellie. The New York critics liked Saville, but often compared her unfavourably to Nellie in their reviews of her performances.

It would seem that Nellie and Saville got on amicably, but the same could not be said about a guest artist Maurice Grau had engaged for the ninth Sunday evening concert at the Met. This was the French cabaret singer Yvette Guilbert, whose fame today survives through drawings and paintings of her by Toulouse-Lautrec. In an interview Guilbert granted to *Le Figaro* on her return to Paris she gave her account of the bitter animosity that had developed with Nellie:

> I had met in New York a friend of Madame Melba, and this friend said to her the next day: 'You are to take breakfast with Yvette Guilbert and me tomorrow'. Melba rose, and said with violent indignation: '*I* take breakfast with *that* singer? You might, at the worst, have invited her to come and sing one of her couplets for pay'. The friend related this to me and I replied simply: 'Well, that is natural. I am of humble origin and Madame Melba belongs to the royal family of France'. The journals reported the incident, and Melba vowed eternal hatred against me.[22]

Guilbert continues by claiming that Nellie demanded Maurice Grau cancel her engagement to sing at the concert but that she insisted on singing and gave her fee of 600 dollars to charity. Nellie never disclosed her version of these events, so the veracity of Guilbert's claims cannot be tested, but Nellie's silence speaks for itself.

With their partnership restored, Nellie sang her familiar roles with Jean de Reszke, and he, Victor Maurel and Pol Plançon supported Nellie when she sang Manon for the first time on 27 January. The following morning Reginald de Koven provided readers of the *New World* with a detailed account of Nellie's performance:

During the first act she was evidently constrained and nervous, and consequently rather gauche. In the second act her action was much more graceful and natural. The first scene of the third act struck me also as too studied and lacking in repose; but in the scene at St. Sulpice she found the note of genuine feeling and passion, and played with real power and convincing sincerity. There were real tears in her voice in the charming little 'Adieu' in the second act. Mme Melba's action was certainly at times lacking in the necessary coquetry but for a first performance of the role hers was unquestionably a remarkable one, and future performances will surely give her greater ease. Unless I am much mistaken 'Manon' will be accounted one of Melba's best roles.

De Koven was mistaken. Nellie sang just one more performance of *Manon* in New York, one in Boston, one at Covent Garden and a few on the Continent, before dropping the role from her repertoire. Despite her avowed love for the opera, the hard work she had put into preparing her role and the success she rightly declared she had enjoyed in it, Massenet's *Manon* must be rated as one of Nellie's failures.

In July the previous year, while Nellie was singing at Covent Garden, Pedro Gailhard had travelled to London to try to persuade her to return to the Paris Opéra, after an absence of three years. Undoubtedly, Nellie explained how busy she was to Gailhard and the generous fees she was receiving in America, before offering to sing a short series of performances of *Hamlet* during May the following year for a fee of 10,000 francs per night. Gailhard capitulated, so on her return from the 1895–96 season in New York, Nellie travelled straight to Paris.

The production of *Hamlet* was staged by Alexandre Lapissida, Nellie's old friend from Brussels, and conducted by the Opéra's new music director Georges Marty. Maurice Renaud was cast in the title role and Blanche Deschamps-Jehin as Gertrude, but the proceedings had a sad element, for Ambroise Thomas had died the previous February. It was planned to use the takings from the opening night to erect a memorial to the composer – but that opening night almost didn't happen.

On 20 May, the evening before the first night of *Hamlet*, the Opéra performed a new work entitled *Hellé*, by Alphonse Duvernoy, starring yet another of Nellie's old colleagues from Brussels, Rose Caron. As the first act of the opera was nearing its end, a flash of light blazed from the central dome above the auditorium, followed by a deafening crash. It was assumed by most of the audience that an anarchist had set off a bomb. Turmoil erupted in the uppermost gallery closest to the disturbance as patrons tried to escape; a few foolhardy individuals even attempted to clamber over the gallery's front wall. Ushers managed to evacuate the area and found the crushed body of an elderly woman and several injured patrons.

It transpired that it was not a bomb but a series of technical mishaps that had caused the horrific accident. An electric wire to the great chandelier in the centre of the dome had fused, starting a small fire, which in turn burned through a cable supporting one of the counterweights that kept the chandelier in place. The counterweight crashed through the roof of the top gallery, bringing down heavy masonry. Fortunately for those below, the chandelier trembled but did not fall.

The incident made the front page of all the Paris newspapers, including *L'Echo de Paris* on 22 May, whose report appeared anonymously. It might have been written by the newspaper's music critic, or if not written by him then certainly read by him. His name was Gaston Leroux and a decade later it provided him with inspiration for his most famous novel: *The Phantom of the Opera*.

By the next evening, when ticketholders turned up to hear *Hamlet*, all the rubble had been removed, the benches in the top gallery had been replaced and no signs of the previous night's horror remained. With commendable *sang-froid* a capacity audience took its place and welcomed Nellie's return with a prolonged ovation. Nellie sang in seven performances of *Hamlet* over three weeks, after which she left for London, where the next Covent Garden season was in full swing and where she was committed to an equally heavy schedule of performances.

Chapter 11

The lure of Wagner

Nellie arrived in London to find the musical community in a Wagner frenzy. The most anticipated event in the Covent Garden season was the first appearance in London of Jean de Reszke as Tristan in *Tristan und Isolde*. The great Polish tenor had sung this role at the Met the previous season and triumphed. London now waited to hear what their matinee idol would make of Wagner's most arduous and romantic tenor part.

In New York de Reszke had been partnered by Lillian Nordica's equally successful Isolde, but London was to hear Emma Albani tackle Isolde for the first time in her long career. A week after Nellie made her reappearance at Covent Garden, de Reszke scored one of the greatest successes of his London career as Tristan, while Albani, committing all that was left of her once-exquisite lyric soprano voice to the part, was deemed an 'adequate' Isolde.

Between them, Albani, Eames and another American, Lola Beeth, had monopolised all the performances of Elsa in *Lohengrin*, Elisabeth in *Tannhäuser* and Eva in *Die Meistersinger*. Nellie desperately wanted a piece of the Wagner action, but if she had lobbied Augustus Harris for an opportunity, it was thwarted by the impresario's sudden and unexpected death from a heart attack four days before 'Tristan' opened. Nellie had to be content, once again, to repeat her familiar roles and to sing *Manon* for the first (and last) time at Covent Garden. Amid all the Wagner hype the Massenet opera slipped by, hardly noticed.

Three weeks after the Covent Garden season closed Herman

Klein broke the news in *The Sunday Times* that Nellie was learning both the roles of Brünnhilde and the Woodbird in Wagner's *Siegfried*, and would be singing them in German at the Met later in the year and at Covent Garden the following year.[1]

The announcement was the culmination of much discussion behind the scenes between Nellie, Marchesi and Jean de Reszke. The tenor was learning the title role in *Siegfried* for the next Met season and opinions differ over whether he encouraged Nellie to learn Brünnhilde or the much lighter music of the Woodbird – or neither – and to share his debut in the opera in New York. Nellie would have argued that if Albani could sing Isolde then surely she could manage the much shorter role of the *Siegfried* Brünnhilde. Marchesi was adamantly opposed to Nellie singing Brünnhilde and considered the tiny role of the Woodbird unworthy of the world's leading lyric soprano, but Nellie ignored her advice. She contacted Henry Abbey and Maurice Grau at the Met and offered to sing both roles. They were happy to schedule her to sing Brünnhilde, but decided that was novel enough without having her sing the Woodbird as well. One person who was upset by the arrangements was Nordica, who accused both Nellie and de Reszke of usurping her right to sing a role for which she was ideally suited. This issue temporarily upset Nellie's friendship with the American star, although later they were reconciled.

Nellie's first engagement when she reached America was another concert with her favourite orchestra: the Boston Symphony. Nellie was not in her best voice at that concert and it marked the beginning of a period of ill health, variously described as 'hoarseness', 'influenza' and even 'blood poisoning' (it was probably the first, brought on by a common cold), which marred her first appearances in the Met season. Four days before Christmas Nellie returned to the role of Violetta in *La Traviata*, for the first time since Palermo, maturity providing the expressiveness in voice and acting that had previously been lacking. On 30 December, the curtain opened on Wagner's *Siegfried*. As well as Nellie and Jean de Reszke, the distinguished cast included Edouard de Reszke as The Wanderer (Wotan, the leader of the gods in disguise). The conductor was Anton Seidl, who had worked with Wagner at Bayreuth and conducted his works throughout Europe. Nellie waited in her dressing room through the first two, long, acts and then settled herself in a sleeping position on the rock where Wotan had imprisoned his disobedient daughter at the end of the previous opera in the cycle.

There are no records of what had transpired at the rehearsals prior to this night, but singing with de Reszke and the full 'Wagnerian' orchestra in rehearsal must have alerted Nellie to the fact that hers was an uphill battle. She was undoubtedly suffering acute nervousness as she lay on the papier-mâché rock waiting for Siegfried to awaken her. Nellie sang her first line: 'Heil dir, Sonne!' ('Hail to thee, oh sun') and, as the long duet developed, Nellie's voice was frequently drowned out by the orchestra. According to the American baritone David Bispham, who was watching the performance from a box, Nellie kept trying to move down to the footlights to be better heard and de Reszke kept restraining her, his action prompting Nellie to conclude that his role in the episode had been malign from the start, a conclusion that enabled her to blame de Reszke for her own inadequacy – blame that was undeserved.[2]

That performance has been described as Nellie's 'Waterloo' and a complete disaster, but it was not. Nellie was too professional to allow herself to be seriously compromised in full view of a capacity audience, but it was a struggle she did not wish to repeat. As soon as the curtain had fallen, Nellie summoned Charles Ellis (who was now officially her American manager) and through him, issued a statement to the press, the essence of which was 'I have been a fool and I shan't do that again'. The promptness and the frankness of that statement probably deterred the critics from being too unkind to her in the next morning's newspapers. Henderson, who had heard every Brünnhilde at the Met since the theatre opened, reported:

This was the first essay of Madame Melba in German opera sung in German and there were evidences that even her experience and self-confidence were not proof against the assaults of nervousness. It is undeniable, and may as well be said now as later, that the quality of her voice and her style of singing are not suited to Brünnhilde, and she can be praised now only for her conscientious effort and for her ambition, which was more potent than wise.[3]

The anonymous critic of the New York *Sun* provided a little more detail and some positive remarks that Nellie no doubt welcomed:

Madame Melba's Brünnhilde will doubtless improve with successive performances, when she, hitherto a singer of what are now considered light, florid parts, will be more at home in this dramatic role. Others who have sung it here have shown greater breadth and power of voice, yet there is a certain charm in the perfect ease with which Madame Melba surmounts all the vocal difficulties of the score, and toward the end, as she gained more confidence in herself, she sang with much greater freedom, and the voice had the true ring of assurance.[4]

Nellie was wise enough to ensure that there were no 'successive performances'. She withdrew from the role and Félia Litvinne took over for the remaining performances of *Siegfried*. Despite her voice suffering audible strain, Nellie sang one more performance of *Roméo et Juliette* in Brooklyn before withdrawing for the remainder of the season. Maurice Grau, who had taken over sole management of the company following Henry Abbey's death just before the season opened, was unimpressed: being forced to reschedule performances and find replacements for Nellie added to the stress he was already suffering. In private he let it be known that he thought Nellie's withdrawal was due to damaged pride rather than damaged vocal cords. The less reputable press got wind of this and began espousing theories about lack of professionalism and prima donna antics. It was not only Nellie's voice she had exposed to risk but also her reputation.[5]

On 24 January Nellie departed for London and a consultation with Felix Semon, who ordered complete rest for several months. Annie Mitchell had returned to Australia so Nellie telegraphed her youngest sister, Dora, asking her to join her and Ernie on the Riviera, where Nellie undertook a long period of rest and recovery. Dora would remain at Nellie's side on both sides of the Atlantic for the next two years.[6]

In the winter sun of Nice, Nellie's voice recovered and her confidence returned. In the years that followed, whether Nellie's voice had suffered any permanent damage from the *Siegfried* misadventure was a topic for debate. A couple of experts claimed that they could discern a difference in the sound Nellie made, but if we discount the period when she was learning and rehearsing the role with piano, it does seem unlikely that two or three orchestral rehearsals and one performance of 30 minutes of music would have caused any permanent physiological change. Another 30 years of successful singing by Nellie also supports that theory.[7]

It had been rumoured in the press previously that Nellie would not be returning to Covent Garden in 1897 because she had accepted a four-month engagement in the spring of that year to sing at the opera in Buenos Aires, a company now led by Francesco Tamagno. Events in New York put paid to those plans and when Nellie offered her services to the Grand Opera Syndicate at Covent Garden, the syndicate expressed the view that their leading soprano had been disloyal to them by giving Buenos Aires preference over London; furthermore, concerns were still being expressed in the press about the condition of her voice. With the support of Gladys de Grey, these issues were resolved, but resulted in Nellie's reappearance at Covent Garden being delayed until the middle of the 1897 season, with her singing only four performances, including a gala to celebrate the Golden Jubilee of Queen Victoria.

When she arrived at Covent Garden, Nellie found Eames claiming to be the company's prima donna, Nordica absent because of illness and Frances Saville consolidating her position with performances of *La Traviata* and as Manon, the role Nellie had sung the previous year.[8] Also in the company was the Tasmanian bass Lempriere Pringle, who had graduated up from the Carl Rosa company, and Maurice Grau, installed as the opera house's new and powerful manager.

For the Jubilee gala on 23 June, Nellie appeared in the third act of *Roméo et Juliette*, teaming up again with Jean de Reszke and supported by Plançon and Bauermeister. That occasion was also the only time that the voices of Nellie and Eames were ever heard together. In front of an audience led by the Prince and Princess of Wales and including half the crowned heads of Europe, Nellie sang the first verse of the National Anthem, Eames sang the second and then both sopranos joined all the other singers on stage for the final verse.[9] Nellie's singing on each of these occasions dispelled any doubts anyone may have had about the state of her voice. The public and the critics had nothing but praise for her.

To compensate for the small number of appearances Nellie made in opera this season, she appeared in a greater number of concerts. In April she dashed over from Paris to oblige an impresario in the Midlands, who had engaged Patti for two concerts and then found himself without a star when the ageing diva cancelled at the eleventh hour. Nellie also gave a highly successful afternoon concert she organised herself at Queen's Hall in London, assisted by Britain's leading operatic tenor Ben Davies, Clara Butt and Butt's future husband, baritone Kennerley Rumford. In October and November she undertook what had now become an annual concert tour of the provinces, with Ben Davies heading her stable of supporting artists.

Perhaps the most interesting and most historic of all the concerts Nellie gave in 1897 was in the Italian city of Bergamo, where a festival was being staged to celebrate the centenary of the birth of its most famous son – Gaetano Donizetti. Joseph Joachim suggested to the organisers that they engage Nellie for one of three planned concerts during the festival and she accepted, singer and violinist happy to renew their professional association and their close friendship.[10]

As well as the concerts, performances of operas by Donizetti were given, presented in the city's opera house, refurbished and renamed in the composer's honour. *La Favorite* was conducted by the young Arturo Toscanini, who in years to come would initiate the era in which conductors dominated the world of opera. *Lucia di Lammermoor* was also performed and the title role sung by a 26-year-old soprano of unprepossessing appearance but with a phenomenal voice – Luisa Tetrazzini.

With little else to do during their stay in Bergamo, it seems likely that Nellie, Dora, Joachim and his daughter, who had accompanied him, would have attended these performances. Nellie may well have watched with casual interest the dynamic Toscanini conducting *La Favorite*, but left us no recollections of that. Her silence about Tetrazzini, the singer who would pose the greatest of all threats to Nellie's supremacy when she arrived at Covent Garden ten years later, is even more regretful.

The death of Henry Abbey, serious financial problems and the responsibilities Grau had taken on in London resulted in the cancellation of the 1897–98 winter season at the Metropolitan Opera in New York. The vacuum this created was filled by the Philadelphia-based Damrosch Opera Company, which expanded its repertoire and its operations to mount seasons in its home city, in Boston, Chicago, Milwaukee, New York and Washington, followed by a tour across the heartland of America, terminating in San Francisco.

The Damrosch company was founded and led by Walter Damrosch, who, along with his late father Leopold, had presided over the Metropolitan Opera during its 'German' years. Damrosch was a devoted Wagnerian and ably equipped to manage and conduct his company's German repertoire but, wisely, decided he needed someone with broader knowledge to manage the Italian and French repertoire in the expanded venture. Charles Ellis was taken on as a partner with that responsibility and the company renamed the Damrosch-Ellis Opera Company.

Nellie knew Damrosch. When singing with the Met in the previous season, Grau had 'lent' Nellie to Damrosch for two performances of *Faust* in Philadelphia. With Ellis now sharing the helm, Nellie was happy to become the company's prima donna, at least until such time as the Metropolitan Opera regrouped and resumed operations. A generous offer from Damrosch of 1500 dollars per performance, with a guarantee of 10 performances per month, sealed the deal.

At the end of her provincial tour of the United Kingdom, Nellie and Dora embarked for America. They celebrated Thanksgiving with Ellis in snow-clad Boston, but Dora was longing for sunny Australia and so departed for home when Nellie travelled to Philadelphia to take her place in the new company.

Over the following six months Nellie would sing a total of 51 performances of *Faust*, *Roméo et Juliette*, *Manon*, *Lucia di Lammermoor*, *La Traviata* and *Rigoletto*. She would also add a new role to her repertoire: Rosina in Rossini's *Il Barbiere di Siviglia*, and return to a role she had not sung for six years – Aida. The leading soprano in the German repertoire was Lillian Nordica, but Nellie's regular collaborators – the de Reszkes, de Lucia, Ancona, Plançon etc. – were not in the company and she had to make do with less famous partners.

The season opened at the Academy of Music in Philadelphia on 29 November with *Faust*. On 27 December Nellie sang Rosina for the first time. In the lesson scene she interpolated the 'Sevillana' from Massenet's *Don César de Bazan* and Tosti's 'Mattinata', accompanying herself at the piano in both items. The audience was enchanted by Nellie's first attempt at a comic role, even if her impersonation of the scheming Rosina had more in common with Nellie

Mitchell, rebellious pupil of Leigh House Ladies College in Melbourne, than it did with Beaumarchais's Seville. The *Philadelphia Inquirer* reported: 'Madame Melba was a delightful Rosina and her marvellous voice wove its way with consummate ease through Rossini's taxing music'.[11]

It may have been her recent successes in *La Traviata* that prompted Nellie to make another attempt at the title role in Verdi's *Aida* and, when she sang the role in Philadelphia on 13 January in a more flattering costume than the one she had worn at Covent Garden in 1892, audiences and the critics were enthusiastic. Buoyed by that success, Nellie sang the role again when the company moved into the Metropolitan Opera House in New York. There the reaction was not so enthusiastic. Henderson in the *New York Times* wrote:

> Madame Melba's assumption of the role of Aida begs the question why she would sing a role so utterly unsuited to her voice, her style and her temperament. Surely this intelligent artist must know that heavy roles like Aida have the potential to wreck her voice, one of the most precious gifts that heaven ever put in a human throat.[12]

Success returned four nights later when Nellie sang Rosina for the first time in New York, also repeating roles that New Yorkers were accustomed to her singing, all of which earned her praise.

Seasons then followed in Boston, Chicago and Minneapolis, after which the company split into two halves, the German artists taking Wagner to the eastern states while the Italian and French artists took their repertoire west under Ellis's management. Cities where they performed included Washington, St Louis, Denver and Salt Lake City, all the while with Nellie harbouring the hope that in some place she might find her son waiting to be reunited with her, but that never happened.

Ellis hired a luxurious railway carriage from the Pullman company for Nellie's travel, with her name emblazoned on each side, emulating the method Patti had used when touring the United

States in former times. As well as luxurious living quarters for Nellie and quarters for her staff, it contained all the most modern conveniences of the day, along with a piano and a harmonium. Travelling in luxury with Nellie were Marnie Bennett, who had taken over from her sister as Nellie's secretary, and the first of many singing protégées Nellie would take under wing: a mezzo-soprano whom she had spotted at one of Marchesi's soirées and whose engagement with the Damrosch-Ellis company Nellie had arranged. The young singer's stage name was Florence Toronto, whose origin is easy to guess.[13]

In April the company reached California. The warm climate, the relaxed lifestyle and the optimism of Californians appealed to Nellie and reminded her of Australia and her compatriots, but the weeks she spent in San Francisco and Los Angeles were plagued by disruptions and mishaps. Nellie opened the season in *La Traviata* at the California Theatre in San Francisco on 19 April and was slightly offended when the audience failed to recognise her on her first entry – she was denied the welcoming burst of applause she had come to expect. Earlier that day the United States had sent an ultimatum to the Spanish Government in Madrid, demanding that Spain recognise the sovereignty of their colony Cuba. Two days later when no answer had been received, war was declared on Spain and the short, bloody Spanish–American War of that year commenced. Anti-Spanish sentiment was running high in San Francisco and the opera scheduled for that night was *Il Barbiere di Siviglia*. Fearing a boycott of an opera with a Spanish setting, or worse, disruption of the performance by demonstrators, Ellis issued a statement to the press reminding San Franciscans that the opera was written by an Italian and that there were no Spaniards in the cast. The curtain rose at 8 pm, with the cast, chorus, conductor and orchestra all nervous and ready to duck for cover if violence broke out. As it turned out, the only demonstration during the performance was some booing when Campanari came on stage as Figaro. That was soon quelled and in the lesson scene Nellie implemented a further appeasement plan, which had been devised by Ellis. Instead of her regular items, Nellie sang Steven Foster's song 'Old folks at home' and then 'The star-spangled banner'. The audience cheered themselves hoarse amid a sea of waving handkerchiefs. A potential disaster had been turned into a triumph.

Other problems were less easy to solve. During a performance of *Rigoletto* a hot water pipe under the stage burst and Nellie was enveloped in clouds of scalding steam and during a performance of *Lucia di Lammermoor* a fire started in the roof of the California Theatre, causing the performance to be abandoned and the theatre evacuated. And not all the mishaps were in the theatre. While being feted as guest of honour at a reception in the home of a San Franciscan socialite, a large bronze bust toppled off its pedestal and struck Nellie on the head. Nellie was knocked unconscious but recovered after a few moments. No permanent harm was done, except to the pride of the hostess.

Upon her return to New York, Nellie met up with Maurice Grau, who offered her a contract to join the new Metropolitan Opera Company he was assembling for the 1898–99 season. Nellie was reluctant to sign because Damrosch wanted to sell his share in the Damrosch-Ellis company and she and Ellis were considering taking over the company themselves. The power this would give her over the company's repertoire and the engagement of singers appealed to Nellie, but she had two concerns. Firstly, she feared that if she rejected Grau's offer and went into competition with the Met, he would block her return to Covent Garden and, secondly, she realised that she would need to expand her repertoire if she was going to continue being the prima donna of what would become the Melba-Ellis Opera Company.

To address the first concern, Nellie signed up with Maurice Grau, but for only four performances, and when she and Ellis took over the former Damrosch-Ellis company it was only Ellis's name that appeared in the title, although everyone (including Grau) must have realised that Nellie was a partner, especially since the press began referring to it as 'Melba's opera company' once it was assembled.

To address her second concern, Nellie stayed on in New York until late May to enable her to attend a performance by a company styling itself the 'Royal Italian Grand Opera Company from La Scala', made up of a few singers who had sung at La Scala and many who had not. The novelty of the company's season at Wallack's Theatre was Puccini's latest opera, *La Bohème*, which had not been seen in New York before. *La Bohème* had been performed in English at Covent Garden by the Carl Rosa company during a short season the previous November when Nellie had been on tour in the midlands and Nellie was now anxious to see a work about which she had heard promising reports.

On the night Nellie attended, the principal soprano role, Mimi, was sung by a second-rate soprano, but Nellie was able to hear enough to discern the potential of this role for herself. Although it offered no opportunity for coloratura fireworks, the part had pathos (the quality Nellie was best at portraying) and the sustained melodies Puccini had written for his latest heroine suited Nellie's voice perfectly. By the time the curtain had fallen on the final poignant act, Nellie knew she had found a new role in a contemporary opera, one that she could exploit and which would add to her prestige. She determined to learn the role and to that end she contacted the composer in Italy and requested she be given opportunity to study the opera with him. Puccini agreed, but before she was able to visit Puccini Nellie had another season at Covent Garden and a series of concerts to perform in London.

When she arrived in London, Nellie took the house near Maidenhead she had previously rented, where she could entertain friends and colleagues, including Haddon Chambers, whose friendship had likely developed into a love affair, despite the playwright being married. She appeared just four times at Covent

Garden: once as Violetta, once as Rosina and twice as Juliette. Alfred de Rothschild, Nellie's financial adviser, invited Adelina Patti to attend the performance of *La Traviata* on 28 June and Nellie watched with satisfaction as her heroine and erstwhile rival applauded generously.

It was the spectre of Patti in her prime that the critics resurrected when reviewing Nellie's first appearance in London as Rosina. While all commended her for tackling a role remembered as a Patti specialty, *The Times* complained that Nellie lacked the exuberance Patti had brought to it.[14] Herman Klein conceded that she was the best Rosina seen in London since Patti, and the *Pall Mall Gazette*'s reviewer proclaimed that Rosina was now 'undoubtedly Madame Melba's best role'.[15]

As in the previous year, Nellie focused on concerts during this London season. For a charity concert organised by the Duchess of Sutherland, Nellie persuaded Joachim to come to London for his only appearance in Britain that year and he stayed with Nellie at Maidenhead. Landon Ronald recalled that the old, ponderous Hungarian violinist and the elegant singer made a very odd couple. Joachim was obviously still smitten with Nellie and Ronald describes how when a man offended her on a railway station, the violinist waited until the train was in motion and then stuck his head out of a window and shouted, 'You blackguard! If you come here I vill punch you on ze nose!'[16] For a concert Nellie gave in the Royal Albert Hall in November, she was joined by Charles Santley, still commanding respect for the beauty of his voice at 64, and two Australians, Ada Crossley and Nellie's old friend and colleague from Melbourne, Johann Kruse. Between these concerts Nellie travelled to Italy to keep her appointment with the composer of *La Bohème*.

At 39, Giacomo Puccini was still establishing the reputation that would eventually see him named the most popular composer of Italian opera of the twentieth century. His first two operas had been politely received and his third – another setting of the 'Manon' story – had alerted impresarios to a new composer of originality, but his fourth opera, *La Bohème*, was in a class of its own. Puccini must have been congratulating himself on having created a work near to perfection both musically and theatrically, but he would also have been canny enough to realise that having the world's most famous soprano take up the work was its surest route to international acceptance.

That summer, Puccini was staying in Monsagrati, a village in the hills above his home city of Lucca, working on his next opera, *Tosca*. Prima donnas don't stay in villages, so when Nellie arrived in Tuscany she took a suite in Lucca's grandest hotel and Puccini was obliged to visit her. He came, willingly, for two hours every morning for about a week and the pair went carefully though the entire score of *La Bohème*, Puccini making copious notes for her in pencil on Nellie's score of the opera.[17] Nellie departed from Lucca convinced that her instincts had been right and she had found a new role in a contemporary opera that would help to dispel any criticism of her repertoire being old-fashioned. She was keen to sing her first Mimi, but that had to wait until December.

In November Nellie sailed for America again, this time to sing at the Met and then to take her place as silent partner and prima donna of the Ellis Opera Company. Nellie sang two performances each of *Roméo et Juliette* and *Faust* at the Met, subsequently relinquishing these roles to Sembrich and Eames.[18] With 7200 dollars earned in four nights in her pocket, Nellie joined the Ellis Opera Company in Philadelphia and sang Rosina in *Il Barbiere di Siviglia* for the company's opening night, a week before Christmas.

The company Ellis had assembled with input from Nellie was not as strong or as star-studded as the Met's, but it did contain some notable names. Two fine sopranos and future stars of the Met, Milka Ternina and Johanna Gadski, sang the soprano leads in the Wagner operas presented, and de Lussan joined Nellie in the French and Italian works.[19] Most of the male principals of the Damrosch-Ellis company had returned and the coup for the new partnership was the engagement of Albert Alvarez, who emulated Jean de Reszke by singing the tenor leads in the Wagner operas and partnering Nellie in some of the French operas.

On 30 December in Philadelphia (during a flu epidemic), Nellie sang Mimi in *La Bohème* for the first time with a young Sicilian tenor named Francesco Pandolfini as her Rodolfo, Zelie de Lussan as Musetta and Maurice Devries as Marcello. The Philadelphia audience was shocked by the modernity of the subject but entranced by the music and the way it was performed. The cast took 20 curtain calls at the conclusion of the performance.

The *Philadelphia Inquirer* reported that Nellie enjoyed 'a triumph of the highest order' and an unnamed freelance journalist, whose review appeared in papers across America, provided more detail:

> From the opening to the last little snatches of song which precede Mimi's death the work of the cantatrice was simply superb. The richness and resources of her voice were sufficiently tested in the love duet in the first act and in the quartet of the third act. No more effective scene has ever been sung upon this stage than the death scene where Mimi recalls little fragments of song from earlier and happier days and finally passes away in a rich crescendo as Melba and Melba alone, knows how to make effective.[20]

After a seven-week season in Philadelphia, the company moved to Washington and then followed a similar route to the previous year, ending up, once again, in California. *La Bohème* proved a hit whenever it was performed and by the end of the tour Nellie was keen to return to Europe and sing the role there.

This cross-continent tour (and the earlier one with the Damrosch company) sealed Nellie's reputation as the leading soprano in the United States. Americans warmed to the image she portrayed of a free-spirited woman from another country where pioneering was still a living tradition, and companies were keen to exploit her popularity. Nellie supplemented her already large earnings by allowing her name (and sometimes her portrait) to be used to endorse a varied range of products: food supplements, hair tonics, throat lozenges, mouth wash, cigars, cigarettes, lipstick, neck warmers, muffs, pianos and a sewing machine proudly named 'The Melba'. After it was realised that the name 'Melba' was an invention, an even greater number of products, including a variety of rose, stoves, mangles and a motor cycle were assigned it without Nellie's approval. 'Melba' also became a popular given name for newborn girls on both sides of the Atlantic and for more racehorses and numerous greyhounds. A small town in Idaho also honoured her by adopting her name.

When Nellie returned to London in May for the next season at Covent Garden, she sang her regular roles and despite the months of heavy performance schedules and tiresome travelling in America, her voice was in superb form. Nellie was no doubt gratified by the response to her familiar roles, but her focus was on exhibiting her Mimi for the first time outside America. A full program of rehearsals was planned before what would be the first performance of the opera sung in Italian in England opened on 1 July. Nellie was supported by a stronger cast than the Ellis Company had been able to muster: Fernando de Lucia sang Rodolfo, Ancona sang Marcello, Zelie de Lussan repeated her role of Musetta and the score came to life more vividly under the baton of the great Mancinelli than under Ellis's conductor Armando Seppelli. Puccini came to London to supervise the rehearsals and to attend the first night.

During the rehearsals Nellie granted another interview to the *Pall Mall Gazette*, in which she described Puccini's opera as having lasting beauty and the role of Mimi as now her favourite and the one she found to be the most sympathetic of all her roles. At the tail end of the interview, Nellie also dropped in the truthless claim that Puccini was writing the role of Tosca *for her*.[21]

Despite all the preparation, the opening night did not proceed faultlessly, with some ragged musical entries in the second act, while at one point a painted backdrop belonging to another opera was lowered to the stage by mistake. Most of the audience had never seen the opera before and they demonstrated their approval of the story and the music, demanding that Nellie and de Lucia repeat the touching love duet that ends the first act. The critics had nothing but praise for Nellie.

Nellie was content – and so was Puccini. Thanks in part to Nellie, *La Bohème* was produced in other major cities across the globe in the following months, establishing it on its path as perhaps the most popular of all operas.

Chapter 12

Campaigns

Despite the success she had enjoyed in America and the phenomenal fees she had earned, Nellie decided not to cross the Atlantic again until the winter of 1900. She feared that she had been neglecting her career on the Continent in recent times and leaving the door open to rivals. Joachim was among those who encouraged her to appear in European cities she had 'overlooked' in the past and assured Nellie she would triumph wherever she sang.

Another provincial concert tour in the United Kingdom had to be completed first and before Nellie left London she purchased the lease on a fine Georgian-style house at 30 Great Cumberland Place, near Marble Arch.[1] Craftsmen were immediately engaged to redecorate the 11 bedrooms, three bathrooms and six reception rooms to Nellie's taste and the result had a decidedly French flavour – reminiscent, one friend commented, of Versailles, complete with its excesses of taste.

This purchase marks a shift in Nellie's principal abode and base of operations from Paris to London and we may assume that she would soon dispose (or had already disposed) of her apartment in the French capital. She did not, however, relinquish her ties with Mathilde and Salvatore Marchesi or her friends in Paris, and proof that events in France were still of interest to her is provided by a letter written by her to the wife of Alfred Dreyfus, the Jewish French Army officer accused of treason. In the letter Nellie offers sympathy and encouragement to Madame Dreyfus and when it was published in *Le Figaro*, no doubt those Parisians who shared Nellie's view that Dreyfus was a scapegoat were grateful for her support.²

Nellie's Continental tour of Europe included concerts and appearances in opera, beginning in Holland in November 1899, but a problem arose even before she embarked for Amsterdam. On 11 October the United Kingdom and its dominions declared war on the Boer republics of South Africa, with troops (including Australians) despatched to the Cape of Good Hope to defend British interests. The Boers were of Dutch descent and so support for them was high in Holland and Nellie feared that she might be the victim of protests or threats if she sang in any Dutch cities. She probably also felt pangs of disloyalty to her homeland, but commitments were commitments and contracts were contracts, so Nellie steeled herself and set out just as casualty lists from South Africa began appearing in the British newspapers.

First in Amsterdam, followed by The Hague and finally Rotterdam, Nellie sang performances of *Faust*, *La Traviata*, *Rigoletto*, *Lucia di Lammermoor* and *Manon*. Pre-occupied as always with rubbing shoulders with royalty, she expressed disappointment that her performances were not patronised by Wilhelmina, the young queen of Holland, and that the monarch's absence had deterred the local aristocracy from attending. She told Agnes Murphy the lack of royal support was attributable simply to logistics: that the queen was engaged elsewhere whenever Nellie appeared, although this is not borne out by Dutch newspapers.³ In fact, Nellie was experiencing just the sort of protest she had feared and it was led from the very top of Dutch society.

From Holland Nellie moved on to Berlin, to be greeted by an ecstatic Joseph Joachim. Berliners heard Nellie for the first time in a concert at the Philharmonic Hall, where Joachim assisted her. As he had done in Bergamo, Joachim played the obbligato to Nellie's singing of the aria 'L'amerò, sarò costante' from Mozart's *Il Ré Pastore*. Karl Muck conducted. At the completion of her offerings of Handel, Verdi and Delibes (as well as the Mozart), the audience was reluctant to allow Nellie to depart until she had sung several encores, including Carl Bohm's song 'Still wie die Nacht', sung in passable German.

After two more concerts Nellie made her stage debut in Germany at the Hofoper, singing *Lucia di Lammermoor*, followed by *Rigoletto* and *Il Barbiere di Siviglia*.[4] The Kaiser attended a performance of 'Lucia' and summoned Nellie to the imperial box after the Mad Scene. With a cloak thrown over her costume and with her hair still dishevelled, Nellie duly presented herself. Nellie told Murphy that the Kaiser was very polite to her and that they discussed various questions of vocal technique. However, in her account of the event after the First World War, she accused the Kaiser of snapping his fingers at his wife, prompting the imperial couple to depart abruptly, with a cursory 'Good evening' directed to Nellie.[5]

German audiences warmed to Nellie, for she offered a different kind of vocalism from that to which they were accustomed. In German opera houses the roles Nellie sang were usually assigned to German singers who affected a 'tighter' and more mechanical way of producing notes, an approach that eliminated the warmth characteristic of singers from south of the Alps. The method Nellie had learned from Marchesi fell somewhere in between the German and the Italian methods, but the freedom and glow of Nellie's sound had probably not been heard in Berlin since Patti's visits. Nellie was hastily booked to return to the Hofoper in the new year for another series of performances.

Nellie returned briefly to Paris before heading to Vienna and Budapest. At the Paris Ritz she was interviewed by a French journalist named Marcel Hutin who got more than he had bargained for. After discussing her success in Berlin, Nellie startled Hutin by questioning why his countrymen rejoiced in Britain's Boer War setbacks. Setting aside the suitability of the circumstances in which it was asked, there was justification for Nellie's question. The French press had expressed concern about what they called British expansionism and for French interests in South Africa and showed support for the position taken by the Dutch. Hutin attempted to convince Nellie that French newspapers made a distinction between art and politics, but when he asked when she expected to sing in Paris again, he received a terse response: 'Do you *really* believe that this is possible right now? An Englishwoman at the Paris Opéra? Perhaps I will sing here again when the war is over and when the French see us as *friends* again.'[6]

Nellie was genuinely disturbed by the Boer War and the toll it was taking on her friends in the United Kingdom and Australia. When a giant fundraising concert was held in London in January to raise money to support the families of British soldiers killed in the early battles of the war, Nellie wrote to *The Times* expressing her deep regret at not being able to appear due to her commitments on the Continent and promising to take part in such events whenever she could in the future.[7]

Nellie made her debut in Vienna in a concert in the Musikverein, then travelling to Budapest for two more concerts. She then returned to Vienna to make her Austrian stage debut at the Imperial Opera, as Violetta in *La Traviata*. An event occurred on the afternoon before that performance similar to the one involving Braga in Palermo. Teresa Carreño was installed in the suite next to Nellie's in their hotel and the great Venezuelan pianist was practising energetically. Nellie sent a message saying that she was singing at the opera that evening and begging for silence so that she might sleep. Carreño was happy to oblige and attended the opera.

La Traviata was conducted by another distinguished conductor, Hans Richter, and after Violetta expired dramatically and numerous curtain calls were taken, Nellie favoured the audience with a performance of the Mad Scene from *Lucia di Lammermoor*, following which the director of the Imperial Opera, Gustav Mahler, was entrusted with presenting Nellie with a laurel wreath on stage as the audience displayed their approval. That duty must have been galling for the famous composer, who had a low opinion of virtuoso singers in general and coloratura sopranos in particular. He was quoted later as saying 'one might as well listen to a clarinet'.

Emperor Franz Joseph, who attended her performance, undoubtedly approved of Nellie's singing, applauding her enthusiastically. Nellie was proud when she was told that this was the first time the old emperor had attended the theatre since his empress had been assassinated in Geneva (on the occasion the assassin had failed to kill Philippe). The following morning Nellie received a summons to the Hofburg and there she and Gemma Bellincioni were both awarded the title 'Kammersängerin', official 'chamber singer' to the Austro-Hungarian court. Nellie was honoured to receive the title because it was seldom given to British singers but, characteristically, in her various accounts of the ceremony, the Italian diva does not get a mention. As a reciprocal gesture, Nellie donated the fee she had received the previous evening to a fund for retired singers of the Imperial Opera.

Nellie then returned to Berlin for her second series of performances at the Hofoper and here she sang the title role in *Manon*, an opera which had not been heard in Berlin before. While in Berlin, a young boy – Fritz Muller – from Australia was introduced to Nellie. The son of the tutor employed by Elise Wiedermann-Pinschof to teach her children in Melbourne, young Fritz was studying piano at the Hochschule für Musik in Berlin but was dejected and homesick. Understanding the boy's feelings, Nellie bought him a camera for his thirteenth birthday. She also contacted Dora in Melbourne asking if her sister would join her again to provide the companionship she too desperately needed; she also wrote to Belle mentioning her desire to tour Australia, indicating that she intended to raise the issue with George Musgrove on her return to London.

Joseph Joachim would no doubt have been happy to provide the companionship on a permanent basis, but Nellie wanted no more than friendship from him. On her departure from Berlin. Joachim presented her with a miniature violin carved from ebony to express his 'mourning' for her leaving.

Concerts in Dresden and with the Gewandhaus Orchestra in Leipzig, conducted by Arthur Nikisch, were given before Nellie headed south to fulfil a long-held commitment to sing at the opera in Monte Carlo. Here she was teamed up with Francesco Tamagno for performances of *La Traviata* and with her colleague from America, Francesco Pandolfini, in *Il Barbiere di Siviglia*. Nellie was also to return (finally) to the role of Desdemona in two performances of Verdi's *Otello*, with Tamagno in the title role, but fate once again intervened, Nellie being forced to withdraw, suffering from influenza.

The *Riviera Daily* accused Nellie of not being ill and abandoning her role in *Otello* because of disagreement over money with Raoul Gunsbourg, the eccentric and autocratic director of the Opéra de Monte Carlo. Nellie wrote an indignant letter to the editor of the *Riviera Daily* denying the charge. Given how keen Nellie was to sing Desdemona, it seems unlikely that she would have voluntarily passed up the opportunity, and her state of health is confirmed by a letter she wrote from Monte Carlo to Herman Klein in London, which begins: 'Excuse the pencil, I am in bed with a bad attack of influenza'.[8]

Nellie completed her Continental campaign with more concerts in Germany and a couple in Prague. There was speculation in the press that she intended to sing in the Rumanian capital, Bucharest, and in the Ottoman capital, Istanbul, but if that was ever her intention time ran out and she was able to manage only a short break in Paris before hastening to London for the 1900 season at Covent Garden.

Nellie's despondency during her time on the Continent was due not only to politics, war or the rigours of travel; she had been confronted by a major personal issue. While in Monaco she had received notification from a law firm in Galveston, Texas, that Charlie was filing for divorce. That communication revealed that Charlie and George (now aged 16) had been living on a cattle ranch Charlie owned near Galveston since 1895. According to Charlie, Nellie had deserted him, he had invited her to join him in Texas but she had declined and that at all times he had supported Nellie 'in good style' and conducted himself 'lovingly' towards her.[9]

Nellie sought legal advice and, based on that, she decided not to contest the divorce. The benefit to her if the divorce was granted would be legal independence from her husband; the downside would be that Charlie would almost certainly be granted sole custody of George under United States law – and she might never see her son again, a bitter pill to swallow, but Nellie would have consoled herself with the knowledge that George would soon reach majority and be able to decide on a future relationship with his mother.

At the divorce hearing Nellie was represented by a lawyer who told the court that his client empathically denied the accusations of wrongdoing on her part made by Charlie, but she would not be laying a counter-claim. On 12 April the divorce was granted, with Charlie given legal custody of George and any claim Nellie may make to a share of her former husband's property denied in advance.[10]

The press in England, Australia and the United States reported on the divorce. The *San Francisco Chronicle* claimed to have a quote from Nellie, in which she said she was delighted with the outcome and that the divorce was something she had longed for.[11] Even before the divorce was granted, there had been rumours and speculation in the press about Nellie remarrying. In February it was widely reported that Nellie would marry Joachim. From Monaco Nellie wrote again to Herman Klein requesting that he publish a denial of that story in *The Sunday Times*.[12]

More credence was put on reports that, as soon as she was free, Nellie would marry Haddon Chambers, but the fact that Chambers was already married seems to have been overlooked. Spurious quotes attributed to Nellie again appeared in the press, this time claiming that she was looking forward to being 'Mrs Haddon Chambers' and to sharing her new house in London with him. Nellie denied these claims in a press statement that was widely circulated: 'Rumours of my approaching marriage', she declared, 'are wild fiction. I will never relinquish my freedom again – not for any man, be he lord, yeoman, troubadour or dramatist!'[13]

Nellie never did marry again, but as a healthy, now single, independently wealthy and attractive woman she would take lovers whenever the right men entered her life. The number of such men has always been exaggerated and argued over. Salacious stories of Nellie's sex life became a weapon in the hands of her critics and, as with the stories about her youthful misdemeanours, Nellie chose to maintain a dignified silence, hoping they would eventually disappear. Most of them did, but even to this day mention of Nellie's name will sometimes prompt the resurrection of some outrageous anecdote from storytellers with more imagination than integrity.

Nellie might reasonably have believed that she need no longer concern herself about Charlie Armstrong, but five months after the divorce she read in the newspapers that a devastating hurricane had hit Galveston, causing widespread damage and loss of life. Her first thought was of George and she was understandably nervous that her son could be among the 1500 reported dead. With the assistance of the newspaper publisher Alfred Harmsworth, Nellie learned that the name Armstrong did not appear among the list of dead or injured, but, as a gesture she probably hoped her son would learn of, she volunteered to sing at a concert organised by Henry Irving at the Theatre Royal Drury Lane to raise money for the hurricane victims.[14]

When Nellie returned to Covent Garden for the 1900 summer season, she found another Australian among the roster of principal sopranos – Lalla Miranda from Victoria. Ten years younger than

Nellie, Miranda came from a musical family and had studied in Paris with Helene Richard. Like Frances Saville, Miranda did not pose any serious threat to Nellie's position, but she did acquit herself respectably in two 'Melba' roles: Gilda and Marguerite de Valois.

Nellie was scheduled to open the season in *Faust* but was ill again and the role of Marguerite was taken by another 'rival', the American soprano and former Marchesi pupil Suzanne Adams. Nellie made her first appearance as Mimi in *La Bohème* and did not share the role with any other soprano during the season.[15] She also sang Rosina and Lucia, with Lempriere Pringle singing Raimondo, the principal bass role in the Donizetti opera. This was also Jean de Reszke's last season at Covent Garden and together they sang in *Roméo et Juliette*, the ticket prices raised for what had become an historic partnership in an opera in which the pair had no equals. Puccini's new opera, *Tosca*, also reached Covent Garden that season but not with Nellie as the protagonist. Milka Ternina, Nellie's colleague from the Ellis company was assigned the role. Nellie attended the first night and as she listened to Ternina singing Puccini's music she became more determined to sing the role herself – one day.

As compensation for missing the opening night of the season, Nellie was granted the closing night. *Faust* was the offering and the role of Marguerite's brother, Valentin, was sung by Antonio Scotti, an Italian baritone with whom Nellie had never before sung, but with whom she would sing regularly in the future. Scotti had triumphed in the villain role of Baron Scarpia in the production of *Tosca* and when Nellie asked him if he thought she would be able to sing Tosca, he is reputed to have replied: 'The great Melba can sing whatever she likes'. Nellie was not sure whether that was encouragement or not.

Before departing for New York and a long engagement with the Met, Nellie spent a few weeks in Dublin as a guest of the Lord Lieutenant of Ireland. Most of her time was allocated to social engagements related to the annual Dublin Horse Show, but she gave a performance at a charity concert at the Royal University. Supporting her at this concert was the famous Irish tenor Joseph O'Mara and her most recently acquired operatic protégée, Regina Nagel, a contralto from the Goulburn Valley in Victoria. Nagel had spent two years at the École Marchesi and Nellie herself had given the young singer some lessons. At the time of the Dublin concert, Nagel enjoyed Nellie's favour, but the young Australian's eccentricities of character exceeded her singing abilities, prompting Nellie to lose interest in her. Nellie's list of protégées was growing and would continue to increase over the next 30 years, although Nellie never found what she claimed she sought: an Australian-born successor.

Of all the ventures Nellie had undertaken in recent years, the one that most resembled a military campaign in terms of mobility, speed and endurance was her six-month tour of the United States, beginning in November 1900 and ending in April 1901. With the demise of both the Damrosch and Ellis companies, Maurice Grau had decided to take his Metropolitan company on a cross-continent tour, covering roughly the same route as those companies had in past years. This was to be followed by the company's regular season in New York and their annual tour of the eastern states. Recognising Nellie's capacity as a drawcard in the Midwest and on the west coast, Grau had engaged her as the company's prima donna and star attraction for the first phase in his venture. The fee of 1350 dollars per performance Grau had offered was the highest ever paid to a female artist at the Met and too tempting to refuse, so despite their past differences Nellie signed up.

Grau certainly got his money's worth. Nellie sang 51 performances during those months. On the cross-continent tour she often sang three times per week and her absence from the United States for almost two years ensured that audiences flocked to hear her again. The 'house full' sign was raised most nights in Minneapolis, Lincoln, Kansas City, Denver, San Francisco and Los Angeles.

The tour began in Los Angeles with the Met's first performance of *La Bohème*. The venue was a stadium normally used for boxing matches. A capacity audience of almost 4000 wept over Mimi's fate and set up a chant of 'Mimi! Mimi!' to draw Nellie out in front of the curtain after every act, rewarding her with cheers and showers of flowers. Nellie returned the compliments with an impromptu performance of the Mad Scene from *Lucia di Lammermoor* (after the Puccini), still dressed in her Mimi costume. A large crowd also filled the streets around the flimsy building and listened to the performance free of charge.

As the tour progressed eastwards through Colorado, Kansas, Nebraska and Minnesota, critics with dubious musical qualifications occasionally pointed out performances where Nellie seemed to be singing below her best, but perhaps, in some instances, the primary purpose of such criticism was to impress readers with the writer's own perspicacity. Audiences were easier to please. As neither Sembrich nor Eames were included in the company that season, Nellie's status as prima donna spilled over into the New York season and the east coast tour. The New York season opened with *Roméo et Juliette* and the distinction of the opening went to her, with the critic W.J. Henderson, who had earlier foreshadowed Nellie's widespread popularity, found nothing to criticise about her Juliette.[16]

On Boxing Day *La Bohème* was performed at the Met for the first time. The critics did not receive the opera with as much enthusiasm as those in London and the west coast, and the reviews must have disappointed and probably angered Nellie. Henderson was reserved in his comments about her Mimi, complaining that she lacked the acting skill to bring off the death scene with the passion it deserved.[17] Henry Krehbiel in the *New York Tribune* displayed no reserve in his comments, dubbing the opera 'foul in subject' and a 'poor man's Traviata' and Nellie as offering nothing more than a beautiful voice and placid singing. Once again audiences did not share these critics' views.[18]

On 16 January Nellie tackled a role she had not sung before: the Infanta in Massenet's *Le Cid*. Jean de Reszke sang the title role, which Massenet had written for him. Like Marguerite de Valois in *Les Huguenots*, the role of the Infanta of Spain is the second soprano part in this opera, but has always had enough appeal to leading coloratura sopranos to allow them to share the stage with another soprano – playing the hero's girlfriend, Chimène. As the singer cast as Chimène – Lucien Bréval from the Paris Opéra – was not in good voice, Nellie had no trouble stealing the vocal honours. Bréval was, however, a better actor than Nellie and when the critics put pen to paper they emphasised this with alacrity. The unnamed critic of the New York *Sun* reported: 'The more Bréval acted, the more waxen Melba became. After the triumph of Bréval's great scene in the third act, the famous soprano looked positively ill.'[19]

This was Nellie's last season at the Met until 1904 and it was historic in another and quite unexpected way: it was the first time anyone attempted to record Nellie singing on stage. Lionel Mapleson – nephew of the impresario Colonel Mapleson – was employed as the Met's librarian. He was also the proud owner of an Edison Phonograph, which not only played cylinder recordings but could record them. Mapleson persuaded the prompter to allow him to sit in the prompt box with the horn of his phonograph pointing towards the stage during performances. Over a 10-week period during the 1900–01 season, Mapleson squeezed in beside the prompter, loaded blank wax cylinders onto his machine and recorded two-minute snippets from several operas. Mapleson undertook these recordings either for his own amusement or so that they could be added to his library's collection – he had no commercial purpose for them in mind.

Based on written records, it appears that he recorded Nellie singing parts of *Le Cid*, *Les Huguenots*, *Lucia di Lammermoor*, *Faust*, *Roméo et Juliette* and *La Traviata*. Only three survive from this group and on the evidence of those, their historic value far outweighs their musical value. Listening to the sound is a tortuous experience. The voice sounds as though in a different building and being heard through a drain pipe; it fades as the singer moves away from the prompt box and the roar and clatter of the machine itself obliterates much of the sound coming from the stage.[20] The prospect of hearing Nellie in full voice during live performances in a great opera house (and in her prime) is enticing, but sadly these and other recordings made by Mapleson in future years offer us only dim and distorted echoes of what audiences were enjoying and acclaiming at the time.[21]

On Nellie's return to Europe, she went first to Paris, where she organised her own 40th birthday party at the Paris Ritz, before continuing on to London. Change was afoot in the British capital. In January, after a 51-year reign, Queen Victoria had died and Nellie's acquaintances and supporters, the Prince and Princess of Wales, had become King Edward VII and Queen Alexandra, although the king's coronation was yet to take place. Nellie also had her new home and a complement of servants to welcome her, but within a month of her arrival she had taken a three-month lease on a substantial house called 'Quarry Wood Cottage' in the Thames Valley in order to escape the summer heat in the city.

Dora had returned to Australia, so Nellie invited Belle to join her. Now Mrs Paterson, Belle arrived with her two small children, Nellie and David. Aunt Nellie delighted in the company of her niece and nephew and the constant flow of guests at the 'cottage', where the long, lazy days of summer were passed with tennis and boating parties and sumptuous feasts on the lawns, which stretched down to the Thames.[22]

Nellie had conceded the opening night of the Covent Garden season to Emma Eames and made her first appearance on 6 June in *La Bohème*. She was in fine voice and partnered this time by Giuseppe Anselmi, a tall, slim tenor who did not need elevated shoes. The performance was marred, however, by a malfunction of the machine that provided the snow in the third act. Despite the efforts of a frantic mechanic, the machine would not shut down, so traces of snow continued to fall in the act that followed. As had become her custom in America, after the opera Nellie offered the audience the Mad Scene from *Lucia di Lammermoor* as an encore – complete with snow. After six more performances (and a week off due to laryngitis), Nellie closed the season with a performance of *Roméo et Juliette*. During the provincial concert tour that followed, she drew what the local press claimed was the largest audience ever assembled in Belfast's Ulster Hall.[23]

At the end of November Nellie left London for an eventful stay in the principality of Monaco, first for a holiday and then to sing again at the Opéra de Monte Carlo. She stayed in the newly opened and luxurious Hotel de l'Hermitage, attended parties and gambled at the casino. Nellie always enjoyed a 'flutter' and during this stay in Monte Carlo, two amusing incidents took place in the casino. She ran out of money one evening and spotted Philippe's friend, Baron de Hirsch. Nellie asked if the baron would lend her 1000 francs and he did so with obvious reluctance. The next day Nellie sent him a cheque for the amount and a couple of days later a small parcel addressed to her arrived at the Hotel de l'Hermitage. It contained a diamond brooch accompanied by a note from de Hirsch saying that the gift was in recognition of the fact that Nellie was the only woman to whom he had ever lent money who had paid him back.

Another evening Nellie entered the casino with Gladys de Grey. They noticed two empty chairs at a table; one on each side of a large, heavily bearded Frenchman. When the Frenchman showed no sign of moving to allow Nellie and Gladys to sit together, they took the chairs on each side of him. The Frenchman was losing heavily and finally stood up and shouted: 'What can I expect? Sitting between two *cocottes*!' Nellie was angry, Gladys delighted. Her companion persuaded Nellie not to challenge the man, saying 'I've never been so flattered in my life'.

She also met the aviator Alberto Santos-Dumont, who had recently won a prize for flying one of his gas-filled dirigibles around the Eiffel Tower. Nellie was intrigued by the young, adventurous Brazilian and suggested that he might collect her after she had visited Haddon Chambers, who was installed in a hotel at Cap Martin, and fly her back to Monte Carlo in his 'machine'. The plan was agreed but the aviator didn't turn up. On her return to Monte Carlo, Nellie found a large crowd on the dock watching Santos-Dumont attempting to retrieve his deflated airship from the bay where it had crashed.

In mid-January Nellie returned to Paris for a few days and organised a dinner to celebrate Salvatore Marchesi's 80th birthday. Among the guests was the Australian painter Rupert Bunny, who had been a regular visitor at Nellie's Thames Valley retreats. Bunny's paintings were popular in Paris and he had embarked on a portrait of Nellie, commissioned by her. The portrait was unveiled in May but did not receive the same praise from the Paris critics to which Bunny was accustomed, and the reason is apparent. Measuring approximately one metre by two and richly painted in oils, the full-length pose shows Nellie standing in a dramatic landscape in the manner of Gainsborough and Lawrence. Her posture and her expression are regal and the stronger aspects of Nellie's character are captured well. What is missing is the warmth and vivacity that tempered those characteristics.[24]

Nellie was contracted to sing three roles at L'Opéra de Monte Carlo, Mimi being the first, in a new production of *La Bohème*, for which Puccini had travelled from Lucca to supervise. Her Rodolfo was to be the Italian tenor Enrico Caruso, with whom Nellie had not sung before.[25] In his biography of Caruso, Stanley Jackson relates how the young tenor had first observed Nellie at the casino and felt intimidated by her regal bearing and the herd of adoring acolytes, who were in constant attendance on her. To Caruso's relief, Nellie was polite and friendly at the first rehearsal and, being a punctual person herself, expressed her appreciation of his early arrival. Just what Nellie thought of or expected of this new partner was not recorded at the time, although in future years she had nothing but praise for Caruso. At their first meeting she probably thought him gauche and lacking Jean de Reszke's charm, but when Caruso opened his mouth all reservations were put aside. Nellie must have realised she was singing with if not de Reszke's direct successor, then with a singer who was better endowed vocally than all the other tenors with whom she regularly sang and who would one day assume de Reszke's mantle as the world's leading tenor.

The performances of *La Bohème* were a triumph for both singers, and in *Rigoletto*, the next opera on offer, Caruso as the Duke of Mantua dominated the performance in a role that suited him perfectly. Further competition for Nellie came in the form of Maurice Renaud, singing Rigoletto for the first time in his career and setting a benchmark by which all future baritones would be judged. Nellie was the equal to her partners and the press claimed no better performance of Verdi's popular opera could ever be expected.[26]

The third opera in which Nellie appeared was not really an opera at all. Hector Berlioz's *Le Damnation de Faust* (based like Gounod's *Faust*, on Goethe's masterpiece) had been written as an oratorio. The composer himself had recognised the potential of the work for transfer from the concert hall to the stage, but that didn't occur until 1893, when Gunsbourg staged it for the first time at Monte Carlo with Jean de Reszke as Faust and Rose Caron as Marguerite.

For this revival Jean de Reszke agreed to repeat his role, Renaud was assigned the role of Méphistophélès and Nellie sang Marguerite for the first time in her career. De Reszke and Renaud were predictably successful in their parts and Nellie, claiming a great affection for this alternative Marguerite, triumphed in hers. The local correspondent of *Le Figaro* reported:

Madame Melba was a delightful Marguerite. One does not know what to admire most: the crystalline voice which can be so exquisitely softened or her dramatic interpretation of Berlioz's touching heroine. Her Marguerite is masterful for its lack of artifice.[27]

This would prove to be the last time Nellie sang on stage with Jean de Reszke, who announced his retirement soon after. She must have been deeply saddened that her association with the singer she admired above all others was over, but the arrival of Enrico Caruso on the scene was compensation. The torch had been passed.

Chapter 13

Home, sweet home?

Nellie had entered into negotiations with George Musgrove for a concert tour of Australia, as she had foreshadowed to her sister Belle. The Australian impresario James Cassius Williamson had also been keen to again attempt to secure Nellie for such a tour, but his terms had not been generous enough for Nellie and she rejected them. Musgrove was prepared to be more financially forthcoming and so a deal was struck. Nellie would spend seven months from mid-September 1902 until April 1903 in Australia and give concerts in all the state capitals. All her expenses would be covered by Musgrove and she would be paid a total of 21,000 pounds – a remarkable sum considering the basic wage in Australia at the time was two pounds per week. A separate deal was also struck with the Tait brothers of J.&N. Tait to manage her concerts in Adelaide, probably because of their control of venues in that city.

But before embarking for Australia, Nellie had more concerts to give in Germany and Switzerland and another season in London to complete. The beginning of the Edwardian era, in which it was hoped long-repressed social issues might find royal support, was heartening to Londoners, and so was the conclusion of the Boer War, although the cost in lives and depleted fortunes (including Nellie's) was still being counted.[1] At Alfred de Rothschild's home she met the hero of the hour, General Kitchener, the defeated Boer leader Lucas Meyer and the South African mining magnate Cecil Rhodes, and at another party the violinist Percy Colsen was introduced to her. Thirty years on, Colsen would write the first 'independent' biography of Nellie, drawing on his personal recollections of his subject and inventing a great deal to fill in the gaps.

The great social event of the season was to be the coronation of the new king, planned for 26 June. Numerous coronation concerts and coronation galas were planned, each trying to outdo the others in their patriotic fervour, with Nellie participating in three of them. On 11 June she sang in the Royal Albert Hall, backed by a choir of 800 and the massed bands of seven regiments of the British Army. She and Clara Butt shared the verses of 'God Save the King' when the new Prince and Princess of Wales (the former Duke and Duchess of York and future King George V and Queen Mary) took their places in the royal box. At the end of the anthem the audience produced thousands of miniature Union Jacks and waved them in a frenzy of patriotic ardour. On 30 June Nellie, Caruso and Renaud sang in one act of *Rigoletto* at a coronation gala at Covent Garden and, 10 days later Nellie was the star attraction at a concert in the Royal Botanical Gardens in Regent's Park during a three-day, 'Coronation Bazaar'.

For the Covent Garden event Edward Elgar had composed a Coronation Ode, for which Nellie was to be the soprano soloist, but when the king came down with appendicitis and the coronation was postponed, Elgar's piece was withdrawn from the program. Such was the king's rapid recovery, however, that other coronation events for which tickets had been sold at inflated prices went ahead.

During the regular Covent Garden season, Nellie and Caruso teamed up for four performances of *La Bohème*, five of *Rigoletto* and two of *La Traviata*. Nellie also appeared in *Faust* and *Roméo et Juliette* supported by Pol Plançon and Albert Saléza, a French tenor with whom she had sung at the Met and in previous seasons at Covent Garden. Maurice Grau had resigned from Covent Garden to concentrate on his duties in America, to be replaced by André Messager, the directeur-général of the Opéra-Comique in Paris. Messager proved to be a more accommodating manager than Grau and spent as little time in London as he possibly could. Nellie's influence at Covent Garden, still strongly backed by Gladys de Grey, continued to grow.

On 2 August Nellie sailed from Liverpool on the SS *Campania*, bound for New York. She was accompanied by 27 large trunks, the contents of which included all her concert gowns and her stage costumes. After a train journey across North America to Vancouver, she boarded the Royal Mail Steamer *Miowera* to transport her to Brisbane. Travelling with her and acting as her companion was an Australian friend from London, May Donaldson, along with an array of servants. Three members of a concert party she had assembled also travelled with them: Ada Sassoli, a 14-year-old Italian harpist, who had appeared in concerts with Nellie in London; Frederic Griffiths, principal flute in the Covent Garden orchestra; and Griffiths's wife, the pianist Llewella Davies. Two singers completed the party but they made their own way to Australia, joining Nellie in Melbourne: the Latvian tenor Louis Arens, with whom she had sung on the Continent and who had sung in Australia before, and the baritone Maurice Bensaude, from the Ellis Company and Covent Garden.[2]

The *Miowera* was due to arrive in Brisbane on 15 September, but when two days passed in Brisbane without news of the ship there was speculation that it might have experienced trouble at sea or even sunk. It arrived in Moreton Bay in the late evening of 17 March and a launch carried local dignitaries out to the ship to greet Nellie. The launch also carried a reporter from the *Brisbane Courier*, who interviewed Nellie on deck. A question about her affair with Philippe was met with silence and a waggle of Nellie's forefinger. On safer ground, the reporter asked about Nellie's views on contemporary Italian opera and she made the claim that Puccini was writing a new opera for her: *Madama Butterfly*.[3] Equally untrue was a subsequent remark of Nellie's – that Brünnhilde in Wagner's Ring Cycle was one of her favourite roles. At the end of the interview the reporter asked if Nellie would like to write a message to the Australian people in his notebook. She obliged. The message read:

> I am happy to be back in my homeland and I am happy to know that my countrymen feel an interest in me. I shall sing to them from my heart; and it is perhaps well that I have not to speak, for I should fail to say all that my heart would dictate.[4]

Nellie stayed overnight at a Brisbane hotel, where 140 telegrams of welcome awaited her, along with the inevitable batch of begging letters. The following morning, Nellie, her attendants and an agent appointed by George Musgrove departed on the Brisbane-to-Sydney train. Nellie's brother Charles joined the train at Hornsby and Belle and Tom Patterson greeted her in Sydney, along with a crowd of 2000 people.

Musgrove had arranged for David Mitchell to travel to the town of Albury on the New South Wales–Victoria border, travelling in what was called the 'royal car' – a splendidly appointed railway carriage that had been used by the Duke and Duchess of York on their visit to Australia in 1901. There Nellie and her father were to be reunited after 16 years, but all the excitement proved too much for the 73-year-old Mitchell. He suffered a mild stroke as the train neared its destination. An Albury doctor was summoned and Mitchell was found to be conscious but suffering minor paralysis. He was taken to a nearby house to be cared for.

Shortly before Nellie's train from Sydney reached Albury, a telegraphic message warned her of what had transpired. As soon as she reached Albury station, she rushed to her father's bedside. Tears flowed and Nellie told her father that she would cancel the rest of her trip and remain at his side, but Mitchell insisted she continue with her itinerary. Nellie obeyed, leaving her father in Albury. David Mitchell's condition improved in the coming days and eventually he was pronounced strong enough to travel home to Melbourne and to his own bed at Doonside.

The platform at which Nellie's train arrived at Melbourne's Spencer Street Railway Station was closed to the public but jammed, nevertheless, with dignitaries and Mitchell family members. Outside the station a vast, excited crowd waited impatiently to catch their first glimpse in 16 years of the city's now most famous daughter. A throng of journalists and photographers were perched on specially erected scaffolding, small boys clung to the top of lamp posts, shouting 'Good on ya, Nellie' and other typically Australian expressions of delight, while a frustrated army of constables (on foot and on horseback) attempted to maintain order.

Nellie was assisted into her waiting carriage by George Musgrove and Tom Patterson and there she stood and waved to the crowd. She also tore up some of the floral arrangements she had been given and cast flowers into the crowd. Men, women and children desperately tried to secure a souvenir of what was the biggest public welcome of any celebrity in living memory.

Nellie's father had hoped she would stay with him at Doonside when the trip was being planned, but wisely Nellie had entrusted Belle and Tom with leasing a house of her own to spare her father the attention her presence would inevitably draw. The politician Robert Harper rented his Caulfield house, Myoora to Nellie for seven months at 200 pounds per month and withdrew to his 'weekender' at Mt Macedon.[5] Crowds and brass bands lined the streets as Nellie progressed across Princes Bridge and along St Kilda Road towards Caulfield. Cable trams were halted to allow her to pass. A passenger in one of these was Nellie's old colleague Armes Beaumont, who stuck his head out of a window to shout 'Welcome back to Melbourne, Nellie!' Nellie recognised the blind tenor and wrote him a note a couple of days later thanking him for his welcome.

Melbourne's *Punch* published an ode to Nellie, which included these words: 'Far away we heard the thunder of applause and fain would wonder, do sweet childhood's memories linger in the far-famed siren singer?'[6] No doubt 'the siren singer' was consumed by 'childhood's memories' on her arrival in Melbourne, tempered by concern for her father. Just as the years had wrought great changes on Nellie, so time had changed her homeland and her home city. The six separate colonies Nellie had left behind in 1886 were now united as the Commonwealth of Australia, and the first Australian parliament had been opened by the Duke of York in the Royal Exhibition Building built by Nellie's father. Australia's population had increased by more than one million. Participation in the Boer War had earned Australia a place in international politics – and yet it had not all been plain sailing: a major economic depression had marred the 1890s and one of the worst droughts in the nation's history was currently gripping the country. And, thanks to Nellie, Australia now occupied a significant place in the international music scene.

So much had changed, and yet so much remained familiar to Nellie. The musical community of Melbourne welcomed her at a reception held in Glen's Concert Hall, where she had sung long before she became famous. A visit to the Presbyterian Ladies College proved more than just an opportunity to meet old classmates. Nellie was greeted by a band playing 'See the conquering hero comes' and, to cope with the rush for her autograph, sandwich labels were commandeered. In years to come proud grandmothers would display small, rather greasy cards with 'Tomato', 'Chicken' or 'Pâté de Foie Gras' printed on one side and 'Nellie Melba' inscribed on the reverse. Baron Tennyson, the Governor-General of the new Commonwealth (based in Melbourne) entertained Nellie to dinner on the instructions of Edward VII. Nellie also requested an extra matinee performance of the play *Sweet Nell of Old Drury*, starring the darling of Australia's theatre, Nellie Stewart, at the Princess Theatre, to enable her to attend. While Nellie Melba lacked any title at this stage in her life, the whole tour began in regal style and with widespread expressions of love, admiration and respect. Sadly, that did not last the full seven months.

Nellie's first concert in the Melbourne Town Hall was managed for maximum effect and maximum profit. One-guinea tickets were sold first and only after this category was exhausted were cheaper tickets offered. The word 'MELBA', picked out in orange and blue electric light bulbs, adorned the front of the building. Nellie was listed to sing just two arias and two songs, but if ticketholders worried they might not get their money's worth, Nellie ensured they did. After singing the Mad Scene from *Lucia di Lammermoor*, Nellie took Llewella Davies's place at the piano and accompanied herself in 'Home, sweet home'. One of the songs was repeated and another added as a final encore after Nellie had sung the *La Traviata* scena sung in the same building at the Elsasser concert in 1884.[7]

In the audience for that first concert was 12-year-old Mabel Emmerton, the future Dame Mabel Brookes. She recalled years later: 'Few people in Australia had heard Melba. It was an incredible concert, everyone was transfixed. Nobody realised she could be as good as she was.'[8]

Four more sold-out concerts followed and, at the second, David Mitchell, in defiance of his doctor's orders, sat in the front row, with Nellie singing 'Comin' thru the rye' for him. Nellie was able to spend time with her father and, while David Mitchell's body had aged, his spirit was intact. In *Melodies and Memories* Nellie reported:

> I remember when I came back to Australia in 1902 my father took me aside and said, 'Well, have you saved any money? I said, hesitating, 'Yes, a little'. He asked, 'How much?' I said (fibbing), 'Perhaps twenty thousand pounds'. He said: 'Well, lass, you're richer than I am'. There was a pause and then he solemnly winked at me and I winked at him. Then taking me by the arm he said, 'You're quite right, lassie. Never tell anybody what you've got. Not even me.'[9]

Concerts followed in Sydney (where Jack Moore was on hand to greet her), Brisbane and Adelaide, with full houses and rapturous reviews, before Nellie took part in what was advertised as the 'Melba Opera Season'. Musgrove was a regular purveyor of opera in Australia so was able to supply an orchestra, chorus, a couple of additional soloists, sets and costumes to enable Nellie, Arens and Bensaude to present three performances in both Melbourne and Sydney of staged excerpts from opera. Single acts from *Faust*, *Rigoletto*, *La Traviata* and *Lucia di Lammermoor* were offered in various combinations and audiences filled the Princess Theatre in Melbourne and the Theatre Royal in Sydney to see and hear their heroine 'in character'. After concerts in Ballarat and Bendigo, and satisfied with the progress of the tour to date, Nellie asked the public and the press to allow her some private time to spend Christmas and the New Year with her family.

Ten days into the new year, Nellie and her party travelled to Western Australia for concerts in Perth and Kalgoorlie, on the goldfields, and a final concert in Adelaide. Nellie's next and last engagement in Australia was for concerts in Tasmania; however, she became seriously ill during a rough crossing of Bass Strait, experiencing bleeding from her throat, forcing her to cancel her Launceston engagement, where she was scheduled to make her first appearance. The local press had got it into their heads that Nellie was not sick at all, only suffering from pique. A crowd who had bought tickets for her concert gathered at the Launceston railway station and booed her as she boarded a train for Hobart. In disgust Nellie cancelled her Hobart concert and embarked for New Zealand.

For Nellie the tour had begun to turn sour in November when a drought relief scheme she had devised with the best of intentions had to be abandoned. Nellie had told the press that she was keen to help her countrymen in distress and had set up a fund, to which she had contributed a large sum. She had also, she said, contacted many of her wealthy friends in Europe seeking donations from them. The federal government objected to a private individual setting up a fund while the government struggled to find subscribers to its own fund. Melba's actions were fiercely debated in parliament and Nellie capitulated, closing her fund and transferring her own donation to the government fund.

In yet a further unpleasant incident a few weeks later, Nellie was sued by one of the Tait brothers, John, who claimed that he had been employed to manage all her appearances in Australia, not merely those in Adelaide. Tait claimed 200 pounds in wasted expenses. Again Nellie capitulated and through her legal representatives agreed to settle out of court for 125 pounds, plus Tait's legal expenses.

The incidents in Tasmania were the last straw for Nellie and also the impetus for Australia's most notorious and unscrupulous newspaper publisher to launch a bitter attack on her character in his Melbourne scandal sheet, *Truth*. In 'An open letter to Madame Melba', John Norton accused her of drunkenness, loose morals, treating her colleagues and her companions badly and being an avaricious and miserly individual who charged Australian audiences exorbitant ticket prices. He ended his letter by challenging Nellie to refute his claims in court.[10]

None of it was true, but so blatantly and confidently were Norton's assertions made that an element in the Australian community believed him and the accusation that she 'caressed the cup' and 'drowned her songs' (his words) in strong drink clung to Nellie for the rest of her days.[11] Nellie was wise enough to ignore Norton's challenge, realising that there would be enough detractors in Australia to bear witness to her sampling wine in her father's vineyards, her occasional outburst of temper when frustrated, her earning power, her affair with Philippe and her recent divorce.[12] Stoic silence was the best way, she reluctantly concluded, to ensure that Norton's campaign did not continue to haunt Nellie outside Australia.

As if fate was conspiring against her, Nellie's concerts in New Zealand were not patronised as well as those in Australia and the warmth she had enjoyed when singing to Australians was missing.

By way of compensation, she was joined in New Zealand by John Lemmoné, whose companionship and support would become increasingly important to Nellie in the years that followed. The New Zealand press was also divided over whether she deserved the title 'World's Greatest Singer', the description that featured in local press advertisements. Nellie was also upset when the New Zealand Government demanded she pay income tax on her New Zealand earnings, which she had not had to do in Australia, Europe or America.

Nellie returned to Sydney and gave one farewell concert before embarking for England. The tour had been a success financially and personally as far as Nellie's reunion with her family was concerned, but the experience also left a bitter taste in her mouth and she had no desire to return to her homeland in the near future.

When Nellie had conquered Covent Garden in 1889 she had been the young challenger to the established soprano stars – Patti, Albani, Nilsson and Sembrich. When she returned to Covent Garden after her Australian tour, she found the tables turned. At 42 Nellie now represented the 'old guard' and a new coterie of younger rivals had arrived on the scene to challenge her.

Having been told by Nellie that she might not be available for the 1903 Covent Garden season because of her trip to her homeland, André Messager had engaged two new sopranos and promoted a couple more to sing the parts Nellie would have sung. The recent arrivals were Erika Wedekind, principal coloratura soprano of the Dresden Opera, and a 19-year-old Spaniard named Maria Barrientos, with a brittle voice but a phenomenal technique. Wedekind was cast as Lucia and Rosina, while Barrientos also sang Rosina. Suzanne Adams and the young Mary Garden, who had joined the company in 1902, were scheduled to share the roles of Gilda and Juliette.

Nellie was exhausted and dispirited after the Australasian tour but when, as the press put it, Gladys de Grey 'persuaded' her to sing in the 1903 season, some rapid rearrangements had to be made. Nellie secured exclusive rights to Mimi in *La Bohème* for the season and conceded Lucia and Rosina to Wedekind and Barrientos, but Adams and Garden had to step aside to allow Nellie to sing some performances of *Rigoletto* and *Roméo et Juliette*. Messager was probably relieved to have Nellie back, for as admirable as all the 'substitutes' were, none offered Nellie's vocal brilliance or enjoyed the patronage of the aristocracy and the wealthy he needed to fill the expensive seats in his theatre.

Caruso did not sing at Covent Garden this season, so Bonci (without his elevated shoes) partnered her in *La Bohème*, with the first of two incidents that did not reflect well on Nellie occurring during the first performance of that opera. At more than half of the 'Bohèmes' Nellie had sung at Covent Garden since 1899, the second soprano role, Musetta, had been taken by a vivacious young Austrian named Fritzi Scheff. Nellie had been content to share the stage with Scheff because she was no real competition, but Scheff's vocal shortcomings finally got the better of Nellie during that performance. When Scheff launched into her showpiece aria (Musetta's 'Waltz Song') during the Café Momus scene she was not in good voice. Nellie, seated with the other 'bohemians' on stage, could not resist the temptation to highlight Scheff's deficiencies.

At the ending of her aria Scheff was experiencing difficulty sustaining a top 'B' and, as she struggled with the note, another voice, pure and steady sang it with her. It was Nellie. Those in the audience who were not familiar with the score probably thought that was how the music was meant to be sung, but aficionados gasped and Scheff was seized with a fit of fury that almost derailed the rest of the act. Scheff glared at Nellie throughout the third act and whatever transpired in the next interval is not recorded but, according to Herman Bemberg, Scheff had tried to scratch Nellie's face. An announcement was made that Miss Scheff had been taken ill, meaning that the fourth and last act of the opera could not be performed. Madame Melba, the announcer continued, had consented to favour the audience with the Mad Scene from *Lucia di Lammermoor* as compensation.

The other incident involved a baritone relatively unknown in Britain who had been invited to sing Figaro, Enrico in *Lucia di Lammermoor* and the title role in *Rigoletto*. At the first rehearsal of *Rigoletto* with Nellie as Gilda, he unleashed what would later be acknowledged as the richest and most voluminous baritone voice of the period. Titta Ruffo was not a subtle singer but so astounding was the sound he made that Nellie realised he would be the focus of the audience's attention at the forthcoming performance – rather than her. Messager was summoned and Nellie announced, 'Signor Ruffo is too young to play my father. He will have to be replaced', the implication being that if Ruffo sang, Nellie would not. Messager complied. Ruffo was replaced by the more modest-voiced Antonio Scotti and Nellie was acclaimed as the star of the performance.

Ruffo always claimed that he had his revenge on Nellie when, years later, she volunteered to sing Gilda to his Rigoletto in Italy and he responded with: 'Melba? She's too *old* to play my daughter.' In fact the pair did sing together in those roles in Philadelphia many years later.[13]

The first of these incidents might be justified as rescuing the performance but jealousy is the only explanation for the second. Both are indicative of the power Nellie could now wield at Covent Garden and, perhaps, of Nellie's realisation that as she aged she needed to fight as well as sing to maintain her supremacy. Fortunately, word of these incidents did not reach Australia, or John Norton might have penned a sequel to his 'Letter to Madame Melba'.

While in London during this season Nellie also sang in the concert with the Queen's Hall Orchestra – mentioned by Henry Wood in his autobiography – performing an aria that had not previously been in her repertoire: 'Zeffiretti lusinghieri' from Mozart's *Idomeneo*. She also sang in the second act of *Roméo et*

Juliette at a gala at Covent Garden to mark the visit of the French President, following which she departed for the United States, where she undertook a 32-concert tour aided by the baritone Charles Gilibert, who had sung Schaunard at most of her Covent Garden 'Bohèmes', along with a tenor from the old Ellis company, Ellison van Hoose, and Ada Sassoli and the pianist Llewella Davies. A week before Christmas, Nellie was soloist in a concert with the Philadelphia Orchestra in Carnegie Hall, New York. Richard Aldrich, who had succeeded W.J. Henderson as critic of the *New York Times*, was not impressed. He wrote:

> Madame Melba seemed to show that neither her voice nor her mood was favourable. The purity of her voice was at times affected by an unpleasant quality that detracted from its charm and smoothness and she sang with carelessness and imperfect intonation.[14]

Aldrich was perceptive in attributing one of Nellie's few moments of failure to her mood. The rollercoaster ride of her Australian tour and the recent contretemps at Covent Garden had left Nellie feeling insecure and slightly despondent, becoming further disheartened when she received no reply from her son George after finally summoning the courage to write to him at Klamath Falls in Oregon.

After a bleak Christmas spent at sea, where many of Nellie possessions (including scores annotated by their composers and some of her costumes) were damaged irreparably when the ship's hold was flooded, Nellie travelled to the south of France, the part of the world most likely to lift her mood, to prepare for another season at L'Opéra de Monte Carlo. Here she was reunited with now-valued colleagues: Caruso, Alvarez, Renaud and Blanche and the Léon Jehin. Also in the company were two new, potentially rival, sopranos. American Geraldine Farrar from the Berlin Opera and the Italian Lina Cavalieri were no match for Nellie in voice or musicianship but both attracted instant attention and approval for their youth and their striking physical beauty.[15] Nellie had to share

Mimi in *La Bohème* with Farrar and Gilda in *Rigoletto* with Cavalieri, but the title role in a new opera, which was the main feature of the season, was Nellie's exclusively.

Camille Saint-Saëns had been a major figure in French musical life for almost half a century: his opera *Samson et Dalila* featured in the repertoire of all major opera companies; his five piano concertos were played by the leading pianists of the day, while the most tuneful extracts of his charming *Carnival of the Animals* were staple fare in drawing rooms worldwide. When Raoul Gunsbourg commissioned Saint-Saëns to write a new opera for Monte Carlo, the composer chose the classical love story of Paris and Helen as his subject and Nellie as the creator of the female lead.

Hélène, as the opera was called, was a one-hour long, single-act work. Reflecting the influence Wagner had exerted on French music in general and Saint-Saëns in particular, it was replete with musical motifs and lacked the showpiece arias Nellie was accustomed to exploiting in other works in her repertoire. It also lacked dramatic action but the music had charm and moments of great power, and the opportunity to create a role in the world premiere of an opera by Saint-Saëns (even one without showpiece arias) appealed to Nellie.

Nellie and Saint-Saëns had met in Paris many times over the years and their friendship blossomed when the composer arrived in Monte Carlo to supervise the rehearsals for the new opera. Saint-Saëns escorted Nellie around town and her company seems to have invigorated the composer. He waxed ecstatic about his new star and she described him as 'the most lively old man she had ever met'.

The premiere of *Hélène* had to be postponed for a couple of days when Nellie came down with a cold, but it was presented for the first time on 18 February 1904 in a double bill with Massenet's *La Navarraise*; Alvarez sang Paris and Léon Jehan conducted. An ultra-fashionable audience, led by Prince Albert, acclaimed the opera and the cast. *Le Figaro* sent the composer Gabriel Fauré to Monaco to review the premiere. The elderly Fauré seems to have been as enraptured by Nellie as his colleague Saint-Säens. He wrote:

> One could not say enough in praise of what Madame Melba offered last night: a noble, pained and passionate *Hélène*, the magnificent and ardent impulse of her cry 'I think I love!' and the delightful tones and exquisite tenderness with which she interpreted the whole last part of the work. Madame Melba remains, more than ever, a very great artist.[16]

The prince hosted a dinner to celebrate Saint-Säens's success, at which Nellie sang Hélène's 'monologue' – the closest thing to an aria in the work – accompanied at the piano by the composer. Following her triumph in Monte Carlo she departed for London.[17]

In her next season at Covent Garden Nellie faced much stiffer competition from Selma Kurz, the leading lyric-coloratura soprano from Vienna. Kurz was an established star on the Continent and before making her Covent Garden debut that year she had spent some time being coached by Marchesi. Covent Garden had offered Kurz the parts of Gilda, Oscar in *Un Ballo in Maschera* (the role Nellie had refused to sing in 1888) and Elisabeth in *Tannhäuser* (opposite Louis Arens). Kurz was an experienced and highly accomplished singer whose voice matched Nellie's in sheer beauty of sound. She enjoyed immediate success in her debut at Covent Garden and Nellie was undoubtedly less than pleased. Kurz came, she sang, she triumphed and then she departed. She returned occasionally in future years, sometimes sharing roles with Nellie, but believed that Nellie's influence prevented her establishing herself in the British capital in the way she had in the Austrian capital.

Caruso was back at Covent Garden that year and, where in the past 'Melba Nights' had been a feature, 'Melba–Caruso Nights' were now popular, occasions when the cream of society filled the boxes – and the city's large Italian community filled the 'gods'. Nellie and Caruso sang in *Rigoletto*, *La Traviata* and *La Bohème*. There was a new Musetta in *La Bohème*, following Scheff's departure for musical comedy and vaudeville. The role was filled by Elizabeth Parkina, a young American protégée of Nellie's and the first of many young singers who would be burdened with the soubriquet 'The Little Melba'. Nellie had recommended Parkina's engagement and she proved worthy of her mentor's support until she suffered a nervous breakdown a couple of years later, spending the remainder of her life in an institution.

From this time onwards, Melba–Caruso nights were also occasionally enlivened by Caruso's propensity for playing practical jokes and even the great Melba was not exempt from his childish tricks. As well as the squeaky toy pressed to her ear mentioned earlier, he also smuggled a large and brightly coloured chamber pot onto the stage in the last act of *La Bohème*, uncovering it so the audience could see it as Nellie collapsed onto her deathbed. His most outrageous prank, however, was to heat up a sausage on a spirit stove in his dressing room and press it into Nellie's hand when he sang 'Che gelida manina' (Your tiny hand is frozen') to Mimi. Nellie forgave the mischievous tenor because of his magnificent voice and its outstanding complementarity with her own, but she almost certainly would have been critical privately of Caruso's antics. She could hardly, however, criticise his sense of humour, which was no more capricious than her own.

On 20 June, Saint-Säens's *Hélène* was presented at Covent Garden with Nellie and the young French tenor Charles Dalmores, but the London critics did not warm to the work or the performers as had their colleagues in Monaco. Reviewers complained that the opera lacked originality and that the role of Hélène did not suit Nellie. It is possible that Nellie was beginning to share their opinions, for she never sang the role again after a second performance in London.[18]

Nellie's performances at Covent Garden were, as they had been in previous seasons, interspersed with concert performances. On 9 June Nellie, Caruso and Gilibert entertained guests at a dinner given by the king and queen at Buckingham Palace for Archduke Frederick of Austria. At the conclusion of the concert the king awarded Nellie the Order of Science, Art and Music and Queen Alexandra pinned the medal on Nellie's chest. Although, at the time, she probably didn't think of it in that way, an even more significant event occurred that year: Nellie made her first commercial recordings.

Chapter 14

The voice preserved

In 1877, the year 16-year-old Nellie played the organ in the Melbourne Town Hall for the Indian famine relief concert, Thomas Edison patented his first voice-recording machine. Edison then set the invention aside and devoted his time to more profitable projects, including the electric light bulb. Its original inventor considered his 'phonograph' (as he called it) to be little more than a novelty, whose only practical application might be as a dictating machine but, as the years passed, others saw its potential for entertainment.

The invention of a flat disc onto which sounds could be recorded (a matrix) and which could be repeatedly duplicated onto shellac (pressings) advanced that concept, but it was not until the beginning of the twentieth century that the sale of discs and what were then called 'gramophones' reached commercial scale. Leading this development was the American Fred Gaisberg, who established the Gramophone and Typewriter Company in London and employed Landon Ronald as his musical adviser. Selling typewriters was part of Gaisberg's business for a few years but his passion was the gramophone. On trips to the Continent Gaisberg recorded the young bass Feodor Chaliapin (then unknown outside his native Russia), Francesco Tamagno, Caruso and the last of the castrati, Alessandro Moreschi, but his sights were set on recording Nellie. Gaisberg realised that having the name 'Melba' in his catalogue would be akin to holding a royal warrant and would escalate his sales to previously unimagined levels.

Through a young and handsome employee of the company named

Sydney Dixon, Gaisberg contacted Nellie while she was still in Monte Carlo with a request that upon her return to London she make some test recordings to see how her voice recorded. Like most singers, Nellie was suspicious of the new medium, fearing that, if recordings did not do justice to her voice, their distribution might harm her career. On the other hand, as the daughter of a canny Scot and a shrewd businesswomen herself, Nellie could also imagine how a successful recording career might add another stream to her income.

Gaisberg invited Nellie to visit his recording studio and business premises in City Road to make the tests. Nellie countered with instructions that Gaisberg or Dixon and their technicians visit her at Great Cumberland Place on a certain date and at a certain time, where their recording equipment could be assembled in her drawing room. Dixon dutifully arrived at the appointed time and a series of tests were made, probably with Landon Ronald accompanying Nellie on her Steinway piano. Exactly what Nellie sang into the recording horn that afternoon has not been identified, but we may assume it was more than a few notes and the odd trill. Although Gaisberg was happy with the results, when pressings from the matrices were played to Nellie her reaction was complete indifference.

Gaisberg awaited a further response from Nellie, but she maintained a strategic silence for many weeks. Finally, Gaisberg summoned the courage to contact her again, suggesting more tests might be made if Nellie was not satisfied with the first set. Nellie agreed and another date for a visit to Great Cumberland Place was arranged. For the second session, Nellie suggested that she might record 'a few arias and songs' and that Gaisberg would give her the recordings so that she could send them to her 'dear daddy' in Australia. She would also require, she explained, Gaisberg to bring the small orchestra he used for recordings and summon the distinguished French flutist Phillipe Gaubert over from Paris to play when required. By this stage in the negotiations, Gaisberg was prepared to do just about anything to please Nellie, so he agreed to all her requests, hoping that if she was satisfied with the second set of recordings he would be able to persuade her to allow him to issue them commercially.

Over one (or possibly two days) in March, it is believed that Nellie recorded 30 items, of which 16 can be identified, some of the others likely being duplicates of identified titles.[1] For at least three items, the dozen or so players Gaisberg had supplied clustered around Nellie to enable the sound of their instruments to be captured, along with her voice. Landon Ronald accompanied Nellie at the piano for the remainder and Philippe Gaubert earned his fee and his fully paid trip from Paris by joining Nellie in the Mad Scene from *Lucia di Lammermoor* and Handel's 'Sweet bird that shunst the noise of folly'.[2]

Pressings were made from the matrices and delivered to Nellie and she, no doubt, expressed her gratitude for being able to send them to her father. At this point Gaisberg proposed she might share the bounty with the general public and allow him to release whichever of the titles she approved commercially. Gaisberg offered a royalty payment on every copy sold and Nellie agreed – but for double the royalty percentage and with three more stipulations. Firstly, the recordings were to retail for one guinea (a shilling more than any others); they were to carry an exclusive mauve label with a facsimile of Nellie's signature; and they were to be presented in a superior-quality double envelope with Nellie's portrait on it. Gaisberg eventually agreed to each condition and a contract was signed on 11 May.

At what point in the process that had begun months earlier, Gaisberg realised he had been systematically outmanoeuvred by Nellie is unknown. Perhaps he never realised it, or if he did he was satisfied, knowing how much might be earned from 'Melba' records. Over the following weeks Nellie approved the release of 15 of the recordings, with the matrices of the rest given to her to do with as she wished.

While the recordings were being manufactured, Gaisberg embarked on a major publicity campaign. On 1 July the discs finally went on sale across the United Kingdom and in Ireland, France, Holland, Belgium, Germany, Austria, Russia, Italy, Spain, Portugal, South Africa and Australia. Nellie did her part in promoting the records by granting an interview to a journalist from *The Sunday Times*. The journalist reported:

> Madame Melba is most pleased with the remarkable fidelity with which the tone, the modulation, the range and expression and the vibration of her marvellously resonant voice have been picked up and reproduced by the gramophone. 'Would you like to hear me sing?' she asked, and led me to the music room. She removed a bowl of roses from a cabinet, lifted the lid and revealed a gramophone. Another moment and the room was filled with melody. It was 'Ah, fors'è lui' from Verdi's *La Traviata* and the record was remarkable.

When the disc had finished playing, the journalist dutifully asked if it and other recordings could be bought. Nellie replied that because she had received so many letters of enquiry from around the world begging for the release of the recordings she had made solely for her father in Australia, she had consented to their release.[3]

Within a week, the first issue of Nellie's recordings had sold out and more pressings were hastily made. The critics and the public (and, apparently Queen Alexandra) were enraptured by them, and listening to them today it is clear why they elicited such a response. While we might question the style of singing compared with what is practised today, there is little to criticise and much to admire about the voice. If perhaps Nellie's coloratura wasn't quite as dazzling as it had been when her career began, the voice is still in pristine condition and a joy to listen to.

It is the recordings of arias from *Lucia di Lammermoor*, *La Traviata*, *Rigoletto* and *Hamlet* that are the most historically important. The three minutes of the 'Lucia' Mad Scene offer little more than the cadenza Marchesi wrote for Nellie in 1887, but the long crescendo trill at the end whets our appetite for more.

The 'Traviata' scena was recorded on two matrices and there was no room on the published discs to include the 'Follia, follia' section, which joins the two halves, but in long-playing disc and compact disc reissues that was restored. The steadiness of Nellie's voice throughout this scena is remarkable and so is her projection of the words and the notes. The scale work and the trills are immaculate. If any criticism can be made, it is that the rollercoaster of emotions Violetta is experiencing when she sings this scena is only vaguely suggested. A retake (this time with orchestra) of the second part of the scena demonstrates perfectly the incredible energy Nellie brought to her singing.

Writers in recent years have accused Nellie of approaching the opening of 'Caro nome' from *Rigoletto* with too much force and also that the wistfulness that Gilda should display as she recalls her first love is lacking, but in my opinion if any criticism is to be made, it is that Nellie sounds a little too mature for the youthful Gilda. Nellie caresses the phrases with great tenderness.

The *Hamlet* Mad Scene is a worthy souvenir of one of Nellie's greatest roles. She makes no attempt to sound 'deranged'; instead, she sings the music with the utmost simplicity and follows the score to the letter. The effect is both beautiful and touching. We may not hear 'insanity' but what Nellie offers is even greater – we hear clearly the withdrawal of sanity.

As well as these, there are recordings of the Countess's aria 'Porgi amor' from Mozart's *Le Nozze di Figaro* and Mimi's 'Farewell' from *La Bohème*. Nellie spins out the long lines of the Mozart aria with perfect poise and amazing breath control. The 'Bohème' aria was not released in the original issue because of excessive surface noise on the matrix, but when it was finally released, it gave listeners their first souvenir of the most famous 'Mimi' of her generation.

Nellie made two recordings of Handel's 'Sweet bird' during

these sessions, having made a mistake in the first. On the original matrix she can be heard stopping and saying: 'No, no ... oh, bother, we'll have to do it again!' Melba started much later in the piece on her second attempt and it was that version that was issued. As an example of virtuosic singing technique the recording is startling.

Among the songs by Tosti, Arditi, Bemberg, d'Hardelot and Hahn are some real gems. Arditi's 'Se Saran Rose' gives Nellie the opportunity to display her full musical armoury (including a ringing laugh) as it trips along with infectious élan and Tosti's 'Goodbye' is sung with genuinely moving inflections.[4]

So successful were these recordings that Nellie willingly made another series later in the year. On this occasion she ventured into the East End and to the Gramophone and Typewriter Company's studio. The throng of journalists waiting outside the building to report on her arrival were allowed to observe her making the recordings – from a distance. Ten more recordings were made, seven of which were issued. They included three more songs by Bemberg, with the composer at the piano, but the *pièce de résistance* was a recording of the Bach-Gounod 'Ave Maria', with the great Czech violinist Jan Kubelik playing the obbligato. Among the operatic items was Juliette's 'Waltz Song' from *Roméo et Juliette*.

Attempts were made at this time to encourage Jean de Reszke to emerge temporarily from retirement and record a duet with Nellie – probably the balcony scene from *Roméo et Juliette*. The now 54-year-old tenor initially agreed but then kept postponing until Gaisberg finally gave up. No one would have been more disappointed with that outcome than Nellie herself. She would not, however, have been disappointed with her new career as a recording artist. Nellie would continue to make recordings for another 22 years and in that time her royalty payments would reach a staggering total of 400,000 pounds.

Between her first and second recording sessions Nellie visited Italy, where she studied the title role in Puccini's *Tosca* with the composer, the experience being both fascinating and frustrating as Nellie tried to negotiate the music of a role she adored, but which was too heavy for her voice. She also spent a couple of weeks in Paris, installing herself in her favourite suite at the Paris Ritz and hiring an automobile with a liveried chauffeur to drive her around. On the afternoon of her second day in Paris, Nellie was involved in a tragedy. She and two of her cousins, who were visiting from New Zealand, were being driven along Boulevard Pereire, a few blocks from Rue Jouffroy, when an old man stepped out in front of the vehicle. He was struck and killed instantly. Nellie was deeply shocked. She returned to the Ritz and took to her bed. The reports of the accident in the press next morning identified the victim as 84-year-old Monsieur Benoit, by coincidence the same name as the Bohemian's aged landlord in *La Bohème*. Nellie and her friends were not accused of any part in causing the accident and by the time it came to court she had left Paris.[5]

After her second recording session in London, Nellie embarked for New York to undertake another concert tour. Heinrich Conried, who had taken over the management of the Metropolitan Opera from Maurice Grau, had tried to engage Nellie for the 1904–05 season at the Met but his offer had been less than Nellie could earn doing concerts during the same period, so she had declined.[6] As a favour to the new manager, however, Nellie agreed to sing four performances as a guest at the Met. The first was on 16 December and the opera was *La Bohème*. Caruso and Scotti sang Rodolfo and Marcello and the Italian Arcangelo Rossi sang Benoit.

Soon after Nellie arrived in New York, a letter was delivered to her at the Manhattan Hotel. It was from George. It's easy to understand Nellie's intense excitement when she recognised the handwriting on the envelope, and after reading the loving words the letter contained she would have been overcome with joy and relief. All the trials and tribulations of the previous couple of years must have seemed of no consequence in those euphoric moments when

Nellie realised her son had asserted his rights on reaching majority, that his love for his mother remained, and that his father seemed reconciled to the changes in their domestic arrangements George was then proposing.

In the letter, George addresses Nellie as 'My darling mother' and says that he has thought of her every day since they were separated. He proposes that in the future he should spend half of each year with his mother and the other half with his father. He also affirms that he will never allow himself to be parted permanently from Nellie again. In a second letter dated four days later, he adds that his father has agreed to drive him to the nearest railhead so that he can catch a train from Oregon to New York and that Nellie should try to be happy until he arrives.[7]

Looking at the situation (without undue cynicism), it would be reasonable to conclude that George Armstrong had worked out, as the old saying goes, 'which side his bread was buttered'. Returning to a life of luxury and privilege (even for half of each year) must have held enormous appeal for the now 21-year-old. The advantages and the prospects for his future were infinitely greater in his mother's company than in his father's. No one would deny the sincerity of George's statements about his love for his mother, but for him the arrangement had practical as well as emotional benefits. None of this would have concerned Nellie when George (now a tall, wiry and weather-beaten young man) arrived and they were reunited at the Manhattan Hotel.

While making extravagant plans for their new life together, Nellie came down with bronchitis and some of her concerts and the remaining performances at the Met had to be cancelled. Bronchitis developed into pneumonia and for the first time in her life Nellie was suffering a potentially fatal illness, but with her son so recently restored to her, she was not going to succumb to any threat. Nellie slowly improved and mother and son spent their first Christmas together in 11 years.

After an (on this occasion) uneventful Atlantic crossing, Nellie returned to London with George at her side and to the comfort of Great Cumberland Place. She was keen to introduce him into London society but first she needed to pace herself carefully while her lungs recovered and her energy returned. When Nellie did, proudly, show off her son to her friends in London, few of them remembered him and those who did only had vague recollections of a small and rather spoiled child kept in the background by a nurse. Thrown back into a milieu to which he was no longer accustomed, George was desperately shy, all of those years in the backblocks of America having made him socially inept. He was also suffering from 'famous-parent syndrome', an affliction that plagues the lives of most sons and daughters of celebrities and he would never entirely recover from that. No matter what he achieved for himself in the future, to the world he would always be 'Melba's son'.

Nellie returned to Covent Garden in May, still the company's pre-eminent soprano but facing stiff competition from Kurz and the Czech soprano Emmy Destinn, who immediately endeared herself to London audiences with her vibrant singing in the British premiere of *Madama Butterfly*. There was also competition from outside Covent Garden. Performing concurrently with Covent Garden at the Waldorf Theatre in the Strand was a rival company featuring Calvé and two of Nellie's former colleagues: Bonci and de Lucia.

Still troubled by the aftermath of her illness. Nellie was forced to cancel her first performance at Covent Garden and did not appear until 22 May, when she joined Parkina, Caruso and Scotti for the first of four sold-out performances of *La Bohème*. She also sang in *La Traviata* with Caruso and in *Faust* with Dalmores. It was announced in the press that she would also sing Tosca during the season, but her common sense prevailed and that performance never took place.[8] Nellie, Parkina, Caruso and Scotti contributed the third act of *La Bohème* to a gala requested by Edward VII for his fellow monarch Alfonso XIII of Spain. That was preceded by act two of

MELBA'S PERSONAL LIFE

Melba's father, David Mitchell.
(Nellie Melba Museum)

Melba's mother, Isabella Mitchell.
(Nellie Melba Museum)

Nellie Mitchell with her younger sisters
Belle and Annie. (Nellie Melba Museum)

Nellie Mitchell (standing) and Janet
Dougal, a friend from Presbyterian
Ladies College, Melbourne. (Johnstone
& O'Shanessy & Co., Melbourne)

Mary Ellen Christian, Melba's first singing teacher.

Pietro Cecchi, Melba's principal singing teacher in Melbourne.

Nellie Mitchell in the outfit she wore at her marriage to Charles Armstrong, Brisbane, 1892.
(Nellie Melba Museum)

Charles Armstrong (in white jacket) with his brothers George and Montague, Littlehampton, England. (White, Littlehampton – Nellie Melba Museum)

Nellie with her son George Armstrong, Brussels, c. 1887. (Nellie Melba Museum)

Melba and Mathilde Marchesi, her singing teacher in Paris. (Reutlinger)

Melba arriving in Melbourne, 19 September 1902, for her first 'homecoming' concert tour of Australia. (*Herald-Sun*)

Prince Louis Philippe Robert, Duc d'Orléans, the great love of Melba's life. (Walery, London)

Melba in Melbourne during her first 'homecoming' concert tour of Australia. (Talma)

Melba and her son, George Armstrong. (Shadwell Clerke)

Melba's favourite photo-portrait of herself. (Shadwell Clerke)

Melba with her daughter-in-law, Evie Armstrong and her granddaughter Pamela.
(Nellie Melba Museum)

Portrait of Melba, 1908.
(Walter Barnett – Nellie Melba Museum)

Portrait of Melba, 1916.
(Nellie Melba Museum)

Melba in Hollywood, 18 February 1916. L. to R.: Lady Susan FitzClarence, Captain Hastings, Stella Power, Frank St Ledger, Melba and Douglas Fairbanks (on the filing cabinet).

'Doonside', the Mitchell home in Richmond, Victoria, where Melba was born.

The manager's house at the Marian sugar mill where Melba spent the first years of her marriage and where her son George was born.
(*Queensland Agricultural Journal*)

Melba's bedroom in one of her Paris apartments. Note the two telephones.

Melba in the garden at Coombe Cottage.
(Nellie Melba Museum)

Melba in the Gramophone Company's London recording studios, date unrecorded, possibly May 1913. (Culver Pictures)

Melba making the first international music broadcast from the Marconi radio studios, Chelmsford, 15 June 1920. (*Daily Mail*)

Melba with tenor Browning Mummery (left) and baritone John Brownlee at the time of her Covent Garden Farewell, London, June 1926.

Melba singing at the opening of Parliament House, Canberra, 9 May 1927.

Melba at the time of her return to Australia, 1927.

Melba with John Brownlee's wife, Donna, and their daughter Isabelle at the child's christening, Paris, 20 September, 1930. The last photograph taken of Melba.

Leading vehicles in Melba's funeral procession, Collins Street, Melbourne, 26 February 1931. (*Herald & Weekly Times*)

MELBA'S OPERATIC ROLES

Melba as Ophélie in Thomas's opera *Hamlet*, Brussels, 1888. (Dupont & Co.)

Melba in the title role of Delibes' opera *Lakmé*, Brussels, 1888. (Dupont & Co.)

Melba in the title role of Donizetti's opera *Lucia di Lammermoor*, Paris, 1889. (Felix Nadar)

Melba as Marguerite in Gounod's opera *Faust*, New York, 1894. (Aimé Dupont)

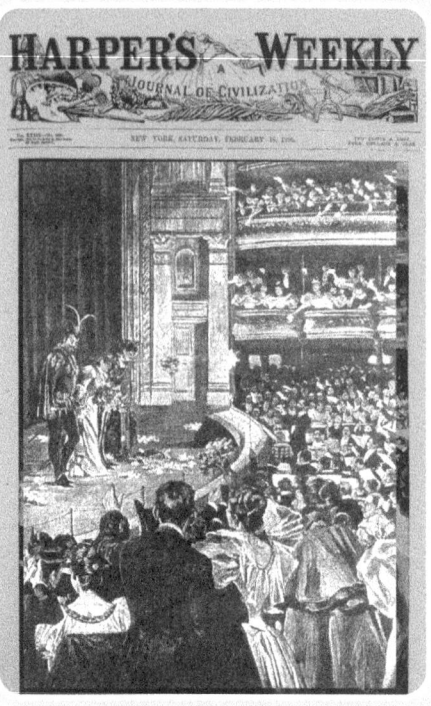

Edouard de Reszke, Melba and Jean de Reszke taking their bows after a performance of Gounod's opera *Faust* at the Metropolitan Opera House, New York, 7 January 1895. (*Harper's Weekly*)

Melba as Juliette in Gounod's opera *Roméo et Juliette*, London, 1889.

Melba in the title role of Verdi's opera *Aida*, c. 1893. (Dupont & Co.)

Melba as Nedda in Leoncavallo's opera *Pagliacci*, London, 1893.

Melba as Elisabeth in Wagner's *Tannhäuser*, New York, 1894. (Davis & Sandford)

Melba in the title role of Massenet's opera *Manon*, New York, 1896.

Melba as Violetta in Verdi's opera *La Traviata*, London, 1905. (Shadwell Clerke)

Melba as Rosina in Rossini's opera *The Barber of Seville*. (Reutlinger, Paris)

Melba in the title role of Saint-Saëns' opera *Hélène*, Monte Carlo, 1904. (Numa Blanc Fils)

Melba as Mimi in Puccini's opera *La Bohème*, 1911.

The Café Momus scene from Puccini's opera *La Bohème*, Melbourne, 1924. L. to R.: Gustave Huberdeau as Colline, Melba as Mimi, Dino Borgioli as Rodolfo and Alfred Maguenet as Marcello.

Roméo et Juliette with Kurz and Dalmores and undoubtedly Nellie sat impatiently in her dressing room as her rival sang one of Nellie's signature roles.[9]

When Mathilde Bauermeister announced that she would be retiring at the end of the season, Nellie organised a farewell benefit matinee for her and persuaded Edward VII, Queen Alexandra and the Prince and Princess of Wales to attend. Significantly, Nellie chose to sing Juliette in the first two acts of *Roméo et Juliette* with Bauermeister as the nurse. Their partnership stretched back to 1888 when Nellie had made her debut at Covent Garden and Bauermeister had sung Alisa to Nellie's Lucia. The 'Bohème' cast offered their services for an act from that opera and at the end of the performance Bauermeister insisted Nellie share her curtain calls. Not all of Nellie's colleagues held Nellie in such high regard as Bauermeister, but the diminutive German mezzo-soprano claimed that Nellie had not only the voice of an angel but the heart of one as well.

A week after the Covent Garden season ended and as Nellie was about to embark on a tour of the provinces, *Le Ménestrel* in Paris reported that there were rumours abroad that she was going to marry Lord Richard Neville.[10] Other newspapers around the world picked up the story. Nellie emphatically denied it, but not until a fortnight later. That story bore the distinct whiff of a publicity stunt and by this stage in her career Nellie was a master of publicity and also adept at covering her tracks and professing aggrieved innocence.

After completing her provincial tour, Nellie made another set of recordings for the Gramophone and Typewriter Company in City Road. Only one was an operatic aria: the 'Jewel Song' from *Faust*, which, surprisingly, had not featured in her earlier sessions. The rest were 'popular' titles, including three recorded with the Band of the Coldstream Guards and three with a small chorus of British singers. Nellie probably insisted on the brass band being placed a considerable distance from her and the recording horn, but somehow the engineers managed to get the balance right, with one of these songs, 'Come back to Erin' by 'Claribel' (Charlotte Barnard) an exquisite piece of singing.

The chorus included the Australian baritone Peter Dawson, a fine singer and perhaps the most prolific recording artist of his day. Nellie probably knew Dawson by reputation but their paths had not crossed before that recording session. When introduced to him, Nellie asked where Dawson came from. When the baritone replied that he was born in Adelaide, Nellie scoffed and said: 'Oh, *that* town of parsons, pubs and prostitutes!' Dawson was more amused than angry by Nellie's rude reference to his birthplace but when she elbowed him out of the way during the run-through of a piece, accompanied by the remark: 'Get out of the way ... you're just one of the bloody chorus!', any respect Dawson might have held for his countrywoman vanished – permanently. Nellie was clearly not in the kind of magnanimous mood she had been in when organising Bauermeister's benefit, but if tempers were frayed it doesn't show in the recordings, all 11 of which were deemed good enough for immediate issue.[11]

Nellie decided not to return to the United States in the autumn of 1905, reasoning that she needed to avoid 'over exposure' and that if Americans were denied her presence for a year or two their appetite for her would grow. She had also been made a generous offer to return to Covent Garden for the autumn season – her first since 1893 – which she accepted.

The managers Frank Rendle and Neil Forsyth had brought an Italian company to Covent Garden the previous autumn and it had enjoyed greater success than the English companies that usually occupied the opera house in that season each year. Rendle and Forsyth decided to repeat the venture in 1905 and assembled a fine collection of singers drawn from the Teatro San Carlo in Naples and La Scala, Milan. The company was strongest in its male singers, and none of the Italian sopranos challenged Nellie's right to the title 'prima donna'. Among the tenors were Emilio de Marchi (the first Cavaradossi in *Tosca*) and Giovanni Zenatello (the first Pinkerton in *Madama Butterfly*). Nellie would sing with both of these talented tenors, but Zenatello impressed her the most. He was, as audiences at La Scala had discovered, second only to Caruso among the younger Italian tenors. Among the baritones were three great 'names': Mario Sammarco, Riccardo Stracciari and the veteran Mattia Battistini, known in Italy as the 'Prince of Baritones'.

This was Nellie's twentieth season at Covent Garden and in seven weeks she sang nine performances, including the opening and closing nights of the season. When news reached London that the Italian province of Calabria had been struck by a series of devastating earthquakes, Nellie took it upon herself to organise a Sunday benefit concert at Covent Garden, which raised 1700 pounds for her colleagues' compatriots.

In the midst of the season a command arrived from Buckingham Palace for Nellie to sing at a concert in Windsor Castle for the Greek royal family, who were visiting London. Zenatello was also summoned, as was Mary Garden, by then an established singing actress. In her autobiography Garden describes how she, Nellie and Zenatello sang their pieces and how the king made a special point of complimenting her, much to Nellie's annoyance. Over dinner Nellie was heard to remark in a loud voice: 'What a dreadful concert this would have been if *I* had not come!' Into the stunned silence, Garden responded with: 'I love Melba's rudeness. It amuses me.' Despite this embarrassing exchange, Garden found herself unable to dislike Nellie. The beautiful Scottish–American soprano was herself a strong personality and in years to come she too would become famous for her verbal putdowns. On the train back to London, Nellie asked Garden to explain how she should act the part of Tosca, and by the time they parted company at Victoria Station they were hugging like sisters.

It would seem that Nellie had discovered that her best non-musical weapon in her struggle to maintain her supremacy was her tongue and her caustic remarks to Dawson and to Garden were typical of the sort of invective for which she would become famous, dispensing it indiscriminately, with the exception of royalty. As the years went by, Nellie's diatribes became more frequent and, while they would be offset by her generosity (where she believed generosity was deserved), the image of a formidable character with powerful connections was growing steadily. Events that took place early the following year also proved just what a tough personality Nellie had become.

While Nellie was focusing on her career in London, an operatic war was being plotted in New York. The plotter was Oscar Hammerstein, grandfather of the 'other' Oscar Hammerstein, who would write the lyrics for *Oklahoma*, *Carousel*, *South Pacific* and *The Sound of Music*. Oscar senior was a German Jew who had emigrated to the United States in the 1860s, made a fortune in the cigar trade and established a theatrical empire in New York. Over the years Hammerstein had promoted vaudeville, straight plays, musicals and occasionally opera, but his ultimate ambition was to build himself a palatial opera house and manage an international opera company in competition with the Met.

In the winter of 1906 Hammerstein began construction on his 'Manhattan Opera House' on Seventh Avenue between Thirty-fourth and Thirty-fifth streets and began to recruit singers.

Heinrich Conried and his shareholders at the Met were worried. In its 23-year history the Met had held a virtual monopoly on opera in New York. The Damrosch and Ellis companies and various groups under different managers at the old Academy of Music had provided brief competition, but Hammerstein's project was the first on a scale that threatened that monopoly. Unlike other competitors, Hammerstein also had capital, initiative, confidence and flair, his impressive figure, elegant clothes and large cigars marking him out as a man of importance in any crowd. Conried began taking pre-emptive steps, even before the first brick had been laid for the new opera house, informing all in the opera world that any singer who entered into negotiations with Hammerstein would be barred from the Met thenceforth. Conried also persuaded George Maxwell, the American agent for Puccini's publishers, Ricordi & Co., to grant the Met an exclusive licence to perform Puccini's operas in New York, thus preventing Hammerstein from producing *La Bohème*, *Tosca* and *Madama Butterfly*, which had become key money-spinners for every opera house worldwide. In anticipation of Hammerstein attempting to engage Nellie, Conried also cabled Nellie with the offer of an engagement for the 1906–07 Met season at what he thought was a generous fee: 2000 dollars per performance.

Undeterred, Hammerstein pressed on. He managed a coup by engaging the great Cleofonte Campanini, who conducted regularly in the major opera houses of Italy, as his musical director. He tried to poach Caruso from the Met, but failed. Alessandro Bonci was more amenable and he and Charles Dalmores were signed up as the new company's principal tenors. Hammerstein also engaged Edouard de Reszke as principal bass, although later, when the company assembled in New York, de Reszke's voice proved to be in such a poor state that Hammerstein tore up his contract. Various female singers were prepared to risk the Met's wrath and signed up, but Hammerstein wanted Nellie as his trump card.

In January 1906 Hammerstein began besieging Nellie with letters and telegrams. In the previous year Nellie had leased a new apartment in Paris – at 162 Boulevard Malesherbes (close, as usual, to Rue Jouffroy) – and it was here that Hammerstein turned up, uninvited, one evening as Nellie was entertaining guests. A little annoyed, Nellie agreed to give her caller 10 minutes and Hammerstein briefly outlined the progress he had made in setting up the company, explaining that without Nellie as his prima donna he would be forced to abandon his plans. Nellie asked him to return the next morning to talk further, but Hammerstein had to leave for Berlin the following day, so in what remained of those 10 minutes terms were discussed. Once again, Nellie set conditions, telling Hammerstein she would only consider singing for him if she could choose her own roles; if he paid her 3000 dollars per performance for ten performances; and picked up the bill for all her travel expenses – and that she would require a non-refundable advance payment of 20,000 dollars against the season not eventuating.

The figures must have shocked Hammerstein and he asked to be given time to consider it. He left, but returned moments later and agreed. The pair drafted and signed a simple written agreement at Nellie's desk and, according to Hammerstein, he returned early the next day with the equivalent of 20,000 dollars in French francs in cash. Nellie claimed Hammerstein scattered the notes at her feet, but Hammerstein gave a more believable version, saying he placed the notes on Nellie's desk and that she shuffled them into a drawer without counting them and turned the key.

Nellie had been impressed by Hammerstein's style and his persistence and she was not averse to, hypothetically, thumbing her nose at the Met. She considered that her relationship with the management of the Met had never been entirely satisfactory, with the power she exercised at Covent Garden never having been replicated in New York. At Covent Garden she could choose the roles she sang; at the Met they were dictated to her. At Covent Garden, while she could not always choose those with whom she sang, she could certainly choose those with whom she would *not* sing. A new company in New York might prove, Nellie reasoned, more fertile ground.[12]

To Hammerstein's relief, Nellie offered not only her voice to his new venture but also her knowledge and her influence. Several artists who had turned down offers of engagement from Hammerstein (Emma Calvé, Maurice Renaud and Elizabeth Parkina among them) changed their minds and signed up when news that Nellie would head the company became public.[13] Hammerstein had gained not only a prima donna but an ally in the opening salvo of an operatic war that would last for four years.

Chapter 15

Oscar and Goliath

Before departing for the United States and the inaugural season of Hammerstein's company, Nellie had nine months of hard work to complete in the United Kingdom and on the Continent. King Alfonso of Spain had kept his promise to Nellie and in January 1906 (a few weeks before her meeting with Hammerstein) she had toured the principal cities of Spain, giving sold-out concerts. Alfonso also invited Nellie to be a guest at the wedding of his sister, the Infanta Maria Therese, to her cousin, Prince Ferdinand of Bavaria, in Madrid.

At the end of the tour she had taken a holiday at Málaga on the southern coast of Spain, where she gave a concert for local charities in the Teatro Cervantes. On the night of the concert Nellie was delighted to find a carpet of flowers stretching from the roadway to the stage door, across which she delicately stepped. At the conclusion of the concert she was showered with bouquets and a flock of doves was released from the stage. She was equally delighted when a bullfight was organised to entertain her during her stay in Málaga, although she insisted there be no blood and no dead bulls to trouble her conscience.

Upon her return to England, Nellie settled into Great Cumberland Place and also leased a house in the Thames Valley to escape the summer heat. This time it was a 60-room mansion, euphemistically called 'Coombe Cottage', located on Kingston Hill. Years later Nellie would choose the same name for the retirement home she built for herself in Australia.

As she had done the year before, Nellie sang in both the 1906 summer and autumn seasons at Covent Garden. For the Grand Opera Syndicate's summer season, she sang her familiar roles, reunited with Caruso, who had recently survived the San Francisco earthquake. Most of Nellie's performances were conducted by Campanini, although she almost missed one of them when her chauffeur was unable to start her car for the drive to London. Showing the 'Aussie' initiative that never deserted her, Nellie hitched a ride in a tradesman's van to the nearest railway station.[1]

During this season Nellie was troubled again by bouts of bronchitis, which probably sapped her energy but, if the critics are to be believed, had little effect on her voice. The role in which she triumphed most conspicuously during this season was Violetta in *La Traviata*, partnered by Caruso and Battistini. After the first performance, *The Times* reviewer wrote a tribute that Nellie would have found gratifying:

> Madame Melba's Violetta always takes us by surprise every time we hear it. For it is surprising as well as refreshing to hear coloratura sung nowadays as she sings it. It all comes pouring out with amazing spontaneity and that splendid sense of enjoyment which makes one feel that here, at any rate, coloratura is not an artificial product, but the natural expression of the person who is singing – just as it was in the eighteenth century. Madame Melba is in fact the link that connects the twentieth century with the golden age of singing.[2]

The autumn season was again under Frank Rendle's management and featured artists from Naples and Milan. Nellie made her *entrée* as Gilda in *Rigoletto* with a now long-forgotten tenor named Giuseppe Krismer as the Duke and Sammarco as the jester. The critics found the 'new' tenor adequate in his part, but he did not and neither did Nellie. It was announced in the press the next day that Krismer had 'withdrawn' from the company. On the other occasions when Nellie sang, she was partnered either by Zenatello or another newcomer, Fernando Carpi, who fared better than Krismer.

One performance of *La Bohème* (with Nellie and Zenatello) was of historic interest as the first-ever 'outside broadcast'. The whole performance was transmitted over telephone lines to Windsor Castle, where it was enjoyed by the king and queen, using what was described as an 'electrophone', presumably some kind of device that amplified the incoming sound.

Towards the end of the autumn season it was announced that Verdi's *Otello* was to be performed with another forgettable tenor, Furio Franceschini, in the title role, Sammarco as Iago and Nellie as Desdemona. Nellie was, at last, going to sing a role to which she had longed to return since her first attempt in 1892. But, once again, that was not to be. It was announced in the press two days before the first performance that the opera had been withdrawn due to the 'unreadiness' of the principals. Which principals were unready was not revealed. It is unlikely to have been Sammarco, it may possibly have been Nellie, but was most likely Franceschini, who was tackling the arduous role of the Moor for the first time.

Nellie also undertook her usual round of concerts both in London and in the provinces. One concert, in Blackpool, threw that city's streets into gridlock and for another – in Stepney – Nellie, her colleagues and an assortment of friends motored down into the 'wilds' of the East End in a cavalcade of expensive motor cars. Nellie also organised a farewell benefit concert for the *opéra-bouffe* star Emily Soldene, who would certainly not have been on Isabella Mitchell's list of acceptable performers when Soldene introduced the can-can to Melbourne in 1877. In several of these concerts Nellie collaborated with other Australian artists whom she deemed worthy of her support.

Nellie's phenomenal success had inspired many younger Australian musicians to pursue careers beyond their homeland and during this season at least four appeared in London – one violinist and three singers. The violinist was Maud MacCarthy, the daughter of a prominent Sydney surgeon and amateur composer. Nellie engaged MacCarthy as a supporting artist for several concerts and also contributed 50 pounds to a fund to purchase a first-class instrument for the young violinist. Another was contralto Eva Mylott, from a small town on the south coast of New South Wales, whom Nellie had auditioned and to whom she offered encouragement.[3]

More prominent was the soprano Amy Castles, from a musical family of Bendigo. Castles had been supported by the Catholic community of Melbourne, keen to find a Catholic rival to the Presbyterian Nellie, and was being touted by them as 'The New Melba' even before she left Australia. When Castles had first arrived in Europe, Nellie had sent her to Marchesi, but when the young singer deserted the École Marchesi to continue her studies with another teacher Nellie in turn abandoned her. By 1906 this rift had been sufficiently repaired for Nellie to recommend Castles as her replacement when illness prevented her singing at a dinner organised by Gladys de Grey. Castles sang at the dinner and earned praise from the guests, including Queen Alexandra, but it was not long before Nellie's support of Castles was again withdrawn. She came to realise, long before others did, that Amy Castles simply did not have the talent to reach the top, and her career, marked by inconsistency, proved Nellie right.

Nellie expended most effort into promoting Irene Ainsley, born Ivy Ansley in Sydney of New Zealand parents. Nellie had heard the young contralto in Auckland in 1903 and had been almost as impressed by her voice as she had been by Ada Crossley's. Nellie had also sent Ainsley off to Marchesi in Paris, but this time the association had been productive.[4] Nellie organised a concert in Bechstein Hall to introduce Ainsley to London audiences.[5] Although Nellie did not sing at the concert, she did accompany Ainsley at the piano in several songs. Marchesi came over from Paris to hear her erstwhile student and Nellie persuaded the Prince and Princess of Wales to attend. The concert was a great success, with the Princess of Wales inviting Ainsley to join Nellie in entertaining guests at a royal dinner a fortnight later. Ainsley's career was launched in style and in years to come she would earn credit in opera, oratorio and concerts.[6]

Two years on from their reunion, Nellie and George's life together had slipped into routine, with mother and son spending as much time together as Nellie's career allowed, with the plan for George to spend half of each year with his father abandoned. Nellie tried hard to help her son make a place for himself in the world. She employed a tutor to prepare George for the entrance examination at an Oxford college, but George's education had been neglected in America and to avoid the embarrassment of certain failure it was decided he would not attempt the examination. Nellie also purchased a commission for her son in a provincial militia regiment and it was her hope that George might move on to a career in the regular army, but before that could happen George dropped a bombshell: he had fallen in love and intended to marry.

The object of George's love was Phoebe Georgina Frances Otway – always known by her nickname 'Ruby' – the 18-year-old daughter of Lieutenant-Colonel Jocelyn Otway, a wealthy army officer and art collector. Ruby's pedigree was impeccable and she was very pretty, but still childlike in many ways. As her prospective groom himself had not managed to outgrow some of the naive elements in his character, the attraction was obvious.

Nellie was concerned about the young couple's ability to build a solid, long-term partnership, and time would prove her concerns well founded. She also probably blamed Charlie for what she perceived as an impulsive decision on the part of her son. However, Ruby seemed to make George happy, so Nellie ignored her misgivings and set about organising a wedding suitable for the son of a prima donna. Nellie gave him a large sum of money and a powerful Emile Mors touring automobile as wedding gifts and her future daughter-in-law a magnificent dressing case in tortoiseshell and gold. Nellie's rich and titled friends also contributed expensive gifts.

On the afternoon of 18 December, George and Ruby were married at St George's, Hanover Square. George's best man was his cousin J.P. Armstrong, Vice-Consul for Burma. Also included among the guests were Charlie's nephew, Sir Andrew Armstrong, who had succeeded to the baronetcy following the death of Charlie's brother, and Prince Francis of Teck, the younger brother of the Princess of Wales, representing the royal family. Conspicuous by his absence was the groom's father. The bride's father hosted a sumptuous wedding breakfast at his home in Park Lane, after which the newlyweds left for a honeymoon in a castle in Dorset, owned by a friend of Nellie's. The following day Nellie set sail for New York to do battle with the Metropolitan Opera on behalf of Oscar Hammerstein.

The new Manhattan Opera House had opened on the evening of 3 December 1906 while Nellie was still in London. The press reported that the tradesmen putting the finishing touches to the theatre had left through the service entrance as the first audience flowed into the auditorium. The opera Hammerstein had chosen to inaugurate his theatre was Bellini's *I Puritani*, which had not been seen in New York for decades. It was an odd choice, but, as well as having novelty value, the role of Arturo was an ideal vehicle for Hammerstein's star tenor, Alessandro Bonci, who was able to deliver the stratospheric top notes in his role with spectacular effect. The capacity audience and the critics were fulsome in their acclaim for the performance, the venue and Hammerstein's enterprise. Performances of Mozart's *Don Giovanni* with Renaud in the title role and *Faust* with Dalmores followed, but attendance figures steadily declined after the opening night. Hammerstein grew ever more anxious for Nellie's arrival, pinning his hopes for the survival of the venture on her popularity.

Nellie arrived in New York on 30 December in a blaze of publicity.

Nellie's clothes, her jewellery and the costumes she would wear were all reported in detail in the press and Hammerstein assured the public that the diamonds Nellie would wear in *La Traviata* – worth a quarter of a million dollars – would be kept locked away in his own safe and guarded by two off-stage detectives when being worn on stage. The press noted that Nellie travelled with an entourage that included Ada Sassoli (brought along to support Nellie in the concerts she undertook between opera performances), Agnes Murphy (now installed as Nellie's secretary), a maid and a burly manservant, who dealt with the vast array of luggage.[7]

Nellie and her retinue moved into the hotel Hammerstein had booked for them, but that establishment was busy, noisy and so cold that Nellie feared her lung problems might return. Five days later they moved to a luxuriously furnished apartment in the Barcelona Building on West 58th Street, with Nellie subsequently cabling London to instruct her cook, her butler and several more of the Great Cumberland Place staff to join their mistress. Missing George and probably worried about how he and Ruby were managing in her absence, she also cabled George inviting him and Ruby to pay her a visit. George and Ruby must have departed immediately, for they arrived in New York ten days later. Agnes Murphy met them at the dock and managed a short conference with the local press. When asked if he played a musical instrument, George replied that he played golf, and when asked which opera he most enjoyed seeing his mother perform he nominated *La Bohème*.

George and Ruby moved in with Nellie at the Barcelona. When time (and Nellie) permitted, they toured around the eastern states of the United States, including a visit to George's old home in Galveston, where George entered a rough-riding competition. Here the newly married couple had one of the violent arguments that would become commonplace in their relationship over the next year.

Nellie made her debut with the Manhattan Opera company on 3 January as Violetta in *La Traviata* with one of Italy's leading tenors,

Amadeo Bassi, as Alfredo and Renaud as the elder Germont. The house was full, including standing room, and ticket scalpers made a fortune. That night the Met gave *Tosca* with Eames, Caruso and Scotti, but New York's high society flocked to the Manhattan, the evening becoming the first gala occasion since the house opened.

The press were generous in their praise of Nellie's singing. The *New York Times* reported: 'Madame Melba's voice has its old-time lusciousness and purity, its exquisite smoothness and fullness'.[8] W.J. Henderson, now writing for the *Sun*, observed that Nellie's voice had lost a little at the top and bottom but gained in the middle and that her figure had also 'gained in the middle'.[9] The only novelty in these comments was the reference to a change in Nellie's figure, which the London critics had been too polite to mention. Photographs of the period do show Nellie as having lost her hourglass figure, probably due to age.

Instead of the 10 performances Nellie had contracted to sing for Hammerstein, she sang 15, keen to help the impresario whom she had come to admire. Every time Nellie's name was advertised, there was a stampede on the box office and the house sold-out sign occasionally appeared many days before each performance. As well as two additional performances of *La Traviata*, she sang Gilda in *Rigoletto* five times, Lucia di Lammermoor twice, Marguerite in *Faust* once and Mimi in *La Bohème* four times.[10]

The first performance of *Lucia di Lammermoor* was marked by a unique response from some sections of the audience. The Australian Society of New York had attended *en masse* and welcomed Nellie with a rousing chorus of 'coo-ees', which Nellie acknowledged with a vigorous wave. When asked for his opinion of this strange call, Hammerstein commented it was not as surprising as the orchestration of Richard Strauss's *Salome*, which the Met had given on 22 January.[11]

La Bohème proved to be both the greatest challenge and the greatest hit of Hammerstein's season. Mimi had been one of the roles Nellie had insisted she be allowed to sing when she struck her deal with Hammerstein in Paris, but the exclusive licence to perform Puccini's operas in New York that had been granted to the Met seemed to be an insurmountable obstacle. Immediately upon his return to New York, Hammerstein had announced that he was going to perform *La Bohème* and the Met promptly mounted a legal challenge to prevent him. Hammerstein claimed that he had made a verbal agreement with George Maxwell (representing Ricordi's) allowing him to perform all of Puccini's works, and that his agreement with Maxwell predated the issue of the licence to the Met. When the case came to court, the presiding judge accepted Hammerstein's claim and dismissed the Met's challenge.[12]

Hammerstein now believed he had approval to proceed, and to plan and cast his production of *La Bohème*, but when he applied to Ricordi's New York office to hire a full score and orchestral parts for the opera, they refused to deal with him. Cleofonte Campanini came to the rescue. He knew the opera well and had conducted it many times, so using a vocal score (singers' parts with piano) he set about reconstructing the orchestration from memory.

On the day before the first performance, Maxwell issued a statement to the press stating that Hammerstein was giving the opera against Puccini's wishes, condemning the orchestration as 'unauthorised' and asking people who attended the performance not to blame Puccini, the house of Ricordi or him for what they heard. Hammerstein immediately responded by questioning how Maxwell could possibly be familiar with the orchestration since he had not attended any of the rehearsals.[13]

Intrigued by the controversy, the public flocked to the first night of *La Bohème* and if any of them – or the critics – knew Puccini's score well, they did not find any aberrations from the original worthy of comment. Supporting Nellie were Bonci as Rodolfo, Emma Trentini, an Italian soprano Nellie had recommended to Hammerstein as Musetta, and Sammarco as Marcello. Concerned about legal action either from Ricordi's or the Met (or both), Campanini declined to conduct, resulting in the performance – and the remaining three – being conducted by his assistant, Fernando Tanara. Henry Krehbiel reported that Nellie was in superb voice, but bore little resemblance to the frail Mimi.[14]

Nellie made her last appearance for the season (in *La Bohème*) on 25 March. It had been advertised that, as a bonus for the audience, she and Dalmores would sing the balcony scene from *Roméo et Juliette* between the second and third acts of the opera, but Dalmores was indisposed, so Nellie gave the audience the Mad Scene from *Lucia di Lammer*moor after the opera. But the audience was unwilling to allow their favourite to depart. Tumultuous applause and shouts for Nellie to reappear continued so she ordered stagehands to push a piano onto the stage and sat down and accompanied herself in Tosti's 'Mattinata'. Still the audience would not depart, so Nellie called for silence and then told them all (in no uncertain terms) to go home. The houselights were dimmed and the audience finally struggled out of the theatre in semi-darkness.

While the evening's public festivities had ended, in private another round was beginning. The stage was cleared, tables were set up and Hammerstein hosted a farewell banquet for Nellie, with Pêches Melba as the dessert. Hammerstein sat between his departing star (Nellie) and his incoming star (Calvé), who had arrived that day and would open in *Carmen* two nights later. Two or three stars from the Met managed to attend without being detected and accused of disloyalty. Eames was not one of them, but Nellie's old arch-rival had attended a performance of *Rigoletto* during the season and had been seen applauding with little enthusiasm. Nellie had not returned the compliment, although she had probably been curious to see how Eames sang Tosca.[15]

Nellie did, however, take a box at the Met for a mid-morning performance of an opera she had not seen before: Wagner's *Parsifal*. She admitted to being tired when she took her place in the box but within minutes was transfixed by the uplifting music of Wagner, sung by a fine cast and conducted by the distinguished Wagnerian Alfred Hertz. That performance had a profound effect on Nellie and rekindled her desire to sing Wagner. Hammerstein had announced earlier that he had reached agreements with Nellie, Renaud and Dalmores to return for his next season, beginning in November, and Nellie now gave her permission for him to tell the press that she would open his next season as Senta in Wagner's 'The Flying Dutchman', sung in French, with Renaud in the title role and Dalmores as Erik. Wisely, Nellie later abandoned that plan. Had she not, a reoccurrence of the 'Siegfried' debacle might have occurred.[16]

Around the time Nellie made her debut with Hammerstein's company, she had been approached by the Victor Talking Machine Company of New York to make a series of recordings for the American market. Victor had offered her a fee of 50,000 dollars in cash, along with royalties on sales of the recordings. It was an offer Nellie could not refuse. Between 1 March and 1 April, Nellie visited their studios seven times and made 35 recordings. Some pieces were recorded twice to ensure a higher-quality version, with a total of 20 ultimately issued. For most of these recordings Nellie was accompanied by a session orchestra, conducted by Victor's 'house conductor', Walter Rogers. On two of them we hear Ada Sassoli playing harp, and in Tosti's 'Mattinata' Nellie accompanies herself at the piano, as she had on stage at the Manhattan. Good copies, sympathetically remastered, reveal that among these 20 issues are some of Nellie's finest and most important recordings. Foremost among them are the first recordings we have of Nellie's Mimi, accompanied by orchestra. She sings 'Si, mi chiamano Mimi' charmingly and when she reaches the section where the seamstress recalls the coming of spring, she rises to the climax with a surety and clarity that few other sopranos have ever matched. 'Mimi's Farewell' is sung with touching resignation but without letting emotion disturb the line. And finally we have the great love duet that ends the first act of the opera, where she is partnered by Caruso. Four takes were made of this duet on two different days, but the first was selected for issue. At the beginning of the duet the balance between the singers favours the tenor but, halfway through, Nellie seems to have moved closer to the recording horn and the balance is improved. As other commentators have observed, listening to Nellie's final top note at the end of the duet confirms the experience that Mary Garden described – the note seems to leave Nellie's throat and hang independently in the air until both singers stop singing.

These recordings also include an excellent version of Tosca's 'Vissi d'arte', superior in sound to one Nellie had made in London. Nellie avoids the histrionics favoured by later singers in this aria and the effect is all the more moving for her discretion. New versions of the 'Jewel Song' from *Faust*, the *La Traviata* scena and the Mad Scene from *Lucia di Lammermoor* were included in this group of recordings. Although she had dropped the role of Ophélie from her stage repertoire a decade earlier, Nellie had retained the *Hamlet* Mad Scene in her concert repertoire and among the group is a new version of that piece, which is among the finest of all Nellie's recordings. Included among these recordings are two duets (one by Giuseppe Blangini and one by Bemberg), where Nellie is joined by Charles Gilibert. Both duets are charmingly sung, the singers listening carefully to one another and blending their voices perfectly.[17]

These American recordings provide evidence of just how remarkably Nellie had preserved her voice as she moved into middle age, and how her singing technique was almost unimpaired by age. The pinpoint accuracy of her intonation, her ability to sing the widest divisions, her fluent scale work and her immaculate trill ensured that she remained – after 23 years as a professional singer – in a class of her own.

Before departing from New York, Nellie had two more duties to perform. The first was to distribute gifts to colleagues at the

Manhattan Opera House. Hammerstein received a gold watch and others were given 'Melba' tiepins carrying the letter 'M' – in gold and diamonds for senior colleagues and in base metal with the letter in blue enamel for obliging dressers and stagehands. The second duty was philanthropic. Soon after her arrival Nellie had told the press that she had been so besieged by autograph hunters that she had decided to charge one dollar for each signature, and that she would give the money to charity before she left the city. The charity selected by Nellie was a home for blind babies in Brooklyn. Nellie dutifully handed over 480 dollars, along with a generous amount from her own pocket. The home used the money to build an extension to their premises, naming it 'The Melba Annex'.[18]

On 2 April Nellie and her entourage sailed for Europe on the Lloyd liner *Kaiser Wilhelm*. Before the vessel departed, Nellie held a reception in one of the ship's saloons, attended by Hammerstein, her American manager, Charles Ellis, and some of the singers from both the Manhattan and the Met. Hammerstein presented Nellie with a canary in a cage to which this piece of doggerel was attached:

> To you, brilliant songstress fairy,
> I give in friendship the canary;
> If ever we should part in rage,
> You will swallow the cage,
> And I the canary.
>
>   Oscar Hammerstein

Chapter 16

Sentimental journeys

When the *Kaiser Wilhelm* reached Cherbourg, Nellie and her party were transferred to shore in a lighter. The weather was cold and the wind blustery. Unfortunately, Nellie developed a severe chill and the congestion on her lungs returned. She had planned to travel immediately to Brussels to sing performances of *La Traviata* and *Rigoletto* in the theatre where she had made her stage debut but, to her intense disappointment, the performances had to be cancelled. She was due to sing at Covent Garden in mid-May, so she spent the couple of intervening weeks recuperating in her apartment in Paris and then travelled to London, although her health was still precarious. For her first scheduled appearance (as Mimi), she had to be replaced by a protégée of Massenet's, Pauline Donalda. Nellie missed as many performances as she sang during this season, providing not only Donalda, but also Selma Kurz and Frieda Hempel, a 'new' German coloratura soprano, with opportunities to build on their popularity.

One engagement Nellie could not refuse was a command from Edward VII to entertain a group of his guests – including the King and Queen of Denmark – at a soirée, and when King Edward asked Nellie to sing in a mixed-program gala at Covent Garden three nights later she obeyed.[1] Another engagement Nellie was happy to accept was to travel to Hayes (just west of London), where she ceremoniously laid the cornerstone for a new Gramophone & Typewriter Company factory. A photo of her arriving at the site was widely circulated and shows Nellie looking as queenly as any monarch.

Next on Nellie's schedule was a sentimental trip to Australia to see her family and to be with her father when he celebrated his seventy-ninth birthday on 16 February.[2] To ensure that she was mobile while in Australia, Nellie had organised for her luxurious Napier touring car and her French chauffeur to be shipped to Australia some weeks earlier. At the close of the Covent Garden season, Nellie rested in Paris, after which she, George, Ruby, Ruby's small dog and a handful of servants embarked from Marseille, bound for Perth via the Suez Canal.

Nellie hoped the sea voyage might improve her health and also Ruby's, George's wife having been recently hospitalised for the removal of her appendix. Arguments between George and Ruby had continued and Nellie witnessed a particularly violent incident as their ship steamed through the Red Sea. She had accepted that her daughter-in-law's lacklustre personality might be trying George's patience; nevertheless, she was concerned about his behaviour. As a husband, he seemed to be displaying some of his father's less attractive character traits and when conflict erupted in the steamy heat of the Red Sea – as it had between Nellie and George's father 21 years earlier – Nellie felt obliged to support Ruby.

Because this was a private tour, Nellie had travelled under the name of Mitchell and, on her arrival in Victoria, she based herself outside Melbourne, taking a six-month lease on a mansion at Ercildoune, 130 kilometres northwest of the city. Ercildoune House was (and is) a large, spacious stone house in the Scottish-baronial style, surrounded by fine gardens and farmland. It was the ideal place for Nellie to entertain her family away from the prying eyes of the press – and of John Norton in particular.[3]

David Mitchell was now white-haired and white-bearded but still pursuing his business interests. He proudly told Nellie that he had just invented a form of cement that was fireproof. Her father's first visit was also an opportunity for George to meet his grandfather, whom he had not seen since he was a small child. After a long engagement, Nellie's sister, Annie, had finally married and was now Mrs Harry Box of St Kilda. Dora had also married. Her husband, Charles Lempriere, was an engineer–businessman and the couple were expecting their first child.

Nellie would have revelled in entertaining her family at Ercildoune, but playing chatelaine in a remote country house soon lost its appeal and she began to appear at social events in Melbourne. The first was a concert given by the husband-and-wife-duo of Clara Butt and Kennerley Rumford, who were touring Australia, and when Nellie entered the Melbourne Town Hall on the arm of her father, she was greeted with applause every bit as enthusiastic as the visiting contralto received. Both divas appeared (rivalling one another in the splendour of their outfits) at a Government House ball and at Flemington Race Course on Melbourne Cup Day.

Ruby contracted diphtheria in Melbourne and was hospitalised for many months as doctors fought to save her life. Nellie pressed on with her busy whirl of social engagements, her actions suggesting that she had decided Ruby was surplus to her son's needs and that if nature removed Ruby from their lives, he might find greater happiness with a new wife – perhaps an Australian girl with a stronger character and a stronger constitution.

In response to public demand, Nellie agreed to give a few concerts before returning to Europe. She recruited the fine Scottish baritone Andrew Black, who was then living in Melbourne, the Australian pianist Una Bourne, the cellist Louis Hattenbach and her old friend John Lemmoné to support her. On consecutive Saturday nights at the end of November, Nellie sang in the Melbourne Town Hall. Two weeks later she gave two concerts in the Sydney Town Hall, then returning to Melbourne for two more concerts, these staged in the Royal Exhibition Building. Remembering the accusations of price-gouging Norton had levelled at her on her previous visit, Nellie ensured that tickets were offered at modest prices.

While Nellie was singing to vast audiences in the cavernous

building her father had built in Melbourne, events were occurring in London that would have a profound effect on her career in the immediate future. To enable her to travel to Australia, Nellie had declined an offer to appear in the autumn season at Covent Garden. This decision had forced Frank Rendle to find another soprano to sing the roles Nellie would have sung. On the recommendation of Campanini, Rendle chose the conductor's sister-in-law and offered her a paltry 120 pounds per performance for 10 performances. The soprano was Luisa Tetrazzini.

Since Nellie had encountered her in Bergamo ten years earlier, Tetrazzini had been consolidating her reputation in Italy, Spain, Portugal and South America, but was virtually unknown in London. The Italian soprano was now 36 and was carrying additional weight, which accentuated her short stature. Before Tetrazzini arrived in London, Rendle was regretting engaging her and when advance ticket sales for her performances were negligible, the managing director of Covent Garden, Harry Higgins, wrote to the soprano suggesting she not come and offering 800 pounds in compensation. Tetrazzini, however, was adamant: she wanted to sing in London and probably realised this would be her only chance.[4]

The weather on the night Tetrazzini made her debut at Covent Garden was similar to that on the night Nellie first sang there in 1888. Fog seeped into the auditorium and the audience was sparse and dispirited. While the other principals, the orchestra and the management had discovered at rehearsal that they had a potential new star in their midst, the public was completely unprepared for the splendour of Tetrazzini's voice and the virtuosity of her singing when she appeared on stage in one of Nellie's favourite roles – Violetta.

Luisa Tetrazzini's voice was larger than Nellie's and her singing technique, although not as perfect as Nellie's, was extraordinary. Experience had given her singing and acting a sense of authority, and the audience soon forgot her unromantic appearance, as exquisite sounds filled the theatre.[5]

The following day the press employed their most extravagant prose to describe the new star's voice and the excitement she had created. Multiple performances of two more of Nellie's favourite roles followed: Gilda and Lucia di Lammermoor. To demonstrate that Nellie had not been forgotten, the critics made frequent comparisons between the younger and the older singer – more often than not in Nellie's favour – but Nellie would find it was Tetrazzini's name that was on everyone's lips when she arrived back in London.

Before returning to Europe, Nellie spent a few weeks more with her family, as well as giving two final concerts in Adelaide. On her journey to Australia she had learned of the death in Berlin of her old friend and admirer Joseph Joachim, and while she was in Adelaide, news arrived that Salvatore Marchesi had also died. Nellie was saddened by the violinist's death and devastated by Marchesi's – the old man who had been a father figure to her in Paris.

Nellie, her party and her automobile sailed from Adelaide on 27 February. They disembarked in Naples and Nellie was driven directly to Paris to console her 'other' mother.[6] Nellie spent as much time as she could with Mathilde Marchesi before continuing to London and settling at Great Cumberland Place to begin rehearsals for the 1908 season at Covent Garden – the year marking the twentieth anniversary of her debut at London's historic opera house.

Nellie had not expected to be living in the house in Great Cumberland Place again. During her time in Australia she had decided that maintaining a mansion in London while she was absent for most of the year was inconvenient and expensive. From Melbourne she had written to a London property agency instructing them to put the house and its furniture and fittings up for sale. The agents arranged an auction and a large assembly attended on the day, but the bidding did not reach the reserve Nellie had set and the property was passed in. In July (after Nellie had taken up residence) it was put up for sale again and again failed to sell. In October it was advertised once more, this time with the comment 'an absolute bargain' added. Finally, towards the end of the year the house was bought by Lady Randolph Churchill (mother of the future prime minister) and Nellie must have breathed an enormous sigh of relief, although the selling price had probably been far below Nellie's original expectation.

This was not Nellie's only domestic problem at the time. Soon after arriving in London, George had begun an affair with a Mrs Hoffmann and that lady's husband had sued for divorce, naming George as co-respondent. At the same time Ruby sued George for divorce and George suffered some kind of nervous breakdown, requiring Nellie to send him off to Marienbad for a cure at a spa resort.[7] And, if all those issues were not enough to try her patience and strength, Nellie was facing the most serious challenge to her supremacy at Covent Garden in 20 years.

Following her success during the autumn season, Tetrazzini had been hastily engaged for the summer season, along with a squad of other impressive sopranos, including Destinn, Cavalieri, the Australian Lalla Miranda and a former pupil of Jean de Reszke's, Louise Edvina. Roles that Nellie had sung previously – Lucia, Rosina and Marguerite de Valois – were assumed by Tetrazzini. Gilda and Violetta had to be shared between the two divas and Marguerite in *Faust* was given to Edvina. Two roles were assigned exclusively to Nellie, those of Mimi and Desdemona.

On 6 July Nellie sang Desdemona at Covent Garden for the first time since 1892. Francesco Tamagno had died in 1905 and his place as the leading exponent of the title role in Verdi's opera had been taken over by Zenatello. Zenatello's presence was reassuring to Nellie; she liked the young Italian and approved of his singing and his acting. Antonio Scotti sang Iago, while the second tenor role in the opera, Cassio, was sung by John McCormack, a young Irish tenor. The critic of *The Times* reported that Desdemona's music had probably never been sung more beautifully.[8] The six performances of *Otello* given by this cast were rated as highlights of the season. Nellie also received liberal praise for her five performances in *La Bohème*, the second on her forty-seventh birthday, when the audience greeted her with a standing ovation before she had sung a note.

Every triumph that Nellie scored during the season was matched by similar triumphs from Tetrazzini, and as the season progressed it became apparent that, while a proportion of the public were still devoted to Nellie, an equal number had transferred their allegiance to the Italian soprano. Nellie was outraged and, while remaining polite to her rival in public, she resorted to ridiculing her in private, referring to Tetrazzini as 'the dwarf' and staggering around on her hands and knees pretending to be the abused horse that carried Tetrazzini on stage in *Les Huguenots*.[9]

In the planning stage for the season it had been decided to celebrate the twentieth anniversary of Nellie's Covent Garden debut with a gala matinee, with Edward VII and Queen Alexandra agreeing to attend. Boxes sold for up to 100 pounds each and the proceeds from the event were to be donated to the London Hospital in Whitechapel. When Tetrazzini was asked to take part, she declined, claiming the invitation had arrived too late for her to accept. Emmy Destinn was happy to offer her services and to sing the first act of *Madama Butterfly*, after which Nellie sang in the first act of *La Traviata*. It was an opportunity for the critics to remark on how miraculously fresh and unimpaired Nellie's voice and her singing had remained, but how little her acting had improved in all those years.[10]

Edward VII, Queen Alexandra, and the Prince and Princess of Wales also attended a concert organised by Nellie in the Royal Albert Hall to raise funds for the League of Mercy, a charity of which the Prince of Wales was patron and which raised money to recruit volunteers for British hospitals. Although he was not singing at Covent Garden that season, Caruso was in London and Nellie persuaded him to sing, along with several other artists from Covent Garden. Nellie also convinced the recently knighted Sir Charles Santley to emerge from retirement and to make one of his final public appearances as a singer. The 74-year-old baritone's reception was even more exuberant than either Caruso's or Nellie's, confirming an adage on which Nellie would rely in years to come: that having once earned the favour of the British public it was never withdrawn.

The honour of closing the season at Covent Garden on 31 July (in *Otello*) was awarded to Nellie. Tetrazzini would continue to challenge Nellie's dominance at Covent Garden for the four summer seasons prior to the outbreak of the First World War. Nellie had weathered the initial threat to her supremacy and, although she might have had reservations at the time, ultimately she would emerge victorious.

In the midst of the Covent Garden season Nellie had returned briefly to Paris to take part in what she later identified as one of the most memorable events in her career. Camille Saint-Saëns had approached Nellie on behalf of the Société des Auteurs et Compositeurs Dramatiques, a long-established organisation whose objective was to protect the intellectual rights of French writers and composers and also maintain a pension scheme. The society was planning a gala fund-raising performance at the Paris Opéra and Saint-Saëns asked if Nellie would sing Gilda in *Rigoletto*, with Caruso as the duke and Renaud in the title role and the opera conducted by a young Tullio Serafin.[11] Nellie happily agreed.

It had been 12 years since Nellie had last sung in opera in Paris and when the cast was announced there was a stampede on the box office. The performance was a complete triumph for the three principals, described by the press as 'an astral trinity'.[12] The press also bemoaned the fact that Parisians had been forced to wait so long to hear Nellie again on stage and wondered wistfully how long it would be before they had another opportunity.[13]

When Nellie had been planning her trip to Australia the previous year she had written to Oscar Hammerstein asking to be excused from the commitment she had made to sing in his second season, adding that she would still come to New York if the impresario really needed her. Hammerstein had written back to say he was prepared to release her and Nellie had been both relieved and a little disappointed that it seemed 'Oscar' could manage without her.[14]

By the time Nellie reached Paris (after the Australian trip) any affront she might have felt about Hammerstein's decision had dissipated and, at his request, she joined him in the Théâtre du Châtelet on several afternoons, auditioning singers for Hammerstein's third season – at the Manhattan in New York and in a new opera house he had built in Philadelphia. Hammerstein had already re-engaged the two sopranos who had emerged as the stars of his second season – Tetrazzini and Garden – and he now added Cavalieri. Nellie agreed to sing 10 performances for Hammerstein over the Christmas (1908) and New Year (1909) period.

On this occasion, Nellie made the trans-Atlantic crossing on the luxury liner *Lusitania*, which, six years later, would be sunk by a German U-boat off the coast of Ireland. Nellie arrived in New York in early December to be met by Oscar Hammerstein, who welcomed her enthusiastically. On 14 December Nellie appeared in *La Bohème* with Trentini, Zenatello and Sammarco. The *New York Tribune* described the evening as 'a sensation of great and general rejoicing',[15] Richard Aldrich in the *New York Times* writing:

> What Madame Melba's voice has lost in silver it has gained in gold. It is still youthful and a warmer, more winning, more touching voice today than it ever was before; and better than all, it is backed by a more beautiful sincerity and a more rounded musicianship.[16]

Three nights later Nellie sang for the first time in Hammerstein's new opera house in Philadelphia in the same opera. On Christmas night at the Manhattan, Nellie, Zenatello and Sammarco gave the company's first-ever performance of *Otello*. Meanwhile, Tetrazzini had been triumphing as Lucia, Gilda and Violetta. Towards the end of her stay, Nellie 'stole' one performance of *La Traviata* from her rival and, for her final appearance with the company, one performance of *Rigoletto*. In both operas, Nellie proved that, while she might no longer be able to match her younger rival in vocal gymnastics, she could still upstage her definitively in beauty of sound and refined musicianship.

On 1 and 6 January, Nellie made 10 new recordings in New York. On four of them she was accompanied by Walter Rogers and the Victor studio orchestra; for the remainder she accompanied herself at the piano. Among the operatic excerpts are impressive versions of Desdemona's two arias from the last act of *Otello* and a new version of 'Mimi's Farewell', which for some reason was only issued in Germany. The third item recorded with orchestra is a song by Landon Ronald that Nellie had sung at the League of Mercy concert in London the previous November: 'O Lovely Night'. The music is old-fashioned and so is the style of singing, and yet the result is enchanting.

At the time Nellie made these recordings, Debussy's *Pelléas et Mélisande* was in rehearsal at the Manhattan, with Mary Garden as Mélisande, a role Garden had created in Paris in 1902, and the forthcoming premiere was tipped to be the hit of the season. Perhaps to prove that she too could sing Debussy, Nellie chose to record 'En sourdine' from the French composer's song cycle 'Fêtes Galantes'. Apart from one over-emphatically sung note towards the end, it is a charming record, demonstrating that Nellie understood the subtlety required to perform Debussy's music. Another French song, 'D'une prison' by Reynaldo Hahn, and the traditional songs, 'Believe me if all those endearing young charms' and 'Ye banks and braes of Bonnie Doon', with Nellie strumming away at the piano, are more reminiscent of a friend's drawing room, where Nellie had been invited to 'give us a song, dear'.

Since her previous trip to Australia, Nellie had been thinking a great deal about her homeland, prompting her to consider three objectives. Firstly, she wanted to undertake an extensive concert tour, not merely of the state capitals but also of the provincial cities and towns, and, secondly, to assemble an international-class opera company to tour the state capitals. Her first objective was aimed at giving as many Australians as possible the opportunity to hear her sing while her voice was still in its prime; the second was to provide city dwellers with the opportunity to hear her in fully staged operas while her stage career was still at its peak. The third objective was to purchase a property in the Melbourne region to which she could retreat when time allowed and there enjoy the pleasures of her youth – sunshine, the smell of eucalyptus, rolling green paddocks and blue hills.

To accomplish her first aim, she entrusted John Lemmoné with organising concerts in any accessible Australian city or town with a suitable venue and which was prepared to outlay a substantial deposit. Lemmoné set about the task early in 1908 and at the conclusion of Nellie's season at Covent Garden that year it was announced that she would not be returning to Covent Garden in 1909, instead undertaking a six-month tour of Australia.

Accomplishing the second objective proved more difficult. When Nellie was earlier helping Hammerstein to audition singers in Paris for his next season in America, the press mistakenly reported that they were developing plans to form a company to tour Australia.[17] Given a choice, Nellie might well have chosen Oscar Hammerstein as a partner in the new enterprise, but the American impresario was fully occupied with his own high-risk ventures in New York and Philadelphia.[18] Nellie wrote to Robert de Sanna, president of the San Carlo company in Naples, who had cooperated with Frank Rendle in organising the recent autumn seasons at Covent Garden. De Sanna expressed interest, but when Nellie visited him in Naples he claimed that ill health prevented his participation in the scheme.[19] Managing the complex arrangements for the opera company continued as the months passed, one obstacle after another being overcome until Nellie's dream finally became a reality in the spring of 1911.

Locating and purchasing a 'bush retreat' had to wait until Nellie reached Australia for the concert tour, but it proved the easiest of her three objectives to accomplish.

To support her on the concert tour of Australia, Nellie recruited Frederick Ranalow, an Irish baritone who had toured the United Kingdom with her the previous year, and Una Bourne. As well as managing the tour, John Lemmoné appeared as a soloist and provided flute obbligatos when Nellie required them. George, Agnes Murphy and a number of servants joined Nellie on the journey, disembarking at Adelaide on 1 March to catch the overnight express to Melbourne.[20]

The familiar pattern of nervous dignitaries making speeches of welcome began the next morning, but at Melbourne's Spencer Street Railway Station the first of the many farcical incidents that would lend spice to the tour occurred. The train stopped at the wrong end of the platform and the only person there to greet her was George Allan of Allan's music house, who happened to be on the spot to catch another train. The welcoming committee (and a choir) were assembled at the other, causing a frantic dash along the platform when Nellie emerged.

The tour opened with four sold-out concerts in the Melbourne Town Hall, at which Nellie sang with an orchestra conducted by George Marshall-Hall, still leading the music department at Melbourne University.[21] For these and subsequent concerts in Australia Nellie felt confident to revive some of the showpiece arias she had dropped from her repertoire in Europe, most notably the Mad Scene from *Hamlet*. She also shrewdly included the song titles she had recently recorded in New York among her encores, the discs now being on sale in local record stores.

As might be expected, the music critics in Australia praised her voice and her singing in such outrageously flattering terms as to make their comments worthless. However, the local press adopted an approach to their reporting that English newspapers would never have contemplated – they filled column after column with descriptions of Nellie's concert attire. After one concert it was reported:

> The dark-haired diva was attired in an Empire gown of emerald green satin with an overdress of black net showered with jets. Here and there were branches of appliqued roses and a coral pink, fringed sash adorned the left side. The bodice of the dress was covered by flashing diamond jewellery.[22]

And after another: 'Madame Melba wore a dress of exquisite cream satin, the sheen of which matched the fortune in pearls at her neck, with a border embroidered with silver and precious gemstones and a tiara of diamonds and turquoises crowning her head.'[23] Nellie was not called 'The Queen of Song' for nothing.

Before departing for concerts in Tasmania and New Zealand, Nellie gave a concert in the Athenaeum Hall in Lilydale. David Mitchell (now 80) greeted his daughter in the foyer of the small hall, along with Nellie's brother Frank, who now managed the limestone quarry. It was an event fraught with emotion. As a final encore Nellie sang 'Home, sweet home' as tears welled in her eyes.

Annie Box accompanied her sister on the trip to Tasmania and to New Zealand. After the rough reception Nellie had received in Launceston on her previous visit, she was nervous about singing there but, as if to redeem themselves, the people of Launceston gave her a tumultuous welcome. On board the steamer bound for New Zealand, Nellie suffered an injury. When the ship was hit by a freak wave, Nellie, who was on deck at the time, fell against a companionway, bruising one knee badly. The knee had to be bandaged and strapped and was painful for weeks, but Nellie carried on with her schedule. In another mishap on the New Zealand leg of the tour, Nellie and her party experienced an earthquake in

Wellington and had to be evacuated from their hotel when a fire broke out in an adjacent building.

Back in Sydney, Nellie gave two concerts in the town hall. In the audience for the first was a group of nuns and among them Sister Mary Paul of the Cross – Nellie's former singing teacher at Presbyterian Ladies College, Mary Ellen Christian. As with the episode in Launceston in 1903, Nellie's public dismissal of Christian's teaching was now 'past history' and the two women enjoyed a joyous reunion. Nellie was delighted to see Christian back at the next concert, this time with a group of her singing students.

Nellie and her party then headed off for concerts in eight provincial cities in western New South Wales, followed by Brisbane and six cities along the coast of Queensland, starting in Townsville and, surprisingly, not including Mackay. More concerts in Sydney and in towns between Sydney and Melbourne, and in Gippsland and the Western District of Victoria completed the tour. Numerous amusing incidents occurred during Nellie's visits to country towns. In one location a large group of people climbed onto the roof of the hall to hear the concert for free, becoming stranded when authorities removed their ladder. At a hall in a different town an equal number crammed themselves underneath the hall, and their subterranean shuffling made Nellie wonder whether she was experiencing another earthquake. Decrepit and out-of-tune pianos confronted Una Bourne when she played and in one venue the piano threatened to fall through the termite-riddled stage. Nellie's favourite anecdote from these adventures involved an old man who accosted her as she was leaving a hall after a concert. 'I've walked 18 miles to hear ye', Nellie reported him as saying, 'and it was worth it. You're all prizes and no blanks. And mind you', the old man added, as he grasped Nellie's arm, 'I know a bit about singin'. I was in a circus meself once.' Back in Melbourne Nellie allowed herself a generous period of rest and recovery, with an assortment of non-singing engagements to keep herself from becoming bored.[24]

One member of the party who was almost continuously bored was George. Ever since his divorce he had been trailing around after his mother, prone to the temptations of having time on his hands and no useful purpose. To create an interest for her son, Nellie purchased a racehorse called Barangkali. George was allowed to choose the horse's racing colours and to register them with the Victorian Racing Club. Either as a compliment to his mother (or to tease her), George chose olive green for the jockey's jacket, mauve for the sash and white for the cap – the colours of the Suffragette Movement, which Nellie supported. The first to wear these colours was George himself, who rode Barangkali in a point-to-point steeplechase during a picnic meeting at Dandenong – and won.[25]

Nellie also set about finding her bush retreat. At the end of October she bought a farm at Coldstream, on what is now the Melba Highway, a few kilometres from Lilydale. The existing farmhouse was inadequate for Nellie's needs so she engaged the architect John Grainger – father of the composer Percy Grainger – to design a new house for her. Nellie might have been expected to choose a design resembling an English stately home or one of those mansions she had rented in the Thames Valley, but she did not. Her brief to Grainger was to create a spacious, comfortable, single-storey house with wide verandahs and which blended with its environment and suited the climate. The one element Nellie did borrow from England was the name: 'Coombe Cottage'. It would be another three years before the house was finished and in later years Nellie would expand the property by purchasing more land, but the process of creating the home to which she would one day retire had commenced.

Before departing, Nellie gave two farewell concerts in the Royal Exhibition Building, followed by a charity concert to raise funds for bush nursing. Lemmoné also hired His Majesty's Theatre in Perth for three nights to allow Nellie to sing in Western Australia on her way back to Europe, but those Perth concerts had to be cancelled when Nellie came down with a cold. In Melbourne at Christmas

George became seriously ill and varicose veins on his bladder were diagnosed. Critical surgery solved the problem, but George was too weak to travel, so Nellie left him to recuperate in the care of a nurse in the farmhouse at Coldstream.

Nellie had achieved two of her three objectives, with only the plan to bring an opera company to tour Australia unfulfilled. During her time in Australia she had talked up the prospect of an opera company's success whenever the press gave her opportunity, identifying a list of operas she hoped the company would be performing when it reached Australia: *Tannhäuser*, *Lohengrin*, 'The Flying Dutchman', *La Traviata*, *Rigoletto*, *Otello*, *La Bohème*, *Tosca*, *Madama Butterfly*, *Lucia di Lammermoor*, 'The Marriage of Figaro' and *Carmen*. One important milestone towards this objective had been achieved while Nellie was in Melbourne. She had commenced negotiations with the firm of J.C. Williamson to collaborate with her in the venture. By the time Nellie had left, a tacit agreement had been reached for Williamson's to share the costs of the tour and for their theatres to be the venue for performances. Nellie must have been pleased, but could not have envisaged that the partnership would result in not one 'Melba-Williamson Grand Opera Company' but three over the next two decades.

Chapter 17

Promises

As soon as Nellie and her party arrived back in London, John Lemmoné was despatched to the Continent to begin recruiting singers for the Australian opera company. Nellie visited Paris and called on Mathilde Marchesi. It was two years since Salvatore had died; Evelyn Scotney had taken lessons with Marchesi and departed and Madame had only a handful of students left. Marchesi's career as a teacher was at an end and according to Nellie she had deteriorated both physically and mentally. In *Melodies in Memories*, Nellie claims that when she arrived at Rue Jouffroy, Marchesi didn't recognise her and even though Nellie explained who she was, Marchesi would not believe her. For Nellie it was a harrowing final encounter with a woman she loved and to whom she credited the greatest contribution that anyone, other than herself, had made to her career.[1] From Paris Nellie travelled to Monte Carlo, Cannes and then Nice, where she and Lemmoné called on Jean de Reszke, who promised to help them to find singers for Australia.

Nellie then settled back into London's Ritz to prepare for the 1910 social and musical season, planning to make her return (after her long absence) with a concert at the Royal Albert Hall on 7 May. The day before the concert, King Edward VII died at Buckingham Palace. London was immediately plunged into mourning and all social and musical events were postponed. From the windows of the Ritz a fortnight later, Nellie and Lemmoné viewed the king's funeral procession passing on its way to Windsor. As she watched the sombre cortège roll by, Nellie's mind would have been filled with memories of the jovial king, who had offered her not only patronage but friendship.

During the mourning hiatus, Nellie used her time well, travelling to the Gramophone Company's studios in City Road to make new versions of some of her old recordings and to add some new titles.[2] The two full-day recording sessions on 11 and 19 May produced some of Nellie's most important recordings, although the occasions were beset by disagreements; in addition, Nellie's voice was not at it best in the afternoons, she having consumed large lunches at the company's expense. Of the 20 sides Nellie recorded, only seven would be issued. Among these are fine versions of Tosca's 'Vissi d'arte' and Elsa's Dream from *Lohengrin*.[3] The outstanding solo disc – and quite possibly the finest recording Nellie ever made – is the aria 'Pleurez, pleurez mes yeux' ('Cry, cry my eyes') from Massenet's *Le Cid*. Nellie had sung the role of the Infanta in this opera at the Met in 1901, but when she came to make this recording she chose the showpiece aria sung by the other soprano in the cast, Chimène. It is a spectacular performance and dispels once and for all the notion that Nellie could not sing passionately. When Massenet heard it he commented: 'Cry, *my* eyes! *Happy* eyes will cry when they hear Melba sing this. It made an unforgettable impression on me.'[4]

Equally unforgettable but for entirely different reasons are the concerted numbers Nellie recorded on the first day. The Gramophone Company recruited John McCormack (who was due to sing with Nellie at Covent Garden), the contralto Edna Thornton and Mario Sammarco to share the recording horn with Nellie. Three pieces were recorded: a duet from *La Traviata* with McCormack, the quartet from *Rigoletto* with Thornton, McCormack and Sammarco, and the final trio from *Faust* with McCormack and Sammarco. The company's expectations of these discs, where four popular singers were combined would have been high – but the results were disappointing. Fred Gaisberg was present at the session and in his memoirs he recounted what happened.[5] Nellie and Sammarco arrived on time to find the orchestra assembled and the conductor ready. Thornton arrived a few minutes late and received a reprimand from Nellie, but another half-hour passed before McCormack sauntered in. Nellie was furious and 'snapped' at the young Irishman. An argument ensued, replete with Irish invective and Aussie expletives. With peace restored, the first item was recorded, the 'Traviata' duet. How that sounded is unknown because, on Nellie's order, the matrix was destroyed. It may be safely assumed that Alfredo and Violetta's love for one another in this duet was not expressed in the recording. The quartet from *Rigoletto* fared little better and the engineers got the balance wrong, so that Thornton's deliciously blousy Maddalena dominates the recording. Success was finally achieved with the 'finale' of *Faust* and here Nellie sings the rising melody of the piece with exciting and rock-steady tones.[6]

Whatever reservations Nellie might have had about John McCormack's character had to be set aside when the Covent Garden season opened and they were rostered to sing six performances of *La Bohème* and two performances of *La Traviata* together. McCormack was 23 years Nellie's junior and his casualness offended her, but his voice did not. Both she and Tetrazzini had come to realise that McCormack's pure lyric tenor voice was the perfect complement to their own. Tetrazzini continued her triumphant run this season and Emmy Destinn, Lalla Miranda, Louise Edvina, Pauline Donalda and Nellie's old colleague from Brussels, Félia Litvinne, scored more successes when neither Nellie nor her Italian rival were on stage.

The first night of *La Bohème* with McCormack and Sammarco drew the largest audience of the season and the consensus of opinion was that Nellie's voice had lost nothing in beauty and power since it had last been heard in London.[7] As well as *La Bohème* and *La Traviata*, Nellie also sang Desdemona in one performance of *Otello*. The title role was sung by a second-rate tenor and his failure dampened the performance and resulted in the cancellation of two more. The honour of closing the 1910 season went to Tetrazzini, singing joyfully as Rosina in *Il Barbiere di Siviglia*. It had not been Nellie's happiest season at Covent Garden, with more factors than the death of the king contributing to her disquiet.

At the end of the Covent Garden season, Nellie, Murphy, Lemmoné and Ada Sassoli set out for the USA, where Nellie was committed to a concert tour and a return to the Metropolitan Opera after an absence of almost five years.

Within days of her arrival in New York, Nellie was back in a recording studio making 28 new recordings for Victor, of which 17 were issued. Most were remakes of earlier titles and some were fresh attempts at pieces that had not been satisfactorily recorded in London three months earlier. John Lemmoné contributed the flute obbligato to a new recording of Bishop's 'Lo, here the gentle lark' and before leaving America later in the year, Nellie volunteered to accompany Lemmoné at the piano in a recording of a flute solo.[8]

The nine-week transcontinental concert tour Nellie then undertook proved to be gruelling and by the time she returned to New York to sing at the Met she was exhausted and suffering from yet another bout of bronchitis.

The Metropolitan Opera was now under the management of Giulio Gatti-Casazza, former head of La Scala, Milan. The highlight of his 1910–11 season was to be the world premiere of Puccini's latest opera: *La Fanciulla del West*, starring Destinn and Caruso. New sopranos were replacing the 'old guard' at the Met, including Geraldine Farrar and Gatti-Casazza's wife, Frances Alda, and yet the new manager was wise enough not to miss the opportunity to exploit Nellie's enduring popularity in the US when the occasion presented itself. He had offered Nellie four performances at 2500 dollars per performance: two of *La Bohème* and one each of *Rigoletto* and *La Traviata*. Nellie's bronchitis prevented her from singing either performance of *La Bohème* and she was replaced by Farrar. In *Rigoletto* on 24 November, Nellie was partnered by the tenor

Florenzio Constantino, with whom she had sung in Hammerstein's company, with her beloved colleague Renaud as the tragic jester, both these artists making their Met debuts that night. The performance was a sell-out. John McCormack was also making his Met debut that season and partnered Nellie in *La Traviata* five nights later. Devoted fans made sure that this performance – Nellie's last at the Met – was a resounding success, although the house was only half-full.

Andreas Dippel, manager of the Chicago Grand Opera Company had also engaged Nellie for four performances with his company following her commitment at the Met, but illness again forced the number down to two. After Nellie sang Violetta, the distinguished critic of the *Chicago Tribune*, Glenn Dillard Gunn invited his readers to:

> Conceive the tone of a clarinet magnified and glorified by the quality of human sympathy. Augment the flexibility and facility of that instrument and remove from it every trace of tonal impurity; perfect its legato until absolute evenness of tone in point of rhythmical, dynamic and qualitative value has been attained, and it will suggest faintly the beauty, purity and sympathy of Madame Melba's voice.[9]

Nellie's star may have begun to dim a little, but when a critic who was himself a distinguished musician was inspired to write such words it is evident her charm had not.

On 1 December Nellie gave a concert with the Boston Symphony Orchestra and intimated to the manager of a new and highly successful opera company that had started up in Boston a year earlier that she might be persuaded to appear as a guest with his company while she was in town. The manager was Landon Ronald's brother Henry Russell, whom Nellie had known for years, but with whom she had never enjoyed the trust that marked her relationship with his brother. At the time she and Russell were not on speaking terms, so the negotiations that followed must have been farcical. Russell's wife Donna may have become involved for, unlike her husband, she had unqualified admiration for Nellie and described Nellie's voice as 'the greatest of all time'.[10] In the end Nellie sang one performance of *La Bohème* in Boston on 15 December and collected another 2000 dollars and another clutch of complimentary critiques. A week later she and her party embarked on the *Mauritania*, reaching London in a record five days, where George was waiting to be reunited with his mother.

Nellie's focus in 1911 had been on the tour of Australia by the opera company she was forming, but before that enterprise began she had another season at Covent Garden to complete – her twenty-sixth – the most notable feature of the season being Nellie's return to a role she had sung first at Covent Garden in 1887 and not sung in its entirety for seven years: Juliette in Gounod's *Roméo et Juliette*. Three weeks before opening night, Nellie had reached her fiftieth birthday. The appearance of a middle-aged Juliette with a spreading waistline must have taxed the audience's sense of credibility, but *The Times* reassured sceptics that 'Madame Melba's voice is scarcely less girlish than it was twenty years ago'.[11]

Nellie also undertook a 25-concert provincial tour. In half of these concerts she was accompanied by Landon Ronald's New Symphony Orchestra and by Ronald at the piano in the remainder. She also gave a concert in the Royal Albert Hall to mark the coronation of the new king and queen and another in the same venue with Henry Wood and his Queen's Hall Orchestra, advertised as 'Madame Melba's Farewell before her departure for Australia'. On 30 July Nellie embarked from Marseille (with George, John Lemmoné, a butler, a chauffeur and five maids), bound for Australia and the intention of fulfilling her final objective.

On arriving in Melbourne, Nellie was keen to see the progress that had been made on Coombe Cottage. Two wings had been added to the house, one containing an elegant music room and a rooftop sundeck had been constructed at one end of the house.[12] The gardens had been redesigned and a tennis court installed, soon to be followed by a swimming pool, described as 'a Roman bathing pool'. The transformation from a nineteenth-century farmhouse to an elegant twentieth-century villa had been completed with the installation of a power generator and a sewerage system. Nellie was pleased with the results, but had little time to enjoy them. It had been decided that the opera company would open in Sydney, so Nellie hastened there to take her place as prima donna of the first 'Melba-Williamson Grand Opera Company'.

The company Nellie and Lemmoné had assembled was not large, even by Australian standards. It was also not of the exalted standard Nellie had originally envisaged and promised on her previous visit. None of the famous singers (Bonci, Renaud, Sammarco etc.), whose names Nellie had let slip to the press as possible recruits, had been signed up. By and large, the company was comprised of young singers of promise, rather than established stars. Of the 33 principals (not including Nellie), only 18 were imported, the remainder being local singers from Australia and New Zealand. Of these 18, only a handful were names familiar to audiences in London or New York, but Nellie could console herself with the fact that Australians would be impressed (as they always were) by a sprinkling of foreign names and that J.C. Williamson's media machine would tout every single one as a star.

The company had just two other principal sopranos: the Pole Janina Korolewicz-Wayda, who had sung at Covent Garden, and a young Russian Marie Axarine, who was a pupil of Jean de Reszke and who had been engaged on his recommendation. Neither soprano would be a threat to Nellie's position as prima donna and that may account for their having been selected. There were two formidable contraltos: Marie Voluntas-Ranzenberg from Vienna and Eleanor de Cisneros, a tall red-headed American, who had sung at the Met and with Hammerstein's company. Outstanding among the 'local' singers was mezzo-soprano Rosina Buckman from New Zealand, who would go on to have a distinguished career at Covent Garden.

The principal tenor was John McCormack and his engagement must have been a bitter pill for Nellie to swallow, but swallow it she must because of the success they had achieved together at Covent Garden and the Met. In addition, the high proportion of Irish among Australia's population would flock to see and hear their compatriot. The other notable tenor in the company was Guido Ciccolini, a young Italian with a fine voice but a tendency to punctuate his singing with numerous sobs and sighs.

Among the lower-voiced male singers were Angelo Scandiani, whose fame now rests on his management of La Scala at the end of his singing career, the Canadian Edmund Burke, with whom Nellie had sung at Covent Garden, and a 28-year-old bass named Vito Dammacco, who contacted lymphadenoma while on tour and died in a Melbourne hospital.

The musical director and chief conductor was Giuseppe Angelini, a dynamic young Roman who was building a successful career in Italy; Marshall-Hall conducted *Lohengrin*, the only German opera in the company's repertoire. The orchestra and the chorus were recruited from scratch in Australia.

Publicly, Nellie towed the line and supported J.C. Williamson's claim that it was the greatest opera company to ever visit Australia, but in her heart Nellie knew she had only partially fulfilled her promise to the Australian people. In private she described the company members as good second-rate singers.

On Nellie's arrival in Sydney, she found the company assembled and ready to begin rehearsals – except for McCormack who had cabled to say he was going to be late. Nellie was furious. 'That man is a pig ... and a low one at that!' Nellie is reputed to have told Lemmoné while accusing the Irish tenor of trying to sabotage the whole venture. In fact McCormack's arrival after most of the other singers was a consequence of his commitments at Covent

Garden, partnering Tetrazzini in *Rigoletto* on one of the last nights of the season.

The company opened at His Majesty's Theatre in Sydney on 2 September with *La Traviata*, sung by Nellie, McCormack and Scandiani. The public and the press were enraptured and that mood was sustained throughout the Sydney season – at least on the evenings when Nellie sang. On other evenings audience numbers were lower.

The shortage of sopranos in the company meant that Nellie had to sing twice a week for eight weeks in Sydney, the same number in Melbourne for six weeks, and again when the company returned to Sydney for two final weeks. She sang Violetta, Gilda, Desdemona, Mimi, Marguerite in *Faust* and Juliette. In the fourth and fifth week in Sydney she contracted bronchitis and missed four performances, but still managed a remarkable 33 performances.[13] Nellie had also planned to fulfil her long-held desire to sing Tosca, but the rehearsal period for that opera coincided with her illness and the role was sung by Korolewicz-Wayda, whose voice was better suited to it. After listening to the Polish soprano – partnered by McCormack and Scandiani – giving the first performance of the opera in Australia, Nellie finally abandoned her ambition to sing Tosca.[14]

For Nellie, the Melbourne season offered the additional pleasure of seeing her father sitting in the stalls and applauding her, but in other ways it was less satisfying. The intention had been for the company to appear for eight weeks in Melbourne, but when ticket sales dropped off after six, the decision was made to cancel the final two weeks and return to Sydney. The Melbourne press were partly to blame. They praised the principal singers, but not the repertoire, complaining that, apart from *Tosca* and Saint-Saëns's *Samson et Dalila*, it offered nothing new and that more Wagner and more 'modern' operas should have been included. The point of the company – to showcase Nellie while she was still close to her prime – seems to have escaped them. The second Sydney season ended three days before Christmas with a mixed offering: the second act of *Aida* (with Korolewicz-Wayda), the fourth act of *Otello* with Nellie, and the last act of *Faust*, with Nellie, McCormack and Burke. And if that was not enough, the Irishman and the Canadian sang songs as encores and Nellie sang what the audience had been waiting for: 'Home, sweet home'.

Soon after the company disbanded, but Nellie stayed on in Melbourne until June 1912, to enable her to enjoy her new country retreat and spend time with her father. David Mitchell would live on for another four years, but Nellie must have feared that when she left she would not see her beloved 'Daddy' again.

Prolonging her stay in Australia had allowed Nellie to observe the work of a second overseas opera company in its tour of Australia. Under the leadership of the impresario Thomas Quinlan, who had managed one of Nellie's concert tours of Ireland, the 160-strong company was comprised of fine British and American singers (including Lalla Miranda and Edna Thornton) and brought its own experienced orchestra and chorus. In its first week of operations, Quinlan's company delivered what Nellie's had been accused of failing to deliver – Australian premieres of four works, including Wagner's *Tristan und Isolde*. Nellie graciously sent a large floral arrangement to Lalla Miranda and a letter of welcome to Quinlan. Another 12 years would pass before Nellie would bring a truly first-class international troupe 'down under' and lessons were already being learned.

As a consequence of her extended stay in Australia, Nellie missed the 1912 season at Covent Garden, but upon her return to England she did embark on yet another marathon tour. This four-month odyssey took her to 39 cities for 47 concerts, with Burke and the German pianist Wilhelm Backhaus as her supporting artists.[15] That the concert-going public in cities like Liverpool, Manchester, Birmingham, Glasgow and Dublin did not tire of parting with five shillings or seven shillings and sixpence to hear Nellie year after year is truly remarkable. Whenever her concerts were announced, ticket queues would form long before daybreak and Nellie would reward the 'faithful' by ordering urns of tea to sustain them and sometimes a piano so they might amuse themselves.[16] The British Empire's own 'Queen of Song', the successor to Adelina Patti and the only contender for the title in the foreseeable future, had become an institution.

In the middle of this tour Nellie returned to celebrate Christmas 1913 in London. George had remained behind in Australia to manage the Coombe Cottage farm, but arrived in London in early January to seek his mother's help in persuading a girl he had fallen in love with to become the second Mrs George Armstrong. This time Nellie approved of her son's choice. In 1909 when Nellie was in Australia she had encountered Evie Doyle, a mezzo-soprano from Brisbane. Nellie had been so impressed by the young singer's voice and character that she invited Doyle to accompany her back to England and had arranged for her to study with Marchesi. Doyle had then returned to Australia and commenced a modest career as a singer. George had become infatuated with the dark-haired and attractive Evie and had been courting her for most of the time they had known one another, but Evie was torn between marriage and a career. Marriage won and with Nellie's blessing, George and Evie were married at Marylebone Registry Office on 2 March 1914.

George's second marriage was as successful as his first had been unsuccessful, although it had a rocky start. While the couple were honeymooning, George developed appendicitis and had to undergo another operation. Evie took her new husband off to the south of France to recover but, while in Nice, George developed double pneumonia and pleural empyema. Doctors had to remove a rib in order to drain his lungs. Nellie's commitments in London kept her from being at her son's side during the nearly two months it took him to recover. George and Evie finally returned to Australia and took up residence at Coombe Cottage.

In April Nellie returned to Paris and gave three highly successful concerts at the Théâtre du Champs-Elysées and was warmly welcomed back by Parisians. While in Paris she also took out a lease on an apartment at 91 Avenue Henri Martin in the fashionable 16th arrondissement. Coombe Cottage was now 'home' to Nellie, but she set about decorating the new apartment luxuriously so that she might have a base from which to continue her career in Europe. As she signed the lease and began visits to the most elegant furniture stores in the French capital, Nellie could not have imagined that, within 15 months, Paris would be under threat of attack from German invaders.[17]

On 22 May Nellie returned to Covent Garden. Tetrazzini had sung for the last time at Covent Garden the previous season, while Nellie was in Australia.[18] It must have given Nellie satisfaction to have outlasted her rival, who would soon abandon her stage career in favour of concerts. At the age of 52 Nellie was firmly back in her place as Covent Garden's leading soprano and Caruso was also back at the house after an absence of seven years.

Nellie's first appearance was advertised as her 'silver jubilee performance'. It took place two days short of the twenty-fifth anniversary of her debut at Covent Garden. The king, who was on a state visit to Germany, sent a message of congratulations to Nellie. On 1 June that anniversary was celebrated again with a concert at the Royal Albert Hall, where Nellie sang arias from the two operas she had first sung in London: *Lucia di Lammermoor* and *Rigoletto*. Percy Grainger joined her for the concert, playing Schumann, Chopin and some of his own piano pieces.[19]

On 19 September, Nellie, along with her personal entourage, Edmund Burke and two French instrumentalists – Marcel Moyce (flute) and Gabriel Lapierre (piano) – embarked from Liverpool for New York and another 100 concerts across the United States and Canada. In New York they were joined by Jan Kubelik, who was to be the principal supporting artist to Nellie on this mammoth tour. For five-and-a-half months the party criss-crossed North America, from north to south and east to west, playing to sold-out houses. Clearly, Nellie had become as much an institution in America as she was in the United Kingdom; the stamina required to sing in city after city and concert hall after concert hall – all of which must have blurred into anonymity – was Olympian.

Touring also promoted record sales. Before leaving London, Nellie had made another batch of new recordings for the Gramophone Company, including a remake of the Bach-Gounod 'Ave Maria' with Jan Kubelik and an organ instead of a piano. It proved unsatisfactory and was soon replaced with a much-improved version, made in America with Kubelik and Lapierre. On the 2, 3 and 4 October (at the beginning of the American–Canadian tour) Nellie recorded 14 more sides in the Victor studios in New Jersey, seven of which were issued. When listening to them it is impossible to ignore the fact the voice is no longer in its youthful prime. On these discs we hear a middle-aged woman with a mature voice, still retaining the 'old-fashioned' style of singing – which was the only method Nellie knew – but the voice is remarkably well preserved. The breath seems inexhaustible (most of the time) and the intrusive 'beat' that afflicts many singers in middle age is absent. In comparisons with Nellie's earlier recordings, we hear that the upper notes still have the ability to thrill and the lower extension of the voice is warmer and richer.

Among these American recordings are a magnificent version of the aria 'Depuis le jour' from Charpentier's opera *Louise* and two more songs by Debussy. There are also some songs sung in English, which have timeless appeal, including: 'John Anderson, my Jo', a setting of a poem by Robert Burns. As she had throughout her career, Nellie avoided trying to dramatise such songs; instead she sings them with utmost simplicity and unexaggerated diction. The results are deeply moving.

In the middle of this most recent tour and while she was in Philadelphia, Nellie agreed to sing Gilda in a single performance of *Rigoletto* for the Philadelphia Grand Opera Company. The title role was sung by none other than Tito Ruffo and it seems neither artist objected to appearing together on this occasion. At the end of the same tour and in the week preceding her fifty-third birthday, Nellie returned to the Boston Opera Company. She appeared in a concert organised by Henry Russell, in which she was soloist with company's orchestra, conducted by the renowned Austrian Felix Weingartner, and in a gala in which she sang acts two and three of *Roméo et Juliette* with the very handsome tenor Lucien Muratore as her Roméo. Russell also persuaded Nellie to sing as a guest with his company when he took the whole enterprise (soloists, chorus, sets and costumes) to the Théâtre du Champs-Elysées in Paris for an eight-week season, commencing in late spring.

Russell's Paris season coincided with the 1914 summer season at Covent Garden, so Nellie found herself commuting between London and Paris. She opened the Covent Garden season in *La Bohème* with a new tenor, Giovanni Martinelli, at that time at the beginning of his long and illustrious career. Rosina Buckman had also joined the company and she sang Musetta, as she had with the Melba–Williamson company, with Nellie sharing some of the floral tributes with her at the opera's triumphant conclusion. Nellie's last appearance for the season at Covent Garden was also in *La Bohème*, this time with Caruso. She also sang the first act of *La Bohème* in a gala to commemorate a visit to London by the King and Queen of Denmark. This event proved remarkable for an entirely non-operatic reason. After Nellie and Martinelli had sung their contribution and the royal party were returning to their seats for the second act of *Aida*, two suffragettes staged a demonstration. One woman stood, waved her fists and shouted abuse at George V and another (in the upper gallery) showered the stalls with pamphlets.

In Paris Nellie sang in three performances of *Otello*, with the Italian tenor Edoardo Ferrari-Fontana in the title role. The first performance was delayed to enable additional rehearsals to be held for another opera. Nellie was nervous and when the curtain rose on *Otello*, it seemed her nerves were justified. A few lively young men in the capacity audience snickered when she appeared. This seems to have spurred Nellie on and when she sang they were silenced. Donna Russell remembered that performance vividly: 'I'll never forget her voice that night. It was divine. I can still hear it. No one has ever matched that quality. When she finished the audience rose in one body to applaud her.'[20]

Henry Russell had agreed to take his company from the Théâtre du Champs-Elysées to the Opéra-Comique for one performance as a benefit for that theatre's retirement fund. Nellie agreed to sing in *La Bohème*, marking her return to a stage on which she had not performed since 1890 and nor would again. The date was 5 June and it was the last time Nellie's voice was heard in opera in Paris. [21]

While she was on tour in America in February, Nellie had received news from home that her father required an operation to remove a papilloma from his bladder, a high-risk procedure for a patient aged 85. Nellie had immediately cancelled all her engagements after the Opéra-Comique performance and embarked for Australia. On board the *Orsova* as it steamed across the Indian Ocean, she received two messages. The first was personal. David Mitchell's surgery had become imperative, the operation had been carried out successfully and the patient was recovering.

The second message was of interest to everyone aboard. On 28 June Archduke Franz Ferdinand, heir to the Austro-Hungarian throne, and his wife had been assassinated by a young Serbian student in the Bosnian capital, Sarajevo. That event proved to be the trigger for transforming what had been an arms race between Germany and the rest of Europe into a war engulfing most of Europe and the Middle East.

Chapter 18

The empress of pickpockets

With her father now out of immediate danger and because she had been forced to cancel her Perth concerts in 1909, Nellie disembarked at Fremantle. John Lemmoné had come to Australia ahead of Nellie and recruited a small concert party, which included the fine Australian bass Malcolm McEachern.[1] This group joined Nellie in Perth, where they gave two concerts, followed by one each in the western goldfields towns of Kalgoorlie and Boulder.

Nellie reached Melbourne at the end of July and spent a happy week with her father at Doonside, delighted to find him recovering and still sprightly in mind and spirit. She then joined George and Evie at Coombe Cottage, her own spirits raised by the signs of an early spring and the flush of yellow wattle blossom across the landscape. But the idyll was soon shattered. On 3 August Germany declared war on France. The following day the United Kingdom and its dominions, including Australia, declared war on Germany and its Axis partners. The conflict described as 'the war to end all wars' had begun.[2]

Initially the Allies believed they could defeat the Axis forces by Christmas but that proved a vain hope. Within days, Belgium and northern France became battlefields, with opposing forces entrenched. On 20 August the Germans captured Brussels. Nellie must have been heartbroken to learn that the city where her stage career had begun was now a scene of destruction, suffering and violent death.

Nellie had planned to stay in Australia for several months, giving concerts and making preparations for the visit of the Boston Opera Company before returning to Covent Garden, but the war changed all that.[3] She now set about using the power of her name and her reputation to assist the war effort, and that meant a fundraising crusade on a grand scale.

The crusade began with a 'Patriotic Concert' in the Melbourne Auditorium. Remembering the fervour engendered at the coronation concert at the Royal Albert Hall in London in 1902, Nellie arranged for every member of the audience to be given a small Union Jack, which they were asked to wave at the end of the singing of the National Anthem. In London in 1902 the singing of that anthem had been shared with Clara Butt; Nellie now asked the Australian contralto Maggie Stirling to join her for the same purpose.[4] Another distinguished Australian bass, Frederick Collier, supported Nellie and the legendary actress Ellen Terry, who was touring Australia and staying at Coombe Cottage, offered her services to recite some verse of Rudyard Kipling. A local scout troop, called 'Melba's Own', formed a guard of honour for the arrival of the Governor-General and the state governors of Victoria and South Australia. The concert raised 1480 pounds.[5]

Nellie followed up with similar patriotic concerts in Sydney, Adelaide and Hobart, interspersed with smaller events in Lilydale, Healesville, at Scots' Church in Melbourne and in Ballarat, Geelong and Launceston. After the first concert, Nellie decided on a new strategy. At the conclusion of each subsequent concert she auctioned off flags of the Allied nations. At a Melbourne concert on the day after Anzac forces landed at Gallipoli, David Mitchell secured a Belgian flag for 100 pounds and was publicly thanked by his daughter. Nellie also offered farthing coins for sale. At the Sydney concert, the wife of department store owner Anthony Hordern contributed another 100 pounds in exchange for a coin valued at a quarter of a penny. At the Ballarat concert Nellie exhorted the young men in the audience to enlist in the army and several pledged to do so, although what some of their wives and mothers might have thought of the diva's intervention is questionable.

Away from the concert hall, Nellie experimented with a variety of schemes to extract money from her compatriots. When she encountered wealthy men socially, she asked them to contribute whatever money they had in their wallets to whichever fund she was currently supporting – but they were not to check the amount before handing it to her. An impressive display of vegetables grown at Coombe Cottage was put on show in a shop window in Melbourne and later auctioned, as was a box of cigarettes sent by Queen Alexandra. This was bought by the Tivoli Theatres boss Hugh McIntosh, who subsequently sold each 'gasper' for five shillings, returning the proceeds to Nellie. Nellie also judged a fundraising competition for dogs costumed in military outfits and auctioned a bulldog wearing a Union Jack at the conclusion of one concert.

Nellie's most substantial fundraiser (outside concerts) was a book compiled by her and which was published by George Robinson & Co. of Melbourne. A 176-page hardcover volume entitled *Melba's Gift Book*, it contained paintings, drawings, poetry and stories by prominent Australian painters and writers. There were literary contributions from Henry Lawson, C.J. Dennis, Aeneas Gunn, Dorothea McKellar and Gordon McCrae. Painters whose works were featured included Arthur Streeton, Frederick McCubbin, E. Phillips Fox, Norman Lindsay, George Lambert, Hans Heysen, Will Dyson and Bertram Mackennal. Many of the paintings were reproduced in colour and 'tipped in', adding to the attractiveness of the book. One or two pretentious critics complained that the content of the book should not have been confined to Australians and that more 'classical' pieces should have been included, but the public embraced it. The first printing sold out in days and further printings followed in quick succession.

By the middle of 1915 it was estimated that Nellie had raised over

30,000 pounds for the Red Cross, Wounded Soldiers' Fund, Belgian and Polish Relief Funds and the Lady Dudley Hospital Ship Fund. As she was leaving a concert hall one night after a patriotic concert, she was stopped by an elderly Scottish clergyman. In *Melodies and Memories* Nellie reported their conversation:

> In his broad burr he said to me, 'Madame, you have been called many flattering names in the course of your career. Do you know what I call you?' I laughed and said I had no idea. 'I call you the Empress of Pickpockets', he said.[6]

That was a title Nellie was proud of.

Being stranded in Australia also gave Nellie the opportunity to renew her practice of teaching talented young singers in Melbourne. George Marshall-Hall had left Melbourne University and established a new conservatorium of music in East Melbourne, an institution known as the Albert Street Conservatorium and later renamed the Melba Conservatorium. It was now directed by another Englishman, Professor Fritz Hart, a devoted admirer of Nellie, who beseeched her to conduct special classes for advanced singing students at the new conservatorium. The association flourished and in March 1915 Hart told the press proudly that 'Madame Melba has consented to head the singing department at the Albert Street Conservatorium for as long as she remains in Australia'.[7]

Among the singers Nellie favoured with her instruction and for whom she predicted great futures were three young sopranos, Stella Power, Gertrude Johnson and Strella Wilson, each of whom would later (like Elizabeth Parkina) have to endure the titles 'the Little Melba' or 'the New Melba'. Each of these young women admitted to being intimidated by Nellie when they first sang for her, but they explained how she put them at ease and how their lessons had been both productive and pleasurable. Gertrude Johnson would later claim that not only did Nellie teach her and her fellow students how to control and project their voices, but also how to deport themselves on stage, how to maintain good health and how to interpret the roles they would eventually sing.[8] In the 'Marchesi' tradition, Nellie organised a concert in the Melbourne Town Hall on 26 July to showcase the talents of 19 of her students, with these three featuring prominently.[9]

After Germany had announced that all Allied shipping – both naval and civilian – was fair game for their navy and following the tragic sinking of the *Lusitania*, Nellie had concluded that a return to Europe was too risky. In contrast, crossing the Pacific was safe and when Charles Ellis suggested a concert tour of the Unites States, Nellie jumped at the offer. The tour, Nellie calculated, would serve two purposes. Firstly, it would allow her to resume her international career and, secondly, to restore her income, which had declined since the outbreak of war.[10] Fearing that she might be accused of abandoning her war charity work by going on tour in the neutral United States, Nellie insisted Canada be included to enable her to stage patriotic concerts there. John Lemmoné was given the task of assembling a concert party and he engaged the American baritone Robert Parker, who had been a principal of the Quinlan Opera Company, the pianist Frank St Leger and the English cellist Beatrice Harrison, who was to join them in America.[11]

In July 1915 Nellie advertised that she would give a farewell concert in the Melbourne Town Hall before leaving for the United States, and that the proceeds would go to the Red Cross to assist their work for wounded Australian soldiers.[12] She personally invited 53 wounded soldiers who had been repatriated to Australia to attend the concert free of charge and arranged transport for them. Yet another distinguished Australian bass-baritone supported her in the farewell concert. On this occasion it was Horace Stevens, still practising as a dentist but destined for a distinguished career in opera and oratorio in the United Kingdom after the war. Also participating was the young Belgian pianist Frances de Bourguignon, who had been gravely wounded in the battle for Brussels. Nellie had generously sponsored de Bourguignon's emigration to Australia, paid his passage and welcomed him as a member of the 'family' at Coombe Cottage.

On 3 August Nellie farewelled her family and friends and travelled to Sydney on the overnight express. Two days later she, Lemmoné, Parker and St Leger embarked for San Francisco via Hawaii.

The tour began with two sold-out concerts in the Honolulu Opera House. Nellie was able to add another monarch to her list of acquaintances when Queen Liliuokalani of Hawaii attended the second concert. A round of concerts in California followed. In Los Angeles Nellie was given a VIP tour of the Keystone movie studios, there meeting Charlie Chaplin. Singer and actor discovered that they were kindred spirits. Chaplin took Nellie for a spin in his new motorcar and presented her with a magnificent travelling rug made of fox tails. When they dined together in an expensive hotel and the bill was presented, Chaplin performed one of his on-screen gags, looking dismayed to find his wallet empty, subsequently pulling out his trouser pockets, from which a cascade of silver dollars spilled.

Concerts on the east coast began with Nellie singing at a music festival in Bangor, Pennsylvania. In Boston she sang again with her favourite orchestra, conducted this time by an old friend from Berlin, Dr Karl Muck. Appearances followed all over the east and the Midwest with a change of supporting artists. Frank St Leger stayed on, but Parker and Harrison departed to fulfil other engagements and were replaced by the familiar Edmund Burke and the faithful Ada Sassoli.[13]

While in Chicago Nellie returned to opera, singing some performances of *La Bohème* and *La Traviata* for the Chicago Opera Association, a new company founded and managed by another old friend, Cleofonte Campanini. In New York she also made what would be her final batch of American recordings. On 12 January 1916 Nellie recorded two versions of the traditional song 'Annie

Laurie' and two versions of Dvořák's 'Songs my mother taught me'. Each piece was recorded with St Leger at the piano and again with orchestra conducted by Walter Rogers. The orchestral versions were published and the Dvořák piece is among Nellie's most beautiful and endearing recordings; the soft entry at the beginning of the second verse is a triumph for a singer on the higher side of middle age.

The patriotic concerts in Canada were accommodated between the 'commercial' concerts in the United States. The first was given in Massey Hall in Toronto; others followed in Montreal and Ottawa. The formula that had worked so well in Australia was revived – flag waving and flag auctioning – and a total of around 30,000 Canadian dollars was raised for the Red Cross. The Ottawa concert took place on 22 December and Nellie, Burke and Sassoli were invited to spend Christmas as houseguests of the Governor-General of Canada, the Duke of Connaught, third son of Queen Victoria. Nellie's old friend Lord Richard Neville was on the Governor-General's staff and his influence may have prompted the invitation. That vice-regal Christmas was also crowned with a special event. On the instructions of King George V, the Duke awarded Nellie the title 'Lady of Grace of the Order of Saint John of Jerusalem' in recognition of her war effort.[14]

George and Evie also spent that Christmas in North America but in less palatial surroundings. Nellie had invited her son and daughter-in-law to join her for the last leg of the tour. They agreed, but before meeting up with 'Madre' (as Evie called Nellie), they visited George's father and spent an icy Christmas in Charlie's cedar-shingle farmhouse on Vancouver Island. Evie was quite taken by Charlie, describing him as a fine-looking man, and Charlie with Evie. Together they trekked through the frozen landscape and Charlie roasted a giant turkey for their Christmas dinner. Tears flowed when the time came for parting.

Son, daughter-in-law and mother were reunited in San Francisco and, after a final round of concerts, all departed for Australia on the

SS *Wilhelmina*. Not long after the ship had made a brief stopover in Honolulu, Nellie received a cable telling her that her father was suffering from acute pleurisy and needed another operation. The procedure was carried out and David seemed to rally, but his condition then declined. On Monday 27 March 1916, the Melbourne *Argus* carried the following report:

> Expressions of regret were widespread on Saturday, when it was learned that Mr David Mitchell, father of Madame Melba, had died early in the afternoon. Mr Mitchell, although he had reached the age of 87 years, attended to his business up until last Tuesday. He then underwent an operation at a private hospital for an internal complaint. For two or three days after this operation his condition encouraged the hope that he would recover. But on Saturday morning his strength failed, and he died shortly after midday.

As the *Wilhelmina* was passing Suva, Nellie received another cable informing her of the sad news. Nellie was devastated. That she, George and Evie would not reach Australia in time for David's funeral was another blow, but there was a degree of consolation in learning that her last letter to her father had reached him before he died and that Nellie had been in her father's thoughts at the last.[15]

When the *Wilhelmina* reached Sydney, Evie disembarked to visit her mother and her brother Bill, who was a doctor, practising in impoverished Glebe. George continued to Melbourne with his mother, where Nellie isolated herself at Coombe Cottage to grieve for the man she claimed had meant more to her than all others. A week later Evie arrived in Melbourne, accompanied by her brother Bill and her mother, staying for a few days at Coombe Cottage, where the cheerful, practical doctor proved to be a spirit restorer for Nellie.

George meantime had tried again to enlist in the AIF and had been rejected a second time on medical grounds. This reminder of the war may well have been the trigger for Nellie to decide she needed to get back to work, resuming her teaching at the Albert Street Conservatorium and continuing to do whatever she could to support the war effort. The company of the young women at the conservatorium cheered Nellie's spirits and while much serious learning was undertaken it was enlivened with laughter and fun, in which Nellie willingly participated.

Nellie took a particular liking to one student, Ruby Gray, and to Ruby's cousin, Tommy Cochrane. Cochrane was gay and as camp in manner as was acceptable in those times. He adored the kudos that came from being a friend of the world's greatest diva, while Nellie for her part found him amusing and great company.

Still in mourning for her father, Nellie did not sing in public for many weeks, gradually easing herself back into concert life, although her return was interrupted in August when she contracted a bad bout of influenza. She took a seaside holiday on the Mornington Peninsula but her health did not improve so she decided to seek a cure further afield – in sunny Hawaii, which she remembered fondly from her visit the previous year.

In her typical style, Nellie gathered around her an entourage to support her on what she planned would be a five-month holiday, before she was due back in the US for more concerts. Evie was pregnant so she and George remained behind at Coombe Cottage. Nellie would have liked new friend Tommy Cochrane to accompany her, but his job as a clerk at the headquarters of the Dalgety Pastoral Company prevented that. Instead she chose her niece Nellie Paterson, Ruby Gray, another young soprano named Peggy Center, whom she had 'discovered' on her last visit to Honolulu and whom she had been teaching in Melbourne, along with her regular team of secretary, butler, chauffeur–minder and maids.

Nellie and her companions took up residence in a comfortable beachside bungalow on Oahu, swimming daily in the warm ocean waters. Sunshine and rest restored Nellie's health but after three months she had tired of Hawaiian society and of the island's voracious insect life, which revived unhappy memories of the sugar mill at Marion and Mackay. In late January 1917 while Nellie Paterson and Ruby Gray returned to Melbourne, Nellie travelled to California and a luxury hotel in Pasadena. There she was joined by a long-term friend from England, Lady Susan FitzClarence, whose husband had been killed at Gallipoli.

Nellie gave concerts in Los Angeles, Pasadena, Oaklands and Santa Barbara and, in April when the United States entered the war, she organised a mammoth charity concert in the San Francisco Auditorium. At the conclusion of the concert Nellie asked the audience to contribute more money and for several minutes a torrent of dollar coins rained down on the platform, with 8000 dollars ultimately raised.

Nellie had now become anxious to return to Australia to be present at the birth of her grandchild, for whom she had already purchased a vast wardrobe of clothes and baby furniture. But before she left the US. a cable arrived informing her that the child had died a few hours after his birth and that the birth had imperilled Evie's life. Once more Nellie was thrown into despair. Lady Susan had lost a child of her own soon after her husband's death and was able to provide some comfort. Nellie arrived back in Australia just in time for her fifty-sixth birthday, but Coombe Cottage saw no celebrations on that occasion.

In September, accompanied by Lady Susan, Nellie returned to the United States, where she was under contract to sing again with Campanini's Chicago Opera Association. Campanini had signed Nellie up for 18 performances of two roles: Mimi in *La Bohème* and Marguerite in *Faust* during a tour of the east and the Midwest, to be followed by a 10-week season in Chicago, a four-week season in New York and a two-week season in Boston. She had also agreed to give concerts under Charles Ellis's management while on tour with the opera company and later on the west coast, after her opera commitments had been fulfilled.

The opera tour was arduous for Nellie, made more so by a series of unfortunate accidents. During a performance of *Faust* in Fort Worth, Texas, a heavy bank of lights fell on her and she was knocked unconscious. One leg was badly cut and it was feared a wrist had been broken. When she regained consciousness and after resting and with her leg bandaged, the performance continued. The painfully lacerated leg was bandaged for several weeks and the bruising concealed by make-up and costumes. Another incident occurred in St Louis. When Nellie and Susan were being driven to a dinner party, their car collided with another and although neither passenger was injured both were deeply shaken. In Dayton, Ohio, Nellie suffered yet another misadventure, with the locomotive pulling the company's train becoming derailed but fortunately remaining upright. A potentially even more serious railroad incident occurred just outside Chicago one night, when Nellie's carriage became detached from the rear of the train and was left stranded on the line. Until assistance arrived, the brakeman warned approaching trains by waving a red lantern. During a performance of Meyerbeer's *Dinorah* Nellie attended in Chicago, an anarchist (or a gangster) detonated a small homemade bomb near her box. Again, no one was seriously injured, but on top of all the earlier mishaps it shattered Nellie's nerves. In the following days she developed a slight speech impediment, which did not affect her singing and may have been the result of exhaustion or some kind of 'mini' stroke. It was a further blow to Nellie's morale.

Bitter rivalry from within the opera company was also a problem Nellie was forced to confront. Among the sopranos Campanini had engaged were Mary Garden, the fine dramatic soprano Rosa Raisa, and a brilliant new star on the American operatic scene, Amelita Galli-Curci. Garden's and Raisa's repertoire did not overlap with Nellie's, but Galli-Curci's did. Campanini had assigned most of the roles Nellie had once sung with unparalleled success to Galli-Curci, and the public adored the younger, sweet-voiced singer as Lucia,

Violetta and Rosina. Nellie resented Galli-Curci's success, but drew some consolation from the comparisons made between them that appeared in print. The consensus of opinion was that the younger singer lacked the virtuosity and brilliance that Nellie had shown in her prime and was unlikely to ever acquire it.

In contrast, Nellie warmed to Rosa Raisa, who would earn fame a few years later as Puccini's first Turandot. Nellie invited Raisa to lunch, praised her singing and gave her good advice on conserving her voice. Raisa was equally impressed with Nellie. After she had attended one of Nellie's performances of *La Bohème*, she echoed Mary Garden's delight at Nellie's rendition of the last note at the end of the first act. Years later she recalled: 'I still remember her exit on the high C. It was like a glittering gem and when she sang 'Mimi's Farewell' in the third act that last F was so beautiful it still rings in my ears.'[16]

The critics in provincial cities shared Raisa's unreserved admiration for Nellie's singing, but when the company reached New York, the more astute critics there noted the changes that time had wrought on Nellie's voice – since 1910, when she had last sung in opera in their city. After her first performance in *Faust* on 4 February 1918, Sylvester Rawling in the *Evening World* noted:

> To say that Madame Melba's voice is as compelling as of yore would not be true. Some of the velvet quality of it has been rubbed off, but it remains a beautiful voice and to hear her is an object lesson to aspiring singers.[17]

Nellie's devoted fans – many of them now white-haired or grey-bearded – filled the Lexington Theatre on the evenings she sang, providing a similar reception to that of her glory days at the Metropolitan in the 1890s, with innumerable curtain calls and a sea of floral tributes. This season, however, marks the time at which Nellie must have come to the realisation that age, nature and a new breed of younger stars were forcing her to consider the time when her stage career would end.

Shortly before the previous Christmas, Stella Power (whose career Nellie believed was ready to begin in earnest), Frances de Bourguignon and Frank St Leger arrived from Australia to support Nellie in her American concerts, to be joined by the American tenor Arthur Hackett. Beginning in January and supported by this group, Nellie interspersed concerts with her appearances in opera, then embarking on the west coast tour. The American public took a liking to Power and admired her voice, which Nellie had helped to train – and that pleased Nellie.

The west coast tour was undertaken on a special train, arranged by Ellis. For the first time in her career Nellie sang in an outdoor venue, entertaining American troops at an army camp near Takoma, Washington. In Portland, Oregon, Nellie received news from George and Evie that they were expecting another child and asking 'Madre' to keep the news a secret. Nellie wrote straight back, expressing her delight and admitting that she had confided in Lady Susan and that her friend had insisted on being the child's godmother.[18]

While in Los Angeles for two concerts, Nellie, Lady Susan, Power and St Leger visited Hollywood and were entertained by Mary Pickford and Douglas Fairbanks. One remarkable photo, taken on that day, shows Fairbanks crouched on top of a tall filing cabinet looking down admiringly at Nellie and her friends. Nellie has a broad smile on her face but whether that was prompted by the actor's antics or the renewed prospect of becoming a grandmother is debatable.

Nellie's speech impediment was still lingering, but after a brief restorative stay in a sanatorium in Pasadena (under an assumed name) and a well-deserved holiday in Santa Barbara, it finally disappeared. At the end of May, Nellie and her companions sailed for Australia.

On Nellie's arrival in Sydney she would be bearing a different title; she would no longer be 'Madame Melba'. During the west coast tour she had read an article in an American newspaper that had surprised her. The paper reported that she had been created a Dame Commander of the British Empire, by King George V, again in recognition of her fundraising for the war effort. Nellie probably didn't believe the report, as she had not been consulted (as protocol required) on whether she would accept the honour *before* it was offered. Investigation proved the report accurate, with Nellie later learning that a bureaucratic bungle had prevented the letter offering the honour from reaching her. Nellie was delighted and overwhelmed with pride. The 'Empress of Pickpockets' had become 'Dame Nellie Melba' and henceforth she would be addressed as 'Dame Nellie'.[19]

Nellie arrived back in Australia in time for the birth of her grandchild. On 12 September, Evie Armstrong gave birth to a strong, healthy daughter. The names Pamela Helen Fullerton were chosen for her and little Pamela became the apple of her grandmother's eye, a focus of her love and attention for the rest of Nellie's life and eventually her heir.[20]

A month later Germany and the other Axis powers surrendered to the allies and an armistice was signed. At 11 am on 11 November the guns fell silent across Europe and the war came to an end. Nellie could look back on four years of turmoil and tragedy, but console herself with the certain knowledge that she had done her bit – and a great deal more.

Chapter 19

Old world, new order

On the day after victory was declared, Nellie sent King George V a congratulatory telegram and received a prompt reply: 'Thank you heartily kind message. Hope to see you soon in England'. Nellie was now determined to return to London to attempt to restore her career to its pre-war glory. Travelling to Europe in the first few months after the cessation of hostilities was difficult and the most feasible route was via the United States. Nellie therefore booked passage for herself and one maid on a ship bound for San Francisco out of Sydney. From there she planned to cross the American continent by train and sail from New York to Liverpool. It was a circuitous route and would take many weeks.

On New Year's Day 1919, Nellie arrived in Sydney, where John Lemmoné had organised a farewell concert for her in the Sydney Town Hall. The concert was to take place on 7 January and Lemmoné had engaged Andrew Black, Frances de Bourguignon and the violinist Leila Doubleday to provide support. Lemmoné himself planned to play a couple of flute solos, but two days before the concert he suffered a stroke. Nellie would have wanted to be at his bedside, but the following day she had an engagement she could not postpone. On 6 January Nellie presented herself at Admiralty House, where the Governor-General (on behalf of the king) invested her with her new title and the regalia of a Dame Commander of the British Empire. The following night the planned concert took place, sadly without Lemmoné.

John Lemmoné had become so important to Nellie that she could not leave without doing all possible to help him, hastily organising another concert at the Sydney Town Hall as a benefit for her long-time manager, friend and confidante. The artists who had appeared at the first concert offered their services free. Lemmoné was popular in Sydney and when the concert was advertised, Sydneysiders decided they also wanted to help, buying all the tickets within hours. On the night of the concert the front of the town hall platform was decorated with greenery, with the words 'OUR JOHN' picked out in pink roses in the centre. The concert raised 2113 pounds, but knowing that Lemmoné would object to accepting charity, Nellie placed the cheque for this amount in the bottom of a silver loving cup and had it filled with plums. On the cup was a note reading: 'Put in your thumb, and pull out a plum and see what your friends have sent you'.[1] A week later Nellie and her maid set out on the first stage of their journey.

The long train trip from the west to the east coast of the US proved arduous, and once in New York she was delayed for several weeks while the papers she needed to enter the United Kingdom were arranged. Equally frustrating for an impatient Nellie was Charles Ellis's inability to organise any concerts for her while she was marking time in New York. Finally, in mid-March, Nellie and her maid were able to board the trans-Atlantic liner *Caronia*.

Nellie arrived in London on St Patrick's Day and moved into the Ritz Hotel. One of her first acts was to contact Louis Philippe, whose wife had died. The touching reunion described in Chapter 8 took place a few days later. Nellie must have been deeply affected to discover that not only were *her* feelings for her former lover unchanged, but that nor were *his* for her – although just about everything else in London had.

In expectation of the arrival of George, Evie and Pamela in London, Nellie moved out of the Ritz and into a house she had leased at 22 Old Queen Street, Westminster. The magnificent residence belonged to an art connoisseur, who had filled it with treasures. It also overlooked St James's Park and would, Nellie had decided, be a perfect temporary home for her little granddaughter. It would also serve admirably as a venue for Nellie to reconnect with her society friends and there entertain them, but to her dismay she found many of the great aristocratic families of her acquaintance were still in mourning for lost fathers, sons and brothers. Behind the veneer of jubilation for the ending of the war hung a pall of sadness over broken lineages and a longing for past, happier, times. Former close friends, including Gladys de Grey and Alfred de Rothschild, were dead and, now in their city, Nellie felt their loss acutely.

Things were much changed at Covent Garden too. For a few years before the war, Thomas Beecham, a brilliant conductor and independently wealthy – thanks to his family's business (Beecham's Pills) – had been mounting innovative opera seasons of his own in London. The competition between Beecham and Covent Garden had been similar to that between Hammerstein and the Met in New York. Eventually the Grand Opera Syndicate had capitulated and invited Beecham to join them. Now, in 1919, Beecham was effectively running Covent Garden single-handedly.

When King George V had expressed a desire for Nellie to sing on the night Covent Garden reopened, the syndicate had complied. Beecham had reluctantly agreed, convinced no doubt by her drawing power and the profit she would undoubtedly generate for the house. Nellie had been offered a total of 12 performances, but as soon as she and Beecham met, sparks flew. Beecham's interests were in the German, Russian and 'modern' operatic repertoire and he had little time for ageing prima donnas who represented what he believed was a decadent branch of the art form. Nellie summed up her opinion of the autocratic Beecham by describing him as a 'dilettante upstart'. When Nellie arrived at Covent Garden for her first rehearsal, she found that the dressing room that had been reserved for her exclusive use for decades had been repainted a shade of green she didn't like. She stormed into Beecham's office to complain, but the conductor was a match for her. He pretended not to recognise her. The clash that followed became one of Covent Garden's legendary tales, recounted for years after. Neither party could claim victory but an armistice was reached out of necessity, because Beecham was to conduct four of Nellie's performances.

The night of Covent Garden's reopening was publicised in the press as the premier event of the 1919 season. When it was announced that King George V and Queen Mary and most other members of the royal family would attend, the demand for tickets was overwhelming. On 12 May 1919, the lights in the red-and-gold auditorium of Covent Garden glowed for the first time in four years, dimming as the great curtains swept back to reveal the setting for act one of *La Bohème*.[2] When Mimi appeared carrying her unlit candle, the audience gave Nellie a reception she would never forget, but sadness pervaded even this happy and triumphant moment. In *Melodies and Memories*, Nellie recalled:

> There has been no occasion on which I have been more satisfied, as far as one is ever satisfied, with my performance and I cannot remember ever receiving a greater ovation. There was so much enthusiasm – but so little brilliance. People in the stalls were wearing shabby tweed coats and while I have no objection to tweed coats (or shabbiness) that would never have happened on a Melba night in the past. And so many familiar faces were missing from the boxes that I felt as if I was singing to ghosts.[3]

In the third and fourth acts when tears were required, real tears flowed easily to Nellie.

Henry Coles, the newly appointed senior music critic for *The Times* wrote this perceptive account of the evening:

> The Royal Opera House syndicate had determined to revive former glories, to carry us back in memory to the time when Madame Melba was ... but there is no need to say what Madame Melba was,

because last night proved that she is just the same today. A 'Melba night' used to mean so many things besides Madame Melba. Last night was a 'Melba night' but only Madame Melba was quite what the phrase used to imply.[4]

Nellie gave three more performances of *La Bohème* during the season. For the first, she was partnered by the young and promising Lancashire tenor Tom Burke; for the remainder, her Rodolfo was the great Giovanni Martinelli. Both singers impressed Nellie and presumably behaved themselves more creditably than had John McCormack, for Nellie permitted them to take some curtain calls with her. Puccini was in London at the time and he attended the second performance of *La Bohème*, visiting Nellie in her (now repainted) dressing room to congratulate her for her service to his music and complimenting her for continuing to follow his score to the letter and singing, as he put it, 'Puccini' – not 'Melba-Puccini'.

Nellie also sang five performances of *Faust*. The title role was shared between Martinelli and the fine Belgian tenor Fernand Ansseau. One performance of *Faust* was also notable for being conducted by a 'replacement' conductor: the young Eugene Goossens, later to become director of the Sydney Conservatorium of Music.[5] Nellie also sang three performances of *Roméo et Juliette* with Ansseau and appeared in one gala performance, in which she sang an act each from *La Bohème* and *Roméo et Juliette*. The critics of all the major papers continued to praise her and Nellie must have felt as if she was back where she most belonged. *The Times* carried this letter from her:

> Since my reappearance at Covent Garden I have been overwhelmed with letters, telegrams, floral tributes and other forms of congratulations from countless people. It is physically impossible for me to acknowledge these individually; but to everyone who has expressed sentiments of appreciation and affection I am now and forever indebted. Will they please accept my warmest and most

heartfelt thanks? My heart is full, and I can only say that my joy at once more being in England is indescribable.[6]

To celebrate Nellie's fifty-eighth birthday, the Guildhall School of Music, of which Landon Ronald was still principal, held a reception for her. Nellie followed her former practice of appearing at concerts during and after the opera season.[7] The impresario Lionel Powell engaged her for five Sunday afternoon concerts at the Royal Albert Hall, where she shared the bill on different occasions with Clara Butt, Tom Burke, violinist Bronislaw Huberman, Vladimir de Pachmann (the pianist Nellie had first heard in 1886), the pianist-composer Ferruccio Busoni and two British pianists, Katharine Goodson and Adèle Verne. On the day before one of these concerts the death of Adelina Patti was announced. Halfway through the concert on the following afternoon Nellie asked the audience to stand in tribute to her erstwhile role model as Adèle Verne played Chopin's 'Funeral March'.

Nellie also sang at a number of charity concerts, including one at 10 Downing Street, and another in the old People's Palace on Mile End Road in East London. In addition, she volunteered to sing for the patients at St Dunstan's Hostel for Blinded Soldiers in Regent's Park. On 23 November Nellie led the applause from a front-row seat in the Royal Albert Hall when Stella Power made her London debut as soloist with the resident orchestra conducted by Ronald.[8]

Having George, Evie and Pamela with her in the Westminster house added to Nellie's sense of wellbeing and happiness and she delighted in strolling along the paths in St James's Park, feeding the ducks on the lake and showing off her granddaughter to passers-by. She also enjoyed attending Wimbledon (her throat protected from the wind with a sable wrap) to watch proudly as her nephew, Gerald Paterson, won the 1919 men's single's final.

In the autumn Nellie undertook a 20-concert provincial tour of the United Kingdom. On a couple of occasions her path crossed with Luisa Tetrazzini's, also on tour, and Nellie noted with satisfaction that, while she sang to full houses, her old rival had to cancel the occasional concert because of poor ticket sales.

In December it was announced that Nellie would sing again at the Opéra de Monte Carlo in the following February. Raoul Gunsbourg, who was still in charge of the company, had signed Nellie up to sing Marguerite in *Faust* and the same part in *Le Damnation de Faust* with her cherished colleague Maurice Renaud. Fate, however, intervened. In January Nellie came down with bronchitis and then began to experience pain in her abdomen. Bronchitis was familiar, but when the pain intensified and blood appeared in Nellie's stools she feared she had developed cancer and would suffer the same agonising death that had claimed Gladys de Grey. While coughing from the bronchitis, Nellie was poked and prodded by doctors, who concluded she was not suffering from cancer but colitis (inflammation of the colon). Medication, abdominal massage, dietary adjustments and rest would eventually cure the condition, but in the meantime, all engagements had to be cancelled, including her return to the Opéra de Monte Carlo.

Monte Carlo still seemed to be the perfect place for Nellie while she recovered, so as soon as she was feeling well enough she travelled there, taking George, Evie and Pamela with her. Bad luck intervened and slightly soured what had been intended as an idyllic holiday. Soon after their arrival at the Hermitage Hotel they were robbed. A gold purse of Nellie's filled with French francs was taken, as was Evie's cash and George's passport. While this incident was being sorted out, a letter arrived for Nellie from Harry Higgins, chairman of the Grand Opera Syndicate. Couched in apologetic terms, the letter explained that plans by the syndicate to re-engage Nellie for the 1920 season at Covent Garden had been vetoed by Beecham.

Having proved that she could still draw full houses at Covent Garden and earn praise from the London critics, Nellie was shocked. She was also angry. After serving Covent Garden well for 29 seasons, Nellie believed she deserved better than to be sacked by that 'dilettante upstart'. Although she did not know it at the time, she would return to Covent Garden after Beecham's departure but, at the time, it must have seemed as if a dark void had descended on her career.

From Monte Carlo Nellie travelled to Paris and installed herself in the Ritz Hotel. But there more health problems assailed her. She developed severe toothache and when she consulted a dentist he advised that her teeth were in a poor state; some would have to be extracted and others repaired. Her son, daughter-in-law and granddaughter had journeyed on to London, with Nellie following in mid-April, determined (despite a swollen face) to uphold her position in the city's musical life while Covent Garden continued without her.[9]

Lionel Powell quickly seized the opportunity and contracted Nellie for more Sunday afternoon concerts in the Royal Albert Hall. As in previous years, Powell surrounded Nellie with first-class supporting artists, including the young pianists Claudio Arrau and Arthur Rubinstein. To celebrate her birthday, Nellie organised a small party in the Old Queen Street house. As they sipped champagne, she sang for her guests and the violinist Jasha Heifetz played for them. Heifetz, aged 19, had made his London debut that season, billed as 'the modern Paganini'. Nellie had attended his debut recital, at the conclusion marching up to the platform and presenting him with a laurel wreath.[10]

Participation in one of the great historic events of the age presented itself to Nellie mid-year. The Marconi Company had been transmitting recorded music and news from their new radio station at Chelmsford for some weeks, which had been picked up by enthusiasts in the local area. When this proved successful, Marconi decided to broadcast a live studio concert at high frequency, which, if all went well, could be heard across Europe. This first international broadcast was being sponsored by the *Daily Mail* and the newspaper's owner, Lord Northcliffe, asked Nellie to provide the music. Nellie's first reaction was to refuse, saying that her voice was not for experimentation, but when Northcliffe offered her 1000 pounds to sing for 20 minutes, she changed her mind.[11]

The broadcast took place on 15 June. Nellie was positioned in front of a microphone in the bare, stone-floored studio. Herman Bemberg, who had travelled from Paris to assist, was seated at an upright piano, and George, Evie and a small group of friends watched from behind a window in an adjoining room. At 7.10 pm Nellie sang a trill to allow listeners to tune their receivers. She then sang Bemberg's 'Nymphes et Sylvains', 'Mimi's Farewell' from *La Bohème* and Bemberg's 'Chant vénitien', finishing off with one verse of the National Anthem. The broadcast was heard across Britain and in France, Italy, Spain, Germany, Poland, and throughout Scandinavia. In Paris, where the signal was strongest, loud speakers were set up in the Champs-Élysées and an estimated 5000 people listened in rapture. Radio would become an important medium in music performance during the next 100 years and it is noteworthy that an Australian was among its pioneers.

In July Nellie spent some time in Paris, there meeting the Swedish ambassador to France, Baron de Wedel-Jarlsberg. The baron and his wife invited Nellie to join them at their castle, Skogen, near Oslo, for a holiday.[12] It was the height of summer and Nellie accepted and revelled in the fresh air and relaxed atmosphere of the Norwegian countryside. The King of Norway, Haakon VII, and Queen Maud (daughter of Edward VII and Queen Alexandra) came to dinner at Skogen and Nellie offered to sing at a gala concert in the National Theatre in Oslo to support the families of Norwegian soldiers who had not returned from the war. The Norwegian royal family and the cream of Oslo society attended and 28,000 kroner was raised. After the concert King Haakon presented Nellie with the Norwegian Royal Gold Medal of Merit.

After her Scandinavian sojourn, Nellie returned to London, but not to 22 Old Queen Street. Her lease on that house had expired. When Evie had found that she was pregnant again, she and George had taken a house of their own in Knightsbridge, and rather than burden them with a houseguest, Nellie moved into the Ladies' Athenaeum Club in Dover Street, just off Piccadilly.

Concerts were resumed and Nellie embarked on another provincial tour, this time with the French-Algerian baritone Dinh Gilly, the violist Lionel Tertis and Una Bourne. Still not fully recovered from her recent health crises, Nellie found the pace of the tour draining both physically and mentally. Her spirits were further crushed when she received a telegram while in Edinburgh to tell her that Evie had given birth to a baby boy but once again the child had only survived a few hours. Nellie was devastated – for herself and for her son and daughter-in-law.

In January 1921 Nellie returned to Monaco – again engaged to sing for Raoul Gunsbourg – but this engagement almost ended the same way as the previous year. Nellie came down with influenza and was bedridden for ten days. So serious was her condition that her regular doctor in London was summoned, willingly coming to her aid.[13] By 1 March she had recovered enough to sing in *Faust* with Fernand Ansseau. In the days that followed she managed one performance each of *Roméo et Juliette* (again with Ansseau) and of *La Bohème*. After Monaco Nellie travelled to Brussels, where she had agreed to appear in a gala at the Théâtre de la Monnaie, the opera house in which she had made her stage debut 34 years earlier. She sang scenes from *Faust* and, for the only time in her career, the role of the Countess Almaviva in the third act of Mozart's *Le Nozze di Figaro*. Audiences in Monte Carlo and in Brussels welcomed her back like an old friend and acclaimed her singing with the same fervour as all those years ago.

Back in London Nellie organised a concert of her own in the Royal Albert Hall. It was billed as her 'farewell concert prior to a world tour' and 'the last time she would sing in England for a year', for Nellie had decided to return to Australia for an extended rest and to resume her teaching duties at the Albert Street Conservatorium.

That concert (on 8 May) proved to be the most memorable of her London appearances in years. Not long after dawn on the day, people queued several deep around the entire perimeter of the great building and into Kensington Road. Police were summoned to manage the traffic. The king and queen, along with their daughter Princess Mary, attended, but the occasion had a decidedly 'Aussie' flavour to it. The Australian national cricket team, in England to play test matches, formed a guard of honour with their bats when Nellie arrived and showered her with wattle flowers. The Australian aviators Sir Ross and Sir Keith Smith sat prominently in the stalls and the polite calls of 'Bravo' were almost drowned out by choruses of 'Coo-ee'. *The Times* described the event as 'enchanting', with no one more enchanted than Nellie. It was the perfect prelude to her return to her homeland.

A week later Nellie returned to the Gramophone Company's studios to make a small batch of new recordings. The company had approached Nellie in 1919 for more recordings but at the time she was feeling too exhausted to agree. Perhaps more from a sense of duty than genuine desire, she turned up on the afternoon of 12 May and recorded five sides. Three were issued, but only one is worthy of her reputation: the 'Chanson Hindoue' from Rimsky-Korsakov's opera *Sadko*. The last piece she recorded, which would prove to be Nellie's last studio recording, was, appropriately, 'Home, sweet home'.[14]

A week later Nellie turned 60 and on the eve of her departure for Australia, Princess Mary (to whom Nellie had given some singing lessons) called on her and presented her with a fan.[15] On 4 June Nellie left Euston Station for Liverpool, carrying a bunch of carnations sent to her from the Buckingham Palace garden. The crowd gathered on the platform to farewell Nellie gave her a hearty send-off. Two days later Nellie left Liverpool on the *Megantic*, bound for Montreal, en route to Australia, accompanied by George, Evie, Pamela, Una Bourne, Susan FitzClarence's brother, Bernard Yorke and the usual squadron of servants.

Chapter 20

Music for the people

Nellie found the long journey to Australia by sea, by land and then by sea again, arduous. She became short-tempered, complaining to the captain of the ship that carried her across the Pacific that the deck games obstructed her daily promenades and that the 'jazzy' music provided by a dance band in the first-class saloon kept her awake at night. Her mood improved when the ship arrived in Sydney and she was greeted at the wharf by John Lemmoné, George Allan, Fritz Hart and her brother Ernie. Nellie was delighted to find Lemmoné fully recovered from his illness and all the arrangements for the concerts she had planned finalised by him in his usual efficient way.

Nellie had been invited to stay at Government House prior to her departure for Melbourne. As she was being driven to the vice-regal residence, Nellie was told that news had just been received of Enrico Caruso's death in Naples. The press sought a reaction from her and the following day a generous tribute to her former partner appeared in the *Sydney Morning Herald* comparing him favourably to Tamagno, as well as to Jean de Reszke.[1]

Nellie gave two sold-out concerts in the Sydney Town Hall, supported by Una Bourne, Lemmoné and the State Orchestra of NSW, conducted by her friend from Brussels, Henri Verbrugghen. At the end of the second concert the orchestra played 'For she's a jolly good fellow' and the audience celebrated Nellie.

A week later Nellie was delighted to be back in the peace and tranquillity of Coombe Cottage, but the house on which she had lavished so much money proved frustratingly inadequate as a place to entertain house guests. Longing for company and diversion, Nellie soon began inviting just about every celebrity who visited Melbourne to stay at Coombe Cottage and there were not enough bedrooms nor bathrooms. Keeping servants at what was then a fairly remote location also proved a problem. When the mistress of the house was absent, only a skeleton staff was required, but when governors, visiting artists of world rank, generals and business tycoons were expected, the work load became gargantuan. Servants arrived and left (exhausted) and family members had to lend a hand, including Nellie herself, who was observed wielding a broom with determination. Among the celebrities who stayed at Coombe Cottage over the following few months were Clara Butt (now also a Dame of the British Empire), Kennerley Rumford, Lionel Powell, Lord Northcliffe and the painter Hans Heysen, whose depictions of gum trees Nellie considered the pinnacle of Australian art.

In September Nellie embarked on concerts in Melbourne, Sydney (again), Adelaide and in provincial towns. The number and frequency of these concerts led to rumours that she was about to retire and was bolstering her financial security by a final burst of work. These rumours spread as far as London, where *The Times* reported that Nellie herself had said she was preparing to make way for new singers. Nellie hastily denied the rumours, explaining her remark had been misinterpreted and that the idea she was ready to retire was 'ridiculous'.[2]

Rumours of retirement were not the only problems Nellie was confronting. Soon after her return from the busy concert tour, she began to experience bleeding from her vagina. Since she was post-menopausal, the fear of cancer loomed once more. Exploratory surgery was recommended, so in mid-October Nellie entered St Ives Private Hospital in East Melbourne. No malignancy was found and a relatively simple surgical procedure to her uterus seemed to remedy the problem. As Nellie was about to leave hospital, she received news that her brother Frank had died of pneumonia at Doonside.

Nellie was well enough to attend the funeral of the first of her adult siblings to die, the solemn service held at Lilydale Cemetery. Nellie placed lilies grown at Coombe Cottage on her brother's grave.

Distressed by the rumours that she had been 'feathering her nest' with her recent concerts, Nellie and Lemmoné planned another series, with the ticket prices set at a uniform five shillings for any seat in the house. Using a phrase that would later become familiar to Melbourne residents – thanks to the labours of conductor Hector Crawford at the Sidney Myer Music Bowl – the concerts were advertised as 'Music for the People', and the people responded gratefully. Over December 1921 and January 1922 Nellie gave 16 more concerts in Melbourne and Sydney, supported by Verbrugghen and his orchestra in Sydney, and by the fledgling Melbourne Symphony Orchestra, conducted by Alberto Zelman.[3]

With these concerts barely over, Nellie embarked on another series, advertised as her farewell concerts before she returned to Europe. Extending north to Brisbane, this farewell tour was made even more remarkable by a publicity stunt managed by Nellie. Upon her arrival in Sydney on the overnight express from Melbourne, she told the press that she had been 'eaten alive' by fleas in her sleeping compartment and that only modesty prevented her from displaying the bites concealed under her clothing. There may well have been a flea or two on the train, but the plague Nellie described was undetected when railway authorities set about cleaning the carriage. The story spread rapidly and featured in almost every newspaper in the country and ticket sales for her concerts skyrocketed.[4]

On her final visit to Sydney, John Lemmoné introduced Lindley Evans, a pianist with whom he had worked, to Nellie. Nellie asked Evans if he knew Debussy's 'Clair de lune', then not as well known as it later became. It happened that Evans knew the piece and was able to play it perfectly from memory. Nellie immediately asked him if he'd like to be her accompanist when she toured Britain in a couple of months. Evans was flabbergasted but leapt at the opportunity.

A working relationship that lasted for as long as Nellie continued to sing was established. Years later, Evans would become a popular figure in Australian musical life as 'Mr Melody Man' on the ABC radio program *Children's Hour* but in 1921 he was a young man about to embark on the adventure of a lifetime.

Despite the success of her Australian concerts, controversy and the accusation that she was an alcoholic resurfaced with distressing frequency. As she was being driven over Prince's Bridge in Melbourne on one occasion, a man called out: 'There goes Champagne Nellie', and after Evans had entered Nellie's employ, a 'lady' approached him one day and whispered in his ear: 'Don't let her spoil you. You know she *drinks*.' These two examples were typical of the many. As she had for 20 years, Nellie deliberately ignored the allegations, but in private they must have hurt her deeply, arising as they did only in her homeland.

One group who would have had no doubts over Nellie's sobriety were her students at the Albert Street Conservatorium. During the 13 months Nellie was in Australia, she taught regularly at the conservatorium when not on tour. Her 'girls' now wore uniforms that Nellie had designed for them, an unbecoming smock with a large 'M' embroidered on the front. In August a group of these young women farewelled Nellie at Spencer Street Railway Station when she departed for Perth on the first leg of her journey back to Europe via the Indian Ocean. Bernard Yorke travelled with her, as did Lindley Evans, who recorded some of his memories of the voyage in his autobiography, *Hello, Mr Melody Man*.

The Viceroy of India, Lord Reading, had invited Nellie to visit India and, consequently, she and her entourage disembarked at Bombay (Mumbai). As their visit coincided with the wet season, Lord Reading and his staff were in residence at Simla (Shimla), forcing Nellie to travel for 48 hours by train to that quaintly English town in the foothills of the Himalayas. There she was an honoured guest at the vice-regal lodge, but the high altitude made her feel lightheaded and slightly nauseous. On 10 October the Viceroy's birthday was celebrated with a party at the lodge. Nellie presented Lord Reading with a copy of *Melba's Gift Book* and sang the 'Jewel Song' from *Faust* and 'Mimi's Farewell' from *La Bohème* for his guests.

For Nellie's journey south to resume her sea voyage, the viceroy provided the carriage that had been used by the Prince of Wales on his tour of India the previous year. Stops were made at Delhi to enable Nellie to view the Red Fort and at Agra, where she was an overnight guest of the Maharajah of Uttar Pradesh. She found the young Maharajah charming but was unnerved by his pet tiger cub, which stalked their footsteps. In the evening when the heat receded, she was taken to view the Taj Mahal, and in the warm, scented twilight she sang a trill that echoed magically through the cavernous building.

As she had planned to stay in Europe for extended periods in the future, upon her arrival in London Nellie purchased the lease on an unfurnished house at 15 Mansfield Street, W1. The house dated from the eighteenth century and had four fine reception rooms, one graced with a ceiling by Robert Adam. Nellie employed an old friend, Marquis Boni de Castellane, to help her to furnish the house, and under his guidance the gilt furniture, bric-a-brac and velvet Nellie had favoured in all her previous houses were rejected. The result when the work was completed was simpler and far more elegant.

This change in Nellie's taste was also reflected in her choice of clothing and accessories. The multilayered trappings of the Victorian and Edwardian modes were finally discarded and she changed how her hair was dyed. Since about 1900 Nellie had been having her hair dyed jet black, but now favoured a more muted shade, which softened her features. She also had some of her jewellery reset into contemporary styles. The new image was still formidable but more in keeping with the 1920s.

As soon as she had settled into her new home, Nellie embarked on a provincial tour of the United Kingdom, but when singing in Scotland the bleeding problem returned. Another surgical intervention was required and when doctors in a Midlands hospital performed the procedure they found a suspicious mark on Nellie's uterus, which they suggested would need further investigation when Nellie returned to London.

Undeterred by this news, Nellie gave two sold-out concerts in London and offered her services to sing again at Covent Garden. Thomas Beecham had departed from the Royal Opera House and his company had been replaced by a new one – the British National Opera. As its name implies, the 'BNOC' as everyone called it, was made up of British singers, including several from Australia and from the other dominions.[5] The aim of the company was to perform all operas in English and at prices working-class people could afford. The intention was commendable, but the execution left a lot to be desired. The reduced income from the lower ticket prices meant that the staging and costumes were often bleak and threadbare and the glamour great international stars had brought to previous seasons was sorely missed. The aristocracy, who had patronised Covent Garden in the past, stayed away and in consequence, missed some wonderful singing. Nellie admired what the company was trying to achieve and, by offering her services free of charge, hoped to draw some of her old fans back to the house and assist the company financially.

The company decided to raise the ticket prices by a few shillings for 'Melba Nights' and the increased cost didn't deter the public, who clamoured for tickets as soon as it was announced that Nellie was returning to Covent Garden after an absence of four years. Also returning were many of Nellie's aristocratic friends, with George V sending a note of apology, explaining that he would be absent from London on the first night Nellie sang and sending his best wishes for her success.

On 17 January Nellie sang in *La Bohème* with a British cast that included the Australian Frederick Collier and was conducted by the company's musical director Percy Pitt. Nellie was permitted to sing in Italian while the rest of the cast sang in English. Pitt also happened to be musical adviser to the newly established British Broadcasting Company and through his auspices the performance was broadcast by the BBC across the south of England, to the Midlands and to the Continent. At the end of the performance Nellie made a speech, encouraging the public to support 'this wonderful, brave company'. The next morning the critics were kind in their remarks, but didn't have much to say about Nellie's performance except that she showed a little more effort in her singing than in times gone by. Readers might well have read more into what the critics *didn't* say than what they had.

The second (and last) 'Melba Night' was to be a gala, in which Nellie would sing in the last two acts of *La Bohème*, preceded by two acts of *Aida* with the Australian Florence Austral in the title role. On the morning before this gala, as Nellie was arriving for a rehearsal, she noticed an enormous crowd waiting to buy tickets. She instructed her driver to stop, got out of her car and for the next 20 minutes mingled with the crowd, shaking hands and signing autographs. The crowd clapped and cheered as Nellie made her 'regal' progress among them. At the conclusion of the gala and surrounded by floral tributes, Nellie made another speech, in which she said that if she was invited she would love to sing with BNOC again.

Nellie also sang in several concerts in London, deliberately choosing fellow Australians to support her, among them Malcolm McEachern, flutist John Amadio and cellist Laurie Kennedy, with Lindley Evans doing sterling work at the piano.[6] The biggest 'Aussie' event in which Nellie participated was a reception at Australia House, followed by a broadcast concert, to celebrate Australia Day. Nellie had promised to sing but had a 'sniffle' on the day. She did attend and mixed with some 1000 guests, including the Prince of Wales (later Edward VIII) and Winston Churchill, and made a short speech at the beginning of the broadcast.[7]

That month Nellie also met another Australian who would feature in her life from then on. As Nellie left the Athenaeum Club one day, she was approached by a young male journalist, who introduced himself as Beverley Nichols. Nichols was working as a reporter for the *Sunday Dispatch* and had been sent to elicit Nellie's opinion on the recent execution of Edith Thompson, convicted of her husband's murder but widely believed to have been innocent. The well-balanced article Nichols subsequently wrote impressed Nellie and she warmed to the handsome, 24-year-old Oxford graduate who, like Tommy Cochrane, was conspicuously gay and therefore no threat to her reputation. She was also impressed by Nichols's service in the Intelligence Department at the War Office during the First World War and his talent as a pianist. Nellie offered Nichols the job of her private secretary and he accepted. Nichols remained in that role and in Nellie's favour for the remainder of her life, although others were suspicious of the new secretary's character and his motive in becoming her confidante and, as one wit put it, 'her handbag carrier'.

Nichols was fascinated by Nellie and especially by her voice. 'Do a trill for me', he would often request in years to come and his employer would willingly oblige. A few months after they had met, Nichols persuaded Nellie to allow a Professor Low to 'photograph' her voice using a device Archibald Low had invented called an 'audiometric camera'. Nichols recalled years later that Nellie was reluctant at first, but when he suggested that the British Museum would surely want copies of the photographs Nellie agreed. As Nichols recounted, Nellie had reasoned that Patti had *not* made it into the British Museum nor had Tetrazzini; therefore, if she agreed, it would be a victory.

The professor turned up at Mansfield Street one afternoon and Nellie sang into his machine. The resulting photographs caught the sonic vibrations of Nellie's voice and resemble the charts generated by a seismograph recorder. Low captured Nellie's trill and several individual notes, and in September that year the photographs were exhibited by the Royal Photographic Society. The photograph of Nellie's trill is especially interesting. Other singer's trills were also photographed and revealed irregular variations in pitch. The efforts of the 61-year-old Nellie display remarkable precision and uniformity as the voice moves between two notes a semitone apart. One can imagine Nellie later tapping her finger against these irrefutable images and muttering something like 'I told you so'.[8]

In Australia the previous year Nellie had discussed with executives of J.C. Williamson's the possibility of bringing another Melba–Williamson opera company to Australia and her idea had been well received. In London Nellie had set to work with Williamson's European representative, Nevin Tait, to sort out the details.

For the manager of the company, Nellie suggested Henry Russell, and Tait agreed. Russell had given up management of the Boston Opera Company and returned to Europe, broke and unemployed. Whatever differences may have marred their relationship in the past, Nellie was prepared to disregard past disagreements in order to take advantage of Russell's proven management skills. At the time Russell and his wife were living in Rome and when agreement was reached, he began auditioning singers there. As soon as she had fulfilled her immediate commitments in London, Nellie set out for the Continent with Nevin Tait to assist Russell in his search. Nellie recognised that she would not be able to bear the lion's share of the soprano roles, as she had with the 1911 company, and wanted to be on hand when a soprano was selected to sing her former roles. Lessons had also been learned from the 1911 company and Nellie was determined to have a greater number of principals in the company to share the work load and provide variety for patrons.

Nellie stopped briefly in Paris in order to visit Sarah Bernhardt. She had been told that the great tragedienne was dying from kidney disease and Nellie hoped to offer what little comfort she could to someone who had helped her at the beginning of her career. Laden with flowers, Nellie returned to the house in Boulevard Pereire, which she had first visited with Mathilde Marchesi 34 years earlier. There she found Bernhardt lying in bed, satin sheets concealing the absence of one leg (amputated some year earlier) and looking desperately ill. In *Melodies and Memories*, Nellie describes the meeting:

> 'Ah! Melba!', she said, clasping my hands in hers. 'Tu as toujours ta voix d'or. Ma voix d'or n'a plus besoin de moi, car je meurs.' ('You still have your golden voice. My golden voice doesn't need me anymore, because I am dying.') But even in the face of death she was acting, with her fair wig, scarlet lips and rouged cheeks. When I said goodbye she clung to me and later I found my own cheeks were covered in Sarah's rouge.[9]

Nellie and Tait met up with Russell in Nice and together they visited Jean de Reszke. The search for singers continued for a month, in Monte Carlo, Milan, Rome and Naples, and by the time Nellie returned to London at the end of March she was satisfied that they had been successful and she was content to leave the remaining details to Tait. Twenty-seven 'foreign' principals had been engaged (compared with 16 in 1911) and among them were several singers in their youthful prime and already major stars in Italy. A soprano had been found to sing the 'Melba' roles – one who met with Nellie's approval, was sure to appeal to Australian audiences and who was so different from Nellie in appearance, personality and voice that direct comparisons between them would likely be avoided.[10]

Nellie's return to London had been required because she had been invited to sing again with the British National Opera and had, as she had promised, agreed. On 14 April *The Times* announced that the company's summer season would open on 14 May with Nellie in *La Bohème* and that she would also sing Marguerite in *Faust*, Juliette in *Roméo et Juliette* and 'several other roles', but that announcement proved premature.

Remembering the advice she had received in the Midlands about the 'mark' on her uterus, Nellie consulted a London gynaecologist before rehearsals began at Covent Garden. The gynaecologist recommended urgent exploratory surgery. Nellie was admitted to a Mayfair private hospital. There the 'mark' was identified as a malignant lesion and Nellie agreed to a hysterectomy as the best option to stop the cancer spreading. The BNOC was advised that Nellie's appearances with them in the forthcoming season would have to be indefinitely postponed.

The high-risk operation was successfully completed, with Nellie assured that no other malignancy had been found. After being discharged from the hospital and rather than returning to her home in Mansfield Street, where the press would have harried her, Nellie travelled to Hove on the south coast of England and took a suite in a quiet hotel under an assumed name. There she slowly recuperated in the care of a specialist nurse. From the hotel Nellie wrote to Evie in Australia, saying that she had been terribly ill but was slowly regaining her strength and wished that she was back at Coombe Cottage, surrounded by her loved ones.

By the end of May Nellie was well enough to commence rehearsals at Covent Garden and, in her opinion, she needed to get back to work urgently. On her return to Mansfield Street from Hove, she had found a bill for 4000 pounds in income tax awaiting her. Nellie paid up reluctantly. The previous October she had written an indignant letter to *The Times* complaining how the new income tax laws could kill opera as an art form: 'People cannot pay exorbitant taxes and support the opera at the same time', she had written and now she was experiencing the new laws firsthand.[11]

Nellie's return to the BNOC on 1 June marked her thirty-first season at Covent Garden. During that month she sang three performances of *La Bohème* with a different Rodolfo each time – Joseph Hislop, then Tudor Davies and finally Charles Hackett, the younger brother of Arthur Hackett, with whom she had sung in America. She also sang in two performances of *Faust* with the Canadian Edward Johnson (future manager of the Metropolitan Opera in New York) in the title role. As they had during the previous season, the critics were kind to Nellie when reviewing her performances, commenting on the remarkable preservation of her voice and the inevitable losses time had imposed.

The concerts Nellie gave in London at this time had a decidedly Russian flavour, due to her association with the bass Alexis Obolensky, whom she had met in the south of France. A former officer in the Tsar's cavalry, who had fled Russia during the revolution with only a violin and a string of his wife's pearls, Obolensky claimed the title 'Prince' and also that his family could trace their lineage back to the ninth century. Photos of him show a rather stern-looking individual with a crop of thick dark hair, impressive eyebrows and a moustache to match.[12]

Obolensky supported Nellie in a Royal Albert Hall concert on 24 June and two days later Nellie hosted a recital by Obolensky in the drawing room at Mansfield Street, attended by Queen Alexandra and her sister, the Dowager Tsarina Marie Feodorovna, who remembered Nellie from St Petersburg. A week later they sang together at a musical party in Carlton House Terrace and Queen Alexandra invited Nellie and Obolensky to sing for her and the Dowager Tsarina at Marlborough House. The interest the former Empress of Russia displayed in the singing prince suggests he may have been her protégée, but the only reason for Nellie's interest in him seems to have been related to her desire to rub shoulders with royalty, his talents being quite unexceptional. That, however, did not stop Nellie inviting Obolensky to join the company touring Australia. After the Marlborough House concert, Queen Alexandra presented Nellie with a necklace and an impressive photograph of herself, her daughter Princess Victoria and the Dowager Tsarina, all three looking incredibly regal above their handwritten signatures.

As soon as the London season ended, Nellie left for the Continent and spent several weeks at Evian, on Lake Geneva, taking the waters and trying to build up her strength before embarking for America and Australia. On 22 September she sailed from Marseilles on the liner *Olympic*, accompanied by Obolensky. Over the next two months the pair gave concerts across Canada, from east to west, travelling across the border for more concerts in northern cities of the United States. Nellie reached Australia in time to spend Christmas at Coombe Cottage and to begin preparations for the 1924 Melba–Williamson opera company's first season, in Sydney in March.

Chapter 21

Tempus fugit

The 1924 Melba-Williamson Grand Opera Company was the finest Italian opera company to perform in Australia up to that time. Not all the singers were Italian, but most of the repertoire was and there was only one novelty: Giordano's *Andrea Chénier*, which had not been performed in Australia previously.[1] The repertoire left the company open to criticism, but the singers did not. Nellie took her place as prima donna, singing Mimi, Marguerite in *Faust* and Desdemona. During the 28 weeks the company performed in Sydney, Melbourne and Adelaide, Nellie missed only a handful of performances when she came down with bronchitis in Sydney, which also prevented her from singing a fourth role she had hoped to sing, Juliette. The 'House Full' sign appeared at every 'Melba Night' and 'Melba Matinee'.

The soprano chosen to sing the other 'Melba' roles was 30-year-old Toti dal Monte, short in stature but with an engaging personality and a bright, birdlike voice, which lacked the richness of Nellie's voice in its prime, but which was used with astonishing virtuosity. The Australian public adored her off stage and on stage as Lucia, Gilda, Rosina, Amina in Bellini's *La Sonnambula*, Norina in Donizetti's *Don Pasquale* and the doll, Olympia, in Offenbach's 'The Tales of Hoffmann'. Nellie probably did not share the public's enthusiasm to the same degree but, according to dal Monte, treated her with kindness and the respect due to her.[2]

The leading tenor was Dino Borgioli, a lyric tenor in the Bonci-de Lucia tradition with a beautiful voice, a patrician singing style and, according to Nellie, 'good legs'. Borgioli sang more frequently with dal Monte than with Nellie, but Nellie had no complaints about Nino Piccaluga, the rich-voiced tenor from La Scala, who partnered her in *La Bohème*, or the Spaniard Antonio Marques, who sang Otello to her Desdemona.

Outstanding among the lower-voiced male singers was Apollo Granforte, probably the best baritone to sing in opera in Australia until Tito Gobbi, a guest with Opera Australia in the 1960s. Granforte's Rigoletto, Iago, Scarpia and Tonio were electrifying – vocally and histrionically.[3] There were also several singers in the company with whom Nellie had sung at Covent Garden and in Monte Carlo and a smattering of Australians, including Stella Power and the tenor Alfred O'Shea, who had recently sung with success in London. Most of the male members of the chorus had been imported from Italy and that caused some protest from local singers and a couple of politicians seeking publicity. The musical director and chief conductor was Cuban-born Franco Paolantonio, who conducted regularly at La Scala. He was supported by Arnaldo Schiavoni, a pupil of Mascagni, who had conducted for Russell in Boston, and Frank St Leger, who took up the baton to lead occasional performances.[4]

Even before the company opened its Melbourne season, a new rift had developed between Nellie and Henry Russell. Russell and his wife were staying at Coombe Cottage when Donna Russell entered for a party one night wearing an almost identical gown (from the same Paris couturier) as Nellie had chosen to wear. That social gaff might have been forgiven in time, but when Russell informed Nellie two weeks later that he, as manager of the opera company, forbade her to sing Marguerite in *Faust*, Nellie's fury was volcanic. Henry Russell's name was removed from all the opera company's publicity and he and his wife departed in haste for Europe, threatening all kinds of legal action.

The company's performances were enthusiastically acclaimed by the public and the critics, and the inevitable problems that beset touring opera companies were overcome by Nevin Tait and his colleagues at J.C. Williamson's, ably assisted by John Lemmoné. Nellie found the pace exhausting, as might be expected, for she had reached her sixty-third birthday during the first Melbourne season.

The company's final performance, on 13 October in Melbourne, featured Nellie and was advertised as her final appearance in opera in Australia. Inevitably, the opera chosen was *La Bohème*. This gala event was planned as a celebration of her achievements and as a benefit for limbless soldiers. The great and the good of Victoria turned out in force to support a worthy cause and pay tribute to Nellie.

At the end of the opera and while the cast took their bows in front of the curtain, the scenery was cleared away and replaced with a six-metre-high circular screen of pink rose petals, with a sea of floral tributes arranged below it. When the curtain ascended again, electric bulbs, set among the petals, burst into light carrying the message 'AUSTRALIA'S GREATEST DAUGHTER – OUR MELBA'. Standing in the midst of the floral tributes was Nellie, looking tired and close to tears. When she stepped forward and bowed, paper streamers thrown from the galleries fell around her. The whole spectacle was brilliantly drawn by Daryl Lindsay and featured on the front page of the *Herald* the next morning, along with a flashlight photo, in which Nellie looks startled.

The Prime Minster, Stanley Bruce, came on stage and made a speech and Nellie responded. She thanked the public for their generous support, also thanking the artists of the company for their hard work and confirming that the performance she had just given would be her last on stage; she was retiring from opera. That announcement was greeted with much regret but probably less surprise – and would prove to be premature.[5]

Nellie spent the next few weeks at Coombe Cottage and then embarked for England. As she steamed across the Indian Ocean, news arrived that Giacomo Puccini had died of throat cancer in

Brussels. Back in her house in Mansfield Street, Nellie entertained a few close friends, but could not shake off the feelings of exhaustion and ennui that had plagued her since the end of the opera season in Australia. She booked herself into a fashionable London nursing home for tests to determine the underlying cause.[6] Diabetes was diagnosed and Nellie put on a regime of two insulin injections per day for the rest of her life. This necessitated employing a nurse full-time to live and travel with her, which Nellie described as 'frightfully expensive'.

As soon as she was well enough, Nellie travelled to Paris to consult an eye specialist about the rapid deterioration of the sight in one of her eyes. The outcome this time proved less dramatic and temporary medication solved that problem. On top of these health issues Nellie discovered she was, once again, under scrutiny by the taxation office.

To earn money without performing, Nellie conceived the idea of writing an autobiography. The London publishers Thornton Butterworth were keen to publish it and probably gave Nellie a substantial advance royalty payment. Beverley Nichols was entrusted with ghost-writing the book and Nellie began recounting details of her life and career to him. He converted what Nellie told him into elegant prose, taking a fair amount of licence in what he wrote. Sensitive issues such as her affair with Philippe, which Nichols wanted to include, were still 'out of bounds' and omitted on Nellie's strict orders. So were Nellie's health problems – and Luisa Tetrazzini, who does not rate a single mention. The substance of the published text is factual, name-dropping is still prevalent and some episodes were embroidered by Nichols to reflect more generously on his employer, but compared with the autobiographies of many other famous singers, *Melodies and Memories* (as the book was called) is refreshingly frank. When it was launched the following October, it was well received by the public, but literary critics (less immune to Nellie's charm than music critics) found it wanting in details.

Also during this year Nellie produced another volume, *The Melba Method*, a singing manual, published by the London music publishers Chappell & Co. In line with *Melodies and Memories*, the content of the manual purported to be Nellie's work, but in fact it was written by Fritz Hart and Mary Campbell (the senior resident singing teacher at the Albert Street Conservatorium), based on what they had observed of Nellie's teaching and what she chose to tell them. The only part that can be reliably attributed to Nellie is the foreword and that was ghost-written by Nichols. Both books served their purpose and earned royalties for Nellie for the rest of her life.

Nellie did not abandon performing; the roar of the crowd if not the smell of greasepaint still held its allure for her. She gave musical parties at Mansfield Street, one of which included the former King and Queen of Portugal. Inevitably, Nellie sang for her guests and, on that royal occasion, so did the Norwegian soprano Eidé Norena, who was singing 'Melba' roles at Covent Garden that year.

At this time it also came to Nellie's notice that the 77-year-old Emma Albani had fallen on hard times. Generously, Nellie did two things to help her old rival. She enlisted the support of some politician friends to petition King George V to bestow a damehood on Albani and she organised a benefit concert for Albani at Covent Garden. George V and Queen Mary attended the concert, as did the Governor-General of Albani's native Canada and the composer Sir Edward Elgar. The Royal Albert Hall Orchestra, under Landon Ronald (recently knighted himself), played and Nellie sang two arias from *Le Nozze di Figaro* ('Porgi amor' and 'Voi che sapete'), as well as two encores. Among the others who sang was the now 67-year-old Ben Davies, who had appeared frequently with Albani when both were in their prime. Albani sat in a box applauding each performer and came on stage at the end of the concert, where Nellie presented her with flowers in the shape of a harp. The money raised by the concert allowed Albani (now Dame Emma) to live comfortably for the five years that remained to her.

Nellie's own retirement had been the subject of speculation in the British press during the summer of that year and not denied by her. Witnessing the aged and almost voiceless Albani reduced to appearing in music halls prior to the benefit concert convinced Nellie that she needed to depart on her own terms – while she could still sing well, avoiding the risk of becoming a figure of ridicule or, as with Albani, a charity case.

Always the pragmatist, Nellie decided that the first step in her move towards retirement was to reduce her living costs. She instructed a London property agent to offer for sale the lease on the large house in Mansfield Street and when that was sold, to auction off the house's contents. As her new European base, Nellie chose an apartment – although small compared with the London house – at 161 Avenue Victor Hugo, in her favoured area of Paris. The building matched the Haussmann-style architecture of its neighbours, but it had only recently been built and offered all the latest modern conveniences.[7] French friends welcomed Nellie back to Paris with a party that included a concert. Nellie sang three French songs: 'Chanson triste' by Duparc, 'Les papillons' by Chausson and Josef Szulc's 'Clare de lune'. Also taking part in the entertainment were Georges Thill, the best of a new generation of French tenors, and a pianist young enough to be Nellie's grandson, Robert Casadesus.

In December 1925 it was announced in the press that Nellie would make a farewell concert tour of the United Kingdom at the beginning of the following year and this would be followed by a farewell performance in opera at Covent Garden. Plans were made, their implementation overseen by Nellie herself.

Nellie arrived in London in the new year and in an interview with *The Sunday Times* she explained that she was keen to bid farewell to her loyal fans in the provinces. After her Covent Garden appearance, she said, she would make farewell appearances at the Paris Opéra in the spring and at the Monnaie in Brussels in autumn. The reference to the Paris Opéra seems to have been a wish rather than a fact and was never realised, and ill health would force her to cancel the arranged appearance in Brussels.

Nellie entrusted the organisation of her provincial tour to the influential agents Ibbs & Tillett and engaged Arthur Hackett and Lionel Tertis to support her.[8] For eight weeks, commencing in mid-January, Nellie criss-crossed England, Scotland and Ireland, giving 23 concerts to capacity audiences as keen to bid her farewell as she was to farewell them. At the end of the tour, Nellie returned to her Paris apartment to gather her strength for the Covent Garden appearance. Keeping her company at this time was the latest in her soprano protégées, Helen Daniels, a young American, who would later adopt the stage name Elena Danieli. Daniels was with Nellie in the apartment one morning when it was announced on the radio that Louis Philippe, Duc d'Orléans, had died in Palermo. Later Daniels recalled how deeply moved Nellie had been and how, as she hurried from the room, Nellie whispered 'Ah ... Philippe'.

As well as the Covent Garden appearance, Ibbs & Tillett had arranged a gala farewell concert for Nellie at the Royal Albert Hall and Nellie herself had planned a full calendar of social events during the 1926 London season, at which she would entertain and be entertained by all her old friends and colleagues. She took a house at Hatfield, 'Camfield Place', the former home of Beatrix Potter's family and later the home of another writer, Barbara Cartland. George, Evie and Pamela arrived from Australia and took a house of their own in Kensington but spent a great deal of time at Camfield Place. When visiting 'Granny', seven-year-old Pamela was, no doubt, intrigued to be sleeping in the house where *The Tale of Peter Rabbit* had been written and where real rabbits lived in the garden.

The farewell concert at the Royal Albert Hall took place six days before Nellie's sixty-fifth birthday and three weeks before the Covent Garden farewell. The vast hall was filled and scalpers profited, with two-guinea and one-guinea tickets changing hands for 10 times their face value. The king and queen attended and led the thunderous applause that followed every item on the program. Their majesties also attended the Covent Garden farewell, tickets for which had sold out many weeks before the event.

The Covent Garden Nellie returned to on 8 June was a very different place from the one she had known in her heyday – and even from when she sang there with the British National Opera Company. International opera had returned and new names such as Lotte Lehmann, Maria Jeritza, Elisabeth Schumann, Frieda Lieder, Fanny Heldy, Lauritz Melchior, Francesco Merli and Mariano Stabile were its stars.

In collaboration with the management, Nellie had chosen to sing a mixed program, comprising the balcony scene from *Roméo et Juliette*, the opening of the last act of *Otello* and the two final acts of *La Bohème*. To sing with her, Nellie was probably allowed to take her pick from the other artists under contract that year, but made a commendable decision to choose (where she could) Australians. Necessity forced a couple of exceptions. Charles Hackett was chosen to sing Roméo and Aurora Rettore, who had sung Musetta with the 1924 Melba–Williamson company, was selected to repeat the role. As her Rodolfo in *La Bohème*, Nellie chose Melbourne-born tenor Browning Mummery, Marcello was assigned to the Geelong-born John Brownlee and Schaunard to Frederick Collier. Each of these Australians was well established in Europe, but Brownlee was a particular favourite of Nellie's – as much for his handsome face and figure as for his fine voice.[9]

As the great evening approached, Nellie was nervous. Beverley Nichols recalled that he had hoped and prayed that she would be fit and in her best voice on the night, and his prayers were answered. The long program was arduous for a singer of Nellie's age, but she came through with flying colours, ably supported by her colleagues and the orchestra conducted by the celebrated maestro Vincenzo Bellezza. The evening was one of the great events in the history of Covent Garden and not only on the stage. Diamonds, rubies, emeralds and starched shirt fronts abounded in the auditorium as they had not done since the beginning of the First World War, with the evening resembling one of the great 'Melba nights' of the 1890s. The king and queen, and most of the royal family, attended and the press commented on seeing faces in the audience unseen there for decades.

At the end of the 'Bohème' acts Nellie came out on stage and was enveloped in a sea of flowers, one arrangement in the shape of a giant kangaroo. Applause and shouts of 'bravo' continued until Lord Stanley of Alderley (the former governor of Victoria) came on stage and beckoned for silence. Stanley made a touching speech commending Nellie's artistry and her charity work during the war, after which Nellie stepped forward to reply.

Nellie had written her speech of reply several days earlier and had read it to Beverley Nichols. Nichols claims that he had told Nellie the speech was dreadful and that it contained so many 'Royal Highnesses' and 'Excellencies' that it sounded like a court circular. After a long argument, Nichols finally persuaded Nellie to omit all those names and include only one – the faithful doorman at Covent Garden. It proved a masterstroke.

As Lord Stanley stepped aside, Nellie addressed the audience in a clear and resonant voice, still showing traces of her Australian accent. She thanked the public for their loyal support for so many years, the management of the opera house, the orchestra and the stagehands and then added: 'And I also have to thank my dear old friend Austin who has been at the stage door for 40 years and for 36 years has put me in my carriage and always bid me goodnight.'

The audience roared their approval.

Nellie continued: 'And now there's only one more word to say and that is 'farewell'. I won't say 'goodbye' because 'farewell' is such a very beautiful word and I'm sure you all know that it is a part of a prayer and means 'fare thee well', which I wish you all … and I feel sure that you wish me the same.' Nellie's voice broke with those final words and the genuineness of her emotions was confirmed by the stagehands who were shedding a tear or two themselves.

Next day the critics commented on the extraordinary preservation of elements of Nellie's voice and of her artistry, but we do not have to rely on their words to judge Nellie's performance. The whole evening was broadcast and recordings made of key items, including the two speeches. The sound is remarkably good on these almost 100-year-old recordings, thanks to the use of the newly improved microphones. What we hear is an aged voice, restricted in its use by failing breath control. The long arching phrases that were one of the hallmarks of Nellie's singing in times gone by are sometimes cut short. High notes lack that starlike quality of earlier times and are sung (by necessity rather than choice) stridently when they might once have displayed a caressing softness.

What remains is, however, remarkable. The voice is still unmistakably and uniquely Nellie's, the tone untarnished. We can hear, as the evening drew on, Nellie tiring, but then in Mimi's 'farewell' and in the quartet in the third act of *La Bohème*, there are breathtaking moments, where it seems as if time has been reversed and once again ethereal sounds float from Nellie's throat. These are recordings of great historical importance, but perhaps more importantly, they are vivid and treasurable mementos of Nellie's singing on stage during a live performance in the aural perspective of a great theatre.[10]

The success of the concert and the Covent Garden performance prompted Ibbs & Tillett to organise a second farewell concert at the Royal Albert Hall. Brownlee and Tertis supported Nellie and the concert was as successful as the first. As a final encore Nellie waved the pianist Harold Craxton from his stool and sat down to accompany herself in 'Home, sweet home'.

A few nights later, another group of Londoners were fortunate enough to hear Nellie sing but without paying for the privilege. A new musical comedy, entitled *Mozart* and based on an episode in the composer's life, opened at the Gaiety Theatre. Nellie took George and Evie to see the show, which had a score by an old friend of Nellie's, Reynaldo Hahn. It was the custom in those days to play the national anthem before any theatrical performance or concert and because *Mozart* was a work created in France, 'La Marseilles' was played first, followed by the British National Anthem. The female star of the show, Yvonne Printemps, came out in front of the curtain and sang the French anthem and then, when the orchestra struck up the British one, Nellie decided it deserved to be sung too. Standing in her box, she launched into 'God save the King' as Printemps and the rest of the audience listened in amazement and delight.

As the London season drew to its close, Nellie took Evie and Pamela off for a long holiday at Evian, now her favourite holiday destination, the resort's charm intensified by old sweet memories of time spent there with Philippe. The holiday was designed to enable Nellie to muster her strength for her farewell in Brussels, but another severe bout of bronchitis sabotaged that plan. In former times Nellie would have made the journey to wherever she was engaged to appear, confident that her recovery would occur swiftly enough to allow her to perform, but those days were past. Reluctantly Nellie advised the Monnaie that she had been forced to cancel her appearance.

Nellie retreated to her apartment in Paris but felt well enough by the end of November to take part in a charity concert at the Théâtre Sarah-Bernhardt, where she sang the songs she had sung at the Paris party at the beginning of the year. It was the last time Nellie sang in public in the French capital.

After that Nellie took herself back to London in order to fulfil two promises made earlier. The first was to make some recordings with Brownlee and the second was to help Lilian Baylis raise funds to establish an opera company at the Old Vic Theatre, near Waterloo Station. Nellie had been following Baylis's valiant efforts to create a new company, one that offered opera at ticket prices the working classes could afford. The two women decided a repeat of the Covent Garden program, but without the *Roméo et Juliette* scene, would draw the maximum crowd. Mummery, Brownlee and Collier offered their services and Gertrude Johnson sang Musetta. Covent Garden lent Baylis some costumes and scenery and the performance took place on 7 December. The evening lacked the glamour of the Covent Garden farewell but served its purpose, raising 300 much-needed pounds towards the establishment of what became the Sadler's Wells Opera Company, known today as the English National Opera.

The London public must have wondered if this was absolutely the last they would hear of Nellie, the word 'farewell' having been used in relation to her so many times during the year that it was raising smiles. It is likely that it was at this time that the expression 'doing a Melba' (meaning giving endless farewells) entered the lexicon, but the sceptics were confounded; that appearance at the Old Vic proved to be Nellie's swansong in London.

The recordings were made 10 days later, not in the Gramophone Company's studio but in the Small Queen's Hall. Harold Craxton accompanied Nellie and Brownlee and together they recorded the duet 'Dite alla giovine' from *La Traviata* and Bemberg's 'Un ange est venu'. Brownlee sings magnificently and seems to have inspired Nellie. The 'Traviata' duet is a splendid souvenir of one of Nellie's great roles and she manages some exquisite soft singing towards the end.

On this occasion, Nellie then recorded two songs: firstly, Szulc's 'Clair de lune', followed by the spiritual 'Swing low, sweet chariot'. In these two solos it is apparent that Nellie is negotiating the difficult sections with caution, but it is testament to her enduring musicianship that she still manages to produce two beautiful recordings. The final notes of what would be Nellie's last recording are of unearthly beauty and a magnificent end to a recording career that had lasted for 22 years.

Despite the disappointment of not appearing at the Opéra or at the Monnaie, Nellie could look back on the year 1926 with pride and a great sense of achievement. She had proved that she had been justified in continuing to sing past the age when most singers retire and doing so where the stakes were highest.

Chapter 22
Evening star

Nellie returned to Australia in early 1927, leaving George, Evie and Pamela in London. It was the height of the Australian summer when she reached Coombe Cottage, where she discovered the house and garden had been neglected in the months since George's departure. The house showed cracks in the walls and leaks in the roof, while the garden resembled a parched wilderness. Daryl Lindsay and his novelist wife, Joan, brought an architect out to Coldstream, who advised Nellie on what needed to be done. Nellie engaged builders to fix the house and the landscape designer Edna Walling to address the garden. Walling brought in three young female gardeners and between them they restored order, although Walling baulked at some of Nellie's suggestions, many of which clashed with the more informal garden style she advocated.

Understanding that the idleness that came with retirement would soon take its toll on her, Nellie had conceived the idea of one last concert tour of Australia, her justification being that her 1924 farewell had been to *opera* in Australia, with no mention of concerts. Before leaving London she had written to John Lemmoné and asked him to make the arrangements. She had also discussed with the young English bass-baritone Stuart Robertson (brother of the actor Anna Neagle) the possibility of him joining her on this tour. Robertson had been surprised and delighted by the offer. By February Lemmoné had made all the arrangements and Nellie cabled Robertson to join her in Australia.

Lindley Evans was re-engaged as pianist and Lemmoné served as flautist, as well as manager. The tour began with a concert in the Melbourne Auditorium on 2 March, with the Melbourne Symphony Orchestra in support. At intervals over the next nine months the touring party gave concerts in Tasmania, rural Victoria (where Nellie travelled in her luxurious black Cadillac tourer), Sydney, Newcastle, Brisbane and towns up the Queensland coast as far as Rockhampton. The tour ended with two concerts in Adelaide in November.[1]

By late autumn that year Parliament House in Australia's new capital, Canberra, was ready to be officially opened. The Duke and Duchess of York (the future King George VI and Queen Elizabeth) came to Australia to perform the ceremony. Nellie volunteered to sing the National Anthem when the royal party arrived and her offer was readily accepted. On 9 May she was stationed at the top of the building's broad steps and cued to sing, but as she opened her mouth to sing a flight of aeroplanes passed over and Nellie had to wait until their sound receded. She then sang the first verse of the anthem, with the prime minister and a choir leading the audience in the second. A few seconds of rare, black-and-white silent newsreel film of Nellie singing that day are available. Flanked by the official party, she looks suitably impressive, standing upright like a guardsman, head held high and wearing her DBE regalia. A month later, in the king's birthday honours, Nellie was elevated to Dame Grand Cross of the Order of the British Empire, the highest rank in that order.

In July, the Russian violinist Efram Zimbalist visited Melbourne on a nationwide concert tour. Nellie invited him and his equally famous soprano wife, Alma Gluck, to stay at Coombe Cottage, and because Zimbalist's concerts had failed to attract large audiences in other cities, Nellie determined to rectify that in Melbourne. For the violinist's opening concert in Melbourne, she booked a large block of seats, inviting some of her students from the Albert Street Conservatorium to join her. After the concert she went on stage and presented Zimbalist with a laurel wreath, as she had for

Leopold Auer's other star pupil, Jascha Heifetz, in London. Nellie also volunteered to sing at Zimbalist's second concert and sang 'L'amerò, sarò costante' from *Il Ré Pastore*, with Zimbalist playing the obbligato. 'I am deeply touched by the spontaneous expressions of Dame Nellie's admiration', the violinist told the *Herald*, his wife adding how delighted she had been to meet Nellie, recalling: 'I was taken to the opera for the first time when I was 14. It was at the Met and Melba was singing. I have worshipped her ever since.'[2]

It had been planned that George, Evie and Pamela would join Nellie in Australia in May, but Pamela became ill and needed an appendectomy. Nellie was terrified that something might go wrong under the surgeon's knife and she would never see her beloved grandchild again. News finally arrived that the operation had been successful and a note from Pamela herself assured her 'Granny' that she was recovering. Plans had been made for the Armstrongs to travel to Australia as soon as Pamela was well enough; in the meantime, news had reached George that his father had suffered a perforated duodenal ulcer and had undergone emergency surgery. The Armstrongs headed to Canada instead and stayed in Victoria, where Charlie was hospitalised until he was able to return to his Vancouver Island home.

When Evie and Pamela arrived at Spencer Street Railway Station, George having arrived in Australia earlier, Nellie was there to greet them, as were a group of journalists, who reported Pamela's first words to her grandmother: 'Do you remember me, Granny?'[3]

To celebrate the reunion of her family, Nellie paid the Melbourne branch of Kodak to send a cameraman out to Coldstream to make a film of them in the garden at Coombe Cottage. On a sunny afternoon in early November the photographer arrived with a 16 mm cine camera and, doubtless following directions from Nellie, filmed her, Pamela, George, Evie, various other guests and Nellie's pets – 'Cocky' the cockatoo and 'Billy' her cocker spaniel. Nellie and Pamela dominate the film and we see grandmother and granddaughter skylarking and thoroughly enjoying each other's company.⁴

Semi-retirement also gave Nellie the opportunity to spend more time at the Albert Street Conservatorium, where she continued to teach and encourage young female students – without a fee. The number who could justifiably call themselves 'Melba girls' became legion, although a successor to Nellie never emerged from among them. The majority became singing teachers, proudly advertising themselves as 'trained by Dame Nellie Melba'. It would take another 32 years before another Australian soprano – Joan Sutherland – would achieve Nellie's exalted status.

Opera was uppermost in Nellie's mind in 1927. Nevin Tait had visited her at Coombe Cottage early in the year. J.C. Williamson's had been keen to repeat the success of the 1924 Melba–Williamson Grand Opera Company and Tait hoped she would lend her voice to another planned for the following year. Tait was on the verge of travelling to Europe to re-engage artists who had been part of the 1924 company, if possible, and to recruit new singers. On behalf of his company, Tait offered Nellie 2000 pounds per week to be nominally a part of the company for the planned 22-week tour. Nellie demanded 3000 pounds per week and got it. The subject of her singing (or not singing) would have been discussed, but irrespective of the outcome of that discussion, Nellie agreed to leave all the arrangements to Tait and his colleagues.

In late April 1928 the 33 principals of the company assembled in Melbourne to begin rehearsals for the opening performance at Her Majesty's Theatre on 12 May. Nevin Tait, aided by one of the partners in J.C. Williamson's, Sir George Tallis, had done his job well, recruiting what was probably the most illustrious roster of singers ever to appear together in Australia. Arturo Toscanini, now musical director at La Scala, was reported to be furious because his company had been 'pillaged' to such an extent by the Australians. Toscanini's boss, Scandiani, took a more collegial approach and actually extended the leave of several of his singers to enable them to remain longer in Australia.

Toti dal Monte, Apollo Granforte and several singers from the 1924 company returned. To these were added several sopranos of international stature, including the great Italian dramatic soprano Giannina Arangi-Lombardi and the Argentinian Hina Spani, possessor of one of the most beautiful voices of all time. The tenors were led by Francesco Merli, Enzo de Muro Lomanto (a young lyric tenor) and Angelo Minghetti, a former sculptor turned singer, who was a popular star across Europe and in the Americas. Browning Mummery and John Brownlee were also included, although assigned fewer performances than their talents deserved. The depth of talent within the company allowed for double or triple casts for some operas and enough understudies to avoid cancellations. The chief conductor was Gaetano Bavagnoli from the Rome Opera, assisted by four other conductors, including Emilio Rossi, Toscanini's assistant at La Scala.

On this occasion criticism of the repertoire was more muted, with 26 operas produced, including the Australian premieres of Puccini's *Turandot, Il Tabarro* and *Gianni Schicchi*, Massenet's *Thaïs*, Mascagni's *Lodoletta* and Montemezzi's *L'Amore dei Tre Re*. Wagner's *Lohengrin* and *Tannhäuser* kept the Wagnerites moderately content and Fritz Hart's opera *Deirdre in Exile* was given in Melbourne, no doubt at Nellie's insistence.

Toti dal Monte enchanted audiences again and, when she married Enzo de Muro Lomanto at St Mary's Cathedral during the Sydney season, thousands of people turned out to wish them well. On the cathedral steps after the ceremony the couple offered the crowd the fascist salute, which had not yet acquired sinister connotations. Nellie gave the couple a generous gift, but declined an invitation to attend the ceremony.

Not having an active role in the opera company frustrated Nellie and in the middle of the Sydney season she volunteered to sing two performances, the first on the evening of 7 August and the second, a matinee, on 11 August. The evening performance was to comprise acts two, three and four of *La Bohème*, followed by the opening scene of act four of *Otello*. The matinee was announced as a complete performance of *La Bohème*. There were risks associated with this and no one would have been more aware of them than Nellie herself. She had not sung regularly in the past nine months and had not appeared in opera since the Old Vic performance in London in 1926. Omitting the first act of *La Bohème* on the first night, she explained, was to allow time for her to sing the Verdi scene, but it is more likely to have been that she was nervous about tackling the top 'C' at the end of the first act of 'Bohème' (the only top 'C' in Mimi's part) for which she was once so famous. An additional risk was a 67-year-old Mimi, which audiences might find too incongruous to accept. Changing the program for the second appearance or cancelling it may have been an option Nellie kept in reserve.

The first appearance was potentially jeopardised after a story in the Australian press that morning that did more damage to Nellie's reputation than anything since John Norton's charges of alcoholism. The English journalist Winifred Ponder had been commissioned to write a biography of Dame Clara Butt, and it had just been released. In it Ponder recounted a purported conversation between Nellie and Butt just before the contralto toured Australia in 1907. According to Ponder, Butt asked Nellie what Australian audiences would most like to hear her sing and Nellie had replied: 'Oh, sing them muck. That's all they understand.'

The story featured in just about every newspaper in Australia on the morning of Nellie's first appearance. Australians believed it and were disappointed and angry. Nellie hotly denied the words that had been attributed to her and a cable from Butt assured her and the press that she had not been the source of the story, nor had the incident occurred. When Ponder was contacted by the press, she stuck to her story.[5]

Nellie was not in the best frame of mind when she turned up at His Majesty's Theatre that night, fearful that there would be some kind of demonstration from the audience when she appeared on stage. Her fear proved unfounded. Supported by Danieli as Musetta and Mummery and Brownlee repeating their familiar roles, Nellie managed to get through the performance if not triumphantly, then highly satisfactorily.[6]

The *Sydney Morning Herald* reported:

> Dame Nellie was a mature Mimi, it is true, and though her vocal quality could not be expected to possess all the beauty of her prime, it proved singularly sweet and fresh, and her artistic powers were undiminished.[7]

The other Sydney newspapers agreed, and reported on the warmth with which the audience greeted Nellie, the masses of flowers and the endless curtain calls she received.

In support of the theory that the first act of *La Bohème* held terror for Nellie, she withdrew from the complete performance four days later and her place was taken by one of the other sopranos in the company. She was, the press were told, suffering from a cold, but appeared at a social function two days later.

After the Sydney performance Nellie was anxious to sing in Melbourne, but, by the time arrangements had been made, the rest of the company was in Adelaide. For this event both acts one and two of *La Bohème* had to be omitted because the chorus were fully occupied in the South Australian capital, as was the company's orchestra. The Melbourne Symphony stepped in and the performance was conducted by Fritz Hart. Danieli, Mummery and Brownlee came across from Adelaide to support Nellie on the afternoon of 27 September in His Majesty's Theatre. The success of the Sydney performance was repeated, with the music critic of the Melbourne *Herald* singling out Nellie's singing of the *Otello* scene for special praise.

Melba reached the highest refinements of her art in the 'Otello' scene, in the reflective 'Salce' and the passionate farewell to Emilia, followed by the 'Ave Maria'. The magic of her Desdemona was reflected in the tense quiet of the audience.[8]

Nellie's third and final appearance with the company took place on the evening of 2 October in Adelaide. The second act of *La Bohème* was restored but Mummery and Brownlee had other commitments and were replaced by Minghetti and the baritone Angelo Pilotto. Remarkably, it was not a full house, although this may have been attributable to the violent electrical storms that swept across the city that evening. Nevertheless, Nellie wove her magic and those present gave her a rousing reception. The company then headed off for a short season in Perth, with Nellie accompanying them, but she did not sing again. She had sung in Australia for the very last time.

Nellie set off for London with Danieli, who had secured a contract to sing small roles at Covent Garden. The journey was broken by a two-day stopover at Shepheard's Hotel in Cairo. Back in freezing-cold London, Nellie rented a house at 34 Cadogan Square in fashionable Belgravia. Influenza and bronchitis were rife in the capital and Nellie soon came down with the former and was bedridden for a fortnight. By 17 December she was well enough to visit Australia House and was photographed by the press stirring a Christmas cake made of Australian produce. The cake was to be a gift to the Duke and Duchess of York and their infant daughter Princess Elizabeth.

The early months of 1929 were spent quietly, with Nellie entertaining a few friends at Cadogan Square. She occasionally attended functions, where she was recognised, including a reception at a Mayfair Hotel to celebrate Ben Davies's seventieth birthday. Before her departure for Australia two years earlier, Nellie had disposed of her apartment in Avenue Victor Hugo but now decided she needed another Paris base. In March she travelled to the French capital and rented an apartment from Princess Catherine Radziwill, at 8 Boulevard de Latour-Maubourg on the Left Bank near Les Invalides. While the former home of the prince and princess was an elegant building, the apartment needed redecorating and Nellie was unable to move in until October. Against the advice of her trusted GP in Paris, Nellie returned to London and set herself up in a suite at Claridge's while the work was carried out in Paris. The London press noted her return and that she had taken Lady de Grey's old box at Covent Garden for the forthcoming season.

Among the newcomers at Covent Garden that year was the American soprano Rosa Ponselle, the possessor of a glorious voice, darker in timbre than Nellie's but with the same kind of radiance that Nellie's had once possessed. Like Alma Gluck, Ponselle had revered Nellie since childhood and asked if she might visit her idol for advice before making her Covent Garden debut. Ponselle arrived at Claridge's on the appointed afternoon to take tea with Nellie. Up to that time Ponselle's career had been largely confined to the Metropolitan Opera and Nellie told her not to expect from London audiences the kind of overt demonstrations New Yorkers delivered when they approved of a singer.

On 28 May, Ponselle made her Covent Garden debut in Bellini's *Norma*, a 'bel canto' masterpiece which had not been heard at Covent Garden for 30 years, and Nellie witnessed a London audience rewarding Ponselle with just the kind of demonstration she had foreshadowed would be unlikely. When the two divas next met, the younger found the elder a little distant towards her and attributed that to envy. Ponselle was probably right.

In June Nellie took a holiday at Evian with Tommy Patterson, after which aunt and nephew toured Switzerland and southern Germany, with Tommy driving the Cadillac. Nellie was delighted to have her nephew as a companion, but she was troubled by financial problems. The Wall Street crash had decimated her investments and the tax office in London was again investigating Nellie's finances, attempting to prove that Coombe Cottage was not her 'primary residence' and therefore she was liable to pay taxes in England.[9]

With her new Left Bank apartment still not ready for occupancy, Nellie moved into the Paris Ritz. Tommy Cochrane turned up there one day and sensing Nellie's despondency organised another motoring tour for her through southern France. Herman Bemberg and Boni de Castellane were invited to join them. The company of three witty and outrageous men raised Nellie's spirits – at least until they reached Chartres, where the party attended a service in the great cathedral. When the choir of young boys sang, Nellie hissed at Cochrane that she 'hated' those 'bloody boys' for the pure sound they made so naturally and which had taken her years to perfect.

In August Nellie travelled to Salzburg to attend the music festival. Accompanying her was Lady Janet Bridges ('Florrie' to her friends), wife of a former governor of South Australia. The two ladies attended performances of *Der Rosenkavalier* and Beethoven's *Fidelio*, with Lotte Lehmann and Richard Mayr leading the casts. They also attended the annual performance of the allegorical play *Everyman* presented in the Domplatz and a concert by the Vienna Philharmonic Orchestra, which featured works by Percy Grainger.

Back in England and aided by Florrie Bridges, Nellie organised a concert on 5 October at the Brighton Hippodrome in aid of the Sussex Eye Hospital and decided to sing herself. Stuart Robertson and two prominent London musicians, the violinist Adila Fachiri and the pianist Irene Scharrer, supported her. Nellie sang songs by Duparc, Chausson, Bemberg and Richard Strauss, 'Mimi's Farewell' and the 'Aubade' from Lalo's *Le Roi d'Ys*. Reluctant to leave the platform, she acquiesced to cries for an encore with 'Swing low, sweet chariot', Tosti's 'Mattinata' and finally 'Home, sweet home'. At the end of the concert she addressed the audience saying: 'I cannot tell you how pleased I am to have sung to you again. I was terrified at first, but it has been a real joy to me.'[10] Nellie spent Christmas 1929 with her old friend Susan Birch and, on Christmas Day, was able to speak to George, Evie and Pamela on the newly opened telephone link between Europe and Australia. Tears were shed on both ends of the line.

The year 1930 marked the beginning of a new decade and the last full year of Nellie's life. The average life span for females in developed countries in the 1930s was 69, the age Nellie would reach in May. Her health was also of ever-growing concern. Not only did she have diabetes and a susceptibility to respiratory illnesses, she was now also suffering from raised blood pressure. It would not have surprised anyone if, at this time, Nellie had retreated to Australia to spend whatever time was left to her in the sunny tranquillity of Coombe Cottage. That Nellie did not choose this path demonstrates that her spirit was still strong and that she was determined to sustain her celebrity status for as long as she could.

In January she was seen in Monte Carlo and from Marseille she took ship for Port Said, accompanying Tommy Paterson on the first leg of his journey back to Australia. From Port Said she moved to Cairo, where Bemberg joined her at Shepheard's Hotel for a two-month holiday. Back in her Paris apartment in May, Nellie hosted a dinner in honour of Prince Christopher of Greece and his new bride, Princess François d'Orléans, a niece of Philippe's. The prince turned up alone, offering his wife's apologies and explaining that she was unwell. Nellie must have wondered (as we might) whether the princess had been reminded at the last moment of Nellie's relationship with her uncle and had chosen diplomacy over dinner. After the meal Nellie sang for her guests.

When the weather became warmer, Nellie returned to London. Encouraged by the compliments she had received from Prince Christopher and her other guests, Nellie was determined to sing in public one more time, arranging an afternoon concert for 10 June in the ballroom of the Park Lane Hotel to raise money for the National Children's Adoption Association. The Duchess of York attended. Nellie was assisted by Lionel Tertis, the French flutist René le Roy (a pupil of Gaubert) and the Russian pianist Nikolai Orlov. Nellie sang the three French songs she had sung at Brighton the previous year and 'Soir païen' ('Pagan Night'), a song for voice and flute by Georges Hue, which she had often sung with John Lemmoné, on this occasion with le Roy playing the flute part. In the audience were Susan Birch, Florrie Bridges, Richard Neville, Beverley Nichols and many other old friends. Nellie sang 'Home, sweet home' as her encore. This was the last time her voice was heard in public.[11]

Nellie's fascination with the music of Wagner remained and at the end of July she took herself off to the Bayreuth Festival in Germany. Her visit to Bayreuth coincided with Siegfried Wagner's last season as director of the festival established by his father. Nellie tried to pay a courtesy call on the director and his English wife, Winifred, but Siegfried was too ill to receive visitors and died in the second week of the festival. Nellie attended performances of *Tristan und Isolde*, the Ring Cycle and *Parsifal*, almost certainly recalling how deeply moved she had been when she heard Wagner's sacred music drama for the first time at the Met in 1905.

From Bayreuth Nellie travelled to Salzburg for her second experience of the city's annual music festival, attending what she described as a 'magnificent' performance of *Don Giovanni* and another of *Der Rosenkavalier*, an opera she had come to love. After Salzburg she stopped in Munich, where she lunched with Richard Strauss, who gave her a signed copy of the score of 'Rosenkavalier' and arranged for her to play a few notes on a spinet that had belonged to Mozart. Next she visited Baden Baden, arriving back in Paris in time to attend the christening of John Brownlee's baby daughter, Isabelle Delphina Nellie. At the christening at Notre-Dame d'Auteuil on 20 September, what is believed to be the last photograph of Nellie was taken by a former member of 'Melba's Own' scout troop. The photo shows Donna Brownlee nursing baby Isabelle, with Nellie standing beside her. Nellie is swathed in a fur coat. She looks shrunken, aged, but happy.[12]

Missing her family, on 19 October Nellie sailed from Marseille on the P&O liner *Cathay*, bound for Australia. As the ship passed through the Red Sea, Nellie developed a rash on her face, which became inflamed, and she felt desperately ill. The ship's doctor diagnosed a staphylococcus infection. Deck games were prohibited near Nellie's state room to ensure that she was not disturbed. When the ship reached Fremantle, the doctor insisted she remain on board, but told the press his patient should make a full recovery.

When the ship reached Adelaide, Nellie decided she was again too ill to go ashore and a cable was sent to George requesting that he make preparations for her arrival in Melbourne. George and Evie and an ambulance were waiting on the dock when the *Cathay* reached Port Melbourne. Nellie was whisked away to Mt Saint Evin's private hospital in Victoria Parade, a couple of kilometres from Doonside, which had recently been demolished. Doctors at the hospital examined her and reported that 'Dame Nellie' was suffering from 'a painful blood disorder', adding that her condition was expected to 'yield to the usual treatment' and that no further bulletins would be issued in the meantime.

By Christmas Nellie was well enough to go to Coombe Cottage with two nurses attending, but her strength was failing and a fear of death haunted her. Evie's brother, Bill Doyle, came to visit but when he had departed Nellie decided he was the only doctor who might save her, but his practice was in Sydney, so she decided that was where she must go. In the New Year she travelled to Sydney and was met by her sister Belle and taken to the property at Mona Vale where Belle and her husband lived. Bill Doyle did what he could, but on 21 January and on his recommendation, Nellie was admitted to St Vincent's Private Hospital in Darlinghurst.

Over the next few days Nellie's condition improved and on 27 January she felt strong enough to hold a press conference in her hospital room, but insisted no photographers be admitted. Sitting up in bed wearing a pink lace-trimmed bedjacket and a matching boudoir cap, she told reporters: 'Considering that I have been in bed now for 17 weeks, I feel wonderfully well. In fact, I am hoping my doctors will allow me to get up for a little while next week.' Asked what her plans for the future were, Nellie said there would be plenty of time to make plans while she was convalescing.[13]

Nellie remained in hospital and on 12 February her condition began to deteriorate dramatically. Four doctors and three nurses were assigned to care for her. George, Evie, Ernie Mitchell and his wife were the only visitors permitted in Nellie's room. On Saturday 22 February her pulse became faint and Nellie began to lapse in and out of consciousness. She asked for a minister of religion and Canon Howard Lee of St Mark's, Darling Point, was summoned. Patient and priest prayed together. During the night George and Evie kept vigil beside Nellie's bed while a doctor fought to keep her alive. In the morning they were joined by Nellie's sister Dora, Dora's daughter and John Lemmoné. Nellie died the following afternoon. She was three months short of her seventieth birthday.

The cause of Nellie's death was septicaemia (blood poisoning) but the origin of the infection, which had been in her body for months and which ultimately led to her death is a mystery. John Lemmoné revealed how Nellie had told him in a letter, written the previous year, that she had 'picked up some germs' in Germany and had sought medical advice there and in Paris, without receiving a definite diagnosis. The mystery deepened in the 1960s when a nursing sister claimed that she had observed the scars of a facelift on the sides of Nellie's head when she was caring for her in St Vincent's Hospital. It was then suggested that the reason for Nellie's visit to Baden Baden the previous year had been to undergo a facelift, performed by a plastic surgeon she had met in Cairo, and that the infection occurred as a result of the procedure being mismanaged. Thereafter, the 'botched facelift' theory gained wide acceptance, but was subjected to little scrutiny.

The theory may well have been based on fact. Before the

discovery of antibiotics, surgery of any kind carried a high risk of complications due to infection. That said, a number of inconsistencies suggest the nursing sister was mistaken, or her memory was unreliable. The nursing sister claimed Nellie had entered St Vincent's immediately on her arrival in Australia when, in fact, Nellie had been in the country for more than two months. The theory also implies a conspiracy on the part of all the attending medical professionals and the journalists who attended the bedside press conference to conceal the facelift.

In the broader sense there are a number of other considerations. Nellie was no vainer than the average person and it would seem improbable that she would have risked undergoing plastic surgery to improve her appearance *after* her retirement. Equally improbable is that any competent surgeon would have performed non-essential surgery on a 68-year-old diabetic with a compromised respiratory system. Timing is also a factor. Three weeks after she had left Baden Baden, Nellie appeared at the Brownlee christening in Paris and there is no sign of bruising or discolouration on the area of Nellie's face visible in that historic photograph. Nellie's family always denied the facelift theory and at this point in time (almost a century later) we will probably never know definitively one way or the other – and it is of little consequence in the vast canvas of Nellie's life.

Nellie's death was reported in newspapers worldwide, usually in long articles recounting the highlights of her career. The *Herald* carried a poem written by C.J. Dennis praising her life and her achievements. Prayers were said for Nellie in churches all over the world and messages of condolence flooded in from world leaders and musical leaders. Flags flew at half-mast across Melbourne. The Governor of Victoria received the following message from Buckingham Palace:

> The Queen and I are grieved to hear that Dame Nellie Melba has passed away. We had known her for many, many years, and

appreciated her beautiful voice, which has given pleasure in all parts of the world. Please convey to her relatives our heartfelt sympathy. George V.

Nellie's body was embalmed before leaving St Vincent's Hospital and placed in a coffin surrounded by roses. Her face was covered with a while veil. The coffin was then put on the Melbourne express. Although suffering from bronchitis himself, John Lemmoné insisted on going with the coffin to Central Railway Station at 6.15 am. At Wodonga, on the state border, the coffin was transferred to a special train for the remainder of the journey. As it passed through each station on the route south, the train slowed so that crowds gathered could pay their respects.

Nellie's body reached Melbourne on 25 February and was taken to Scots' Church, where it lay in state, draped with an Australian flag and surrounded by a sea of floral tributes, including white roses on top of the coffin, from Pamela. Two men in long black cloaks shepherded 6000 people through the church. On the following day the Rt Rev. Dr William Borland conducted Nellie's funeral service.[14]

Inner city streets were closed as the cortège, which stretched for three blocks, began its journey to Lilydale, where the coffin was transferred to a gun carriage. Nellie was buried close to her parents and those of her siblings who had predeceased her. Her gravestone carries the words 'Addio senza rancour' ('Goodbye without bitterness'), part of 'Mimi's Farewell' from *La Bohème*.[15]

When Nellie's estate was registered for probate, it was valued at 200,000 pounds, less than most people expected. The principal beneficiaries were George and Pamela; 8000 pounds went to the Albert Street Conservatorium, with bequests to other charities and institutions. Sums of money, jewellery, furniture and art works were left to Nellie's living siblings and her nieces and nephews. Small bequests were made to former servants.

In the years that followed Nellie's death the practice of calling little girls, race horses and streets after her declined, but her reputation as a singer and a pioneer among Australian musicians steadily grew. The proliferation of books about her began to appear, with Percy Colson's unreliable biography the first, published just a year after Nellie's death. In the same year a novel by Beverley Nichols was published. Titled *Evensong*, it told the story of two rival prima donnas – one old and the other young. The two protagonists were obviously modelled on Nellie and Toti dal Monte and if it was ever intended as a tribute to Nichols's former friend and employer it was a seriously misguided one. In 1961 and 2011 Australia Post issued commemorative postage stamps featuring Nellie and currently her portrait appears on the Australian 100 dollar bill.

The other principals in Nellie's life departed as the years went by. Charlie Armstrong died in 1948. George Armstrong died in 1971 and Evie Armstrong two years later. Pamela married Captain William Howarth Vestey, who was killed in action during the Second World War. Pamela was granted the rank of a baron's wife and thereafter known as Lady Vestey. She became chatelaine of Coombe Cottage and lived there until her death in 2011. Lady Vestey gave most of her grandmother's stage costumes to the Performing Arts Museum in Melbourne, where they form a magnificent and important collection. Following her death, Coombe Cottage was opened to the public as a museum and an elegant function venue.

That Nellie's home should now be open to the public is fitting. She was, after all, the most renowned Australian woman of her generation and, arguably, remains so. A consequence of that fame was that many who encountered her felt obliged to comment on her character, and many published their comments. The most extraordinary aspect of this excess of commentary is the plethora of contradictions it contains. Some found Nellie kind and compassionate; others found her arrogant and sometimes aggressive. Some note her generosity; others her parsimony, and so on. The preceding chapters report on instances of Nellie displaying most of these characteristics. Given the credibility of many of these commentators and the irrefutable evidence on record, the only plausible conclusion is that she probably displayed these often-conflicting attributes at various times, dependent on her mood and the circumstances – like most of us, no doubt.

One quality most commentators highlight is that she was egotistical. She was born with a robust sense of her own worth and her own capabilities, and as her fame and power grew so did her ego. 'I am Melba!' was a statement she is reported as using frequently to justify ordering other people about, rearranging furniture in hotel lobbies and, if some of her rivals are to be believed, influencing the management of opera houses. Nellie never denied that she had a powerful ego, and it was certainly an essential component in her success. The gift of a magnificent voice determined her path, but had Nellie chosen to become a doctor, a lawyer or a businesswomen, she would have been equally determined to achieve success.

So what, almost a century after her death, can we conclude about her character. She was, as this account of her life has shown, a very *human* being, blessed with great talent and many estimable qualities, but possessed of a raft of equally human shortcomings, few of which she ever tried to address. If we met Nellie today, the first thing we would observe was that in manner and bearing she was a product of her era, as we all are. Next, we would probably feel intimidated by the obvious manifestations of her fame and star status. We would feel that we had to be on our mettle when her gaze fell on us and if she engaged us in conversation we would know we were being judged. If she found us wanting, Nellie would have passed us over very quickly but, if she recognised sincerity, intelligence and respect, the kinder side of her nature would probably have emerged. Either way, at the end of the encounter, we would likely feel the compulsion to join the legion of other commentators and add our remarks to everyone else's.

Contradictions are rare in the comments her contemporaries

made about Nellie as an artist. Within the boundaries of what she attempted, all agreed that she succeeded spectacularly. It should, however, be remembered (as observed earlier) that the style of singing and the standards of performance by which her contemporaries judged Nellie are not today's standards. Fashions and taste have changed, and accepting that allows us to fully appreciate Nellie's art for what it was, rather than for what we think it should have been.

Listening to Nellie singing on record more than 100 years ago, and exploring her remarkable career, makes me proud to be a fellow Australian and I hope that the preceding pages will make other Australians equally proud. For others, I trust that this book will help you to understand why Australians are so proud to have given the world one of the greatest 'Queens of Song'.

Notes

Chapter 1 – Nellie Melba
1. Nellie Melba, *Melodies and Memories*, Butterworth, London, 1925, p. 9.
2. ibid., p. 11.
3. North Meathie seems to have disappeared off the maps of Angus. It was located not far from the present town of Gateside, just off the A90.
4. J.M. Barrie was born in Kirriemuir a year before Melba was born in Australia. The creator of Peter Pan once told the press that if Melba's father had remained in Kirriemuir and she had been born there, they might have been playmates, a prospect that delighted him.
5. In later years other members of the Mitchell family would choose the same course. David's brother, Charles, immigrated to Canada and three more brothers followed David to Melbourne. In 1887, a sister, Anne, along with her husband and seven children, chose Western Australia as their destination, but the ship on which they were travelling collided with another on the voyage out and there were no survivors.
6. *Argus* (Melbourne), 26 July 1852.
7. The land was subdivided last century but the general location of Mitchell's property can be identified by the names Doonside Street and David Street.
8. A small, bellows-operated organ that did service in small churches and was a popular accoutrement in the parlours of wealthy Victorians.
9. Mitchell was paid £7760 for the work on the cathedral, but before it was finished the decision was made to demolish the old building and replace it with a new one, so Mitchell's work had been in vain. In the years that followed Mitchell would be responsible for the construction of numerous large buildings in Melbourne, often working in conjunction with Melbourne's leading firm of architects, Reed & Barnes.
10. Not 1856 as many references state.
11. Melba, *Melodies and Memories,* p. 12.
12. The year of Melba's birth was given by different writers (during her life and after) as 1859, 1864 or 1865; 19 May 1861 is the correct date,

confirmed by her birth registration in the state of Victoria (Entry No. 12520/61) and by the announcement of her birth in the *Argus*, 25 May 1861.

13   Until Doonside was demolished in 1930, it was possible to pick out the name 'Nellie Mitchell' scratched into the glass of one of the front windows.

14   In 1878, when the Prince of Wales Theatre was built in Melbourne and Lyster assumed its management, David Mitchell purchased 50 shares in the enterprise.

15   Nellie was engrossed in the works of Charles Dickens at the time of Dora's birth and insisted that her new sister be named after David Copperfield's wife.

16   Agnes G. Murphy, *Melba – A Biography*, Doubleday, Page & Co, New York, 1909, da Capo edition, pp. 2–3.

17   There are no press advertisements or reports of this concert, so the date is lost, but it must have been between June 1867 and June 1868.

18   Melba would later make two memorable recordings of 'Comin' thro the rye', one in 1904 and one in 1913 (see Appendix 2: Melba's recordings).

19   At different times Nellie gave different versions of this story. For Agnes Murphy she toned down the friend's remark to 'Nellie Mitchell, I could see your garter'. She also occasionally said that she accompanied herself at the piano, but that would likely negate the story of the visible undergarment. To Beverly Nichols in 1925 she said that she sang the two songs in the reverse order and that the concert took place in the Richmond Town Hall, although that building was not constructed until 1869.

20   *Richmond Australian*, 16 October 1869.

21   The third favourite song was Stephen Foster's 'Nellie Bly', Nellie Mitchell probably imaging herself as 'Nellie with the voice like a turtle-dove and a heart as warm as a cup of tea'.

22   *Richmond Australian*, 11 December 1869.

23   When the soaring spire on the building was partly completed, Mitchell invited Nellie to ascend to the top in a basket, suspended on ropes and pulleys; it was used by the building workers to carry material aloft. Scots' Church remains one of Melbourne's most elegant churches. A plaque bearing Melba's portrait and information about the Mitchell family is affixed to the stonework at street level.

24   Guenett seems to have been a favourite teacher of Melba's. Years later, when she was famous, she sent him a cigarette case, on which were engraved the signatures of several famous opera singers. Accompanying the gift was a note expressing the hope that the recipient had not forgotten 'the naughty little girl to whom he was so kind'. The gift and note were reported in the *Lilydale Express*, 24 December 1896.

25 Melba, *Melodies and Memories*, p. 14.
26 Murphy, *Melba*, da Capo edition, pp. 4–5 (edited).
27 Another aquatic anecdote concerns a visit Nellie made in the company of a female friend to Stubbs's Sea Baths at Port Melbourne on a blistering hot summer's day. The approach to the baths Nellie insisted they use involved tiptoeing over a narrow wooden plank spanning a muddy ditch. Excited by the challenge, Nellie ran back and forth across the plank until the inevitable happened and she fell into the mud. Amid gales of laughter from the two girls and a storm of complaints from other bathers, Nellie then dived into the baths fully clothed to wash away the mud.
28 Long after she became the world's revered 'Queen of Song', Melba would shock listeners by seasoning her speech with 'Aussie' expletives. When someone suggested to her one day that she resembled Queen Victoria, Melba's response was: 'Don't say that. I hated the *bloody* woman!'
29 One can also imagine Nellie feeling envious of her brothers, who were as rebellious as she, but whose behaviour was tolerated because of their gender. Frank and Charlie Mitchell had to leave one school after another as pranks misfired on them. David and Isabella finally employed tutors for their two eldest sons, but Frank and Charlie managed to force a succession of these men into resigning from their posts.
30 The three-storeyed building with arched windows and turret looked more like the seat of a minor Scottish baronet than a school. It was demolished in 1958 when the school moved to new premises in Burwood.
31 Nellie was enrolled as student number 166 and her given name incorrectly recorded as 'Ellen'.
32 Humming and whistling had always been favourite occupations of Nellie's from her infancy and her sister Belle and brother Ernie were also virtuoso whistlers. One can imagine a cacophony of whistling around the house at Doonside, which might not have always been appreciated by the non-whistlers.
33 Alice Charbonnet, born in Cincinnati in 1858, was a pupil of Félix Le Couppey at the Paris Conservatoire. She arrived in Australia in 1878 on a concert tour and stayed for 30 years. Her daughter, Annette Kellermann, became a champion swimmer and a Hollywood film star.
34 Mary Ellen Christian, born in 1848, arrived in Australia in 1871. In 1894 she abandoned her career and entered the Sisters of Charity in Sydney. As Sister Mary Paul of the Cross, she continued to teach singing until just before her death at the age of 93.
35 Melba, *Melodies and Memories*, da Capo edition, p. 5.
36 *Sydney Morning Herald*, 1 January 1927 (edited).

37 In 1889 when Melba was appearing in her second season at London's Covent Garden Opera House, a journalist from the *Pall Mall Gazette* (no doubt fishing for a juicy scoop) contacted PLC and asked for a comment about their former student. These extraordinary words appeared in the 1 August issue of that journal: 'The grave and reverend authorities at Presbyterian Ladies College regard with conflicting emotions the celebrity which their former pupil has achieved. They are pleased at having had the early training of such a musical prodigy, and displeased at seeing her delicate talents devoted to the abhorrent operatic stage.' In later years there was a story disseminated that Melba had been expelled from PLC, but when that was published her former mathematics teacher, Dr Wilson, leapt to her defence, refuting the claim in letters to the press.
38 Melba, *Melodies and Memories*, da Capo edition, pp. 14–15.
39 Cecchi's high opinion of Nellie's talent is confirmed by one of his other students, contralto Margaret Laidlaw, who recalled arriving early for a lesson and listening to an outstanding soprano voice singing an aria. On entering the studio for her own lesson, Laidlaw commented to Cecchi: 'What a glorious voice that girl has!' 'Si', Cecchi replied with a contented smile, 'that voice is going to enthral the world one day'. Nellie's swimming companion, Billy Neilson, also studied with Cecchi and over the years Cecchi produced many singers who went on to have successful careers, but none on the scale of Melba's.
40 The Cave Hill quarry operated until the 1970s.
41 The Royal Exhibition Building, which is now a World Heritage-listed building, and Scots' Church, are the most impressive remaining memorials to David Mitchell's talent and skills. On 9 March 1901 the opening of the Federal Parliament of Australia took place in the Royal Exhibition Building.
42 On the afternoon of Isabella's funeral a violent storm hit Melbourne and part of the Royal Exhibition Building was damaged. Isabella was interred in Melbourne General Cemetery, but later transferred to the Lilydale Cemetery, where David Mitchell had purchased a large family plot. Margaret Mitchell's tiny coffin was also transferred to the Lilydale plot and she was laid beside her mother.

Chapter 2 – Mrs Armstrong

1 *Mackay Mercury and South Kennedy Advertiser*, 31 May 1882.
2 Some writers have stated that Annie Mitchell accompanied her father and sister, but her name does not appear on the passenger lists of any of the ships on which they travelled. It is likely that Annie, now 19, was entrusted with the care of the younger children, who remained behind

at Doonside. We also know that Annie commenced taking singing lessons with Cecchi while her father and sister were in Mackay.
3   Letter to Pietro Cecchi, 15 September 1882 (edited), quoted in Thorold Waters, *Much Besides Music* (Georgian House, Melbourne, 1951, p. 110–11). Oreste Nobili was a concert and opera manager in Melbourne, and 'Bracchi' was probably Signor Baracchi, a representative of the Italian Government in Melbourne.
4   *Mackay Mercury and South Kennedy Advertiser*, 20, 30 September 1882.
5   Letter to Pietro Cecchi, 15 October 1882 (edited), quoted in Waters, *Much Besides Music*, p. 111.
6   Family legend has it that the Armstrongs were originally Scottish and had fled to Ireland in the 17th century after an ancestor had been hanged for raiding English communities across the border. That Charlie Armstrong might have had Scottish blood in his veins would have added to his appeal for Nellie.
7   One of those properties was historic 'Jimbour' near Dalby. Charles Armstrong's brother-in-law John Alexander Bell had served as a member of the Queensland Legislative Council from 1866 to 1872.
8   Finding young men of pedigree (such as the son of a baronet) or of diverse talents working as jackaroos or drovers in colonial Australia might seem surprising to us today, but it would not have to their contemporaries. Among the team of drovers that accompanied Armstrong on the drive to Mackay were Thomas Chataway, a former Charterhouse student who later became mayor of Mackay and served as a senator for Queensland in the federal parliament, and William Cresswell who ended up as a vice-admiral in the Royal Australian Navy.
9   Not to be confused (as other writers have) with the same composer's song 'Goodbye', which was not written until 1885 and which later became a staple of Melba's song repertoire.
10 *Courier Mail* (Brisbane), 21 January 1947. A photograph of Nellie wearing the outfit she wore at her wedding will be found among the illustrations.
11 Quoted in John Hetherington, *Melba, a Biography* (Faber & Faber, London, 1967).
12 Evidence for this and other acts of domestic violence allegedly perpetrated by Armstrong on his wife are based on testimony Melba gave (under oath) some years later when she was applying for legal separation from Charlie. More about this will be found in Chapter 8.
13 Letter to Pietro Cecchi, 12 April 1883 (edited), quoted in Waters, *Much Besides Music*, p. 112. The 'Mr Ampt' referred to was possibly Gustave Ampt, a prominent member of the German community in Melbourne who had recently moved to Sydney. The opera season Nellie referred to was put on at the Gaiety Theatre by a touring Italian opera company under the musical directorship of Paolo Giorza, who had come to

Australia with the same company as Cecchi. The performance Nellie attended was of Gounod's *Faust*. Alice Rees was a talented young Australian lyric soprano, whom Nellie then admired, but by the time Rees made her debut in the Sydney season, Nellie had departed for Mackay.

14 Quoted in Hetherington, *Melba, a Biography,* p. 31.
15 Letter to Pietro Cecchi, 11 May 1883 (edited), quoted in Waters, *Much Besides Music*, p. 112–13. The request in this letter for Cecchi to send her the sheet music of a song in a 'low' key suggests it was a gift for some local contralto.
16 Murphy, *Melba*, da Capo edition, pp. 13–14.
17 Melba, *Melodies and Memories*, pp. 17–18 (edited). Ironically it was Charlie who would have been most alarmed by the presence of snakes. He feared few things but had a pathological fear of snakes.
18 John Ewan Davidson was one of the pioneers of the sugar industry in Queensland but is better remembered today for some of his less commendable actions: leading armed raids on Indigenous communities and sending Aboriginal artifacts to the British Museum. Charles Rawson had been the mayor of Mackay when Nellie and her father had first visited. The Rawsons tried to create a 'little piece of England' at Mirani through the elegance of the interior of their homestead, a tennis court and formal gardens, an effect Nellie undoubtedly approved of and enjoyed.
19 The other operas performed were Verdi's *Il Trovatore*, Wallace's *Maritana*, Gounod's *Faust* and Flotow's *Martha*. Montague and Turner sang the principal soprano and tenor parts and Saville sang the principal mezzo-soprano parts in each opera.
20 Letter to Pietro Cecchi, 4 July 1883 (edited), quoted in Waters, *Much Besides Music*, p. 113.
21 See Note 12.
22 Undated letter to Pietro Cecchi (edited), quoted in Waters, *Much Besides Music*, pp. 114–15. The 'Madame Elmblad' referred to is Maggie Menzies-Elmblad a popular concert pianist and the composer of a hit song 'God be with you'.
23 Despite this statement of his intentions, Charlie turned up in Melbourne a few weeks later, arriving without warning at Doonside. Presumably, he came to try to persuade Nellie to return to Mackay with him but, after several violent arguments, Charlie conceded failure and retreated to Mackay.
24 An 'obbligato' is a solo instrumental part (usually played by a string, woodwind or brass instrument) added to the voice and accompanying instruments in a song or aria. Its purpose is to complement the voice.

Chapter 3 – One voice in ten thousand

1. Liedertafel were amateur choral societies, sometimes with their own orchestras, which existed in most cities and many provincial towns in Australia. Begun by German immigrants (hence the name) but not exclusively German in membership, there were two in Melbourne: the Melbourne Liedertafel, founded in 1868, and the Metropolitan Liedertafel, founded in 1870. Both were major contributors to the city's musical life.
2. Other writers have stated that Nellie sang two items, replacing an indisposed singer in a vocal quartet, but as there was no vocal quartet in the advertised program, nor is one mentioned in the reviews, that is erroneous.
3. As is the custom when this *scena* is performed in concert, the three lines sung by the tenor singing the part of Alfredo, were omitted. The first and second sections of this piece (minus the 'Follia, follia! part) would be among the first recordings Melba made in 1904 and she would record the whole piece twice more in America (see Appendix 2: Melba's recordings).
4. One of these floral tributes was heart-shaped and made of white flowers. When she arrived home and looked at the attached card Nellie discovered it bore the name of a young man she had detested when they were both teenagers and whom she remembered always calling her 'Nellie Longdrawers'. The card was torn up and the flowers given to a maid. The reference to nerves affecting Nellie's first notes is taken from a review of the concert in the *Argus*, 19 May 1884.
5. *Australasian* (Melbourne), 24 May 1884 (edited).
6. *Con Amore*, no.13 (Journal), 1946, Melba Memorial Conservatorium Archive.
7. Melba later claimed that she organised the Sorrento concert. Her contribution was going around the little community, putting up posters for the concert and helping to decorate the hall with bunches of fresh eucalyptus leaves.
8. As well as the arias and *scena* already mentioned, Nellie sang 'Regnava nel silenzio' from *Lucia di Lammermoor*; the cavatina 'Ma la sola, ahimè!' from Bellini's *Beatrice di Tenda*; 'Qui la voce' from Bellini's *I Puritani*; 'Caro nome' from Verdi's *Rigoletto*; 'Ombre légère' ('Shadow Song') from Meyerbeer's *Dinorah*; 'The Jewel Song' from Gounod's *Faust*; 'The Waltz Song' from Gounod's *Mireille*; and arias from *Maritana* and *The Bohemian Girl*. When the opportunity arose, she also sang duets from *Lucia di Lammermoor* and *Rigoletto* and the trio 'Guai se ti sfugge un moto' from Donizetti's *Lucrezia Borgia*.
9. Haydn's Mass No. 11 in D minor, known today as the *Nelson Mass*, was called the *Imperial Mass* at that time.

10 David Mitchell's attitude towards his daughter singing in a Catholic church didn't soften. There is a wonderful story about how he would insist Nellie came with the rest of the family when he drove them to church on Sundays. Nellie, and a young Catholic maid from Doonside, would be dropped off first, outside St Francis's, and in full view of the public he would say loudly to his daughter, 'Shame on you Nellie! You ought to be singing at your own kirk.' As a sequel to that story, it is said that on one occasion when Nellie had sung at Scots' Church she asked her father as he carved the Sunday roast, what he thought of her performance. 'I dinna like your hat' was the reply she received.
11 Letter from Annie Mitchell to S. Arthur Hilliger, 1 October 1885 (Mitchell Library).
12 *Australasian*, 27 June 1885 (edited).
13 Letter dated 7 July, quoted with an incorrect date in Waters, *Much Besides Music,* p. 115. 'Mrs. Fisher' was Sarah Jane Fisher, wife of the conductor–composer Wilhelm Carl Fisher. In fact, the only negative that Fisher's review of their first concert contained was the adjective 'metallic', applied to Nellie's voice. Two days after Nellie wrote this letter, Fisher reviewed their fourth concert in Sydney and was effusive in her praise of Nellie. Alice Rees seems to have been demoted from someone worthy of admiration to the status of a rival.
14 Quoted in Ann Blainey, *I am Melba*, Blank Inc., Melbourne, 2009, p. 38.
15 There is an air of secrecy about Nellie's surviving correspondence with Hilliger. That may have been prompted by the risk of scandal attached to a young married woman writing to a bachelor, or of Nellie's husband becoming aware of their correspondence. There is also evidence that neither Nellie nor Annie was aware that the other was corresponding with Hilliger and with Moore.
16 Information from an article Moore wrote (anonymously) for the *Sydney Morning Herald*, 16 October 1926.
17 *Argus*, 10 August 1885.
18 *Table Talk* (Melbourne), 14 August 1885.
19 Letter dated 16 August 1885 from Doonside (Performing Arts Museum, Melbourne). Nellie's frustration and depression may have resulted in the period of illness she suffered this month and which forced her to cancel some (but not all) engagements, although influenza was rife in Melbourne at the time and that may have been the cause.
20 The exhibition halls are long gone, but their location is still marked by the name Exhibition Road.
21 Letter from Annie Mitchell to Arthur Hilliger, 31 July 1885.
22 Despite this success, Melba only sang *Messiah* once more in her long career when an English cathedral city offered her a very large fee for one performance. Her pure and bright soprano proved well suited to

how Handel was performed in the nineteenth and early twentieth centuries when she occasionally performed other pieces by Handel, but Melba came to realise that perhaps Professor Ives had been right, and she was better suited to the stage. This trip to Sydney was spoiled for Nellie by Arthur Hilliger avoiding her – perhaps because he had decided that their friendship was too much of a risk for *him*. Jack Moore had no such reservations and escorted Nellie to and from each of her Sydney engagements. Seven years later Moore visited Paris and had a joyful reunion with Nellie.

23   The last time Nellie's voice was heard in Australia for the following 16 years was at an afternoon reception held in one of the buildings her father had built: the Masonic Hall in Collins Street. The event was an official farewell for David Mitchell.
24   Melba, *Melodies and Memories*, pp. 22–23.
25   Melba, *Melodies and Memories*, pp. 18–20 (edited).
26   Quoted in Waters, *Much Besides Music*, p. 119.

Chapter 4 – Pomp and mixed circumstances

1   The writers of these last three letters are unknown, but it is likely that some (or all of them) were penned by Lady Loch, wife of the Governor of Victoria who had patronised Nellie's farewell concert in the Melbourne Town Hall. Lady Loch's sister was married to Robert Bulwer-Lytton, British ambassador to France between 1887 and 1891. When Nellie lived and performed in France during those years, Lady Lytton continued her sister's practice of offering support and patronage to Nellie.
2   *Herald* (Melbourne), 11 March 1886.
3   Letter, 13 May 1886 (National Library of Australia).
4   See Note 12, Chapter 2.
5   ibid.
6   Melba, *Melodies and Memories*, p. 25 (edited).
7   See Note 3.
8   Some other writers have claimed that Nellie forgot her letter to Marchesi, that she only remembered it after she had presented her other letters in London and that she then went to Paris unannounced, but all this is disproved by her May letter to Rudolph Himmer (see Note 3).
9   At the time Sullivan was working on *Ruddigore*.
10   Later when Melba became friends with both Sullivan and Randegger, she teased them both about their initial rejection of her.
11   Wilhelm Ganz, *Memories of a Musician: Reminiscences of seventy years of musical life*, John Murray, London, 1913, p. 315.
12   See Note 12, Chapter 2.
13   Quoted in Hetherington, *Melba, a Biography*, pp. 53–4.

14 Nellie was not the first Australian-born singer to appear in Europe. The first was the contralto Lucy Chambers (1834–1894), daughter of a town clerk of Sydney. Chambers sang successfully in Italy (including La Scala), Germany, Spain, Portugal and Belgium in the 1860s. Chambers was followed much later by Tasmanian-born Amy Sherwin (1855–1935), who began her career in the United States and then sang with the Carl Rosa company in Britain.
15 *Musical World* (London), 5 June 1886.
16 Herman Klein, *Thirty Years of Musical Life in London, 1870–1900*, William Heinemann, London, 1903, p. 238 (edited).
17 Other writers have suggested that 'Colonel' James Mapleson, another influential English opera impresario of the time was present, but Mapleson's name does not appear in the list of guests published in the press.
18 Henry J. Wood, *My Life of Music,* Victor Gollancz, London, 1938, p. 240 (edited).
19 Letter to Cecchi, 27 June 1886. Antoinette Sterling was a famous American contralto. Sullivan wrote his song 'The lost chord' for her.
20 The widely accepted story that Charles Armstrong became an officer with the rank of captain in the regular British Army is untrue. He did later hold the rank of captain in the volunteer Mackay Mounted Infantry.
21 See Note 12, Chapter 2. That was not the only mishap Nellie suffered at this time. While alighting from a train she had boarded by mistake, she fell and hit her head on the platform and had to spend two days in bed.
22 Undated letter to Wilhelm Ganz, quoted in Ganz, *Memories of a Musician*, pp. 318–19.
23 Oddly, Nellie does not mention this concert in her letter to Cecchi. Perhaps she had begun the letter before the concert and forgot to add it later. Rose Hersée was the first to sing the role of Carmen in Australia.
24 Because his family were aristocrats, Salvatore used the stage name Marchesi and when he married Mathilde she adopted that as her professional name. After his singing days were over, Salvatore Marchesi became famous for his translations of the German texts of Wagner's music dramas into Italian – of which the composer did not approve.
25 Other students from this period included Antonietta Fricci, Gabrielle Krauss, Célestine Galli-Marié, Emma Calvé, Emma Abbott, Emma Nevada, Blanche Arral and Marchesi's own daughter, Blanche. Later students would include (as well as Melba), Emma Eames, Suzanne Adams, Francis Saville, Sybil Sanderson, Mary Garden, Frances Alda, Selma Kurz and Australians Ada Crossley, Amy Castles and Evelyn Scotney.

26 Rue Jouffroy, was renamed Rue Jouffroy-d'Abbans in 1994 and is located in the 17th arrondissement, about one kilometre northeast of the Arc de Triomphe.
27 'Salvatore, at last I have a star!' This literal translation and the inclusion of the word *enfin* ('at last') suggests that, despite having produced so many stars in the past, Marchesi was anxious to find another as her career entered its last phase. Melba's phenomenal success when it came and which the singer attributed entirely to Marchesi, gave Marchesi's reputation a massive boost, which lasted until her death, 27 years later. Three years before Melba gave her interview to the *Musical Age* in New York, she also described her first meeting with Marchesi to the novelist George Moore, whom she met at a dinner in London. Moore's next novel, *Evelyn Innes*, contains a fictional scene which is unmistakably based on what Melba described to him, although no one reading the novel at the time would have recognised it as such.
28 Melba, *Melodies and Memories*, p. 29.
29 When Marchesi wrote her own memoirs a decade later (Mathilde Marchesi, *Marchesi and Music – Passages from the Life of a Famous Singing Teacher*, Harper & Brothers, New York, 1898), she commented at length on Melba, praising her extravagantly and beginning with: 'When I heard Madame Melba's soprano voice for the first time I was charmed with its pure tones, and at once recognized in her a future star'.
30 See Note 12, Chapter 2.
31 It would appear that Charlie never contributed anything to his wife and son's upkeep during their time in Paris and to Nellie's credit, she never asked her father for additional funds, resisting the temptation to spend money on anything other than the bare essentials of living and studying. There is a story of Marchesi complaining to Nellie after her lessons began that her new student wore the same unfashionable blue-and-white striped serge dress every day. As Nellie was the wife of an army officer and the daughter of a rich man, Marchesi demanded Nellie go out and buy some more clothes. When Nellie explained that she was living frugally, Marchesi offered to pay for a new dress, but Nellie's pride made her refuse the offer and Marchesi had to put up the blue and white creation for many months more.
32 One of these was Lucien Petipa, a former principal dancer at the Paris Opéra, who taught the students how to enter and exit a room, how to sit, how to eat and drink, and how to conduct themselves in society in ways that brought credit on the school. Another was a stage director from the Opéra named Pluque, who gave the students acting lessons. Part of the school's routine also covered how students paid their fees. On the same day each month a special vase was placed on the studio piano and students were expected to place their month's fees (in an

envelope with their name on it) in the vase. This way Madame did not have to handle the money.

33   Murphy, *Melba*, p. 25.
34   Emma Eames, *Some Memories and Reflections*, Appleton, New York, 1927, pp. 58–9.
35   It is generally accepted that the human voice is divided into two different registers – called 'chest' and 'head' – although experts with differing views have claimed there are three or even four registers. The lower notes in a singer's vocal range are generally produced using the chest register; that is, employing the part of the singing mechanism which feels, to the singer, as if it originates from the torso. The head register is used for the upper part of a singer's range. It involves exploiting the resonating cavities in the part of the head called 'the mask'. More volume and greater weight of tone can be achieved by producing notes using the chest register and this has led many singers into bad practices, resulting in vocal crises. The greatest singers perfect the skill of transitioning from one register to the other at the right point in their vocal range and without their listeners being aware of the change, rather like a motorist shifting smoothly through a vehicle's gears.
36   The Australian contralto Ada Crossley is perhaps the only one remembered today. Crossley went to Marchesi on Melba's recommendation, but not before she had studied for a long period with Charles Santley.

Chapter 5 – Madame Melba

1   Much to Emma Eames's disgust, she was not invited to sing a solo on this occasion and her enmity towards Nellie must have increased as she saw her rival praised by the famous composer.
2   *Le Ménestrel* (Paris), 9 January 1887. Melba would later make four recordings of the Mad Scene from *Hamlet*, the best of which are among the finest of her recordings (see Appendix 2: Melba's recordings).
3   Maurice Strakosch, born 1825, was a pianist, former tenor (pupil of legendary soprano Giuditta Pasta), composer and later, impresario and noted voice teacher. He managed Adelina Patti's early career in the USA and was married to Patti's sister Amelia.
4   Murphy, *Melba*, p. 26.
5   Melba would later claim that the contract was for ten years and some other writers have accepted that.
6   Letter to S. Arthur Hilliger, 29 March 1887.
7   In French newspapers and some reference books, Gailhard is referred to as 'Pierre' rather than Pedro. As Pedro Gailhard, he had enjoyed a very

successful career in Paris and London singing bass roles, before taking over the co-directorship of the Opéra.
8 That cadenza can be heard on the recording Melba made of the Mad Scene from *Lucia di Lammermoor* in London in 1904 (see Appendix 2: Melba's recordings). Emma Eames finally shared top billing with Nellie at this soirée and Heugel wrote that both sopranos were destined for brilliant careers (*Le Ménestrel*, 19 June 1887).
9 Reported a year later in *Le Ménestrel*, 8 April 1888.
10 Melba refers to Professor Gevaert by his familiar name 'Félix'. His correct name was François Auguste Gevaert and both he and his wife were to prove staunch friends to Nellie. Melba also described Gevaert as 'the ugliest man she had ever seen', but photographs of him do not support that. He is quoted as saying: 'Melba's art is as spontaneous as the murmur of a brook. She sings because she must sing.'
11 This version of how Strakosch was to be appeased comes from Melba, in both Murphy's *Melba* and *Melodies and Memories*, and effectively lays the blame for what ultimately transpired on Marchesi. It relies on Marchesi showing a degree of naivety that would have been uncharacteristic of her, especially if Strakosch had begun paying Nellie her monthly fee. As no alternative version has come down to us, it has been accepted, but elements of it remain questionable.
12 Letter to S. Arthur Hilliger, 31 August 1887.
13 At different times in the future Melba gave the address of her apartment in Brussels as 'Avenue Louise' and 'Rue de Bec', but Rue de Bailly is correct.
14 See Note 12, Chapter 2.
15 *Le Ménestrel*, Paris, 2 October 1887.
16 Mixed-language performances such as this were not uncommon in the nineteenth century and audiences of the time seemed little troubled by them. The author can remember performances sung in English here in Australia as late as the 1970s where guest artists were permitted to sing in Italian.
17 Lapissida may well have spoken those words, but it was later revealed that Strakosch had given the soprano Sigrid Arnoldson a singing lesson at his apartment in the evening, and then fainted while preparing for bed and died in his sleep around midnight. Strakosch's heirs made a legal bid some months later to hold Nellie to the contract she had signed but as payments to her had ceased after Strakosch confronted Nellie in Paris, their claim was dismissed.
18 Melba, *Melodies and Memories*, p. 46 (edited).
19 ibid. p. 47 (edited).
20 *Étoile Belge* (Brussels), 14 October 1887.
21 *Indépendence Belge* (Brussels), 14 October 1887.

22 *La Patriote* (Brussels), 18 October 1887.
23 *Le Ménestrel*, 23 October 1887 (edited).
24 Nellie's success was also reported in Germany, Italy, the United States and Australia.
25 Melba, *Melodies and Memories*, p. 46 (edited).
26 While in Paris Nellie confided to her 'loving old mother' that she was suffering from some kind of gynaecological disorder, which was sapping her energy and causing her concern. Marchesi berated her for not having the condition treated earlier. Eventually the condition (whatever it was) was either treated or disappeared of its own accord.
27 Wauters's portrait of Melba is now in the collection of the Musée Charlier in Brussels. It is charming and captures both Nellie's physical attractiveness and her determination. A welcome guest at the apartment on another occasion was the great pianist Ignace Paderewski, who was brought to meet Nellie by Monsieur Elkin, the music lover who had originally recommended her to Lapissida and Dupont.
28 Such works had to wait until the middle of the twentieth century when firstly Callas, and then Sutherland, Montserrat Caballé and Beverly Sills proved their merit in modern revivals.
29 Later that comment got expanded into: 'She can sing *Lakmé* in French, in Italian, in German, in English or even in Chinese for all I care, but she must sing it!' The original, as quoted here, appeared in *Le Ménestrel*, 23 October 1888. The expanded version was offered by Nellie to the press when she toured Australia in 1902.
30 Litvinne would have another encounter with an Australian soprano more than 40 years later and long after she had retired from the stage. When the Australian Wagnerian soprano Marjorie Lawrence was studying in Paris, Litvinne gave Lawrence advice and presented her with some of the stage costumes she had worn during her own career. Those interested in Marjorie Lawrence's remarkable life and career should read the author's biography of her: *Wotan's Daughter*, published by Wakefield Press in 2012 and reprinted in 2021.
31 Among those who attended the opening night of *Hamlet* (and probably some of Nellie's earlier performances) was a 15-year-old prodigy violinist. He went backstage to congratulate Nellie and was given a signed photograph of her as Ophélie. His name was Henri Verbrugghen and 27 years later he would be appointed the first director of the New South Wales State Conservatorium of Music. He and Nellie remained casual friends for the rest of Nellie's life and Verbrugghen's admiration for Nellie never wavered.
32 During her first season at the Monnaie, Nellie had sung a total of 30 performances: eight of Gilda in Verdi's *Rigoletto*, seven of Ophélie in Thomas's *Hamlet*, six each of the title roles in Donizetti's *Lucia di*

Lammermoor and Delibes's *Lakmé* and three as Violetta in Verdi's *La Traviata*.

Chapter 6 – Covent Garden

1. The theatre did not adopt its present name, 'The Royal Opera House, Covent Garden', until 1892.
2. *Times* (London), 25 May 1888 (edited). Nellie was the first Australian to sing at Covent Garden and in the decades that followed dozens more would follow.
3. Nellie's debut was five days after her own 27th birthday.
4. *Times*, 25 May 1888.
5. *Sunday Times* (London), 27 May 1888.
6. Other writers have stated that the role of Oscar was offered in the next season when Nellie returned to London, but *Un Ballo in Maschera* was not in Covent Garden's repertoire for the 1889 season.
7. Nellie would always be grateful to Lapissida and Dupont for providing her with the chance to lay the foundations of her stage career. Their reward, in the form of sold-out houses and increased international attention, was acknowledged when Jacques Isnardon, a bass with the company, wrote his history of the Monnaie in 1890 (see bibliography).
8. *Le Ménestrel*, 16 September 1888 (edited).
9. Engel sang Roméo and Renaud sang Capulet. It was also announced that Nellie would sing the Queen of the Night in Mozart's *Die Zauberflöte* this season with Landouzy as Pamina, but when the production reached the stage, Landouzy sang the Queen of the Night and Rose Caron sang Pamina. A possible revival of Meyerbeer's *Les Huguenots* with Nellie as Marguerite de Valois, was also mooted, but failed to materialise. In her second season at the Monnaie Nellie sang 42 performances of opera: ten of *Lakmé*, nine each of *Hamlet* and *Roméo et Juliette*, seven of *Rigoletto*, five of *Lucia di Lammermoor* and two of *La Traviata*. This was Lapissida's and Dupont's last season in charge of the Monnaie. Dupont stayed on as a conductor and Lapissida was engaged by Harris as a stage director at Covent Garden.
10. Another whom Nellie had hoped would be in attendance at her first attempt at Juliette was Queen Marie Henriette, but she was in mourning for a relative: Crown Prince Rudolph, heir to the Austro-Hungarian throne who, along with his mistress, had committed suicide at Mayerling.
11. That evening was one of the great nights in the history of the Paris Opéra. The glittering audience included a 'who's who' of European society and many famous musicians of current and past generations. It is believed that Patti received a fee of 25,000 francs (about £1000) for each of her three performances.

12 After the concert featuring the Handel work, King Leopold presented Nellie with the medal of the Brussels Conservatoire.
13 On this trip to Paris, Nellie took the opportunity to attend another performance of *Roméo et Juliette* at the Opéra, where Emma Eames was making her debut in the role of Juliette. According to Eames, Nellie had been responsible for the long delay in her making her debut in Paris. She also claimed that Nellie called on her on the morning after her debut for the sole purpose of telling her how badly she had sung. A very large grain of salt is required if Eames's claims are to be considered as factual.
14 The history and the current whereabouts of that portrait are unknown.
15 *Le Figaro* (Paris), 9 May 1889. On 22 May, *Le Figaro* also published a four-verse ode to Nellie of such banality as to disqualify it from being quoted here.
16 The institution's copy of the contract appears not to have survived in the archives of the Paris Opéra, but subsequent events suggest it was for three seasons, or one with options for two more, covering the years up until 1892.
17 *Sunday Times*, 9 June 1889 (edited).
18 *Pall Mall Gazette* (London), 3 July 1889, gives a detailed description of how Covent Garden was decorated for this occasion with roses, carnations, shrubs and blocks of ice in the foyer, through which coloured lights shone. Programs printed on silk were issued.
19 In this season at Covent Garden Nellie had sung nine performances: six of *Roméo et Juliette* (not seven as stated in some histories of Covent Garden), two of *Rigoletto* and one of *Faust*. She and Harris may have planned for her to sing more, but the illness that prevented her singing at Buckingham Palace and the bout of 'hoarseness' reported in the press may have prevented that.
20 During her stay in London the press announced that Nellie had cancelled her engagements to sing in Berlin, Madrid and St Petersburg, although she would later sing in each of those cities.
21 See note 12, Chapter 2. Charlie did return to Australia for an extended period, began draining the land at Sarina and built a house at what is now called Armstrong Beach. There is now a Melba Street at Armstrong Beach.
22 Annie and Belle would remain in Australia for most of the rest of their lives. In 1892 Belle married Tom Paterson, a Melbourne real estate agent and one of their sons, Gerald Paterson, became a champion tennis player. When she was 45, Annie married Harry Box, son of socialite Mrs Henry Box of 'Iramoo', East St Kilda.
23 As might have been anticipated there were rumblings in the press about Donizetti's 'old-fashioned' opera, but not about Nellie's singing of the title role.

24 Melba, *Melodies and Memories*, p. 63. Prompted by that incident, Nellie arranged to take lessons in make-up from a dancer in the Opéra ballet.
25 Murphy, *Melba*, pp. 50–2.
26 Melba, *Melodies and Memories*, pp. 61–2.
27 Nellie promptly set about furnishing the apartment in regal style, with a clutter of gilt furniture, crystal chandeliers, silver tableware, paintings, mirrors, a bed for herself that looked like it might have been borrowed from the Palace of Versailles and a telephone cubicle with two telephones.
28 In years to come Nellie would recount her version of the circumstances surrounding her first engagement at Monte Carlo. Her version does not mention Louis Jehin or his recommendation and does not tally very well with historical fact. According to Nellie, she had heard that the principal soprano engaged for the season had failed, so she took herself (and George) off to Monte Carlo, where she had tea with the director of the Opéra de Monte Carlo. The director tried to persuade her to join his company. She demurred until the director made a generous offer. Nellie claims she then said that if the offer was trebled she might accept. 'Done', the director replied (according to Nellie, anyway).

Chapter 7 – Le cœur cède à l'amour

1 *Sunday Times*, 8 June 1890.
2 ibid.
3 Emma Eames was also accused of coldness in her acting. Her performance of Aida at the Metropolitan in New York drew one of the most memorable lines ever written by a critic: 'Last night there was skating on the Nile'. None other than Sir Arthur Sullivan, who had rejected Nellie when she first sang for him, summed up what Nellie could achieve by purely vocal means: 'So perfect is Melba's vocal utterances, that by the mere emission of tone, she can express the whole gamut of human feeling' (Quoted in Murphy, *Melba*, p. 121).
4 *Times*, 12 June 1890.
5 Jean Philippe Worth (son of the founder of the House of Worth, Charles Frederick Worth) designed the cloak. It was made of green silk, shot with gold and lined in flesh-coloured silk, and featured a broad Byzantine-style border with nine hand-painted angels set in gold velvet. Today it takes pride of place in the Melba Collection at the Performing Arts Museum in Melbourne.
6 *Pall Mall Gazette*, 11 July 1890.
7 One of Nellie's other performances at Covent Garden that season deserves to be mentioned. This was *Hamlet* on 21 July. The short but important part of the ghost of Hamlet's father was played on that

occasion by Orme Darvall, a Brisbane-born bass and the second Australian (after Nellie) to sing at Covent Garden.

8   When Melba recounted this event to Murphy for *Melba*, she correctly named the accompanist as Mancinelli, but when she recounted it to Nichols for *Melodies and Memories* she named the accompanist as Paolo Tosti. Court circulars confirm it was Mancinelli.

9   Melba, *Melodies and Memories*, p. 79.

10 In her biography of her grandmother, Pamela Vestey states that the queen subsequently requested information about Nellie and a secretary reported: 'She is Madame and married to Mr. Armstrong, who belongs to a very respectable English family. He went to Australia, fell in love and married her. She has been, to some extent spoilt by her success but may also pass as respectable.'

11 Les Avants had another role to play in Australian musical history. In the mid-1960s Dame Joan Sutherland and her husband Richard Bonynge chose to establish their home there.

12 The costume was comprised of a velvet bodice in blue and maroon with drop-away white sleeves embroidered in gold and black. The short (by contemporary standards) skirt was in blue with a red trim. A black lace mantilla crowned the outfit. It purported to be traditional dress for a girl from Aragon but was far too grand to qualify for that description.

13 *Le Ménestrel*, 14 December 1890.

14 It was widely rumored that Gladys de Grey was Jean de Reszke's mistress.

15 *Le Ménestrel*, 12 October, 28 December 1890.

16 Amelie Materna (1844–1918) had been chosen by Wagner to sing Brünnhilde in the first Ring Cycle at Bayreuth in 1876 and had created the role of Kundry in Wagner's *Parsifal* at Bayreuth in 1882.

17 When Percy Colson wrote his *Melba – An Unconventional Biography* the year after Nellie died, he claimed that he had drawn on information given to him by Nellie for most of the content of his book. In his version of this incident in Vienna he states that Ernest van Dyck, who was singing the tenor lead in the opera that night, spotted Nellie and Philippe when he was peeping through the curtain before the performance and that he alerted his friend, the editor of the *Wiener Tagblatt*. Colson claims it was in that newspaper that the article appeared, but there are two flaws in this version. Colson gets the opera wrong (saying it was *Lohengrin*) and while the *Wiener Tagblatt* for January 1892 does mention Nellie in other contexts there is no article linking her name to Philippe. A search carried out by the author failed to identify the name of the journalist or the newspaper involved, but the article undoubtedly once existed, for its content was copied by other papers outside Austria, including *L'Evénement* (Paris), 2 November 1891.

18 Melba, *Melodies and Memories*, pp. 102–3.
19 *Le Figaro*, 25 January; *Pall Mall Gazette*, 29 January; *Le Ménestrel*, 1 February 1890.
20 There is an unconfirmed story (*L'Evénement*, 2 November 1891) that at the final performance of *Roméo et Juliette* and after Nellie had thrown off a particularly scintillating rendition of the 'Waltz Song', Philippe, sitting in the stalls, jumped to his feet and led the audience in their applause. Alexander III was again present and protocol demanded that whenever the Tsar attended a theatre, the privilege of leading the applause was reserved for him. One of the Tsar's equerries challenged Philippe about his behaviour and the Duke demanded an audience with the Tsar, saying he had paid for his ticket and had every right to show his approval however and whenever he wished. The story goes that Philippe tried to gain entry to the Imperial box but was waylaid by a grand duchess and next morning an Imperial order arrived at the Hôtel de France instructing Philippe to leave St Petersburg. There is another story (also unsubstantiated) that during this visit (and before the above event) Philippe had offered his military services to the Tsar and the offer had been politely declined.
21 After Nellie's death, the parasol handle – salmon-coloured Guiloche enamel, gold trim and set with diamonds – was acquired by Sir Thomas Beecham. In 2017 it was auctioned by Christie's and bought by the Metropolitan Opera Guild for $US23,750. It is now in the Bispham Operatic Memorabilia Collection at the Met. The bracelet given to Nellie by the Tsar became a favourite piece of jewellery of hers, worn regularly and its source proudly explained if anyone inquired.
22 *Sunday Times*, 29 March 1891.
23 Choosing what music to perform and who to perform it proved unexpectedly difficult for Harris. Atrocities committed during the Franco-Prussian war were still raw in the memories of several of the French artists on his roster and they refused to take part, Victor Maurel, Jean Lassalle and Pol Plançon among them.

Chapter 8 – The storm breaks

1 *L'Evénement*, 2 November 1891.
2 Nellie used the word 'abducted' to describe Charlie's removal of George from his school; however, in her biography of her grandmother, Pamela Vestey expresses the opinion that it was done with Nellie's reluctant approval.
3 Several of Melba's biographers stated that, after the affair, Philippe was sent by his father on an extended trip to Africa but, as Blainey revealed in her biography of Melba, it was Philippe's brother, Henri, who made that journey. Philippe stayed on in London and it is likely that their

paths crossed from time to time. We know, for example, that in June 1895 both Nellie and Philippe were guests at the Savoy Hotel, she in London to sing at Covent Garden and he to organise the wedding of his sister Hélène to the Duke of Aosta.

4   Australian-born Lady Maie Casey was the widow of Richard, Baron Casey, Governor-General of Australia from 1965 to 1969. Lady Maie does not reveal the source of the letter, dated 25 March 1919, but it was most likely shown to her by Nellie's granddaughter Lady Vestey.
5   The widely reported story that Philippe died after being bitten by a monkey in Africa is untrue.
6   Joseph Wechsberg, *Red Plush and Black Velvet*, Weidenfeld & Nicolson, London, 1962, pp. 196–7. The closest Nellie ever came to another scandal occurred just a year after her separation from Philippe and it was no fault of hers. The 30-year-old Prince Alois Schwarzenberg, a lieutenant in the Austrian army, absconded from his regiment and spent a month in Italy with, it was believed, a mistress. Later he faced a court martial, with his career only saved by the intervention of the Austrian emperor. For some unexplained reason, elements in the press speculated that the prince's mistress was Nellie. At the time Prince Alois was in Italy, Nellie was singing at Covent Garden (*Le Figaro*, 24 December 1892, 11 January 1893).
7   *Giornale di Sicilia* (Palermo), 22 January 1892.
8   It had been reported in the Paris press that Nellie would return to the Monte Carlo opera at this time, but there is no available evidence that Monte Carlo was included in her appearances in the spring of this year.
9   *La Stampa* (Turin), 5 March 1892.
10 Victoria's disapproval seems to have been real and lasting. Two years later when a command performance of *Faust* was given at Windsor Castle, the queen informed Harris that she did not want 'that woman' to sing and would prefer Emma Albani. These rumours and that injunction were probably the cause of the remark of Nellie's about hating Queen Victoria quoted earlier.
11 Calvé described Nellie's voice as like that of an angel.
12 *World* (London), 3 August 1892.
13 During the second performance of *Elaine*, practical joking resurfaced. Bemberg, whom Harris had brought over from Paris to attend the rehearsals and the performances, had got into the habit of using Nellie's dressing room as a repository for whatever he brought with him to the theatre. Nellie found this inconvenient when she came to change costumes and decided to teach her friend a lesson. In Melba's *Melodies and Memories* (pp. 84–5) she related: 'I cut his hat almost completely round the brim, covered the inside of it with black grease paint, cut his umbrella so that it would fall to pieces when it was opened and put two

eggs in his overcoat pockets. At the end of the third act Bemberg rushed around for his hat and his other belongings telling me that he had to hurry to Lady de Grey's box, where there was a particularly august assembly of persons waiting for him. Gladys de Grey told me afterwards that he arrived in her box with a face like a nigger [sic] and that when he took off his hat it fell down at her feet.'

14 The published score of *Elaine* survives, but the only part of it ever recorded is the ballad Elaine sings with a group of minstrels in act 1: 'L'amour est pur comme la flamme'. Nellie made a recording of this in London in 1906 with a female chorus and the composer at the piano. The recording was not issued at the time but has since appeared in various forms. Like Bemberg's songs, the music has charm, but little else. Nellie's singing of the ballad however is delightful and the 'cleanliness' with which she takes the final note should be a lesson to all sopranos.
15 Significantly, when Nellie was photographed in her Aida costume in a studio, she left off the skin make-up and the wig.
16 *Times*, 7 November 1892 (edited).
17 *Sunday Times*, 27 November 1892.
18 Letter postmarked Paris, December 1892, quoted in Murphy, *Melba* (edited).

Chapter 9 – Italy and America

1 The absence of Helen Mearns's name in the press in the United Kingdom and Australia *after* this tour, suggests her career did not progress beyond it.
2 Melba, *Melodies and Memories*, pp. 112–13 (edited).
3 *Corriere della Sera* (Milan), 17 March 1893.
4 When relating the details of this trip to Milan to Agnes Murphy, Nellie claimed that she also met Giuseppe Verdi at this time, but that is incorrect. She did eventually meet 'the grand old man' of Italian opera, but that did not happen until the following year.
5 A photograph exists of Nellie at the time of her La Scala debut signed 'Melbrizzina', an Italian diminutive of 'Melba' that she coined (or was coined for her) and used only while in Italy.
6 Henry J. Wood, *My Life of Music,* Victor Gollancz, London, 1938, p. 241. Both Fernando de Lucia and Mario Ancona recorded their respective arias from *Pagliacci*. Regrettably, Nellie did not record Nedda's *ballatella* 'Stridono lassù' about soaring birds, which would have completed a historic group of recordings.
7 *Sunday Times*, 14 May 1893.
8 Nellie's birth date in the advance publicity is given as 1865. This may have been an error, or evidence of Nellie following the common practice

among prima donnas of lopping a few years off their age as they matured.
9   Quoted in Blainey, *I am Melba*, p. 136.
10 Three years late Oscar II turned up unexpectedly at Nellie's apartment in Paris. At first her butler would not believe who the visitor claimed he was, but eventually he was admitted. The pair spent the afternoon drinking tea and singing duets.
11 *New York Times*, 5 December 1893.
12 *New York Tribune*, 5 December 1893.
13 *New York Times*, 12 December 1893.
14 Contrary to modern practice, *Pagliacci* was given first.
15 In her *Melodies and Memories* (p. 147), Nellie claimed that she did not know that she was to sing in *Tannhäuser* until she saw it advertised in the press and that she learned the role from scratch in three days. Such feats are not unheard of in operatic annals, but the story is undermined by the fact that Nellie brought her costume for Elisabeth to New York with her. The three days of 'learning' was probably three days of intense preparation before singing a role she had been studying for some time. The only recording we have of Nellie singing Wagner is one she made in 1910 of 'Elsa's Dream' from *Lohengrin*. Sung in Salvatore Marchesi's Italian translation and accompanied by an orchestra that could have been fitted into an elevator, it does not sound 'Wagnerian' by modern standards, but the way Nellie spins out the long phrases on an apparently endless supply of breath is both remarkable and beautiful (see Appendix 2: Melba's recordings).
16 Melba, *Melodies and Memories*, pp. 115–16. One of Verdi's biographers, Mary Jane Phillips-Matz (see bibliography) cast doubt on whether this encounter ever happened and suggested it was invented by Nellie to compensate for Verdi's refusal to see her two years earlier. Apart from the fact that the story has the ring of truth, there is evidence to support it. Verdi had not been in Milan when Nellie first sang there in 1893 but was in the city in May 1894 and despite his advanced age he would likely have been curious to hear one of the most famous interpreters of Gilda. The definitive piece of evidence, however, is the existence of the photograph Nellie mentions Verdi giving her. After Nellie's death it was passed on to her heirs. Ann Blainey inspected it when writing her biography of Melba and reported that the inscription (in French) reads: 'To my celebrated – [the next word is indecipherable] Nellie Melba. G. Verdi'.

Chapter 10 – Rivals, old and new

1. *Flutist*, November 1926 issue.
2. Quoted in Roger Neill, *Divas – Mathilde Marchesi and her Pupils*, University of NSW, Sydney, 2016, p. 296.
3. Perhaps prompted by the visits from Lemmoné and Crossley, Nellie conceived the idea of touring Australia after she completed her next season at the Met. The impresario J.C. Williamson told the Australian press that he had signed Nellie up for this tour and that she had broken their engagement by, in his words, 'not turning up', but there is no documentary evidence to support this claim. Other commitments and more generous offers prevented Nellie touring Australia until 1902.
4. Escoffier was also responsible for creating the thin oven-dried toast which came to be known as 'Melba Toast'.
5. For the remaining six performances of *Lucia di Lammermoor*, Nellie was partnered by the more modest-voiced tenor Giuseppe Russitano.
6. In some versions of this story, it is stated that it was Nellie who called on Tamagno and discovered what was being eaten, but it was Mancinelli.
7. *Sun* (New York), 19 December 1894.
8. The role of Marguerite de Valois in *Les Huguenots* contains only one show-stopping aria, but that aria elevates the short role of the queen to equal footing with the much longer (and more arduous) roles of the other principals. It proved a perfect vehicle for Nellie and for her compatriot Joan Sutherland at La Scala 67 years later.
9. *New World* (New York), 27 December 1894.
10. *New York Times*, 28 April 1895.
11. Before quitting New York, Nellie wrote an article for the April edition of *Lippincott's Magazine*. On the subject of singer's fees, she observed: 'There is nothing improper or ungraceful in the plan that the singer should sell his or her voice at the topmost price that it will bring in the market. One thing is certain, no manager is going to pay more than it is worth. The measure of value is fixed by the box offices, and these are the only standards that managers can be guided by. This does not prove that art is mercenary. The labourer everywhere is worthy of his hire.'
12. From a review of Melba's performance of Marguerite in *Faust* on the opening night of the 1894 Covent Garden season (*World*, London), 6 June 1894.
13. Murphy, *Melba*, p. vii.
14. ibid., p. 64; Thérèse Radic, *Melba – The Voice of Australia*, Macmillan, Melbourne, 1986, p. 44n.
15. Mary Garden & Louis Biancolli 1951, *Mary Garden's Story*, Simon & Schuster, New York, 1951, pp. 93–4.

16 During this performance of *Les Huguenots*, Nellie had one of her rare memory lapses, forgetting a line and a couple of bars of music. She substituted some made-up words and ended with a stunning cadenza. Pol Plançon, singing St Bris, replied by singing 'J'irai le dire à Meyerbeer!' ('I will go and tell Meyerbeer!').
17 Jean de Reszke had taken time off to learn the role of Tristan in Wagner's *Tristan und Isolde*, which he was to sing the following year at the Met and at Covent Garden in 1896.
18 That was not the only incident involving fire that Nellie experienced at around this time. The following year in America she was travelling in a carriage when the coals in an iron foot warmer set fire to her cloak. Nellie leapt out of the stationary carriage into the snow and discarded the burning garment.
19 A week after the end of the Covent Garden season, the *Pall Mall Gazette* featured an article entitled 'Juliet at Home' purportedly based on an interview with Nellie. The article appeared anonymously but was probably written by Murphy. In it Nellie reveals that she is planning to write a treatise on singing, that she is learning the role of Eva in Wagner's *Die Meistersinger* and may not return to Covent Garden the following year. It would be another 30 years before the treatise appeared, Nellie never sang Eva and the reference to Covent Garden was probably a ploy to gain better terms from Augustus Harris for the 1896 season.
20 Chicago was the scene of yet another incident a few months later when Nellie was singing there on the Met tour. During a performance of *Faust*, a deranged man climbed onto the stage and appeared to be about to attack Nellie. Jean de Reszke (singing Faust) held him at bay with his stage sword until police officers restrained him. Landon Ronald made his debut as a conductor at Covent Garden on 3 July 1896, no doubt promoted by Nellie and directing a performance of *Faust* with her, Bonnard, Ancona and Plançon.
21 Louie's younger sister, Marnie, soon replaced her as Nellie's secretary until she was succeeded by Agnes Murphy.
22 *Le Figaro*, 8 February 1896.

Chapter 11 – The lure of Wagner

1 *Sunday Times*, 23 August 1896. In *Siegfried* Brünnhilde does not appear until the final scene and then has a long and impassioned duet with Siegfried, considered by many who sing the role to be the most arduous part of Brünnhilde's role in the Ring Cycle. The Woodbird has only a few lines to sing in a different act of the opera and is sung by a lyric-coloratura soprano. In the famous 1962 recording of the Ring Cycle, conducted by Georg Solti and produced by John Culshaw, Joan Sutherland sang the Woodbird.

2   Nellie later concluded that she had been incorrect in accusing Jean de Reszke of any wrongdoing and exonerated him in an interview she gave to the *Pall Mall Gazette* in Paris the following February (*Pall Mall Gazette*, 13 February 1898).
3   *New York Times*, 31 December 1896 (edited).
4   *Sun*, 31 December 1896.
5   In the interview with the *Pall Mall Gazette* previously referred to, Nellie claimed her subsequent vocal problems in New York had been due to 'pestilential emanations' from drains and gas mains being repaired in Fifth Avenue, compounded by a bout of 'malarial fever' and not from trying to sing Brünnhilde! (*Pall Mall Gazette*, 13 February 1898).
6   12 years younger than Nellie, Dora had by all accounts as forceful a personality as her eldest sister, which occasionally caused friction between them. Like Nellie and Annie, Dora also had a promising soprano voice. Encouraged by her eldest sister, Dora studied singing in Paris (but not with Marchesi) and later in Melbourne, but never pursued a career.
7   Six years on and with the memory of this debacle fading, Nellie actually contemplated singing another Wagner role – for her, the most incongruous of all: Isolde in *Tristan und Isolde*. According to a letter from Nellie to Marchesi held by the National Library of Australia, Gailhard approached her to sing Isolde in French with Jean de Reszke at the Paris Opéra in the winter of 1902–03. The tone of the letter suggests Nellie was seriously considering the offer when she wrote, but in the end common sense prevailed and she declined the offer.
8   The press had speculated months before that Nellie might create the title role in the Covent Garden premiere of the opera *Inèz Mendo* by Frédéric d'Erlanger, but when it was produced this season, the role was assigned to Saville.
9   Those with a horticultural interest might like to know that next day the press waxed lyrical about the floral arrangements that adorned Covent Garden for the gala. The three tiers of boxes were faced with roses, not in masses as was customary for such events, but arranged on trellis work covered with foliage. The roses were complemented by large bouquets of white flowers, hung above each box of the grand tier. The 10 central boxes were joined to create an enormous royal box, overhung by festoons of yellow silk and a large crown formed of red roses and yellow orchids. One imagines sufferers of hay fever must have avoided such events.
10 At the concert on 17 September, Nellie sang the aria 'L'amerò, sarò costante' from Mozart's *Il Ré Pastore*, with Joachim playing the violin obbligato, and the Mad Scene from *Lucia di Lammermoor*. Both artists were presented with one of the gold medals that had been struck to mark the centenary of Donizetti's birth.

11 *Philadelphia Inquirer*, 28 December 1898 (edited).
12 *New York Times*, 25 January 1898.
13 Florence Toronto sang professionally for only a couple of years and then married and retired from the stage.
14 *Times*, 9 July 1898.
15 *Sunday Times*, 10 July 1898; *Pall Mall Gazette*, 8 July 1898.
16 Landon Ronald, *Variations on a Personal Theme*, Hodder & Stoughton, London, 1922, pp. 61–2. Ronald does not name Joachim in this anecdote, but it is believed to have been him.
17 At various times Nellie claimed the time she spent with Puccini in Lucca amounted to 'nearly a week', 'ten days' and 'six weeks'. In a letter to Marchesi (quoted by Blainey in *I am Melba*), Nellie described the period as 'nearly a week' and that would seem the most likely.
18 When Nellie was 'lent' to Damrosch, she appeared 'by courtesy of Mr Maurice Grau' and now, when she a appeared at the Met it was 'By courtesy of Mr Charles Ellis'.
19 Sopranos complimenting one another is rare, but Ternina admired Nellie and presented her with a signed photograph inscribed: 'To Madame Melba, the great artist, the favourite of the gods, my highest and sincerest admiration'.
20 *Philadelphia Inquirer*, 31 December 1898; *Topeka State Journal*, 4 January 1899.
21 *Pall Mall Gazette*, 30 June 1899. Five months later in another interview with the same newspaper (6 November 1899), Nellie was more circumspect and stated that she *hoped* that Puccini was writing the role with her voice 'in mind'.

Chapter 12 – Campaigns

1 The press initially reported that Nellie had rented this house, but she states quite clearly in the November interview with the *Pall Mall Gazette* that she has bought the house – meaning that she had bought a 22-year lease on it. Nellie would pay 250 pounds per annum to the freeholders for as long as she held the lease. The house was located in the crescent end of Great Cumberland Place.
2 *Le Figaro*, 26 September 1899.
3 Murphy, *Melba*, p. 153.
4 Nellie was to have been partnered in *Lucia di Lammermoor* by the celebrated Italian tenor, Francesco Marconi, but he was ill and had to be replaced by a young Czech tenor named Karl Burrian, whose career was to end abruptly some years later when a husband he had cuckolded replaced the beer in his stein with bleach.
5 Murphy, *Melba*, p. 155; Melba, *Melodies and Memories*, p. 171.

6 *Le Figaro*, 2 January 1900.
7 *Times*, 29 January 1900.
8 Reprinted in part in *Sunday Times*, 4 March 1900.
9 *Table Talk*, 10 April 1900, suggested that Charlie's action had been prompted by his forming a relationship with an American lady whom he wanted to marry. Likely though that story might be, there was no evidence to support it.
10 Soon after, Nellie made her own arrangements to protect her property from Charlie. George was the principal beneficiary in Nellie's will and she feared that if she should die and her fortune pass to her son before he reached maturity, Charlie would get his hands on it. To prevent that, George's legacy was turned into a trust to mature on his twenty-first birthday.
11 *San Francisco Chronicle*, 17 April 1900.
12 *Sunday Times*, 4 March 1900. Among Nellie's friends there was speculation that the story had come from Joachim himself, the violinist hoping that seeing the reports in print might make Nellie feel obliged to marry him.
13 *Australasian*, 9 June 1900.
14 Soon after this Nellie learned that Charlie and George had quit Texas and moved to the remote town of Klamath Falls in Oregon.
15 In two of the three performances Nellie sang of *La Bohème*, she was partnered by the Italian tenor Alessandro Bonci. Short in stature, Bonci found himself having to crane his neck upwards to meet Nellie's gaze when they sang together during stage rehearsals. To overcome this, the tenor wore a pair of shoes with extravagantly elevated heels at their first performance. Legend has it that Nellie complained that the shoes were a distraction to both her and the audience and the embarrassed tenor was instructed to dispense with them at the second performance.
16 *New York Times*, 19 December 1900.
17 ibid., 27 December 1900.
18 *New York Tribune*, 27 December 1900.
19 *Sun*, 17 January 1900 (edited).
20 More details about these recordings will be found in Appendix 2: Melba's recordings. Mapleson's efforts did serve a commendable purpose in capturing a few moments of Jean de Reszke singing on stage, for no commercial recordings of the great tenor were ever issued – and possibly none ever made.
21 Mapleson may not have been the first to record Nellie's voice. In the mid-1890s an Italian named Gianni Bettini, who was married to a wealthy New York socialite, acquired a phonograph capable of making recordings. When members of the Metropolitan Opera Company visited his home, Bettini persuaded some of them to leave a musical souvenir of

their visit in the form of a cylinder recording. Bettini claimed that Nellie was among these, but when he later turned his hobby into a business her name did not appear in his catalogue. No recording of Nellie has ever turned up in the small number of Bettini cylinders discovered over the years.

22 Nellie was always fond of mechanical things and her pride and joy at Quarry Wood Cottage was an electric-powered motor launch named the *White Swan*, in which she and her friends cruised the river between Henley-on-Thames and Windsor. She was also one of the first among her set to purchase a motor car.

23 During this period a schedule of the fees Nellie demanded for appearances at soirées in London's great private houses was revealed in the press. For singing three songs, Nellie's fee was 500 guineas, enough money to buy a street of smaller houses.

24 The portrait is in the collection of the National Gallery of Victoria.

25 In Melba's *Melodies and Memories* (p. 185), she claims that she had already sung with Caruso in London but this is incorrect. Caruso did not make his debut at Covent Garden until the summer season following this one in Monte Carlo.

26 In *Melodies and Memories* (p. 185), Nellie claims that during one performance of *La Bohème* in Monte Carlo Caruso played his first practical joke on her – squeezing a rubber 'squeekie' toy in her ear during Mimi's death scene. That story is repeated in Stanley Jackson's *Caruso* (W.H. Allen, London, 1972) and no doubt Caruso did play such a trick on Nellie at some time, but it seems unlikely that he would have risked playing any practical jokes on her as early as this in their association.

27 *Le Figaro*, 4 March 1902 (edited).

Chapter 13 – Home, sweet home?

1 At one of Nellie's forthcoming appearances in London a group of Australian soldiers recently demobilised following the end of the war presented her with a bouquet to which was attached the regimental badges they had worn in South Africa. Nellie was deeply touched (*Brisbane Courier*, 6 September 1902).

2 Towards the end of the long tour, Arens and Bensaude had to leave to fulfil overseas engagements and Griffiths became ill. New artists had to be recruited, including Lempriere Pringle (who happened to be visiting his homeland), contralto Elva Rogers, tenor Walter Kirkby and pianist Benno Scherek.

3 Nellie repeated this claim in Murphy's *Melba* (p. 212), adding that circumstances had prevented her singing the role, 'as yet'.

4 *Brisbane Courier*, 18 September 1902.

5   Robert Harper's household staff had also been retained, but when Nellie discovered that Australian servants in the new century were not nearly as subservient as her own staff in London, friction developed, and replacements had to be engaged. Two local constables were also assigned to provide security at Myoora and to protect the collection of jewellery Nellie had brought with her.
6   *Punch* (Melbourne), 18 September 1902.
7   Among the hundreds of floral tributes brought onto the platform after the concert was what the press called a 'ladder of fame' made from pink plum blossom and surmounted by 'an electric star' sent by Nellie Stewart, a floral boomerang from Charles Mitchell, a basket of flowers from her old friend and colleague Rudolph Himmer and a harp-shaped arrangement from the employees of her father's Cave Hill Quarry. During this visit Nellie would make a sentimental visit to Lilydale.
8   Quoted in Thérèse Radic, *Melba – The Voice of Australia*, Macmillan, Melbourne, 1986, p. 6.
9   Melba, *Melodies and Memories*, p. 13.
10 *Truth* (Melbourne), 28 March 1903.
11 Nellie did enjoy a glass of wine or champagne, but no sensible person would believe that a singer could sustain a long career and continue to sing admirably into their 60s, if they subjected their body to excessive drinking.
12 The accusation that she treated her colleagues badly may have had its origin in Nellie's dismissal of the local tenor Walter Kirkby, whom she found to be an inadequate replacement for Louis Arens when the latter departed. The 'loose living' accusation was, perhaps, fuelled by Nellie's appearances in public in Melbourne escorted by Lord Richard Neville, the Governor-General's handsome secretary, with whom she had become acquainted in London, an association of which the Governor-General's wife did not approve.
13 See Chapter 17.
14 *New York Times*, 19 December 1903 (edited).
15 Cavalieri was dismissed by Nellie as of no musical consequence, but she liked Farrar, who had sung for her and Nordica in America. Nellie had recommended that Farrar study in Europe but had not been pleased when Farrar rejected Marchesi as a teacher. Farrar admired Nellie's voice unreservedly: 'The Australian songstress had been miraculously endowed with the finest natural vocal equipment since Patti, which was not even rivaled by the dizzy cadenzas of the flute she shamed, to the delirious delight of astonished listeners' (Geraldine Farrar, *Such Sweet Compulsion*, Greystone Press, New York, 1938, p. 26). Farrar would go on to become the most popular soprano at the Metropolitan Opera until her early retirement in 1922. The only sour note in their relationship

was a comment by Farrar after her retirement, when she hinted that she believed Nellie's influence may have kept her out of Covent Garden.
16   *Le Figaro*, 19 February 1904 (edited).
17   The title role in Saint-Säens's *Hélène* would be the last new role Nellie would add to her repertoire and perform.
18   The work was given at the Opéra-Comique in Paris in 1905 and the Paris Opéra in 1919 but lapsed into obscurity after that. Because of Nellie's association with it, the Melbourne-based company Melba Records made an excellent recording of it in 2008 with Rosamund Illing and Steve Davislim.

Chapter 14 – The voice preserved

1   See Appendix 2: Melba's recordings.
2   The flautist, composer and conductor Philippe Gaubert would play a significant role in the early career of Marjorie Lawrence a quarter of a century later.
3   *Sunday Times*, 26 June 1904 (edited).
4   From the beginning of the long-playing vinyl era and into the compact disc era, most of this first batch of issued recordings have been reissued in various compilations. The sound quality has been variable. By far the best sound can be found on the ABC Classics CD *Dame Nellie Melba – The First Recordings* (476 3556), issued in 2008. For this, the original matrices were used and for the first time we can hear something close to what the recording engineers must have heard in Nellie's drawing room all those years ago. The voice emerges clearly and with a presence that no earlier reissues achieved. I have used this CD in making my assessments of the recordings.
5   Later it was revealed that the victim had been wrongly identified in the initial reports and his name was not Benoit but Dussellier. The chauffeur was accused of causing the accident by speeding but denied the charge. He was convicted but sentenced to only one month in jail.
6   Nellie told Murphy that she had signed up with Conried but that ill health prevented her joining the company upon reaching New York. This does not tally with relevant documents held in the Metropolitan Opera Archives, although she did become ill while in the USA.
7   These letters was published for the first time in Pamela Vestey's, *A Family Memoir* (Phoebe, Melbourne, 1996).
8   *Sunday Times*, 11 June 1905.
9   Either that evening or at the charity concert attended by the 19-year-old Spanish king at which Nellie sang a few nights later, Alfonso asked her if she had ever sung in his country. When she replied that she had not, the king asked why. Nellie explained that she had not been asked. The king said he would remedy that on his return to Madrid and he did.

10 *Le Ménestrel*, 30 July 1905.
11 The following July Nellie returned to the Gramophone & Typewriter Company's studios to record six more titles. These included the 'ballad' from Bemberg's *Elaine* and a new version of the Bach-Gounod 'Ave Maria', this time with the cellist W.H. Squire playing the obbligato. The latter was needed because the recording of this piece with Kubelik had proved so popular the matrix had been worn out making tens of thousands of pressings. With four of these new recordings issued, the 'Melba' catalogue then stood at 36 titles; full details of all these recordings can be found in Appendix 2: Melba's recordings. At this time, the Gramophone & Typewriter Company also marketed a 'top of the range' gramophone with the name 'The Melba', retailing for 25 pounds.
12 After striking a deal with Hammerstein, Nellie cabled Conried at the Met declining his offer. No doubt Conried would have liked to have had Nellie in his roster of singers for the 1906-07 season, but even without her, he mustered a strong company, including Sembrich, Eames, Farrar, Cavalieri, Caruso, Scotti, Stracciari and Plançon. He also engaged a team of outstanding German singers to perform Wagner's works (which Hammerstein did not attempt) and staged the American premiere of Richard Strauss's *Salome*.
13 One singer Hammerstein had approached and who was keen to be engaged by him was the granddaughter of Fanny Simonsen, Frances Alda. Although born in New Zealand, Alda was brought up in Australia and always referred to herself as an Australian. Later Hammerstein decided not to engage Alda, and she blamed Nellie, but some bad reviews the young singer had received at the time were probably the true reason for Hammerstein's change of heart. Alda would go on to have a long and illustrious career at the Met.

Chapter 15 – Oscar and Goliath

1 The story of Nellie hitching a ride in a tradesman's van appears in her own account of her life given to journalists and is dated to various different times, the vehicle sometimes referred to as a butcher's van; 1906 and Kingston Hill are the correct time and place of origin for the story.
2 *Times*, 9 July 1906 (edited). The only aspect of Nellie's Violetta that drew criticism was her insistence on wearing costumes that were too *moderne* for the period in which the opera is set. Nellie took note of this and after the first performance wore more appropriate dress. For the final performance of *La Traviata* this season Battistini was replaced by Eugenio Giraldoni, the creator of the role of Scarpia in the world premiere of *Tosca*. Compared with the elegant Battistini, Giraldoni was a crude singer and one can imagine which of the two baritones Nellie would have preferred as her singing partner.

3   Mylott is best remembered today as Mel Gibson's grandmother.
4   The only note of discord had been when Nellie learned that Marchesi had persuaded Ivy Ansley to change her name to Ivy Zealandia. On Nellie's advice that was changed again to Irene Ainsley.
5   Now Wigmore Hall.
6   When Ainsley retired to New Zealand, she took up teaching and among her students was Sister Mary Leo. Sister Mary subsequently taught Kiri Te Kanawa, who portrayed Melba in an episode of *Downtown Abbey*.
7   During this stay in New York various stories released to the press about Nellie were attributed to the former journalist Agnes Murphy. The most notable claimed that Nellie had been approached by a group of disgruntled shareholders from the Met offering to bankroll her to build another opera house in New York, which would replace both the Met and the Manhattan. Heinrich Conried emphatically denied this, and the story proved to be nothing more than a piece of propaganda in the war between him and Hammerstein. Other stories kept the publicity machine well fuelled throughout Nellie's stay in New York, including a demand that the city corporation should clean up their streets where Nellie claimed she had spotted dead cats and dogs.
8   *New York Times*, 3 January 1907.
9   *Sun*, 6 January 1907.
10 It was also announced that Hammerstein would be producing Saint-Saëns's *Hélène* during this season with Nellie and Dalmores, but that never eventuated.
11 *New York Tribune*, 24, 29 January 1907. The single performance of Strauss's lurid masterpiece had so shocked the audience and the critics that it was also the last at the Met until 1934.
12 The result of this case reached Hammerstein the day after Nellie had made her debut in *La Traviata*.
13 *New York Tribune*, 1 March 1907. During these altercations, Puccini himself had been in New York to oversee the productions of his *Manon Lescaut* and *Madama Butterfly* at the Met but had maintained a dignified silence on Hammerstein's activities and departed for Europe the day before *La Bohème* opened at the Manhattan Opera House.
14 *New York Tribune*, 2 March 1907.
15 During rehearsals for *Rigoletto*, Nellie had an altercation with the conductor. After she had sung a particular phrase, Campanini stopped the rehearsal and informed Nellie that he did not like the way she had sung the phrase and required her to sing it differently. If she did not, the conductor said, she would not be singing the role at all. The scene that followed can be imagined, but Nellie had the grace to accede to Campanini's wishes. Such exchanges would become common in 'the

age of the conductor', but in Nellie's time and with her as one of the participants, they were extremely rare.
16 As well as Senta, Hammerstein also announced that Nellie would sing Hélène, Desdemona and Tosca.
17 Among the recordings not issued is a duet from *Rigoletto* with Giuseppe Campanari. Details of all these recordings will be found in Appendix 2: Melba's recordings.
18 Nellie continued this policy in London where she raised large sums for charity, charging half a crown per autograph.

Chapter 16 – Sentimental journeys

1 This event was marred by a sad incident. Just as the British and Danish royals were arriving, General Sir Arthur Ellis, a hero of the Crimean War and one of Edward VII's equerries, collapsed; later, as Destinn, Caruso and Scotti were opening the proceedings with the first act of *Madama Butterfly*, the general died in a room off the Crush Bar.
2 Other writers, including Murphy, have identified David Mitchell's 1908 birthday as his eightieth, but that is incorrect.
3 By this time John Norton was a member of the Legislative Assembly of New South Wales, but still destroying other people's reputations and lives.
4 In her autobiography, *My Life of Song* (Cassell, London, 1921), Tetrazzini hints that Covent Garden's desire to cancel her contract may have been due to 'influence' from 'someone I had offended', but if by that she meant Nellie she was mistaken. Whether Nellie even remembered Tetrazzini is doubtful, and she was far away in Australia at the time of these negotiations.
5 Unlike many of Nellie's rivals, Tetrazzini had never been near the École Marchesi, so the characteristics of the Marchesi 'method' were absent from her singing. On the negative side that meant that she lacked the equalisation and seamless transition between registers of which Nellie's voice was capable and there was a weakness in the middle of Tetrazzini's voice, which critics described as sounding 'infantile' compared with her glorious upper notes. Listening to the recordings Tetrazzini soon began making, we hear a more 'modern' style of singing than Nellie's, devoid of the outdated features of the 'Patti' era, and anticipating singers (Callas, Sutherland and Caballé) of the twentieth century *bel canto* revival.
6 While in Paris Nellie also visited the Paris branch of the Gramophone & Typewriter Company. It is believed she went there to make a series of recordings in French (for the French market) of pieces she had already recorded in Italian or English. As no written records survive of the visit, the date and the titles she recorded have always been the subject of speculation. Proof that the visit occurred is provided by the survival

of one title: 'On m'appelle Mimi' ('Sì, mi chiamano Mimi') from *La Bohème*, which was issued. Details will be found in Appendix 2: Melba's recordings.

7   Ruby's grounds for seeking a divorce were George's adultery and his alleged cruelty towards her. As Nellie had done when seeking a divorce from George's father, Ruby gave precise details of the occasions when she claimed her husband had publicly humiliated her and inflicted physical violence on her. These can be found in a press report of the divorce hearing published in *The Times*, 14 November 1908. At the conclusion of that hearing the presiding judge granted Ruby the divorce she sought and ordered George to pay all her costs.

8   *Times*, 2 July 1908.

9   It is believed that Tetrazzini became aware of some of Nellie's comments about her and returned like for like. There is a story that Tetrazzini was being escorted to her suite in the Savoy one day by the manager and heard Nellie practising as they passed the door to Nellie's suite. 'Have you *many* cats in your hotel?' Tetrazzini asked.

10 After the event, the profit of £2000 was sent to the hospital in the form of a cheque from Nellie. Earlier in the season Tetrazzini had offered no excuse to avoid sharing the stage with Nellie when Covent Garden mounted a gala performance commanded by the King to mark the visit of the French President to London.

11 Half a century later Serafin would conduct the historic performances of *Lucia di Lammermoor* at Covent Garden that launched Joan Sutherland's international career.

12 *Le Ménestrel*, 13 June 1908.

13 At the conclusion of the Covent Garden season Nellie embarked on a concert tour of the provinces and Ireland. While in Plymouth she visited two Australian rugby league football players (Peter Burge and Peter Flanagan), who were in hospital after breaking their legs in matches during what became known as the first 'Wallabies' tour of the United Kingdom.

14 For his second season at the Manhattan Opera House Hammerstein was not short of first-rate sopranos. On the strength of her success in the autumn season at Covent Garden, he had 'snapped up' Tetrazzini, along with Calvé, Nordica, Garden and the Italian Giannina Russ. At the end of the first season, Alessandro Bonci had defected to the Met and, on Nellie's recommendation, Hammerstein had engaged Zenatello to replace him. The impresario also retained Campanini as his musical director and chief conductor for his second and third seasons.

15 *New York Tribune*, 15 December 1909.

16 *New York Times*, 15 December 1909.

17 *Le Ménestrel*, 15 February 1908.

18 Hammerstein's opera company survived one more season (1909–10) – without Nellie. Having decided it could not afford to compete with him any longer, in April 1910 the Met offered Hammerstein 1.2 million dollars for the Philadelphia Opera House, all his scenery and costumes and the rights he held to perform the operas of Strauss and Massenet. A clause in the agreement prohibited Hammerstein from producing opera in New York, Philadelphia, Boston and Chicago for 10 years. Hammerstein accepted and then turned his attention to building a new opera house and forming a new opera company in London.
19 It is believed that while Nellie was in Naples, de Sanna took her to the opera to hear Titta Ruffo and it was then that Nellie offered to sing Gilda to Ruffo's Rigoletto and the baritone replied: 'Melba is too old to play my daughter' (see Chapter 13). While in Naples Nellie also planned to give a concert to raise funds for victims of a recent earthquake, but there is no evidence of the concert taking place. Nellie did, however, take part in a concert for the earthquake relief fund in London.
20 Agnes Murphy now occupied an ever-increasingly important role in Nellie's entourage. As well as being Nellie's secretary and spokesperson in dealing with the press, she had become her 'trouble-shooter' and 'fixer' for matters professional and personal. Before the party left London, Murphy's biography of Nellie had been published. The book had received generous reviews and boosted Nellie's profile. Tetrazzini does not get a single mention in the 300-odd pages.
21 Around this time, Nellie offered to pay for a full set of new standard pitch orchestral instruments for the Marshall Hall Orchestra, a generous gift that was received with delight and deep appreciation.
22 *Sydney Morning Herald*, 2 June 1909.
23 ibid., 7 June 1909.
24 These included auditioning a soprano from Ballarat named Evelyn Scotney, who had been studying with Elise Wiedermann-Pinschof. Nellie was impressed by the young singer and Scotney was packed off to the École Marchesi. Of all Nellie's Australian soprano protégées, Scotney was the most successful. She went on to have a long career in the United Kingdom and in America, singing at the Met in 1920. At the request of Professor Marshall Hall, Nellie also gave some singing lessons to selected students at Melbourne University.
25 Nellie also made the owner of an entrant in the Melbourne Cup ('Knox') an offer of 1000 guineas for the horse but the owner refused to sell.

Chapter 17 – Promises

1 Melba, *Melodies and Memories*, p. 36. Two years later, Marchesi would move to London to live with her daughter Blanche in St John's Wood. She died on 17 November 1913 while Nellie was on tour in America.

2 The Gramophone & Typewriter Company had dropped the last half of its name and was no longer involved in selling typewriters. Most of these recordings were accompanied by the New Symphony Orchestra, conducted by Landon Ronald.
3 The recording referred to in Note 15, Chapter 9.
4 Quoted in the booklet accompanying the EMI LP set, *Nellie Melba – The London Recordings*.
5 F.W. Gaisberg, *Music on Record*, Robert Hale, London, 1946, pp. 105–6.
6 Details of all these recordings will be found in Appendix 2: Melba's recordings.
7 Legend has it that at the end of the first act that evening, as an usher held one curtain back so the artists could step out to acknowledge the applause, Nellie extracted her revenge on McCormack. When the tenor moved forward to join Nellie in the first curtain call, she hissed at him: 'No one takes curtain calls with Melba at Covent Garden!'
8 Details of all these recordings will be found in Appendix 2: Melba's recordings.
9 Reprinted in *The Times*, 25 December 1910.
10 Quaintance Eaton, *The Boston Opera* Company, Appleton-Century, New York, 1965, p. 262.
11 *Times*, 10 June 1911. Nellie's 'Roméo' for these performances was the French tenor Paul Franz, who was still around 22 years later to sing Lohengrin when Marjorie Lawrence made her debut at the Paris Opéra as Ortrud.
12 The speed with which these extensions had been completed would be revealed in later years when structural repairs were required. As Pamela Vestey observes in her biography of her grandmother, if David Mitchell had still been in the building trade and given the work such problems would have been avoided.
13 Rumours that Nellie's absence was not due to illness but alcohol (born out of John Norton's scurrilous accusations of 1903) resurfaced. Nellie wrote to J.C. Williamson's publicist, Claude McKay, bemoaning the unfairness of the rumours. Without seeking Nellie's approval, McKay gave the letter to the press and that scotched the rumours.
14 Testament that Nellie had planned to sing Tosca in Australia is a diamante headdress she had had made for the role and brought with her to Australia. It is now in the Australian Performing Arts Collection at the Melbourne Arts Centre.
15 Philippe Gaubert, cellist Arnold Trowell and Gabriel Lapierre (piano accompanist) completed the concert party.
16 Such announcements would also be followed by requests in the personal columns of newspapers, such as 'Single lady wishes to find companion to attend Madame Melba's concert'. Some of these may have been discreet

advertisements for prostitution, but not all. The genuine ones usually appended: 'Will pay for both tickets'.
17 By coincidence the apartment Nellie leased was only a few steps from another in which Maria Callas spent the last tragic years of her life.
18 Among the other sopranos at Covent Garden this and subsequent seasons was Elsa Stralia, born Elsa Fisher in Adelaide and a former pupil of Elise Wiedermann-Pinschof.
19 Percy Grainger had strong opinions of Nellie, as he did about most topics. He later wrote: 'I loved her voice as truly as I disliked her person' (Quoted in John Bird's *Percy Grainger*, Macmillan, Melbourne, 1976, p. 70).
20 Eaton, *The Boston Opera* Company, p. 262 (edited).
21 The *Times* in London (7 May 1914) reported that Nellie and Russell were negotiating at this time for the Boston Opera Company to visit Australia in 1915 and Nellie referred to this plan when she was in Australia the following July but, if a deal was reached, war prevented it from happening.

Chapter 18 – The empress of pickpockets

1 Malcolm McEachern was listed as a baritone for these concerts, and he sang baritone arias, but soon his voice would descend until it became that rarest of vocal phenomena: the *basso profondo*. Nellie was still distributing her now famous tiepins. A gold, enamel and diamond one was bestowed on McEachern.
2 George Armstrong immediately tried to enlist but was rejected on medical grounds. His father had settled on Vancouver Island, British Columbia, and as soon as war was declared Charlie Armstrong rushed to the nearest British Army recruiting office, but at 56 he too was rejected. According to family legend, Charlie was furious about the decision and when a young man with a German-sounding name who had also turned up to enlist was accepted, Charlie punched him to the ground.
3 Word had come from London that Covent Garden was closing indefinitely and had been requisitioned by the government to be used as a furniture repository.
4 Maggie Stirling is one of those once-popular Australian singers who have been forgotten. She was born in Geelong in the same year as Nellie, studied with Cecchi and Marchesi and had a respectable career in Britain as a concert singer before returning to Australia.
5 Remembering the criticism she had received during the Boer War, this time Nellie 'played it safe' and channelled the money she raised from this and all subsequent sources into established charities.
6 Melba, *Melodies and Memories*, p. 288.
7 *Herald*, 25 March 1915.

8   Johnson to the author, 1972.
9   Stella Power had a modest career as a concert singer in the US and in the UK between 1917 and 1924. She then returned to Australia and continued to sing until the beginning of the Second World War. Gertrude Johnson had a successful career with the British National Opera Company after the First World War and then returned to Australia to establish the National Theatre movement in Melbourne. Strella Wilson began her career in opera but later achieved fame in Australia in operetta and musical comedy. Each of these women left behind a few rare recordings.
10 Nellie was still a very rich person and had the resources to retire in comfort if that had been her choice, but her investments had been sharply devalued by the war and maintaining the lifestyle to which she had become accustomed required a substantial cash flow.
11 Robert Parker was one of several American singers who specialised in Wagner and had built their careers in Germany, but were now unable to stay there or, in Parker's case, return there.
12 Announcements of this concert appeared in the newspapers on 8 July alongside advertisements for the first screening in Australia of the movie *Neptune's Daughter* starring Alice Charbonnet's daughter, Annette Kellermann.
13 The departure of Beatrice Harrison from the party may have been hastened by a practice of Nellie's, explained by the cellist to the accompanist Gerald Moore. According to Harrison, Nellie would instruct the lighting technicians in the various venues to adjust the lights to her advantage before she sang – and while Harrison was on stage playing to the audience. Others supporting artists made similar claims, but this tour seems to have been the origin of this much-repeated story.
14 Previous recipients of this award included Florence Nightingale.
15 David Mitchell's funeral was conducted in the music room at Doonside on 27 March. A funeral cortège then proceeded to Melbourne General Cemetery. A car with only a driver and no passengers was included in the cortège, representing the absent Nellie. Later his coffin was removed to the Mitchell plot at Lilydale Cemetery. David Mitchell's estate, valued at almost £300,000, was divided between his seven surviving children. Each received their share in the form of a trust, from which they derived income until their deaths, after which each individual's share would go to their children.
16 Quoted in Charles Mintzer, *Rosa Raisa*, Northeastern University Press, Boston, 2001, p. 40.
17 *Evening World* (New York), 5 February 1918 (edited).

18 Pamela Armstrong eventually acquired an impressive list of godparents. As well as Lady Susan FitzClarence, Lady Stanley (wife of the Governor of Victoria, Lord Stanley of Alderley) was named as joint godmother, and Sir Ronald Ferguson (Governor-General of Australia) and Lord Richard Neville were named as joint godfathers.
19 Nellie received other awards for her war work. Most notable were the Queen Elizabeth Medal awarded to her in September 1919 by King Albert I of the Belgians, for her tireless work raising money for the relief of his country during the German occupation, and the Royal Gold Medal of Merit from the King of Norway (See Chapter 19).
20 Pamela was baptised in a ceremony in the music room at Coombe Cottage. John Lemmoné played the flute, and Nellie, backed by a choir comprised of students from the Albert Street Conservatorium, sang Mendelssohn's 'O for the wings of a dove'.

Chapter 19 – Old world, new order

1 Lemmoné recovered from the stroke and was able to resume his career after a few months. He continued to play until 1927 and then concentrated on managing other artists. He died in 1949.
2 The performance nearly didn't take place when, in the spirit of those new times, most of the chorus went on strike at the final dress rehearsal, demanding more pay. The dispute was not resolved until later, but the chorus agreed to sing on the night.
3 Melba, *Melodies and Memories*, pp. 302–3 (edited).
4 *Times*, 13 May 1919 (edited).
5 In his autobiography, *Overture and Beginners* (Methuen, London, 1951, p. 142), Goossens recalls visiting Nellie's dressing room before the performance to ask if she wanted any changes to the traditional tempi, receiving the following reply: 'None whatsoever. I sing it exactly as Gounod wrote it and I hope you conduct it the same way.' Goossens goes on to say that Nellie did exactly that in the performance which made it, in his words, 'a refreshingly musical experience'.
6 *Times*, 16 May 1919 (edited).
7 A few days after her birthday Nellie received an unexpected letter that revived old memories. It was written by the one surviving Hyland sister – the sisters who had helped her when she first moved to Paris to study with Marchesi. May Hyland wrote that she had followed Nellie's career with interest for the past 33 years and signed herself 'Ever your sincere friend'. Next time Nellie was in Paris she visited May Hyland in the 'Maison de Retreat' at St Clovis.
8 Soon after this, Stella Power's relationship with Nellie soured. Power had married against Nellie's advice and at the time of this concert told

her mentor she was pregnant. Nellie is reported to have shouted to Lionel Powell, 'The bloody little fool is going to have a bloody baby!'
9   Among those who sang Melba roles at Covent Garden in the 1920 winter season was Rosina Buckman, promoted from Musetta to Mimi.
10 Heifetz had been taught by Leopold Auer, the star pupil of her old friend Joachim.
11 There is a story (probably apocryphal) that when a Marconi executive showed Nellie a photo of the 137-metre high transmission mast on the top of the Chelmsford building she said: 'Young man, if you think I am going to climb up there, you are very much mistaken'.
12 Oslo was then called Christiania.
13 To the press in Sydney a few months later Nellie described the illness she had contracted as 'Spanish influenza', the disease which had ravaged communities around the world since the end of the First World War. That may well have been the case and it should also be noted that the various bouts of bronchitis and influenza Nellie had suffered in recent years had often coincided with epidemics and pandemics.
14 For details see Appendix 2: Melba's recordings.
15 Princess Mary later became the mother of the 7th Earl of Harewood, a major figure in the musical arts from the middle of the twentieth century until his death, and the contributor of the foreword to the author's biography of accompanist Geoffrey Parsons.

Chapter 20 – Music for the people
1   *Sydney Morning Herald*, 4 August 1921.
2   *Times*, London, 24, 28 September 1921.
3   In his book about Zelman (Don Fairweather, *Your friend Alberto Zelman*, Zelman Memorial Symphony Orchestra, Melbourne, 1984, p. 40), Don Fairweather records a couple of amusing incidents during these Melbourne concerts. On the outermost seat of the third desk of violins sat the future leader of the orchestra, Bertha Jorgensen, then aged 16 but looking even younger. As Nellie arrived on the platform at the start of each concert in Melbourne, she would pat Bertha on the head – to the delight of the audience and the intense embarrassment of the violinist. Also, on one occasion when the orchestra failed to join the audience in applauding her, Nellie hissed as she moved through their ranks, 'Clap, damn you, clap!'
4   Another anecdote believed to have its origin on this tour concerned John Lemmoné. After Nellie had given a highly successful concert in Ballarat, a large crowd gathered outside her hotel demanding she make an appearance on the balcony of her room. Nellie was tired, so Lemmoné donned a velvet dressing gown, tied a towel around his head like a toque and stepped out onto the balcony. From a distance

he resembled Nellie enough for the crowd to cheer, but when he told them to 'Bugger off home you lot', the cheering ceased and the crowd dispersed muttering imprecations. On her arrival in Marseilles on her return to London, Nellie told the press that she had calculated that she had sung to approximately 97,000 people during this extended stay in Australia.
5   Australians in the company included Florence Austral, Gertrude Johnson, Beatrice Miranda, Elsy Treweek, Browning Mummery, Frederick Collier and the conductor Aylmer Buesst.
6   For one concert, in the East End, the local paper (*Daily Graphic*, 25 January 1923) commented: 'Ain't it lovely. Nellie Melba for one bob and thruppence.'
7   Just about every notable Australian living in London at the time attended this event. Among the musicians who performed in the concert were: Ada Crossley, Gertrude Johnson, Stella Power, Clara Serena, Peter Dawson, Harold Williams, Malcolm McEachern, Alfred O'Shea, violinist Daisy Kennedy and composer–pianist William G. James.
8   Three of these photographs appear among the illustrations in Beverley Nichol's book *The Sweet and Twenties*.
9   Melba, *Melodies and Memories*, pp. 65–6 (edited).
10 On 15 June 1923, *Le Ménestrel* in Paris reported that Mary Garden was in negotiations with Russell to join the company but if that is the case, no agreement was reached, for Garden did not join the company.
11 *Times*, 1 November 1922.
12 Another member of the Obolensky family, Prince Serge Obolensky, had a protracted love affair with Marjorie Lawrence in the United States in the late 1930s.

Chapter 21 –Tempus fugit
1   The reason for the lack of more recently composed works, more French works and for any by Wagner was attributed (by Williamson's) to the high cost of securing performing rights.
2   Dal Monte, Toti, *Una voce nel mondo*, Longanesi, Milan, 1962, p. 131.
3   The voices and artistry of each of these great singers – dal Monte, Borgioli and Granforte – can be sampled on numerous recordings. After his singing career ended, Borgioli became a prominent singing teacher in London. His pupils included the New Zealand-born Australian Joan Hammond, Australians June Bronhill and Kevin Miller, and the English tenor Robert Gard, who made his career in Australia.
4   Alexis Obolensky had arrived in Australia with Nellie and supported her in a couple of concerts she gave before the opera season commenced. During the season he sang only minor roles.

5   This performance and the post-performance ceremony were broadcast by the newly opened Australian Broadcasting Company, based in Melbourne and part-owned by J.C. Williamson. There seems to have been no attempt to preserve the broadcast with recordings.

6   The term 'nursing home' in Nellie's time (and up until the middle of the last century) did not mean an aged care facility; instead, it was a place where patients went to convalesce after surgery, to recover from non-life-threatening illnesses and to give birth.

7   Nellie kept enough of her favourite pieces of furniture and artworks to furnish the new apartment and donated a bust of herself, which had stood in the entry hall at the Mansfield Street house, to Covent Garden. This elegant portrait in white marble had been commissioned by Nellie from the Australian sculptor Bertram Mackennal in 1895. The sculptor had produced two versions of the bust. One had gone to the National Gallery of Victoria and the second went to Covent Garden. Gratefully accepted, it was placed on a pedestal halfway up the Grand Staircase, where it sits to this day. A portrait of Nellie was also painted in oils by John Longstaff.

8   For these concerts Arthur Hackett was styled as 'A. Granville Hackett', probably to distinguish him from his brother.

9   In a conversation I was privileged to have with Browning Mummery in 1972, he recalled being chosen to sing on this occasion as a great honour but added that Nellie paid little attention to him off stage and paid much to Brownlee: 'I was shy, a bit chubby and moonfaced and I couldn't compete with John's movie star looks'. The tenor also recalled that the first time he rehearsed *La Bohème* with Nellie and tried to follow the stage direction to embrace her, she whispered to him, 'Don't touch me.' That, Mummery put down to Nellie's concern about the difference in their ages, but also observed that he believed he and John McCormack were the only Rodolfos on whom such a restriction was placed. Mummery had learned his role while studying in Italy, but Brownlee did not know his role and had never seen *La Bohème* performed on stage. Nellie enlisted the help of her old colleague Maurice Renaud to teach Brownlee the role and Renaud lent Brownlee his own Marcello costume.

10 The earlier Mapleson cylinders of Nellie singing 'live' are anything but 'vivid' in sound and do not bear comparison with these recordings. The *Roméo et Juliette* scene was not committed to disc because Charles Hackett was not under contract to the Gramophone Company. Of the 11 sides recorded, only three were initially issued commercially, but all have been issued on LP and CD. Details will be found in Appendix 2: Melba's recordings.

Chapter 22 – Evening star

1. By the time of the Adelaide concerts, Stuart Robertson had returned to England and for them he was replaced by another English baritone, Clive Carey, a former student of Jean de Reszke. At the time, Carey was professor of singing at the Elder Conservatorium in Adelaide. He later became one of Joan Sutherland's teachers.
2. *Herald*, 25, 29 July 1927 (edited).
3. ibid., 1 September 1927.
4. This film was discovered just a few years ago when an Adelaide law firm was having a clean-out. It was donated to the National Film and Sound Archive and part of it can now be viewed on the internet. The date on the film storage can is 'November 1927'. One of the guests filmed is Stuart Robertson, who left to return to England before 10 November, so the date can be narrowed down to the first part of that month. Earlier that year the Melbourne photographer Spencer Sheer also visited Coombe Cottage and took some film of Nellie on the verandah at Coombe Cottage and in the garden singing to 'Cocky'. Part of Sheer's film can also be viewed on the internet.
5. Unsold copies of the first printing were withdrawn from sale, no doubt because of fear that Nellie would sue. When the book went back on sale the passage had been removed. Copies of the first printing are now desirable collectors' items. Giving credence to the story was Australians' familiarity with the writer; Ponder had spent many years in Australia working as a journalist and was well respected. Friendly relations between Nellie and Butt were restored with exchanged letters, but when Nellie was asked months later if the story was true, she is rumoured to have replied: 'I didn't need to tell Clara to sing muck ... that was all she ever sang.'
6. The performance was broadcast by two Sydney radio stations (2BL and 2FC) but neither seems to have attempted to record any part of it.
7. *Sydney Morning Herald*, 8 August 1928.
8. Evening edition of the *Herald*, 27 September 1928 (edited).
9. Ann Blainey in her *I am Melba* quotes a marvellous story about an English tax official suggesting to Nellie that Coombe Cottage was just a shack in the bush, providing a tax dodge. 'Does this Coombe Cottage have a bathroom?' the tax official asked. 'Eight!' Nellie replied indignantly.
10. Reported in *The Sunday Times*, 6 October 1929.
11. A couple of weeks later Nellie attended a welcome dinner at the International Sportsmen's Club for the Australian cricket team, in England to play for the Ashes. Richard Neville escorted her and she chatted with members of the team, including the 21-year-old Don Bradman, playing in England for the first time.

12 Nellie was so pleased with this 'snap' that she asked the former Boy Scout to send her a quantity of enlargements of it and sent them to the press; hence the survival of an amateur photograph that would prove to be of historical importance.
13 *Herald*, 27 January 1931 (edited). On the same day the Governor-General received a telegram from the king inquiring after Nellie's health and the king was reassured that Nellie was improving.
14 The service was broadcast on radio 3LO.
15 At a memorial service held in London, Ben Davies came out of retirement to sing and Maggie Teyte sang Gounod's 'Ave Maria' and 'Mimi's farewell'.

Chronology of Melba's life and career

1861 Born Helen Porter Mitchell at Richmond, Victoria, first surviving daughter of Isabella and David Mitchell.

c. 1867 Made her public debut as a juvenile singer.

1873 Began her formal education and commenced learning the organ and piano.

1875 Continued her education at Presbyterian Ladies College, Melbourne. Studied piano there with Alice Charbonnet-Kellermann and singing with Mary Ellen Christian.

1877 Public debut as an organist in Melbourne.

1878 Commenced studying singing with Pietro Cecchi.

1882 Travelled to Mackay, Queensland, with her father and there met Charles Armstrong; married Armstrong in Brisbane.

1883 Lived with Armstrong beside the sugar mill he managed at Marion, near Mackay; their son, George, born.

1884 Left Armstrong and returned to Melbourne with her son. Made her first public appearance in Melbourne as an adult singer and undertook her first professional engagements.

1885 Appointed soprano soloist at St Francis' Roman Catholic Church, Melbourne and toured Australia with the violinist Johann Kruse.

1886 Departed for London, where David Mitchell served as a Commissioner to the Indian and Colonial Exhibition. Auditioned for various prominent musicians in London and appeared in concerts there; travelled to Paris to audition for Mathilde Marchesi.

1887 Moved to Paris and commenced her studies with Marchesi. Made her operatic debut at the Théâtre de la Monnaie in Brussels as Gilda in Verdi's *Rigoletto* and followed up with other roles.

1888 Made her debut at Covent Garden in London in the title role in Donizetti's *Lucia di Lammermoor*, but was only partially successful.

1889 Made her debut at the Paris Opéra as Ophélie in Thomas's *Hamlet* and met Sarah Bernhardt, who gave her tips on acting. Returned to Covent Garden and triumphed as Juliette in Gounod's *Roméo et Juliette* and in other roles.

1890 Sang at the Opéra de Monte Carlo, at the Paris Opéra and at Covent Garden. Developed a small nodule on one of her vocal cords and rested until it disappeared. Met Louis Philippe, Duc d'Orléans, and they became lovers.

1891 Sang at the Imperial Opera in St Petersburg. Charles Armstrong sued for divorce naming the Duc d'Orléans as co-respondent. A settlement was reached.

1892 Nellie made her debut in Italy at Palermo, followed by Rome and Turin. Returned to Covent Garden for both the summer and winter seasons and appeared in the world premiere of *Elaine* by Bemberg. Was to have made her debut at the Metropolitan Opera in New York this year, but the opera house was destroyed by fire.

1893 Sang at La Scala, Milan, and was introduced to Verdi, Puccini and Leoncavallo. Also sang in Florence and Genoa. Sang in the British premieres of Leoncavallo's *Pagliacci* and Mascagni's *I Rantzau* at Covent Garden and also sang in Stockholm and Copenhagen. Made her debut at the Metropolitan Opera in New York as Lucia and went on tour in the United States with the Metropolitan Opera.

1894 Sang more performances at La Scala and studied the role of Desdemona in Verdi's *Otello* with the composer. In London, chef Auguste Escoffier created the dessert 'Pêches Melba'. Returned to the Met for her second season.

1895 Appeared at Covent Garden and then undertook a long concert tour of the US and Canada before returning to the Met.

1896 Returned to the Paris Opéra, Covent Garden and the Met, where she took on the role of Brünnhilde in Wagner's *Siegfried* and temporarily damaged her voice.

1897 Sang in a concert in Bergamo to celebrate the centenary of the birth of Donizetti. Returned to the US to appear with the Philadelphia-based Damrosch Opera Company.

1898 Returned to Covent Garden and visited Lucca to study the role of Mimi in Puccini's *La Bohème* with the composer. Made her debut in that role in Philadelphia with the Ellis Opera Company.

1899 Sang Mimi at Covent Garden for the first time. Sang in opera and concerts in Holland and Germany.

1900 Sang in concerts and opera in Vienna and was named a Kammersängerin by the Austrian emperor. Sang in concerts in Hungary. Charles Armstrong was granted a divorce from Melba in a Texas court. Returned to Covent Garden and New York where, she sang in the first Met performance of *La Bohème*.

1901 Some short passages of performances featuring Melba were recorded by Lionel Mapleson on stage at the Metropolitan Opera.

1902 Sang with Enrico Caruso for the first time in Monte Carlo. Returned to Australia for a concert tour; sang in most states and then New Zealand. Accused by the editor of Melbourne's *Truth* of being an alcoholic.

1904 Created the title role in Saint-Saëns' opera *Hélène* in Monte Carlo. Made her first commercial recordings for the Gramophone & Typewriter Company in London. Undertook a long concert tour of the US.

1906 Sang in Spain. Made a second series of recordings in London.

1907 Sang with Oscar Hammerstein's Manhattan Opera Company in New York and made a series of recordings for the Victor Company.

1908 Returned to Covent Garden for her twenty-fourth season and faced stiff competition from the Italian soprano Luisa Tetrazzini. Sang in *Rigoletto* with Caruso at the Paris Opéra and in another season for Oscar Hammerstein in New York.

1909 Undertook another long concert tour of Australia and New Zealand. The first biography of Melba (by Agnes Murphy) was published.

1910	Made further recordings in London. Sang again at Covent Garden and the Met, toured the US and made her debut with the Boston Opera Company.
1911	Brought the first Melba–Williamson Grand Opera Company to Australia.
1912	Undertook her longest provincial tour of Great Britain and returned to Covent Garden.
1913	Undertook a marathon concert tour of the US and Canada with the violinist Jan Kubelik and made more recordings for the Victor Company.
1914	Returned to Covent Garden and sang with the Boston Opera Company in Paris. She was in Australia when the First World War commenced and gave patriotic concerts to raise money for the war effort.
1915	Toured the neutral US and Canada, where she gave more fundraising concerts.
1916	Continued to give concerts in the US and Canada and made more recordings for Victor.
1917	Sang with the Chicago Opera Association opera company on an extensive tour of the US.
1918	Created a Dame of the British Empire.
1919	Returned to London for her twenty-ninth season at Covent Garden.
1920	Sang for the first international radio broadcast, from the Marconi studio in London. Sang in a royal gala concert in Oslo.
1921	Sang in *Faust* and *La Bohème* at Monte Carlo and returned to the Monnaie in Brussels for a gala concert. A further concert tour of Australia followed.
1922	Visited India on her way back to Europe and sang at the Vice-Regal Lodge in Simla.
1923	Returned to Covent Garden singing without a fee to support the British National Opera Company. Gave more concerts in the US and Canada and toured Europe, helping to select singers for another Melba–Williamson Grand Opera Company.
1924	Sang with the second Melba–Williamson Grand Opera Company in Australia.

1925   Diagnosed with diabetes. Engaged Beverley Nichols to ghost-write her autobiography *Melodies and Memories* and put her name to a singing manual, *The Melba Method*.
1926   Gave a farewell performance at Covent Garden, which was recorded, and made her final appearance in opera in London at the Old Vic Theatre. Made her last recordings in London.
1927   Undertook a farewell concert tour of Australia and sang the National Anthem at the opening of Parliament House in Canberra. Elevated to Dame Grand Cross of the Order of the British Empire. Agreed to be a partner in another Melba–Williamson Grand Opera Company in Australia.
1928   Sang three performances with third Melba–Williamson Grand Opera Company, one each in Sydney, Melbourne and Adelaide. Returned to Europe.
1929   Sang in a concert at the Hippodrome, Brighton.
1930   Sang in a concert at the Park Lane Hotel in London – her final public appearance. Became ill at sea as she was returning to Australia.
1931   Admitted to St Vincent's Private Hospital in Sydney, where she died.

Appendix 1

Melba's repertoire

Stage repertoire

Melba performed 26 complete operatic roles on stage during her career. It is believed that she learned another 12, but was not given the opportunity to perform any of those in their entirety, or she abandoned them by choice before performing them. At different times various opera companies proposed that Melba should sing other roles, which she either rejected outright or abandoned after beginning to study them. These included a few that would have suited her, such as Philine in Thomas's *Mignon*, some rarities (the title role in Fournier's *Stratonice* as an example) and some that were entirely unsuited to her voice, including the 'Mount Everest' of the soprano repertoire: Isolde in Wagner's *Tristan und Isolde*.

Of the composers of the 26 operas in which Melba did perform, only one (Donizetti) had died before she was born; and all but 10 of the 26 operas were composed during Melba's lifetime. We may not think of her as a performer of contemporary music, but Melba undoubtedly was, although this came about not entirely by choice. Rather, it was the result of Melba's life coinciding with a flowering in opera composition (Verdi, Wagner, Puccini etc.) and the resulting rejection of repertoire from earlier periods.

Melba also studied 14 of her roles with their composers, which makes what we can glean from reviews and recordings about how she sang their music of immense historical importance. Recordings reveal many instances of Melba singing phrases or individual notes differently from the way they are routinely sung today, and careful study of original scores shows that Melba's approach is often the composer's approach. A good example appears in her recordings of 'Ah, fors' è lui' from *La Traviata*, which she studied with Verdi. Melba discriminates clearly between the passages marked 'staccato' and 'marcato' and the semiquaver rests in the first few bars are observed but not allowed to disturb the smooth shape of the phrase – as Melba would, no doubt, have claimed Verdi had told her was his wish.

Melba quickly dropped dramatic roles such as the title role in *Aida* and Elisabeth in *Tannhäuser* from her repertoire and, as the years passed and her voice aged, she also dropped most of the 'coloratura' roles which had made her famous, concentrating instead on 'lyric' roles. By the end of the First World War, her stage repertoire had contracted to two roles in operas by Gounod: Juliette in *Roméo et Juliette* and Marguerite in *Faust*, as well as Desdemona in Verdi's *Otello* and Mimi in Puccini's *La Bohème*. As the 1920s rolled on and Nellie entered her 60s, Marguerite, Desdemona and Mimi were the only parts she felt confident singing on stage. The one part she had come to love more than any other and which served her better than any other in her declining years, Mimi in *La Bohème*, was the last she ever performed.

Roles Melba sang

Opera	Composer	Role	First performed
Rigoletto	Verdi	Gilda	13 October 1887, Théâtre de la Monnaie, Brussels
La Traviata	Verdi	Violetta	9 November 1887, Théâtre de la Monnaie, Brussels
Lucia di Lammermoor	Donizetti	Lucia	4 January 1888, Théâtre de la Monnaie, Brussels
Lakmé	Delibes	Lakmé	8 March 1888, Théâtre de la Monnaie, Brussels
Hamlet	Thomas	Ophélie	25 April 1888, Théâtre de la Monnaie, Brussels
Roméo et Juliette	Gounod	Juliette	21 February 1889, Théâtre de la Monnaie, Brussels
Faust	Gounod	Marguerite	21 July 1889, Covent Garden, London
Lohengrin	Wagner	Elsa	10 June 1890, Covent Garden, London
Esmeralda	Goring Thomas	Esmeralda	12 July 1890, Covent Garden, London
Carmen	Bizet	Micaëla	11 December 1890, Opéra-Comique, Paris
Elaine	Bemberg	Elaine	5 July 1892, Covent Garden, London
Aida	Verdi	Aida	4 November 1892, Covent Garden, London
Otello	Verdi	Desdemona	22 November 1892, Covent Garden, London
Pagliacci	Leoncavallo	Nedda	19 May 1893, Covent Garden, London
I Rantzau	Mascagni	Luisa	7 July 1893, Covent Garden, London

Semiramide	Rossini	Semiramide	12 January 1894, Metropolitan Opera, New York
Tannhäuser	Wagner	Elisabeth	29 January 1894, Metropolitan Opera, New York
Les Huguenots	Meyerbeer	Marguerite	26 December 1894, Metropolitan Opera, New York
Manon	Massenet	Manon	27 January 1896, Metropolitan Opera, New York
Siegfried	Wagner	Brünnhilde	30 December 1896, Metropolitan Opera, New York
Siegfried	Wagner	Forest Bird	Unknown, private performance, London
Il Barbiere di Siviglia	Rossini	Rosina	27 December 1897, Academy of Music, Philadelphia
La Bohème	Puccini	Mimi	30 December 1898, Academy of Music, Philadelphia
Le Cid	Massenet	Infanta	16 January 1901, Metropolitan Opera, New York
Le Damnation de Faust	Berlioz	Marguerite	2 March 1902, Opéra de Monte Carlo, Monaco
Hélène	Saint-Saëns	Hélène	18 February 1904, Opéra de Monte Carlo, Monaco

Roles Melba is believed to have learned but did not sing in their entirety

Opera	Composer	Role
Le Nozze di Figaro	Mozart	Susanna
		Countess
		Melba sang the countess in act three of Le Nozze di Figaro at a gala at the Théâtre de la Monnaie, Brussels on 14 April 1921.
Don Giovanni	Mozart	Zerlina
		Elvira
Les Pêcheuer de perles	Bizet	Leila
Mireille	Gounod	Mireille
Martha	Flotow	Lady Harriet
La Sonnambula	Bellini	Amina
Il Trovatore	Verdi	Leonora
Die Meistersinger von Nürnberg	Wagner	Eva
Tosca	Puccini	Tosca
Madama Butterfly	Puccini	Cio-Cio-San

Concert repertoire

Melba was not a song recitalist in the sense we use that term today. Songs were, however, a major component in her concert repertoire, invariably mixed in with operatic arias. She seldom sang German lieder and when she did, she only chose the most popular songs, usually singing them in English translations. The bulk of Melba's song repertoire was comprised of ballads and 'salon' songs of the type exemplified by the works of Paolo Tosti.

The one area in the song repertoire where she was adventurous was the works of contemporary French composers. Not only did she sing the rather inconsequential songs of her friend Herman Bemberg, but she also made a feature in her programs of songs by Duparc, Chausson, Debussy and Ravel. Although her French accent may not have been entirely idiomatic, Melba showed a clear understanding of this genre and her pure tone gave an ethereal quality to her singing of those with an impressionistic flavour.

Listing Nellie's complete song repertoire here would take too many pages, but a representative cross-section can be identified from what she recorded and will be found in Appendix 2: Melba's recordings.

Once Melba's stage career was established, she declined many offers to appear as a soloist in oratorio or in other large scale concert works, only once (as noted in Chapter 3) agreeing to sing *Messiah* in a provincial town in England and unimpressed by the experience. This decision may have been prompted by the much higher fees she could earn in opera, but it also may have been because she knew she was at her best on stage or in concerts of miscellaneous works.

Oratorios and other concert works in which Melba took the principal soprano part

Title	Composer	First performed
Mass in G major	Alfred Plumpton	24 May 1885, St Francis' Church, Melbourne
Nelson Mass	Haydn	14 June 1885, St Francis' Church, Melbourne
Mass in G, Opus 76	Weber	28 June 1885, St Francis' Church, Melbourne
Messe Solennelle	Gounod	25 October 1885, St Francis' Church, Melbourne
Lalla Rookh	Frédéric Clay	8 December 1885, Town Hall, Melbourne
Messiah	Handel	25 December 1885, Exhibition Building, Sydney
Saint François	Edgar Tinel	13 January 1889, Théâtre de la Monnaie, Brussels
Ode for Saint Cecilia's Day	Handel	14 April 1889, Conservatoire, Brussels
Coronation Ode, Opus 44	Elgar	June 1902, Rehearsed in London, but not performed

Appendix 2

Melba's recordings

Between 1904 and 1926 it is documented that Melba made 183 commercial recordings. Another 18 were made of her performing live on stage, the earliest in 1901. There is also evidence that Melba recorded items at some recording sessions for which there is no documentation other than a number missing from a matrix series. The titles of these are, therefore, unknown; some may have been repeats of other titles recorded at the same sessions. These 'missing' recordings would probably push the total of commercial recordings to well over 200.

All but one of Melba's recording sessions took place in England or America, the exception being a single recording session in Paris. Rumours that Melba made recordings in Australia are untrue.

Of the recordings of which we have knowledge, 111 were issued commercially on 78 rpm discs, mostly 12 inches in diameter and single- or double-sided (one item on each side). The original issues of the first series (1904) bore the exclusive Melba lilac label. Reissues and first releases of some previously unissued recordings were made on 78s and proliferated in the long-playing disc era. Outstanding among the LP reissues were two multi-disc boxed sets from EMI and RCA. *Nellie Melba – The London Recordings* (EMI RLS 719), issued in 1976, assembled all the surviving recordings Melba had made in London and the only known one from the Paris session. This set also included several that had never been issued before. Six years later the Australian branch of RCA, in partnership with the Australian Broadcasting Commission, issued all of Melba's

American recordings under the title *Melba – The American Recordings 1907–1916* (RCA VRL5 0365). One of the 1901 live recordings was included in this latter set.

The proliferation of reissues continues to this day on compact disc and on the internet.

The sonic quality of Melba's recordings is consistent with the technology of their time, the later ones made electrically being superior in sound to the earlier acoustic ones. Some patience is required to listen through the hiss and crackle and the unnatural ambience of early recording studios, but the rewards are many. As noted in the text, the best and most accurate reproduction of Melba's voice can be heard on those CD reissues where unworn original matrices have been used and modern technology applied to remove extraneous noises and enhance the sound.

Melba's recordings document the sound of her voice and the standard of her singing from the middle of her career to its end. They are also important in an historical sense because she was the first great soprano to be recorded while still in her prime. As well as giving listening pleasure, Melba's recordings provide a fascinating glimpse into the musical world of the late-Victorian and Edwardian eras.

On the following pages, all known Melba recordings are listed under the composer's names (alphabetically) and with each title listed alphabetically. Where more than one recording was made of a piece, they are listed chronologically, according to the recording dates, and numbered. An incomplete recording date (month, but no day) indicates that the written records are incomplete.

ARDITI, Luigi

Se saran rose

(1) With Landon Ronald (piano), recorded by the Gramophone & Typewriter Company, Great Cumberland Place, London, March 1904. Matrix: Melba 9; original issue: 03019

(2) With orchestra conducted by Walter B. Rogers, recorded by the Victor Company, New York, 29 March 1907. Matrix: C-4356-1; original issue 88076

(3) With orchestra conducted by Walter B. Rogers, recorded by the Victor Company, Camden, New Jersey, 23 August 1910. Matrix: C-4356-2; original issue 88076 (replacing the 1907 Victor recording)

BEMBERG, Herman

Chanson Hindou

With Herman Bemberg (piano), recorded by the Gramophone & Typewriter Company, City Road, London, 20 October 1904. Matrix: 405c; original issue: 03036

Chant vénitien

(1) With Herman Bemberg (piano), recorded by the Gramophone & Typewriter Company, City Road, London, 20 October 1904. Matrix: 6149B; unissued and destroyed

(2) With Herman Bemberg (piano), recorded by the Gramophone & Typewriter Company, City Road, London, 20 October 1904. Matrix: 6150B; original issue: 3575

(3) With Gabriel Lapierre (piano), recorded by the Victor Company, Camden, New Jersey, 4 October 1913. Matrix: C-13908-1 (with Les anges pleurent on the same matrix); unissued

Elaine: L'amour est pur

With female chorus and Herman Bemberg (piano), recorded by the Gramophone & Typewriter Company, City Road, London, 7 July 1906. Matrix: 690c; unissued

Les anges pleurent

(1) With Herman Bemberg (piano), recorded by the Gramophone & Typewriter Company, City Road, London, 20 October 1904. Matrix: 6151B; original issue: 3576

(2) With Gabriel Lapierre (piano), recorded by the Victor Company, Camden, New Jersey, 4 October 1913. Matrix: C-13908-1 (with Chant vénitien on the same matrix); unissued

Nymphs et Sylvains
    With Landon Ronald (piano), recorded by the Gramophone & Typewriter Company, Great Cumberland Place, London, March 1904. Matrix: Melba 2; original issue: 03016

Sur le lac
    With Herman Bemberg (piano), recorded by the Gramophone & Typewriter Company, City Road, London, 5 September 1905. Matrix: 520c; original issue: 03046

Un ange est venu
(1) With Charles Gilibert and orchestra conducted by Walter B. Rogers, recorded by the Victor Company, New York, 28 March 1907. Matrix: C-4348-1; original issue: 89012
(2) With John Brownlee and Harold Craxton (piano), recorded by the Gramophone Company, Small Queen's Hall, London, 17 December 1926. Matrix: Cc9551; original issue: DB987

BISHOP, Henry

Bid me discourse
(1) With Landon Ronald (piano), recorded by the Gramophone Company, City Road, London, 11 May 1910. Matrix: 4193f; original issue: 03188
(2) With Christopher H.H. Booth (piano), recorded by the Victor Company, Camden, New Jersey, 26 August 1910. Matrix: C-9374-1; unissued

Home, sweet home
(1) With Landon Ronald (piano), recorded by the Gramophone & Typewriter Company, City Road, London, 5 September 1905. Matrix: 523c; original issue: 03049
(2) Accompanying herself at the piano, recorded by the Gramophone Company, Hayes, Middlesex, 12 May 1921. Matrix: Cc151; original issue: 03049

Lo, here the gentle lark
(1) With Landon Ronald (piano) and Albert Fransella (flute), recorded by the Gramophone & Typewriter Company, City Road, London, 5 September 1905. Matrix: 521c; original issue: 03047
(2) With Charles K. North (flute) and orchestra conducted by Walter B. Rogers, recorded by the Victor Company, New York, 27 March 1907. Matrix: C-4350-1; unissued

(3) With Charles K. North (flute) and orchestra conducted by Walter B. Rogers, recorded by the Victor Company, New York, 28 March 1907. Matrix: C-4350-2; original issue: 88073

(4) With John Lemmoné (flute) and orchestra conducted by Walter B. Rogers, recorded by the Victor Company, Camden, New Jersey, 23 August 1910. Matrix: C-4350-3; original issue: 88073 (replacing the 1907 Victor recording)

BIZET, Georges

Pastorale

With Landon Ronald (piano), recorded by the Gramophone & Typewriter Company, City Road, London, 7 July 1906. Matrix: 691c; original issue: 03070

BLANGINI, Giuseppe

Per valli per boschi

With Charles Gilibert and orchestra conducted by Walter B. Rogers, recorded by the Victor Company, New York, 28 March 1907. Matrix: C-4347-1; original issue: 89011

CHARPENTIER, Gustave

Louise: Depuis le jour

(1) With orchestra conducted by Walter B. Rogers, recorded by the Victor Company, Camden, New Jersey, 2 October 1913. Matrix: C-13900-1; unissued

(2) With orchestra conducted by Walter B. Rogers, recorded by the Victor Company, Camden, New Jersey, 3 October 1913. Matrix: C-13900-2; original issue: 88477

(3) With Gabriel Lapierre (piano), recorded by the Victor Company, Camden, New Jersey, 3 October 1913. Matrix: C-13903-1; unissued

CHAUSSON, Ernest

Le temps de lilas

(1) With Gabriel Lapierre (piano), recorded by the Gramophone Company, Hayes, Middlesex, May 1913. Matrix: Z7325f; original issue: 2-033037

(2) With Gabriel Lapierre (piano), recorded by the Victor Company, Camden, New Jersey, 4 October 1913. Matrix: unnumbered; unissued

'CLARIBEL' (Charlotte Barnard)

Come back to Erin
 With the Band of HM Coldstream Guards conducted by Lt Mackenzie Rogan, recorded by the Gramophone & Typewriter Company, City Road, London, 4 September 1905. Matrix: 7202½b; original issue: 3616

D'HARDELOT, Guy

Three green bonnets
 With Landon Ronald (piano), recorded by the Gramophone & Typewriter Company, Great Cumberland Place, London, March 1904. Matrix: Melba 25; original issue: 03027

DEBUSSY, Claude

En sourdine
 Accompanying herself at the piano, recorded by the Victor Company, New York, 1 January 1909. Matrix: C-6697-1; unissued

Romance **and** *Mandoline (recorded on the same matrix and issued on the same disc)*
 (1) With Gabriel Lapierre (piano), recorded by the Victor Company, Camden, New Jersey, 2 October 1913. Matrix: C-13899-1; unissued
 (2) With Gabriel Lapierre (piano), recorded by the Victor Company, Camden, New Jersey, 3 October 1913. Matrix: C-13899-2; original issue: 88456

DONIZETTI, Gaetano

Lucia di Lammermoor: Verrano a te sull'aura
 With Albert Saléza and the orchestra of the Metropolitan Opera, conducted by Luigi Mancinelli. Recorded by Lionel Mapleson at a public performance in the Metropolitan Opera House, New York, 2 March 1901. In the collection of the New York Public Library

Lucia di Lammermoor: Ardon gl'incensi (part of the Mad Scene)
 With John Lemmoné (flute) and orchestra conducted by Walter B. Rogers, recorded by the Victor Company, Camden, New Jersey, 24 August 1910. Matrix: C-4349-3; original issue 88071 (replacing the 1907 Victor recording of 'Del ciel clemente')

Lucia di Lammermoor: Del ciel clemente (part of the Mad Scene)
(1) With Landon Ronald (piano) and Philippe Gaubert (flute), recorded by the Gramophone & Typewriter Company, Great Cumberland Place, London, March 1904. Matrix: Melba 12; original issue: 03020
(2) With Charles K. North (flute) and orchestra, conducted by Walter B. Rogers, recorded by the Victor Company, New York, 29 March 1907. Matrix: C-4349-1; unissued
(3) With Charles K. North (flute) and orchestra conducted by Walter B. Rogers, recorded by the Victor Company, New York, 30 March 1907. Matrix: C-4349-2; original issue: 88071

Lucia di Lammermoor: Spargi d'amaro pianto (part of the Mad Scene)
(1) With the orchestra of the Metropolitan Opera, conducted by Luigi Mancinelli. Recorded by Lionel Mapleson at a public performance in the Metropolitan Opera House, New York, 2 March 1901. In the collection of the New York Public Library
(2) With the orchestra of the Metropolitan Opera, conducted by Luigi Mancinelli. Recorded by Lionel Mapleson at a public performance in the Metropolitan Opera House, New York, 8 March 1901. In the collection of the New York Public Library

DUPARC, Henri

Chanson triste
(1) With Gabriel Lapierre (piano), recorded by the Gramophone Company, Hayes, Middlesex, May 1913. Matrix: Y16572e; original issue: 7-33004
(2) With Gabriel Lapierre (piano), recorded by the Victor Company, Camden, New Jersey, 3 October 1913. Matrix: C-13906-1; unissued

Phidylé
With Gabriel Lapierre (piano), recorded by the Victor Company, Camden, New Jersey, 3 October 1913. Matrix: unnumbered; unissued (recorded for Melba, not for issue)

DVOŘÁK, Antonín

Songs my mother taught me
(1) With orchestra conducted by Walter B. Rogers, recorded by the Victor Company, Camden, New Jersey, 12 January 1916. Matrix: C-17002-1; unissued
(2) With orchestra conducted by Walter B. Rogers, recorded by the Victor Company, Camden, New Jersey, 12 January 1916. Matrix: C-17002-2; original issue: 88485

(3) With Frank St Leger (piano), recorded by the Victor Company, Camden, New Jersey, 12 January 1916. Matrix: C-17004-1; unissued

FOSTER, Stephen

Old folks at home

(1) With chorus (Gwladys Roberts, Ernest Pike, Peter Dawson) and Landon Ronald (piano), recorded by the Gramophone & Typewriter Company, City Road, London, 4 September 1905. Matrix: 7203b; original issue: 3617

(2) With orchestra conducted by Walter B. Rogers, recorded by the Victor Company, Camden, New Jersey, 3 October 1913. Matrix: C-13904-1; unissued

(3) With orchestra conducted by Walter B. Rogers, recorded by the Victor Company, Camden, New Jersey, 3 October 1913. Matrix: C-13904-2; original issue: 88454

GOUNOD, Charles

Ave Maria (arrangement of Bach)

(1) With Landon Ronald (piano) and Jan Kubelik (violin), recorded by the Gramophone & Typewriter Company, City Road, London, 20 October 1904. Matrix: 400c; unissued and destroyed

(2) With Landon Ronald (piano) and Jan Kubelik (violin), recorded by the Gramophone & Typewriter Company, City Road, London, 20 October 1904. Matrix: 401c; original issue: 03033

(3) With Landon Ronald (piano) and W.H. Squires (cello), recorded by the Gramophone & Typewriter Company, City Road, London, 7 July 1906. Matrix: 689c; original issue: 03069

(4) With Ada Sassoli (harp), violin and organ, recorded by the Victor Company, New York, 30 March 1907. Matrix: C-4259-1; unissued

(5) With Ada Sassoli (harp), violin and organ, recorded by the Victor Company, New York, 30 March 1907. Matrix: C-4259-2; unissued

(6) With Jan Kubelik (violin) and Stanley Roper (organ), recorded by the Gramophone Company, Hayes, Middlesex, May 1913. Matrix: Z7321f; unissued and destroyed

(7) With Jan Kubelik (violin) and Stanley Roper (organ), recorded by the Gramophone Company, Hayes, Middlesex, May 1913. Matrix: Z7323f; original issue: 03333

(8) With Jan Kubelik (violin) and Gabriel Lapierre (piano), recorded by the Victor Company, Camden, New Jersey, 2 October 1913. Matrix: C-13897-1; unissued
(9) With Jan Kubelik (violin) and Gabriel Lapierre (piano), recorded by the Victor Company, Camden, New Jersey, 2 October 1913. Matrix: C-13897-2; original issue: 89073

Faust: Ah! Je ris de me voir, si belle (Jewel Song)
(1) With the orchestra of the Metropolitan Opera, conducted by Luigi Mancinelli. Recorded by Lionel Mapleson at a public performance in the Metropolitan Opera House, New York, 28 March 1901. In the collection of the New York Public Library
(2) With Landon Ronald (piano), recorded by the Gramophone & Typewriter Company, City Road, London, 5 September 1905. Matrix: 522c; original issue: 03048
(3) With orchestra conducted by Walter B. Rogers, recorded by the Victor Company, New York, 27 March 1907. Matrix: C-4338-1; unissued
(4) With orchestra conducted by Walter B. Rogers, recorded by the Victor Company, New York, 27 March 1907. Matrix: C-4338-2; original issue: 88066
(5) With orchestra conducted by Walter B. Rogers, recorded by the Victor Company, Camden, New Jersey, 22 August 1910. Matrix: C-4883-2; unissued
(6) With orchestra conducted by Walter B. Rogers, recorded by the Victor Company, Camden, New Jersey, 22 August 1910. Matrix: C-4883-3; original issue: 88066. (Replacing the 1907 Victor recording)

Faust: Alerte! Alerte! (Trio)
(1) Part only, with Albert Saléza, Edouard de Reszke and the orchestra of the Metropolitan Opera, conducted by Luigi Mancinelli. Recorded by Lionel Mapleson at a public performance in the Metropolitan Opera House, New York, 4 March 1901. In the collection of the New York Public Library
(2) With Albert Saléza, Pol Plançon and the orchestra of the Metropolitan Opera, conducted by Luigi Mancinelli. Recorded by Lionel Mapleson at a public performance in the Metropolitan Opera House, New York, 28 March 1901. In the collection of the New York Public Library
(3) With John McCormack, Mario Sammarco and the New Symphony Orchestra conducted by Landon Ronald, recorded by the Gramophone Company, City Road, London, 11 May 1910. Matrix: 4188f; unissued

(4) With John McCormack, Mario Sammarco and the New Symphony Orchestra, conducted by Landon Ronald, recorded by the Gramophone Company, City Road, London, 11 May 1910. Matrix: 4190f; unissued in the UK

Roméo et Juliette: Je veux vivre le rêve (Waltz Song)
(1) With the orchestra of the Metropolitan Opera, conducted by Luigi Mancinelli. Recorded by Lionel Mapleson at a public performance in the Metropolitan Opera House, New York, 9 March 1901. In the collection of the New York Public Library
(2) With Landon Ronald (piano), recorded by the Gramophone & Typewriter Company, City Road, London, 20 October 1904. Matrix: 404c; original issue: 03035
(3) With orchestra conducted by Walter B. Rogers, recorded by the Victor Company, New York, 29 March 1907. Matrix: C-4257-1; unissued

HAHN, Reynaldo

D'une prison
Accompanying herself at the piano, recorded by the Victor Company, New York, 1 January 1909. Matrix: C-6700-1; original issue: 88151

Si mes vers avaient des ailes
(1) With Landon Ronald (piano), recorded by the Gramophone & Typewriter Company, Great Cumberland Place, London, March 1904. Matrix: Melba 27; original issue: 03029
(2) With Ada Sassoli (harp), recorded by the Victor Company, New York, 29 March 1907. Matrix: C-4352-1; original issue: 88080

HANDEL, George Frideric

L'Allegro, il Penseroso ed il Moderato: Sweet bird that shunst the noise of folly
(1) With Landon Ronald (piano) and Philippe Gaubert (flute), recorded by the Gramophone & Typewriter Company, Great Cumberland Place, London, March 1904. Matrix: Melba 14; unissued
(2) With Landon Ronald (piano) and Philippe Gaubert (flute), recorded by the Gramophone & Typewriter Company, Great Cumberland Place, London, March 1904. Matrix: Melba 15; original issue: 03021
(3) With Charles K. North (flute) and orchestra, conducted by Walter B. Rogers, recorded by the Victor Company, New York, 30 March 1907. Matrix: C-4358-1; original issue: 88068
(4) With John Lemmoné (flute) and orchestra conducted by Walter B. Rogers, recorded by the Victor Company, Camden, New Jersey, 24

August 1910. Matrix: C-4358–2; original issue: 88068. (Replacing the 1907 Victor recording)

HENSCHEL, George

Spring

(1) With Landon Ronald (piano), recorded by the Gramophone Company, City Road, London, 19 May 1910. Matrix: 4210f; unissued and destroyed

(2) With Landon Ronald (piano), recorded by the Gramophone Company, City Road, London, 19 May 1910. Matrix: 4213f; original issue: 03328

HUE, Georges

Soir païen

With John Lemmoné (flute) and Landon Ronald (piano), recorded by the Gramophone Company, City Road, London, 19 May 1910. Matrix: 4209f; unissued

LALO, Édouard

Le Roi d'Ys: Aubade

(1) With Landon Ronald (piano), recorded by the Gramophone & Typewriter Company, City Road, London, 7 July 1906. Matrix: 693c; original issue: 03072

(2) With orchestra conducted by Walter B. Rogers, recorded by the Victor Company, Camden, New Jersey, 25 August 1910. Matrices: C-9372–1; original issue: 88250

(3) With orchestra conducted by Walter B. Rogers, recorded by the Victor Company, Camden, New Jersey, 25 August 1910. Matrices: C-9372–2; unissued

LEHMANN, Liza

Magdalen at Michael's Gate

With Gabriel Lapierre (piano), recorded by the Victor Company, Camden, New Jersey, 2 October 1913. Matrix: C-13898–1; original issue: 88452

LIEURANCE, Thurlow

By the waters of Minnetonka

With Landon Ronald (piano), recorded by the Gramophone Company, Hayes, Middlesex, 12 May 1921. Matrix: Bb149; original issue: 2-3568

LOTTI, Antonio

Pur dicesti, o bocca bella
With Landon Ronald (piano), recorded by the Gramophone Company, City Road, London, 19 May 1910. Matrix: 4214f; unissued

MASSENET, Jules

Don César de Bazan: Sevillana
(1) With the New Symphony Orchestra, conducted by Landon Ronald, recorded by the Gramophone Company, City Road, London, 11 May 1910. Matrix: 4184f; unissued
(2) With the New Symphony Orchestra, conducted by Landon Ronald, recorded by the Gramophone Company, City Road, London, 19 May 1910. Matrix: 4206f; unissued
(3) With the New Symphony Orchestra, conducted by Landon Ronald, recorded by the Gramophone Company, City Road, London, 19 May 1910. Matrix: 4207f; unissued
(4) With orchestra conducted by Walter B. Rogers, recorded by the Victor Company, Camden, New Jersey, 24 August 1910. Matrix: C-9370-1; original issue: 88252 & 88662

Le Cid: Allez en paix ... Allelulia! (part only)
With the orchestra of the Metropolitan Opera, conducted by Luigi Mancinelli. Recorded by Lionel Mapleson at a public performance in the Metropolitan Opera House, New York, 16 January 1901. In the collection of the New York Public Library

Le Cid: Pleurez, pleurez mes yeux
With the New Symphony Orchestra, conducted by Landon Ronald, recorded by the Gramophone Company, City Road, London, 19 May 1910. Matrix: 4208f; original issue: 2-033020

MENDELSSOHN, Felix

O for the wings of a dove
(1) With Landon Ronald (piano), recorded by the Gramophone Company, City Road, London, 19 May 1910. Matrix: 4211f; unissued and destroyed
(2) With Landon Ronald (piano), recorded by the Gramophone Company, City Road, London, 19 May 1910. Matrix: 4212f; original issue: 03199

MEYERBEER, Giacomo

Les Huguenots: Cabaletta from the aria 'A ce mot seul s'anime' (part only)
With the orchestra of the Metropolitan Opera, conducted by Philippe Flon. Recorded by Lionel Mapleson at a public performance in the Metropolitan Opera House, New York, either 28 January or 11 March 1901. In the collection of the New York Public Library

MISCELLANEOUS

Vocal lesson No.1
Melba accompanying herself at the piano. Recorded by the Victor Company, Camden, New Jersey, 4 October 1913. Matrix: C-13909-1; unissued

MOZART, Wolfgang Amadeus

Il Ré Pastore: 'L'amerò, sarò costante
(1) With Jan Kubelik (violin) and Gabriel Lapierre (piano), recorded by the Gramophone Company, Hayes, Middlesex, May 1913. Matrix: Z7322f; original issue: 2-053083
(2) With Jan Kubelik (violin) and Gabriel Lapierre (piano), recorded by the Victor Company, Camden, New Jersey, 2 October 1913. Matrix: C-13896-1; unissued
(3) With Jan Kubelik (violin) and Gabriel Lapierre (piano), recorded by the Victor Company, Camden, New Jersey, 2 October 1913. Matrix: C-13896-2; original issue: 89074

Le Nozze di Figaro: Porgi amor
With Landon Ronald (piano), recorded by the Gramophone & Typewriter Company, Great Cumberland Place, London, March 1904. Matrix: Melba 26; original issue: 03028

Le Nozze di Figaro: Voi che sapete
(1) With piano (pianist unidentified), recorded by the Victor Company, New York, 27 March 1907. Matrix: C-4337-1; unissued
(2) With orchestra conducted by Walter B. Rogers, recorded by the Victor Company, New York, 29 March 1907. Matrix: C-4353-1; original issue: 88067
(3) With orchestra conducted by Walter B. Rogers, recorded by the Victor Company, Camden, New Jersey, 23 August 1910. Matrix: C-4353-2; original issue: 88067. (Replacing the 1907 Victor recording)

PUCCINI, Giacomo

La Bohème: Si, mi chiamano Mimì
(1) With Landon Ronald (piano), recorded by the Gramophone & Typewriter Company, City Road, London, 7 July 1906. Matrix: 692c; original issue: 03071
(2) With orchestra conducted by Walter B. Rogers, recorded by the Victor Company, New York, 5 March 1907. Matrix: C-4281-1; unissued
(3) With orchestra conducted by Walter B. Rogers, recorded by the Victor Company, New York, 24 March 1907. Matrix: C-4281-2; original issue 88074
(4) Sung in French with orchestra. Recorded by the Gramophone and Typewriter Company, Paris, 9 May 1908. Matrix: 602i; original issue 033062
(5) With orchestra conducted by Walter B. Rogers, recorded by the Victor Company, Camden, New Jersey, 22 August 1910. Matrix: C-4281-3; unissued
(6) With orchestra conducted by Walter B. Rogers, recorded by the Victor Company, Camden, New Jersey, 22 August 1910. Matrix: C-4281-4; original issue 88074 (replacing the 1907 Victor recording)

La Bohème: O soave fanciulla
(1) With Enrico Caruso and orchestra conducted by Walter B. Rogers, recorded by the Victor Company, New York, 24 March 1907. Matrix: C-4326-1; original issue 95200
(2) With Enrico Caruso and orchestra conducted by Walter B. Rogers, recorded by the Victor Company, New York, 24 March 1907. Matrix: C-4326-2; unissued
(3) With Enrico Caruso and orchestra conducted by Walter B. Rogers, recorded by the Victor Company, New York, 1 April 1907. Matrix: C-4326-3; unissued
(4) With Enrico Caruso and orchestra conducted by Walter B. Rogers, recorded by the Victor Company, New York, 1 April 1907. Matrix: C-4326-4; unissued

La Bohème: Entrate ... C'e Rodolfo
With John Brownlee and the orchestra of the Royal Opera House, Covent Garden, conducted by Vincenzo Bellezza. Recorded live at Covent Garden, 8 June 1926. Matrix: CR411; unissued

La Bohème: Donde lieta usci (Mimi's Farewell)
(1) With Landon Ronald (piano), recorded by the Gramophone & Typewriter Company, Great Cumberland Place, London, March 1904. Matrix: Melba 28; unissued
(2) With Landon Ronald (piano), recorded by the Gramophone & Typewriter Company, City Road, London, 20 October 1904. Matrix: 406c; original issue: 03037
(3) With orchestra conducted by Walter B. Rogers, recorded by the Victor Company, New York, 27 March 1907. Matrix: C-4341-1; original issue: 88072
(4) With orchestra conducted by Walter B. Rogers, recorded by the Victor Company, New York, 6 January 1909. Matrix: C-4341-2; issued only in Germany 053111
(5) With orchestra conducted by Walter B. Rogers, recorded by the Victor Company, Camden, New Jersey, 23 August 1910. Matrix: C-4341-3; original issue: 88072 (replacing the 1907 Victor recording)
(6) With orchestra conducted by Walter B. Rogers, recorded by the Victor Company, Camden, New Jersey, 23 August 1910. Matrix: C-4341-4; unissued
(7) With the orchestra of the Royal Opera House, Covent Garden, conducted by Vincenzo Bellezza. Recorded live at Covent Garden, 8 June 1926. Matrix: CR412; original issue: DB943 & DB1500

La Bohème: Addio dolce svegliare alla mattina (Quartet)
With Aurora Rettore, Browning Mummery, John Brownlee and the orchestra of the Royal Opera House, Covent Garden, conducted by Vincenzo Bellezza. Recorded live at Covent Garden, 8 June 1926. Matrix: CR413; unissued

La Bohème: Gavotta ... Minuetto
With Aurora Rettore, Browning Mummery, John Brownlee, Frederic Collier, Edouard Cotreuil and the orchestra of the Royal Opera House, Covent Garden, conducted by Vincenzo Bellezza. Recorded live at Covent Garden, 8 June 1926. Matrix: CR414; unissued

La Bohème: Sono andati?
With Browning Mummery and the orchestra of the Royal Opera House, Covent Garden, conducted by Vincenzo Bellezza. Recorded live at Covent Garden, 8 June 1926. Matrix: CR415; unissued

La Bohème: Io Musetta ... Oh, come è bello e morbido!
 With Aurora Rettore, Browning Mummery, John Brownlee, Frederic Collier, Edouard Cotreuil and the orchestra of the Royal Opera House, Covent Garden, conducted by Vincenzo Bellezza. Recorded live at Covent Garden, 8 June 1926. Matrix: CR416; unissued

Tosca: Vissi d'arte
(1) With orchestra conducted by Walter B. Rogers, recorded by the Victor Company, New York, 5 March 1907. Matrix: C-4282-1; unissued
(2) With orchestra conducted by Walter B. Rogers, recorded by the Victor Company, New York, 24 March 1907. Matrix: C-4282-2; original issue 88075
(3) With the New Symphony Orchestra conducted by Landon Ronald, recorded by the Gramophone Company, City Road, London, 11 May 1910. Matrix: 4183f; original issue: 2-053020
(4) With the New Symphony Orchestra, conducted by Landon Ronald, recorded by the Gramophone Company, City Road, London, 11 May 1910. Matrix: 4186f; unissued
(5) With orchestra conducted by Walter B. Rogers, recorded by the Victor Company, Camden, New Jersey, 24 August 1910. Matrix: C-4282-3; unissued
(6) With orchestra conducted by Walter B. Rogers, recorded by the Victor Company, Camden, New Jersey, 25 August 1910. Matrix: C-4282-4; original issue 88075 (replacing the 1907 Victor recording)

RIMSKY-KORSAKOV, Nicolai

Sadko: Chanson hindoue
 With orchestra conducted by Landon Ronald, recorded by the Gramophone Company, Hayes, Middlesex, 12 May 1921. Matrix: Cc147; original issue 03759

RONALD, Landon

Away on a hill
(1) With Landon Ronald (piano), recorded by the Gramophone & Typewriter Company, City Road, London, 4 September 1905. Matrix: 7205b; original issue: 3619
(2) With Landon Ronald (piano), recorded by the Gramophone Company, Hayes, Middlesex, 12 May 1921. Matrix: Cc148 (2 items on the same matrix); unissued

Down in the forest
(1) Accompanying herself at the piano, recorded by the Victor Company, New York, 1 January 1909. Matrix: C-6698-1; unissued
(2) With Landon Ronald (piano), recorded by the Gramophone Company, Hayes, Middlesex, 12 May 1921. Matrix: Cc148 (2 items on the same matrix); unissued

O lovely night
(1) With orchestra conducted by Walter B. Rogers, recorded by the Victor Company, New York, 6 January 1909. Matrix: C-6706-1; original issue: 88182
(2) With orchestra conducted by Walter B. Rogers, recorded by the Victor Company, Camden, New Jersey, 26 August 1910. Matrix: C-6706-2; original issue: 88182 (replacing the 1909 Victor recording)

Sounds of earth
With Landon Ronald (piano), recorded by the Gramophone Company, City Road, London, 11 May 1910. Matrix: 4194f; unissued

White sea mist
(1) With Landon Ronald (piano), recorded by the Gramophone & Typewriter Company, City Road, London, 11 July 1906. Matrix: 8473b; unissued
(2) Accompanying herself at the piano, recorded by the Victor Company, New York, 1 January 1909. Matrix: C-6699-1; unissued
(3) Accompanying herself at the piano, recorded by the Victor Company, New York, 1 January 1909. Matrix: C-6699-2; unissued

ROSSINI, Gioacchino

Stabat Mater: Inflammatus
With orchestra conducted by Walter B. Rogers, recorded by the Victor Company, Camden, New Jersey, 26 August 1910. Matrix: C-9373-1; unissued

SCOTT, Lady John

Annie Laurie
(1) Accompanying herself at the piano, recorded by the Gramophone Company, Hayes, Middlesex, 12 May 1921. Matrix: Bb150; unissued
(2) With orchestra conducted by Walter B. Rogers, recorded by the Victor Company, Camden, New Jersey, 12 January 1916. Matrix: C-17001-1; original issue: 88551

(3) With Frank St Leger (piano), recorded by the Victor Company, Camden, New Jersey, 12 January 1916. Matrix: C-17003-1; unissued

SCOTT-GATTY, Alfred

Goodnight

With chorus (Gwladys Roberts, Ernest Pike, Peter Dawson) and Landon Ronald (piano), recorded by the Gramophone & Typewriter Company, City Road, London, 4 September 1905. Matrix: 7204b; original issue: 3618

SPEECH

Melba's farewell speech, recorded live at Covent Garden, 8 June 1926. Matrix: CR421; original issue: DB943

SZULC, Josef

Clair de lune

With Harold Craxton (piano), recorded by the Gramophone Company, Small Queen's Hall, London, 17 December 1926. Matrix: Cc9552; original issue: DB989

THOMAS, Ambroise

Hamlet: Mad Scene

(1) With orchestra conducted by Landon Ronald, recorded in two parts by the Gramophone & Typewriter Company, Great Cumberland Place, London, March 1904. Matrices: Melba 20 & 21; original issue: 03023 & 03024

(2) With orchestra conducted by Walter B. Rogers, recorded by the Victor Company, New York, 29 March 1907. Matrices: C-4354-1 & C-4355-1; original issue: 88069 & 88070

(3) Two phrases only, sung as a distance test, with Landon Ronald (piano), recorded by the Gramophone Company, City Road, London, 11 May 1910. Matrix: 4195f; unissued

(4) With orchestra conducted by Walter B. Rogers, recorded by the Victor Company, Camden, New Jersey, 25 August 1910. Matrix: C-9371-1; original issue: 88251

TOSTI, Paolo

Goodbye

(1) One stanza only. With Landon Ronald (piano), recorded by the Gramophone & Typewriter Company, Great Cumberland Place, London, March 1904. Matrix: Melba 16; original issue: 03022

(2) Two stanzas. With Landon Ronald (piano), recorded by the Gramophone & Typewriter Company, City Road, London, 5 September 1905. Matrix: 524c; original issue: 03050

(3) With orchestra conducted by Walter B. Rogers, recorded by the Victor Company, New York, 27 March 1907. Matrix: C-4340-1; original issue: 88065

(4) With orchestra conducted by Walter B. Rogers, recorded by the Victor Company, Camden, New Jersey, 22 August 1910. Matrix: C-4340-2; unissued

(5) With orchestra conducted by Walter B. Rogers, recorded by the Victor Company, Camden, New Jersey, 26 August 1910. Matrix: C-4340-3; original issue: 88065 (replacing the 1907 Victor recording)

La Serenata

(1) With Landon Ronald (piano), recorded by the Gramophone & Typewriter Company, City Road, London, 20 October 1904. Matrix: 402c; original issue: 03034

(2) With Ada Sassoli (harp), recorded by the Victor Company, New York, 27 March 1907. Matrix: C-4342-1; unissued

(3) With Ada Sassoli (harp), recorded by the Victor Company, New York, 27 March 1907. Matrix: C-4342-2; original issue: 88079

Mattinata

(1) With Landon Ronald (piano), recorded by the Gramophone & Typewriter Company, Great Cumberland Place, London, March 1904. Matrix: Melba 1; original issue: 03015

(2) Accompanying herself at the piano, recorded by the Victor Company, New York, 30 March 1907. Matrix: C-4360-1; original issue: 88077

TRADITIONAL

Auld lang syne

With chorus (Gwladys Roberts, Ernest Pike, Peter Dawson) and the Band of H.M. Coldstream Guards conducted by Lt. Mackenzie Rogan, recorded by the Gramophone & Typewriter Company, City Road, London, 4 September 1905. Matrix: 7201½b; original issue: 3615

Believe me, if all those endearing young charms
(1) Accompanying herself at the piano, recorded by the Victor Company, New York, 1 January 1909. Matrix: C-6701-1; original issue 88156
(2) Accompanying herself at the piano, recorded by the Victor Company, New York, 1 January 1909. Matrix: C-6701-2; unissued

Comin' thro' the rye
(1) With Landon Ronald (piano), recorded by the Gramophone & Typewriter Company, Great Cumberland Place, London, March 1904. Matrix: Melba 7; unissued
(2) With Gabriel Lapierre (piano), recorded by the Victor Company, Camden, New Jersey, 4 October 1913. Matrix: C-13907-1; original issue: 88449

God save the King (first verse only)
With the Band of H.M. Coldstream Guards conducted by Lt. Mackenzie Rogan, recorded by the Gramophone & Typewriter Company, City Road, London, 4 September 1905. Matrix: 7200b; original issue: 3625

Swing low, sweet chariot (arr. Burleigh)
With Harold Craxton (piano), recorded by the Gramophone Company, Small Queen's Hall, London, 17 December 1926. Matrix: Cc9553; original issue: DB989

Ye banks and braes o' Bonnie Doon
(1) Accompanying herself at the piano, recorded by the Victor Company, New York, 6 January 1909. Matrix: C-6707-1; original issue: 88150
(2) Accompanying herself at the piano, recorded by the Victor Company, New York, 6 January 1909. Matrix: C-6707-2; unissued

VERDI, Giuseppe

La Traviata: Ah! fors' è lui
(1) With Landon Ronald (piano), recorded by the Gramophone & Typewriter Company, Great Cumberland Place, London, March 1904. Matrix: Melba 6; original issue: 03017
(2) With orchestra conducted by Walter B. Rogers, recorded by the Victor Company, New York, 27 March 1907. Matrix: C-4339-1 (continues with 'Sempre libera'); original issue: 88064
(3) With orchestra conducted by Walter B. Rogers, recorded by the Victor Company, Camden, New Jersey, 22 August 1910. Matrix: C-4339-2 (continues with 'Sempre libera'); unissued

(4) With orchestra conducted by Walter B. Rogers, recorded by the Victor Company, Camden, New Jersey, 23 August 1910. Matrix: C-4339-3 (continues with 'Sempre libera'); original issue: 88064 (replacing the 1907 Victor recording)

La Traviata: Sempre libera

(1) With orchestra conducted by Landon Ronald, recorded by the Gramophone & Typewriter Company, Great Cumberland Place, London, March 1904. Matrix: Melba 23; original issue: 03026

(2) With orchestra conducted by Walter B. Rogers, recorded by the Victor Company, New York, 27 March 1907. Matrix: C-4339-1 (preceded by 'Ah! fors' è lui'); original issue: 88064

(3) With orchestra conducted by Walter B. Rogers, recorded by the Victor Company, Camden, New Jersey, 23 August 1910. Matrix: C-4339-2 (preceded by 'Ah! fors' è lui'); unissued

(4) With orchestra conducted by Walter B. Rogers, recorded by the Victor Company, Camden, New Jersey, 23 August 1910. Matrix: C-4339-3 (preceded by 'Ah! fors' è lui'); original issue: 88064 (replacing the 1907 Victor recording)

La Traviata: Un di felice

(1) With Andreas Dippel and the orchestra of the Metropolitan Opera, conducted by Philippe Flon. Recorded by Lionel Mapleson at a public performance in the Metropolitan Opera House, New York, 16 March 1901. In the collection of the New York Public Library

(2) With John McCormack and the New Symphony Orchestra conducted by Landon Ronald, recorded by the Gramophone Company, City Road, London, 11 May 1910. Matrix: 4187f; unissued and destroyed

La Traviata: Dite alla giovine

With John Brownlee and Harold Craxton (piano), recorded by the Gramophone Company, Small Queen's Hall, London, 17 December 1926. Matrix: Cc9550; original issue: DB987

Otello: Piangea cantando (Willow Song)

(1) With orchestra conducted by Walter B. Rogers, recorded by the Victor Company, New York, 6 January 1909. Matrix: C-6704-1; original issue: 88148

(2) With orchestra conducted by Walter B. Rogers, recorded by the Victor Company, Camden, New Jersey, 25 August 1910. Matrix: C-6704-2; original issue: 88148 (replacing the 1909 Victor recording)

(3) With Jane Bourguignan and the orchestra of the Royal Opera House, Covent Garden, conducted by Vincenzo Bellezza. Recorded live at Covent Garden, 8 June 1926. Matrices: CR417 (Part 1) & CR418 (Part 2). Part 1 original issue: DB1500; part 2 unissued

Otello: Ave Maria piena di grazia (Prayer)
(1) With orchestra conducted by Walter B. Rogers, recorded by the Victor Company, New York, 6 January 1909. Matrix: C-6705-1; original issue: 88149
(2) With orchestra conducted by Walter B. Rogers, recorded by the Victor Company, Camden, New Jersey, 25 August 1910. Matrix: C-6705-2; original issue: 88149 (replacing the 1909 Victor recording)
(3) With the orchestra of the Royal Opera House, Covent Garden, conducted by Vincenzo Bellezza. Recorded live at Covent Garden, 8 June 1926. Matrix: CR419; unissued

Rigoletto: Caro nome
(1) With orchestra conducted by Landon Ronald, recorded by the Gramophone & Typewriter Company, Great Cumberland Place, London, March 1904. Matrix: Melba 22; original issue: 03025
(2) With orchestra conducted by Walter B. Rogers, recorded by the Victor Company, New York, 5 March 1907. Matrix: C-4283-1; unissued
(3) With orchestra conducted by Walter B. Rogers, recorded by the Victor Company, New York, 5 March 1907. Matrix: C-4283-2; original issue 88078

Rigoletto: Tutte le feste al tempio
With Giuseppe Campanari and orchestra, conducted by Walter B. Rogers, recorded by the Victor Company, New York, 1 April 1907. Matrix: C-4361-1; unissued

Rigoletto: Bella figlia dell'amore (Quartet)
With Edna Thornton, John McCormack, Mario Sammarco and the New Symphony Orchestra conducted by Landon Ronald, recorded by the Gramophone Company, City Road, London, 11 May 1910. Matrix: 4189f; original issue: 2-054025

WAGNER, Richard

Lohengrin: Elsa's dream (sung in Italian)
With the New Symphony Orchestra conducted by Landon Ronald, recorded by the Gramophone Company, City Road, London, 11 May 1910. Matrix: 4185f; original issue: 2-053019

WETZGER, Paul

By the brook – Idyll for flute and piano (Instrumental piece)

(1) John Lemmoné (flute) and Nellie Melba (piano), recorded by the Victor Company, Camden, New Jersey, 26 August 1910. Matrix: C-9375-1; unissued

(2) John Lemmoné (flute) and Nellie Melba (piano), recorded by the Victor Company, Camden, New Jersey, 26 August 1910. Matrix: C-9375-2; unissued

(3) John Lemmoné (flute) and Nellie Melba (piano), recorded by the Victor Company, Camden, New Jersey, 7 November 1910. Matrix: C-9375-3; original issue: 70023

(4) John Lemmoné (flute) and Nellie Melba (piano), recorded by the Victor Company, Camden, New Jersey, 7 November 1910. Matrix: C-9375-4; unissued

WHITE, Maude Valerie

John Anderson, My Jo

With Gabriel Lapierre (piano), recorded by the Victor Company, Camden, New Jersey, 3 October 1913. Matrix: C-13905-1; original issue: 88455

Bibliography

Albani, Emma 1911 (1977), *Forty Years of Song*, Arno Reprint, New York
Alda, Frances 1937, *Men, Women and Tenors*, Houghton Mifflin, Boston
Beecham, Thomas 1944, *A Mingled Chime*, Hutchinson, London
Bird, John 1976, *Percy Grainger*, Macmillan, Melbourne
Blainey, Ann 2009, *I am Melba*, Black Inc., Melbourne
Brisbane, Katharine (ed.) 1991, *Entertaining Australia – An Illustrated History*, Currency Press, Sydney
Brownrigg, Jeff 2006, *A New Melba? The Tragedy of Amy Castles*, Crossing Press, Sydney
Campbell, Joan 1974, 'David Mitchell', in *Australian Dictionary of Biography*, vol. 5, Melbourne University Press, Melbourne
Cane, Anthony (ed.) 1982, *Melba – The American Recordings 1907–1916* (Booklet accompanying the reissue of Melba's American recordings on LP, RCA VRL5 0365)
Cargher, John 1980, *Melba: Melodies and Memories–An edited and annotated edition*, Thomas Nelson, Melbourne
Cargher, John 1977, *Opera and Ballet in Australia*, Cassell, Sydney
Casey, Maie 1975, *Melba Revisited*, published privately, Melbourne
Christiansen, Rupert 1995, *Prima Donna – A History*, Pimlico, London
Colson, Percy 1932, *Melba – An Unconventional Biography*, Grayson & Grayson, London
Cone, John F. 1966, *Oscar Hammerstein's Manhattan Opera Company*, University of Oklahoma Press, Norman, OK
Connan, Bryan 2000, *Beverley Nichols – A Life*, Timber Press, Portland, OR
Dal Monte, Toti 1962, *Una voce nel mondo*, Longanesi, Milan
Davis, Richard 2012, *Wotan's Daughter – The Life of Marjorie Lawrence*, Wakefield Press, Adelaide

Dawson, Peter 1951, *Fifty Years of Song*, Hutchinson, London

Dizikes, John 1993, *Opera in America – A Cultural History*, Yale University, New Haven, CT

Douglas, Nigel 1992, *Legendary Voices*, Andre Deutsch, London

Douglas, Nigel 1994, *More Legendary Voices*, Andre Deutsch, London

Drake, James A. 1997, *Rosa* [Ponselle] *– A Centenary Biography*, Amadeus Press, Portland, OR

Eames, Emma 1927, *Some Memories and Reflections,* Appleton, New York

Eaton, Quaintance 1965, *The Boston Opera* Company, Appleton-Century, New York

Evans, Lindley 1983, *Hello, Mr Melody Man*, Angus & Robertson, Sydney

Fairweather, Don 1984, *Your friend Alberto Zelman*, Zelman Memorial Symphony Orchestra, Melbourne

Farrar, Geraldine 1938, *Such Sweet Compulsion*, Greystone Press, New York

Foster, Roland 1947, *Come Listen to my Song*, Collins, Sydney

Foxall, Raymond 1963, *John McCormack*, Robert Hale, London

Gaisberg, F.W. 1946, *Music on Record*, Robert Hale, London

Game, Peter 1976, *The Music Sellers*, Hawthorn Press, Melbourne

Ganz, Wilhelm 1913, *Memories of a Musician: Reminiscences of seventy years of musical life*, John Murray, London

Garden, Mary & Biancolli, Louis 1951, *Mary Garden's Story*, Simon & Schuster, New York

Gattey, Charles Neilson 1979, *Queens of Song*, Barrie & Jenkins, London

Gatti-Casazza, Giulio 1941, *Memories of the Opera*, John Calder, London

Gilbert, Susie 2009, *Opera for Everybody – The Story of English National Opera*, Faber, London

Glennon, James 1968, *Australian Music and Musicians*, Rigby, Adelaide

Goossens, Eugene 1951, *Overture and Beginners*, Methuen, London

Guilbert, Yvette 1929, *The Song of My Life*, Harrap, London

Gyger, Alison 2005, *Australia's Operatic Phoenix*, Pellinor, Sydney

Gyger, Alison 1999, *Civilising the Colonies*, Pellinor, Sydney

Gyger, Alison 1990, *Opera for the Antipodes*, Currency Press & Pellinor, Sydney

Hadden, J. Cuthbert 1913, *Modern Musicians*, Foulis, Edinburgh

Hamilton, David (ed.) 1987, *The Metropolitan Opera Encyclopedia*, Simon & Schuster, New York

Hetherington, John 1967, *Melba, a Biography*, Faber & Faber, London

Hibbert, Jack 1976, *A Toast to Melba: A play*, Outback Press, Melbourne

Holmes, Paul (ed.) 1976, *Nellie Melba – The London Recordings 1904–1926* (Booklet accompanying the reissue of Melba's London recordings on LP, EMI RLS719)

Isnardon, Jacques 1890, *La Théâtre de la Monnaie*, Schott Frères, Brussels

Jackson, Stanley 1972, *Caruso*, W.H. Allen, London

Klein, Herman 1903, *Thirty Years of Musical Life in London 1870–1900*, William Heinemann, London

Ledbetter, Gordon T. 1977, *The Great Irish Tenor – John McCormack*, Duckworth, London

Love, Harold 1981, *The Golden Age of Australian Opera*, Currency Press, Sydney

Mackenzie, Barbara & Mackenzie, Findlay 1967, *Singers of Australia: From Melba to Sutherland*, Lansdowne Press, Melbourne

Marchesi, Blanche nd, *Marchesi's Vocal Method*, Enoch, London

Marchesi, Blanche 1923, *Singer's Pilgrimage*, Da Capo Reprint, New York, 1978

Marchesi, Mathilde 1898, *Marchesi and Music – Passages from the Life of a Famous Singing Teacher*, Harper & Brothers, New York

Melba, Nellie nd, *Melba's Gift Book*, George Robertson, Melbourne

Melba, Nellie 1925, *Melodies and Memories*, Butterworth, London

Melba, Nellie 1926, *The Melba Method*, Chappell, London

Mintzer, Charles 2001, *Rosa Raisa*, Northeastern University Press, Boston, MA

Moore, Gerald 1962, *Am I Too Loud?* Hamish Hamilton, London

Moran, William R. (ed.) 1985, *Melba – A Contemporary Review*, Greenwood, Westport, CT

Murphy, Agnes G. 1909, *Melba – A biography*, Doubleday, Page & Co, New York

Neill, Roger 2016, *Divas – Mathilde Marchesi and her Pupils*, University of NSW, Sydney

Nellie Melba Museum, Lilydale, Vic., https://nelliemelbamuseum.com.au/

Newton, Ivor 1966, *At the Piano*, Hamish Hamilton, London

Nichols, Beverley 1949, *All I Could Never Be*, Jonathan Cape, London
Nichols, Beverley 1932, *Evensong*, Jonathan Cape, London
Nichols, Beverley 1972, *Father Figure – An uncensored autobiography*, Heinemann, London
Nichols, Beverley 1958, *The Sweet and Twenties*, Weidenfeld & Nicolson, London
O'Connor, Garry 1979, *The Pursuit of Perfection – A Life of Maggie Teyte*, Victor Gollancz, London
Phillips-Matz, Mary Jane 1996, *Verdi: A biography*, Oxford University Press, Oxford
Pleasants, Henry 1967, *The Great Singers*, Victor Gollancz, London
'A provisional Mapleson cylinder chronology' 1981, *ARSC Journal*, vol. 13, no. 3
Pullar, Philippa 1978, *Gilded Butterflies – The Rise and Fall of the London Season*, Hamish Hamilton, London
Radic, Thérèse 1986, *Melba – The Voice of Australia*, Macmillan, Melbourne
Rasponi, Lanfranco 1990, *The Last Prima Donnas*, Limelight, New York
Reid, M.O. nd, *The Ladies Came to Stay*, published privately, Melbourne
Riemans, Leo & Kutsch, K.J. 1962, *A Concise Biographical Dictionary of Singers*, Chiltern, New York
Ronald, Landon 1922, *Variations on a Personal Theme*, Hodder & Stoughton, London
Rosenthal, Harold 1967, *Opera at Covent Garden – A Short History*, Gollancz, London
Rosenthal, Harold 1958, *Two Centuries of Opera at Covent Garden*, Putnam, London
Rushmore, Robert 1971, *The Singing Voice*, Hamish Hamilton, London
Scott, Michael 1977, *The Record of Singing*, Duckworth, London
Sheean, Vincent 1956, *The Amazing Oscar Hammerstein*, Weidenfeld & Nicolson, London
Smith, Russell & Burgis, Peter 2001, *Peter Dawson*, Currency Press, Sydney
Steane, John 1974, *The Grand Tradition*, Duckworth, London
Tetrazzini, Luisa 1921, *My Life of* Song, Cassell, London
Todd, R.H. 1938, *Looking Back – Some Early Recollections*, Snelling, Sydney
Van Straten, Frank 1994, *National Treasure – The Story of Gertrude Johnson and the National Theatre*, Victoria Press, Melbourne

Vestey, Pamela 1996, *A Family Memoir*, Phoebe, Melbourne

Vickery, Marian (ed.) 1982, *They call me Melba*, Victorian Arts Centre, Melbourne

Walsh, Thomas J. 1975, *Monte Carlo Opera 1879–1909*, Gill & Macmillan, Dublin

Wander, Tim 2020, *From Marconi to Melba*, Marconi, London

Warrender, Maud 1933, *My First Sixty Years*, Cassell, London

Waters, Thorold 1951, *Much Besides Music*, Georgian House, Melbourne

Wechsberg, Joseph 1962, *Red Plush and Black Velvet*, Weidenfeld & Nicolson, London

Westlake, Donald 1997, *Dearest John – The story of John Lemmoné, flute virtuoso, and Nellie Melba*, Bowerbird Press, Sydney

Wood, Henry J. 1938, *My Life of Music*, Victor Gollancz, London

Index

A

Abbey, Henry 136, 149, 152, 158, 159, 160, 163, 168, 174, 176, 179
Abbott, Emma 362
Adams, Suzanne 198, 216, 362
Ainsley, Irene 242–243, 384
Albani, Emma 59, 61, 62, 89, 99, 120, 138, 149, 163, 164, 173, 174, 216, 325, 326, 372
Albert I, King of Belgium 391
Albert I, Prince of Monaco 220–221
Albert Street Conservatorium, Melbourne 286, 291, 306, 311, 325, 335, 337, 349, 391
Alboni, Marietta 138–139
Alda, Frances 271, 362, 383
Aldrich, Richard 219, 260
Alexander III, Tsar of Russia 117, 118, 371
Alexandra, Queen 98, 99, 113, 118, 121, 178, 202, 223, 227, 233, 241, 242, 258, 285, 305, 319
Alexei, Grand Duke of Russia 117, 118
Alfonso XIII, King of Spain 232, 239, 382
Allan, George 263, 308
Alvarez, Albert 164, 165, 187, 219, 220
Amadio, John 314
Ancona, Mario 144, 145, 151, 152, 180, 188, 373, 376
Andrade, Francesco d' 91
Angelini, Giuseppe 275
Anselmi, Giuseppe 202
Ansseau, Fernand 301, 306
Arangi-Lombardi, Giannina 338
Arditi, Luigi 229, 411

Arens, Louis 209, 214, 221, 380, 381
Argentina, Teatro (Rome) 131–132, 398
Armstrong, Sir Andrew (father-in-law) 27–28
Armstrong, Sir Andrew (nephew by marriage) 244
Armstrong, Charles Nesbitt Frederick ('Charlie') (husband) 27–34, 36–39, 43–45, 51, 56, 57–59, 64, 65, 69, 75, 78–79, 81, 85, 98, 101–103, 105, 114–115, 122–126, 153, 195–196, 197, 231, 243, 244, 289, 336, 350, 357, 358, 360, 362, 363, 368, 369, 370, 371, 379, 386, 389, 397, 398, 399
Armstrong, Sir Edmund (brother-in-law) 65, 244
Armstrong, Evie (daughter-in-law) 278, 283, 289, 290, 291, 292, 295, 296, 298, 302, 303, 304, 305, 306, 307, 318, 327, 331, 334, 336, 344, 346, 347, 350
Armstrong, Lady Frances (mother-in-law) 58–59, 78, 98, 102, 112
Armstrong, George (son) 37–39, 44, 50, 55, 56, 57–58, 65, 69, 73, 78–79, 85, 94–95, 98, 101–102, 103, 105, 112, 123–124, 126, 153, 196, 197, 219, 230–232, 243–244, 245, 253, 254, 257, 263, 266, 267, 273, 278, 283, 289, 290, 291, 295, 298, 302, 303, 304, 305, 306, 307, 327, 331, 334, 336, 344, 346, 347, 349, 350, 363, 371, 379, 386, 389, 397
Armstrong, J. P (cousin by marriage) 244
Armstrong, Montague (brother-in-law) 122, 124
Armstrong, Pamela (Lady Vestey) (granddaughter) 2, 296, 298, 299, 302,

303, 304, 307, 327, 331, 334, 336, 337, 344, 349, 350, 370, 371, 372, 382, 388, 390
Armstrong, Phoebe Georgina Frances ('Ruby') (daughter-in-law) 243–244, 245, 253, 254, 257, 386
Arnoldson, Sigrid 365
Arral, Blanche 362
Arrau, Claudio 304
Aubigne, Lloyd d' (Thomas Lloyd Dabney) 167
Augusta Victoria, Empress of Germany 121
Austral, Florence 314, 393
Axarine, Marie 274

B

Backhaus, Wilhelm 277
Balfe, Michael
 The Bohemian Girl 36, 359
Ballarat Liedertafel 45
Barbier, Jules 87
Barrie, J.M. 353
Barrientos, Maria 216
Bassi, Amadeo 246
Battistini, Mattia 235, 240, 383
Bauermeister, Mathilde 167, 178, 233, 234
Bavagnoli, Gaetano 338
Baylis, Lilian 331–332
Bayreuth Wagner Festival 175, 345, 370
Beaumont, Armes 40, 43, 211
Beecham, Thomas 299–300, 303–304, 313, 371
Beeth, Lola 173
Beethoven, Ludwig van
 Fidelio 343
Bell, John Alexander 357
Bellezza, Vincenzo 328, 422, 423, 424, 430
Bellincioni, Gemma 163, 164, 194
Bellini, Vincenzo 21, 86
 Beatrice di Tenda 359
 I Puritani 244, 359
 La Sonnambula 321, 406
 Norma 342

Bemberg, Herman 134, 158, 217, 229, 250, 305, 332, 343, 344, 372–373, 407, 411, 412
 Elaine 134–135, 139, 158, 372, 373, 383, 398, 404, 411
Benardaky, Maria Pavlovna 98
Benedict, Julius 43
Bennett, Louise 130, 141, 142, 148, 153, 168, 376
Bennett, Marnie 182, 376
Bensaude, Maurice 209, 214, 380
Berlin Philharmonic Orchestra 46, 165
Berlioz, Hector
 Le Damnation de Faust 205–206, 303, 405
Bernhardt, Sarah 61, 98, 103–105, 107, 133, 316–317, 398
Bertrand, Eugène 129, 144
Bettini, Gianni 379–380
Birch, Susan 343, 345
Bishop, Henry 39, 59, 271, 412–413
Bispham, David 175
Bizet, Georges 113, 134, 413
 Carmen 112, 113, 120, 133, 149, 158, 163, 165, 168, 248, 267, 362, 404
 Les Pêcheurs de Perles 406
Black, Andrew 254, 297
Blangini, Giuseppe 250, 413
Boer War 191, 192–193, 207, 212, 380, 389
Boito, Arrigo 141
 Mefistofele 145
Bonci, Alessandro 217, 232, 237, 244, 247, 274, 321, 379, 386
Bonnard, Charles 164, 376
Bonynge, Richard 370
Booth, Christopher H.H. 412
Borgioli, Dino 321–322, 393
Borland, Rt. Rev. Dr. William 349
Bosisto, Joseph 50
Boston Opera Company 272, 281, 284, 316, 389, 400
Boston Symphony Orchestra 152, 166, 174, 272, 288
Bourguignan, Jane 430
Bourguignon, Frances de 287–288, 295, 297

Bourne, Una 43, 254, 263, 265, 306, 307, 308
Boyle, Frank 47
Box, Harry (brother-in-law) 254, 368
Bradman, Sir Donald 395
Braga, Gaetano 130, 193
Bréval, Lucien 201
Bridges, Lady Janet 343, 345
Brinsmead, John 56, 60
British National Opera (Company) 313–314, 317–318, 328, 390, 400
Bronhill, June 393
Brookes, Dame Mabel 213
Brownlee, Donna 345
Brownlee, Isabelle 345
Brownlee, John 328, 330, 332, 338, 340, 341, 348, 394, 412, 422, 423, 429
Bruce, Stanley 323
Brussels Conservatorium of Music 78, 86, 93, 408
Buckman, Rosina 275, 281, 392
Buddee, Julius 15, 41, 45, 61
Buesst, Aylmer 393
'Buffalo Bill', 79
Bunny, Rupert 204
Burke, Edmund 275, 277, 279, 288, 289
Burke, Tom 301, 302
Burrian, Karl 378
Busoni, Ferruccio 302
Butt, Clara 156, 178, 208, 254, 284, 302, 309, 339, 395

C
Caballé, Montserrat 366, 385
Callas, Maria 1, 366, 385, 389
Calvé, Emma 133–134, 135, 136, 145, 149, 151, 155, 158, 162, 163, 164–165, 168, 232, 238, 248, 362, 372, 386
Campanari, Giuseppe 167, 182, 385, 430
Campanini, Cleofonte 237, 240, 247, 248, 255, 288, 292, 293, 384–385, 386
Campbell, Mary 325
Carey, Clive 395
Carlo Felice, Teatro (Genoa) 143
Caron, Rose 80, 81, 171, 205, 367

Carpi, Fernando 241
Carreño, Teresa 193
Caruso, Enrico 101, 204–205, 206, 208, 217, 219, 221, 222, 224, 230, 232, 235, 237, 240, 246, 250, 258, 259, 271, 279, 281, 308, 380, 383, 385, 399, 422
Casadesus, Robert 326
Casey, Lady Maie 126–127, 372
Castellane, Boni de 312, 343
Castles, Amy 242, 362
Cavalieri, Lina 219–220, 257, 260, 381, 383
Cecchi, Pietro 20–23, 24–26, 31, 32, 33, 36, 38, 39, 40, 41, 47–48, 49, 53–55, 63, 64, 71, 73, 356, 357, 358, 362, 389, 397
Cellier, Alfred 56, 60
Center, Peggy 291
Chaliapin, Feodor 224
Chalot, Anna 95
Chambers, Haddon 128, 184, 196–197, 204
Chambers, Lucy 362
Champs-Elysées, Théâtre de 279, 281, 282
Chaplin, Charlie 288
Charbonnet-Kellermann, Alice 19, 20, 355, 390, 397
Charpentier, Gustave 413
  Louise 280, 413
Chausson, Ernest 326, 343, 407, 413
Chicago Grand Opera Company 272
Chicago Opera Association 288, 292, 400
Christian, Mary Ellen 19–20, 21, 40, 54, 73, 265, 355, 397
Christopher, Prince of Greece 344
Churchill, Lady Randolph 257
Churchill, Winston 257, 314
Ciccolini, Guido 275
Cisneros, Eleanor de 274
'Claribel' (Charlotte Barnard) 234, 414
Clay, Frédéric
  Lalla Rookh 408
Cochrane, Tommy 291, 315, 343

Coldstream Guards, Band of the
233–234, 414, 427, 428
Coles, Henry 300
Collier, Frederick 284, 313, 328, 332, 393, 423, 424
Colsen, Percy 207–208, 350, 370
Comédie Française, Paris 95
Connaught, Duke of 289
Conried, Heinrich 230, 236–237, 382, 383, 384
Constantino, Florenzio 272
Coombe Cottage, Coldstream, Victoria 266, 267, 273–274, 278, 279, 283, 284, 285, 287, 290, 291, 292, 308–309, 310, 318, 320, 322, 323, 334, 335, 337, 343, 344, 346, 350, 388, 395
Coppin, George 45
Corrigan, Archbishop Michael 168
Cossira, Emile 103
Cotogni, Antonio 90
Cotreuil, Edouard 423, 424
Covent Garden, Royal Opera House 11, 36, 63, 83, 88, 89–92, 94, 98–101, 107–109, 110, 111, 113, 116, 119, 120–121, 122, 127, 129, 133–135, 136–138, 140, 143, 144–146, 155, 156, 157, 160, 163, 167, 170, 172, 173, 174, 177, 179, 181, 183, 184–185, 188–189, 195, 197–198, 202–203, 208–209, 216–219, 221–222, 232–233, 234, 238, 240–241, 252, 253, 255, 256, 257–259, 262, 269, 270–271, 273, 274, 275, 276, 277, 279, 281, 284, 299–301, 303–304, 314–315, 318, 322, 325, 326, 327–330, 332, 341, 342, 356, 367, 368, 369–370, 372, 375, 376, 377, 380, 382, 386, 388, 389, 392, 394, 398, 399, 400, 401, 404, 422, 423, 424, 426, 430
Crawford, Francis Marion 128, 153
Crawford, Hector 310
Craxton, Harold 330, 332, 412, 426, 428, 429
Crossley, Ada 156, 185, 242, 362, 364, 375, 393
Crystal Palace 155

D
Dalmores, Charles 222, 232, 233, 237, 244, 248, 249, 384
Dammacco, Vito 275
Damrosch, Walter 179–180, 183, 378
Damrosch & Ellis Opera Companies 179–184, 186–187, 399
Danieli, Elena 327, 340, 341
Darvall, Orme 370
Davidson, Amy 29, 35
Davidson, John Ewen 35, 358
Davies, Ben 178, 325, 341, 395
Davies, Tudor 318
Davies, Llewella 209, 213, 219
Dawson, Peter 234, 236, 393, 416, 426, 427
Debussy, Claude 66, 261, 280, 310, 407, 414
  Pelléas et Mélisande 261
Delany, John Albert 36
Delibes, Léo 66, 76, 86, 97, 98, 105, 120, 129, 191, 366
  Lakmé 77, 86, 87, 97, 98, 105, 120, 123, 366, 367, 404
Dennis, C.J. 285, 348
Dereims, Étienne 106
Deschamps-Jehin, Blanche 80, 106, 170, 219
Destinn, Emmy 232, 257, 258, 270, 271, 385
Devries, Maurice 187
Dippel, Andreas 272, 429
Dixon, Sydney 224
Donalda, Pauline 252, 270
Donaldson, May 209
Donizetti, Gaetano 21, 86, 178–179, 377, 399, 402, 414–415
  Don Pasquale 321
  La Favorite 179
  Lucia di Lammermoor 11, 43, 62, 70, 76, 77, 85–86, 87, 89–91, 103, 107, 112, 120, 123, 131–132, 141, 142–143, 147, 148, 149, 151, 157–158, 163, 179, 180, 183, 191, 192, 193, 198, 200, 201, 203, 213, 214, 216–217, 218, 226,

227–228, 233, 246, 248, 250, 256,
257, 261, 267, 279, 293, 321, 359, 365,
366–367, 368, 375, 377, 378, 386, 398,
404, 414–415
   Lucrezia Borgia 359
Doubleday, Leila 297
Doucet, Jacques 166
Dow, Alice (maternal aunt) 9, 12
Dow, Elizabeth ('Lizzie') (maternal aunt) 9, 12
Dow, Isabella Ann, see Mitchell, Isabella
Dow, James Foot (maternal grandfather) 9, 11
Dow, Jean (maternal grandmother) 9, 11, 13
Doyle, Dr. Bill 290, 346
Dreyfus, Alfred 190–191
Drury Lane Theatre (Theatre Royal) 145, 197
Dufriche, Eugéne 149, 151
Duparc, Henri 326, 343, 407, 415
Dupont, Joseph 76, 77, 80, 81, 82, 83–84, 86, 87, 96, 366, 367
Duvernoy, Alphonse
   Hellé 171
Dvořák, Anton 289, 415–416
Dyck, Ernest van 135–136, 370
Dyson, Will 285

E

Eames, Emma 71–72, 103, 120, 121, 124, 133, 138, 149, 155, 157, 163, 173, 177, 178, 186, 200, 202, 246, 248, 362, 364, 365, 368, 369, 383
Edison, Thomas 224
Edward VII, King 49, 59, 99, 101, 109, 113, 133, 178, 202, 208, 212, 223, 232, 233, 235, 241, 252, 258, 268–269, 305, 386
Edward VIII, King 312, 314
Edvina, Louise 257, 270
Elgar, Edward 208, 325
   Coronation Ode 208, 408
Elizabeth, Empress of Austria 126, 194
Elizabeth, Queen ('Queen Mother') 335, 341, 344

Elizabeth II 341
Elkin, Mons. 76, 366
Ellice, Pauline 62
Ellis, Charles 166–167, 175, 180, 181, 183, 185, 251, 287, 292, 295, 298, 378
Elmblad, Maggie (Menzies-Elmblad) 38, 43, 358
Elsasser, Carl Gottlieb 40
Engel, François Pierre-Émile 80, 84, 103, 367
Erard, Sallé 76
Erlanger, Frédéric d'
   Inèz Mendo 377
Escoffier, Auguste 156–157, 375, 398
Escott, Lucy 11, 21
Evans, Lindley 310–311, 314, 335

F

Faccio, Franco 141
Fachiri, Adila 343
Fairbanks, Douglas 295
Farrar, Geraldine 219–220, 271, 381–382, 383
Fauré, Gabriel 220–221
Faure, Jean-Baptiste 98
Feez, Arthur 30, 33
Ferguson, Sir Ronald 391
Ferrari-Fontana, Edoardo 281
Ferrier, Paul 134
Fisher, Sarah Jane 47, 360
Fittipaldi, Eduardo 45
FitzClarence, Susan 292, 295, 307, 391
Flon, Philippe 421, 429
Flotow, Friedrich von
   Martha 358, 406
Forsyth, Neil 234
Foster, Stephen 39, 183, 354, 416
Fournier, Émile 129
   Stratonice 129, 402
Fox, E. Phillips 285
Franceschini, Furio 241
Franck, César 65
Francis, Prince of Teck 244
Fransella, Albert 412

Franz, Paul 388
Franz Joseph, Emperor of Austria 194, 399
Fricci, Antonietta 362

G
Gadski, Johanna 186
Gailhard, Pedro 75-76, 77, 80, 87-88, 94, 96, 97, 103, 116, 170, 364-365, 377
Gaisberg, Fred 224-227, 229, 269-270
Galli-Curci, Amelita 293-294
Galli-Marie, Celestine 113, 362
Ganz, Wilhelm 56, 60-61, 62-63, 64, 362
Garcia, Manuel (the younger) 19-20, 63, 66
Gard, Robert 393
Garden, Mary 72, 162-163, 216, 235, 236, 250, 260, 261, 293, 294, 362, 386, 393
Gatti-Casazza, Giulio 271
Gaubert, Phillipe 225, 226, 344, 382, 388, 415, 418
George Robinson & Co 285
George V 146, 208, 210, 212, 233, 243, 258, 273, 279, 281, 289, 296, 297, 299, 300, 307, 313, 325, 327, 329, 348-349, 395
George Vl 335, 341
Gevaert, Félix (François) 78, 81, 86, 93, 365
Gewandhaus Orchestra, Dresden 195
Gilibert, Charles 219, 222, 250, 412, 413
Gilly, Dinh 306
Giordano, Umberto
  Andrea Chénier 321
Giorgi, Carlo di 129, 131
Giorza, Paolo 357
Giraldoni, Eugenio 383
Gluck, Alma 335-336, 342
Gluck, Christoph Willibald von
  Armide 116
  Orfeo ed Euridice 121
Gobbi, Tito 322
Goddard, Arabella 17
Goodson, Katharine 302
Goossens, Eugene 301, 391

Gounod, Charles 65, 76, 92, 93, 96, 97, 103, 104, 109, 134, 148, 391, 403, 416-418
  Ave Maria 46, 63, 229, 280, 383, 395, 416-417
  Faust 61, 101, 104-105, 110, 118, 135, 136, 147, 148, 149, 152, 159, 163, 164, 165, 168, 180, 186, 191, 198, 201, 205, 208, 214, 232, 233, 244, 246, 250, 257, 269-270, 276, 277, 292, 293, 294, 301, 303, 306, 311, 317, 319, 321, 322, 358, 359, 368, 372, 375, 376, 400, 403, 404, 417-418
  Mireille 97, 359, 406
  Messe Solennelle 46, 408
  Roméo et Juliette 92, 100, 101, 103, 106, 107-108, 113, 118, 120-121, 128-129, 133, 146, 147, 148, 152, 157, 163, 165, 167, 168, 176, 178, 180, 185, 186, 198, 200, 201, 203, 208, 216-217, 218-219, 229, 233, 248, 273, 276, 281, 301, 306, 317, 321, 328, 332, 367, 368, 371, 394, 398, 403, 404, 418
Grainger, John 266
Grainger, Percy 266, 279, 343, 389
Gramophone & Typewriter Co. (Gramophone Co.) 224, 229, 252, 269-270, 280, 307, 332, 383, 385-386, 388, 394, 399, 409-431
Granforte, Apollo 322, 338, 393
Grau, Maurice 119, 136, 146, 149, 152, 158, 159, 160, 163, 168, 174, 176, 178, 179, 180, 183-184, 199, 208, 230, 378
Gray, Ruby 291, 292
Green, Richard 144
Grey, Earl de 123-124
Grey, Gladys de 83, 88, 92, 98-99, 121, 126, 146, 177, 203, 209, 216, 242, 299, 303, 342, 370, 373
Griffiths, Frederic 209, 380
Gromzeski, Victor di 150
Guenett, Thomas Harbottle 14, 15, 41, 354
Guilbert, Yvette 169
Gunn, Aeneas 285
Gunsbourg, Raoul 195, 205, 220, 303, 306

H

Haakon VII, King of Norway 305, 391
Hackett, Arthur 295, 318, 327, 394
Hackett, Charles 318, 328, 394
Hahn, Reynaldo 229, 261, 331, 418
Hammerstein, Oscar I 236-238, 239, 244-249, 251, 260, 262, 272, 299, 383, 384, 385, 386, 387, 399
Hammerstein, Oscar II 236
Hammond, Joan 393
Handel, George Frideric 155-156, 191, 418-419
   L'Allegro, il Penseroso ed il Moderato 155, 165, 226, 228-229, 418-419
   Ode for Saint Cecilia's Day 93, 368, 408
   Messiah 51, 52, 59, 360-361, 407, 408
   Samson 155
Hardelot, Guy d' 229, 414
Harewood, Earl 392
Harmsworth, Alfred 197
Harper, Robert 211, 381
Harris, Augustus 63, 83, 88, 89, 91, 98, 99, 100, 111, 112, 120, 121, 133, 134, 136, 138, 143, 144, 145, 155, 163, 164, 165, 173, 367, 368, 371, 372, 376
Harrison, Beatrice 287, 288, 390
Hart, Fritz 286, 308, 325, 340
   Deirdre in Exile 338
Hattenbach, Louis 254
Haydn, Joseph
   Nelson Mass 46, 359, 408
Heifetz, Jasha 304, 336, 392
Heldy, Fanny 328
Hempel, Frieda 252
Henderson, William James ('W.J.') 150, 151, 175-176, 181, 200, 219, 246
Henschel, George 419
Hersée, Rose 65, 362
Hertz, Alfred 249
Heugel, Henri 74-75
Heunerbein, Charles 52
Heysen, Hans 285, 309
Higgins, Harry 255, 303

Hilliger, Sylvester Arthur 48, 50, 51, 75, 360, 361, 364, 365
Himmer, Rudolph 57, 59, 61, 361, 381
Hirsch, Maurice de 125, 203
Hislop, Joseph 318
Hofoper, Berlin (Berlin State Opera) 192, 194
Hofoper, Vienna (Vienna State Opera) 36, 116, 193, 194
Hoose, Ellison van 219
Hordern, Mrs Anthony 284
Huberman, Bronislaw 302
Hue, Georges 345, 419
Hutcheson, Ernest 43, 46
Hutin, Marcel 192-193
Hyland, the Misses 69, 391

I

Ibbs & Tillett 327, 330
Indian and Colonial Exhibition 1886 49-50, 59, 397
Irving, Henry 197
Isnardon, Jacques 106, 367
Ives, Joshua 51, 361

J

James, William G. 393
Jehin, Léon 105-106, 219, 220, 369
Jeritza, Maria 328
Joachim, Joseph 46, 93, 162, 178-179, 185, 190, 191, 194-195, 196, 256, 377, 378, 379, 392
Johnson, Edward 319
Johnson, Gertrude 286, 332, 390, 393
Jorgensen, Bertha 392

K

Kellermann, Annette 360, 395
Kennedy, Daisie 393
Kennedy, Laurie 314
Kirkby, Walter 380, 381
Kitchener, General Herbert 207
Klein, Herman 63, 91, 100, 107-108, 138, 145, 173-174, 185, 195, 196
Korolewicz-Wayda, Janina 274, 276, 277

Koven, Reginald de 159, 169-170
Krauss, Gabrielle 362
Krehbiel, Henry 150, 200, 248
Krismer, Giuseppe 240-241
Kroll Theatre, Berlin 94
Kruse, Johann 46-49, 51, 54, 93, 185, 397
Kubelik, Jan 229, 279, 280, 383, 400, 416-417, 421
Kurz, Selma 221, 232, 233, 252, 362

L

Lalo, Édouard 419
   Le Roi d'Ys 343, 419
Lambert, George 285
Lamoureux, Charles 143
Landouzy, Lise 80, 367
Lang, Anna 63
Langtry, Lily 61
Lapierre, Gabriel 279, 280, 388, 411, 413, 414, 415, 417, 419, 421, 428, 431
Lapissida, Alexandre 76-77, 80, 81, 86, 87, 96, 100, 170, 365, 366, 367
Lara, Isidore de 65
Lassalle, Jean 95, 99, 100, 101, 109, 110, 112, 113, 149, 371
Lawrence, Marjorie 366, 382, 388, 393
Lawson, Henry 285
Lee, Canon Howard 347
Lehmann, Liza 419
Lehmann, Lotte 328, 343
Leigh House Ladies College, Richmond 15, 181
Lemmoné, John 40, 42-43, 128, 156, 165, 216, 254, 262, 263, 266, 268, 271, 273, 275, 283, 287, 297-298, 308, 310, 323, 334-335, 345, 347, 349, 375, 391, 392-393, 413, 414, 418-419, 431
Lempriere, Charles (brother-in-law) 254
Leoncavallo, Ruggiero 143, 144, 398
   Pagliacci 143, 144-145, 151, 322, 373, 374, 398, 404
Leopold II, King of Belgium 83, 368
Leroux, Gaston 171
Lieder, Frieda 328
Lieurance, Thurlow 419

Liliuokalani, Queen of Hawaii 288
Lind, Jenny 15, 61
Lindsay, Daryl 323, 334
Lindsay, Joan 334
Lindsay, Norman 285
Litvinne, Félia 80, 87, 176, 270, 366
Lloyd, Edward 61
Loch, Lady 361
Lotti, Antonio 420
Low, Professor Archibald 315-316
Lucia, Fernando de 144-145, 151, 180, 188, 189, 232, 321, 373
Lussan, Zelie de 112, 158, 186, 187, 188
Lyster, William Saurin 11, 21, 65, 354
Lytton, Lady 361
Lytton, Lord 120, 361

M

McBurney, Dr. Robert 37, 44
MacCarthy, Maud 242
McCormack, John 257, 269-270, 272, 275-276, 277, 301, 388, 394, 417, 418, 429, 430
McCrae, Gordon 285
McCubbin, Frederick 285
McEachern, Malcolm 283, 314, 389, 393
McIntosh, Hugh 285
McKay, Claude 388
McKellar, Dorothea 285
Mackennal, Bertram 128, 285, 394
McKenzie, Alexander 25
Mahler, Gustav 133, 193-194
Mancinelli, Luigi 90, 100, 110, 111, 149, 158, 165, 188, 370, 375, 414, 415, 417, 418, 420
Manhattan Opera House 236, 237, 244, 245, 246, 249, 251, 260, 384, 386, 399
Mapleson, 'Colonel' James Henry 120, 201, 362
Mapleson, Lionel 201-202, 379, 394, 399, 414, 415, 417, 420, 421, 429
Marchesi, Blanche 70, 116-117, 362, 387
Marchesi, Mathilde 20, 54, 56, 60, 65, 66-73, 74-78, 81-82, 85, 91, 93, 95, 96, 97, 101, 104, 116-117, 123, 133, 136, 140,

141, 146, 156, 168, 174, 182, 190, 192, 198, 199, 221, 228, 242–243, 256, 268, 278, 287, 317, 361, 362, 363, 363, 365, 366, 377, 378, 381, 384, 385, 387, 389, 391, 397
Marchesi, Salvatore 66, 67, 68, 75, 78, 81, 95, 123, 129–130, 146, 190, 204, 256, 268, 362, 363, 374
Marchi, Emilio de 235
Marconi Company 304–305, 400
Marconi, Francesco 378
Maria Feodorovna, Tsarina of Russia 118, 319
Marie Henriette, Queen of Belgium 83–84, 87, 367
Mariinsky Theatre, St Petersburg 94, 116, 117
Marques, Antonio 322
Marshall Hall, George 167, 263, 275, 286, 387
Martinelli, Giovanni 281, 301
Marty, Georges 170
Mary, Princess (Princess Royal) 307, 392
Mary, Queen 146, 208, 210, 233, 243, 244, 258, 273, 300, 306, 325, 327, 329, 348
Mascagni, Pietro 133, 145–146, 322
    Cavalleria Rusticana 133, 145, 149, 151
    I Rantzau 145, 398, 404
    L'Amico Fritz 133
    Lodoletta 338
    Romana 145–146
Mason, Kenyon 168
Massenet, Jules 66, 76, 109, 134, 162, 166, 201, 252, 269, 387, 420
    Don César de Bazan 180, 420
    Hérodiade 129
    La Navarraise 220
    Le Cid 201, 269, 405, 420
    Manon 166, 169–170, 173, 177, 180, 191, 194, 405
    Thaïs 338
Materna, Amelia 116, 370
Maud, Queen of Norway 305
Maurel, Victor 120, 143, 157, 159, 164, 168, 169, 371
Mayer, Daniel 140, 156, 165

Mayr, Richard 343
Maxwell, George 237, 247
Mearns, Helen 140, 373
Melba Conservatorium, see Albert Street Conservatorium
Melba, Nellie
    accent 77, 79–80, 86, 132, 329, 407
    acting 82, 84–85, 92, 100, 105, 107, 108, 135, 151, 159, 170, 174, 200, 201, 258
    adult debut as a singer 25–30, 397
    affair with the Duc d'Orléans 113–117, 119
    ancestry 5
    autobiography 1, 5, 324–325
    awards and decorations 148, 194, 223, 289, 296, 297, 305, 335, 368, 391, 399, 400, 401
    birth 11, 353–354, 397
    birth of son 37, 397
    character ix, 5, 15–18, 19, 28, 55, 84, 99, 218, 236, 350–351, 355
    Covent Garden debut 89–91
    death 347–348, 401
    divorce 195–196, 215, 398, 399
    early interest in music 12
    final appearance as a singer 345, 401
    first music lessons 12
    first press notices 13
    first professional music lessons 19–20
    general education 12, 15, 18–19
    health 111–112, 115, 123, 174, 195, 198, 214, 220, 231–232, 240, 252, 266, 271, 276, 291, 293, 295, 303, 304, 306, 309, 313, 318, 321, 324, 331, 341, 344, 346–348, 360, 368, 382, 392, 398, 401
    Italian debut 130–131, 398
    juvenile debut as a singer 12–13, 354, 397
    La Scala debut 140–142
    legacy ix, 212
    London concert debut 62–63
    marriage 30, 357, 397
    'Melba', origin of the name 73
    Metropolitan Opera debut 149–150

nerves 41, 81, 95, 132, 175, 282, 293, 328, 359
organ lessons 13-14, 397
Paris Opéra debut 95-96
physical appearance 16, 28, 82, 96, 99, 115, 132, 246, 264, 312, 366
piano lessons 12, 13, 15, 19, 397
radio (first broadcast) 304-305
recordings 2, 154, 155-156, 161, 166, 201-202, 223, 224-230, 233-234, 249-250, 261, 263, 269-270, 271, 280, 288-289, 307, 329, 331, 332, 352, 359, 364, 365, 373, 379, 382, 383, 385, 386, 388, 394, 399, 400, 401, 403-403, 409-431
St Petersburg debut 118
stage debut 81-82, 397
vocal technique 19, 20, 21, 22, 26, 61, 68, 71, 72, 75, 83, 100, 108, 111, 133, 159, 161-163, 219, 227-229, 240, 250, 272, 314, 316, 330, 332, 343, 410
voice 20, 21-22, 26, 49, 68, 71, 72, 75, 83, 100, 107-108, 109, 111, 132, 136-137, 160, 161-163, 219, 227-228, 246, 250, 258, 260, 270, 272, 273, 280, 282, 294, 316, 319, 330, 332, 339, 340, 363, 369, 381, 403, 407, 410
whistling and humming 19, 355
Melba-Williamson Grand Opera Company 1911 267, 273, 274-277, 281, 316, 317, 400
Melba-Williamson Grand Opera Company 1924 316, 319, 320, 321, 328, 334, 337, 338, 393, 400
Melba-Williamson Grand Opera Company 1928 337-341, 401
Melbourne International Exhibition 1880 22
Melbourne Liedertafel 40, 359
Melbourne Symphony Orchestra 310, 335, 340
Melbourne University 167, 263, 286, 387
Melchior, Lauritz 328
Mendelssohn, Felix 420
Merli, Francesco 328, 338
Messager, André 208-209, 216, 217, 218

Metropolitan Liedertafel, Melbourne 43, 45, 359
Metropolitan Opera, New York 36, 119, 129, 136, 146, 149-153, 155, 157-160, 166, 167, 173, 174, 179, 180, 181, 183, 186, 198, 199-202, 208, 230, 236-238, 246, 247, 248, 251, 269, 271- 272, 274, 275, 294, 299, 319, 336, 342, 345, 369, 371, 376, 379, 381, 382, 383, 384, 386, 387, 398, 399, 400, 405, 414, 415, 417, 418, 420, 421, 429
Meyer, Lucas 207
Meyerbeer, Giacomo 159, 376, 421
   Dinorah 293, 359
   Les Huguenots 121, 158-159, 163, 198, 201, 257, 258, 367, 375, 376, 405, 421
   Robert le Diable 159
Miller, Kevin 393
Minghetti, Angelo 338, 341
Miranda, Beatrice 393
Miranda, Lalla 197-198, 257, 270, 277
Mitchell, Andrew (paternal uncle) 11
Mitchell, Anne (aunt) 353
Mitchell, Anne (paternal grandmother) 6, 7
Mitchell, Anne Fraser ('Annie') (sister) 11, 18, 29, 46, 47, 48, 50, 56, 57, 73, 79, 81, 85, 94, 95, 101, 102, 103, 112, 156, 167, 168, 177, 254, 264, 356-357, 360, 368, 377
Mitchell, Charles (uncle) 353
Mitchell, Charles James ('Charlie') (brother) 11, 210, 355, 381
Mitchell, David (father) 5-10, 12, 14, 15, 16, 17, 18, 22, 23, 24-25, 27-32, 40, 41, 45, 49, 50-51, 52-53, 55, 59, 64, 65, 69, 73, 85, 210, 212, 213, 225, 226, 227, 253, 264, 276, 277, 282, 283, 284, 290, 291, 353, 354, 355, 356, 360, 361, 363, 381, 385, 388, 390, 397
Mitchell, Dora Elizabeth Octavia (sister) 11, 177, 179, 180, 194, 202, 253, 347, 354, 377
Mitchell, Francis David ('Frank') (brother) 11, 264, 309-310, 355
Mitchell, Helen Porter, see Melba, Nellie

Mitchell, Isabella (mother) 9–11, 12, 15, 16, 18, 22–23, 29–30, 241, 355
Mitchell, Isabella Ann ('Belle') (sister) 11, 50, 56, 57, 73, 94, 95, 101, 102, 103, 112, 156, 194, 202, 207, 210, 211, 346, 355, 368, 397
Mitchell, John Watt (paternal uncle) 17
Mitchell, Margaret Walker (sister) 10, 356
Mitchell, Victoria Florence Maude Vere ('Vere') (sister) 11, 22–23
Mitchell, William (paternal grandfather) 6
Mitchell, William (paternal uncle) 11, 17
Mitchell, William Henry Ernest ('Ernie') (brother) 11, 112, 115, 167, 177, 308, 347, 355
Mitchell, William James (brother) 10
Monnaie, Théâtre de la (Brussels) 76–77, 79–88, 92–93, 97, 106, 123, 168, 252, 306, 326–327, 331, 333, 366–367, 397, 400, 404, 406, 408
Montague, Annis 33, 36, 358
Monte Carlo, Opéra de 106, 195, 203–206, 219–221, 303, 306, 369, 372, 380, 398, 399, 400, 405
Monte, Toti dal 321, 322, 338, 350, 393
Montemezzi, Italo
    L'Amore dei tre re 338
Moore, George 363
Moore, Gerald 390
Moore, Jack 48, 213, 360, 361
Moorhouse, James 57
Moreschi, Alessandro 224
Mornay, Comte de 134
Moyce, Marcel 279
Mozart, Wolfgang Amadeus, 345, 421
    Die Zauberflöte 367
    Don Giovanni 163, 244, 345, 406
    Idomeneo 218
    Il Ré Pastore 191, 336, 377, 421
    Le Nozze di Figaro 228, 267, 306, 325, 406, 421
Muck, Carl 191, 288
Muller, Fritz 194

Mummery, Browning 328, 332, 338, 340, 341, 393, 394, 423, 424
Muratore, Lucien 291
Muro Lomanto, Enzo de 338
Murphy, Agnes 1, 12, 15, 34, 53–55, 67, 70, 75, 82, 84, 104, 126, 128, 141, 164, 165, 191, 192, 245, 263, 271, 354, 370, 373, 376, 382, 384, 385, 387, 399
Murska, Ilma di 16–17, 49, 66
Musgrove, George 46, 47, 194, 207, 210, 211, 214
Musikverein, Vienna 193
Mylott, Eva 242, 384

N

Nagel, Regina 199
Nápravník, Eduard 118
Neilson, William ('Billy') 16, 356
Nevada, Emma 362
Neville, Lord Richard 233, 289, 345, 381, 391, 395
Nichols, Beverley 1, 53, 67, 75, 82, 84, 128, 141, 315, 324–325, 328, 329, 345, 350, 354, 370, 393, 401
Nield, James 42, 43, 47
Nightingale, Florence 390
Nikisch, Arthur 165, 195
Nilsson, Christine 61, 62, 82, 149, 216
Nordica, Lillian 89, 99, 149, 159, 168, 173, 174, 177, 180, 381, 386
Norena, Eidé 325
Normanby, Marchioness of 20
North, Charles K. 412–413, 415. 418
Northcliffe, Lord 304–305, 309
Norton, John 215, 218, 253, 254, 339, 385, 388

O

Obolensky, Alexis 319–320, 393
Offenbach, Jacques
    Les Contes d'Hoffmann 321
Ogg, Rev. Charles 30
Ogg, Margaret 30
O'Mara, Joseph 199

Opéra-Comique (Paris) 76, 112–113, 164, 282, 382, 404
Orleans, Princess François d' 344
Orléans, Prince Louis Philippe Robert, Duc d' 113–117, 119, 122–128, 132, 133, 135, 146, 194, 203, 209, 215, 298, 324, 327, 331, 344, 370, 371, 372, 398
Orlov, Nicolai 345
Oscar II, King of Sweden and Norway 147–148, 374
O'Shea, Alfred 322, 393
Otway, Lieutenant-Colonel Jocelyn 243, 244

P

Pachmann, Vladimir de 61, 302
Paderewski, Ignace 98, 366
Paglioni, Teatro (Teatro Verdi), Florence 143
Pandolfini, Francesco 187, 195
Paolantonio, Franco 322
Paris, Comte de 113, 115, 125, 126, 371
Paris Conservatoire of Music 119
Paris Opéra, 75, 76–77, 87, 93, 94–95, 96–97, 101, 103, 105, 106, 112, 116, 120, 123, 128–129, 144, 170–172, 193, 201, 259, 326, 333, 363, 365, 367, 368, 388, 398, 399
Parker, Robert 287, 288, 390
Parkina, Elizabeth 222, 232, 238, 286
Parliament House (Old), Canberra 335, 401
Parry, Hubert 56, 60
Pasta, Giuditta 364
Paterson, David (nephew) 202
Paterson, Gerald (nephew) 302, 368
Paterson, Nellie (niece) 202, 291, 292
Paterson, Tom (brother-in-law) 210, 211, 346, 368
Paterson, Tommy (nephew) 342, 344
Patti, Adelina 61, 62, 64, 75, 82, 92–93, 94, 106, 107, 128, 132, 136, 141, 149, 150, 152, 163, 164, 178, 181–182, 185, 192, 216, 278, 302, 315, 364, 367, 381, 385
Patti, Amelia 364
Paul, Grand Duchess of Russia 118
Peach Melba 156–157, 248, 398

Pearson, Charles 18
Petipa, Lucien 363
Philadelphia Grand Opera Company 280–281
Philadelphia Orchestra 219
Piccaluga, Nino 322
Pickford, Mary 295
Pike, Ernest 416, 426, 427
Pilotto, Angelo 341
Pitt, Percy 314
Plançon, Pol 95, 100, 133, 152, 157, 158, 159, 164, 165, 168, 169, 178, 180, 208, 371, 376, 383, 417
Plumpton, Alfred 45–46
   Mass in G major 408
Pluque, Mons. 363
Politeama, Teatro (Palermo) 129, 398
Ponder, Winifred 339, 395
Ponselle, Rosa 342
Potter, Beatrix 327
Power, Stella 286, 295, 302, 322, 390, 391–392, 393
Powell, Lionel 302, 304, 309, 392
Presbyterian Ladies College, Melbourne 18–20, 212, 265, 355, 356, 397
Pringle, Lempriere 178, 198, 380
Printemps, Yvonne 331
Puccini, Giacomo 143, 145, 184, 185–186, 188–189, 204, 209, 229–230, 237, 247, 301, 323–324, 378, 384, 398, 399, 402, 422–424
   Gianni Schicchi 338
   Il Tabarro 338
   La Bohème 162–163, 184, 185–186, 187, 188–189, 198, 200, 202–203, 204, 205, 208, 217, 219, 220, 221–222, 228, 230, 232, 233, 237, 241, 245, 246–248, 249–250, 252, 257, 258, 260, 261, 267, 270, 271, 273, 276, 281, 282, 288, 292, 294, 300–301, 305, 306, 311, 313–314, 317, 318, 321, 322, 323, 328, 329, 330, 339–340, 341, 343, 349, 379, 380, 384, 386, 392, 394, 395, 399, 400, 403, 405, 422–424
   La Fanciulla del West 271

Madama Butterfly 209, 232, 235, 237, 258, 267, 384, 385, 406
Manon Lescaut 185–186, 384
Tosca 186, 188, 198, 229–230, 232, 235, 237, 246, 248, 250, 267, 269, 276, 322, 385, 388, 406, 424
Turandot 294, 338

Q
Queen's Hall Orchestra 63, 178, 218, 273
Quinlan, Thomas 277

R
Radziwill, Princess Catherine 342
Raisa, Rosa 293–294
Ranalow, Frederick 263
Randegger, Alberto 56, 60, 99, 361
Ravel, Maurice 407
Ravelli, Luigi 90
Ravogli, Giulia 137–138
Rawson, Charles 35, 38, 102, 123–124, 358
Rawson, Winifred 35, 38, 102
Reading, Lord 311–312
Real, Teatro (Madrid) 94
Rees, Alice 32, 48, 358, 36
Renaud, Maurice 80, 86, 170, 205, 208, 219, 238, 244, 246, 249, 259, 272, 274, 303, 394
Rendle, Frank 234, 240, 255, 262
Reszke, Edouard de 98, 100, 101, 107, 108, 110, 116, 117, 118, 120, 121, 133, 149, 157, 159, 168, 175, 180, 237, 417
Reszke, Jean de 91, 93, 98, 100, 101, 107, 108, 109, 110, 111, 112, 113, 116, 117, 118, 120, 121, 133, 134, 144, 146, 149, 150, 152, 157, 158, 159, 162, 163, 164, 168, 169, 173–174, 175, 178, 180, 187, 198, 201, 205–206, 229, 257, 268, 274, 308, 317, 370, 376, 377, 379, 395
Rettore, Aurora 328, 423, 424
Rhodes, Cecil 207
Richard, Helene 95, 198
Richter, Hans 193
Ricordi & Co. 237, 247, 248
Rimsky-Korsakov, Nicholai 424
 Sadko 307, 424

Ritt, Eugène 87, 94, 96, 97, 103, 116, 129
Roberts, Gwladys 416, 426, 427
Robertson, Stuart 334, 343, 395
Rogan, Lt. Mackenzie 414, 427, 428
Rogers, Elva 380
Rogers, Walter B. 249, 261, 289, 411–430
Romani, Pietro 21
Ronald, Landon 165–166, 167, 185, 224, 225, 226, 261, 272, 273, 302, 325, 376, 378, 388, 411–430
Roper, Stanley 416
Rosa, Carl 62
Rossi, Arcangelo 230
Rossi, Emilio 338
Rossini, Gioachino 21, 86, 138, 425
 Il Barbiere di Siviglia 86, 138, 163, 180–181, 182–183, 185, 186, 192, 195, 198, 216–217, 257, 271, 294, 321, 405
 Semiramide 151–152, 405
 Stabat Mater 46, 425
Rothschild, Alfred de 185, 207, 299
Roy, René Le 344
Royal Albert Hall 59, 61, 185, 208, 258, 268, 272, 279, 284, 302, 304, 306, 319, 327, 330
Rubinstein, Anton 118
Rubinstein, Arthur 304
Ruffo, Titta 218, 281, 387
Rumford, Kennerley 178, 254, 309
Russ, Giannina 386
Russell, Donna 273, 282, 316, 322
Russell, Henry 166, 272–273, 281, 282, 316, 317, 322, 389, 393
Russitano, Giuseppe 375

S
Sadler's Wells Opera Company (English National Opera) 332
St James Hall 91, 114, 135–136
St Leger, Frank 287, 288, 289, 295, 322, 416, 426
St Petersburg Imperial Opera 116, 118, 119, 398
Saint-Saëns, Camille 66, 220–221, 259

449

Hélène 220–221, 222, 382, 384, 385, 399, 405
Samson et Dalila 220, 276
Saléza, Albert 208, 414, 417
Salzburg Festival 343, 345
Sammarco, Mario 235, 240, 241, 247, 260, 269–270, 274, 417, 418, 430
San Carlo, Teatro (Naples) 234, 262
Sanderson, Sybil 362
Sanna, Robert de 262, 387
Santley, Charles 61, 185, 259, 364
Santos-Dumont, Alberto 204
Sassoli, Ada 209, 219, 245, 249, 271, 288, 289, 416, 418, 427
Saville, Frances 36, 168–169, 178, 198, 358, 362, 377
Scala, Teatro alla (Milan) 140–143, 153, 157, 184, 234, 234, 271, 275, 322, 337, 338, 362, 373, 373, 398
Scalchi, Sofia 152, 159, 167
Scandiani, Angelo 275, 276, 337–338
Scharrer, Irene 343
Scheff, Fritzi 217, 222
Scherek, Benno 380
Schiavoni, Arnaldo 322
Schumann, Elisabeth 328
Scotney, Evelyn 72, 268, 362, 387
Scott, Lady John 425–426
Scott-Gatty, Alfred 426
Scotti, Antonio 198, 218, 230, 232, 246, 257, 383, 385
Séguin, Arthur Henri 80, 82, 84, 87, 100
Seidl, Anton 175
Sembrich, Marcella 149, 150, 163, 164, 186, 200, 216, 383
Semon, Dr Felix 111, 112, 177
Seppelli, Armando 188
Serafin, Tullio 259, 386
Serena, Clara 393
Shaw, George Bernard 135, 161
Sheer, Spencer 395
Sherard, Robert 95–97
Sherwin, Amy 362
Sills, Beverly 366

Simonsen, Fannie 40, 55, 383
Smith, George 24–25
Smith, Jane 25
Smith, Sir Keith 307
Smith, Leila 25, 34
Smith, Sir Ross 307
Soldene, Emily 241
Spani, Hina 338
Squire, W.H. 383, 416
Stabile, Mariano 328
Stanley, Lord 329, 391
States, Agatha 21
Sterling, Antoinette 64, 66, 362
Stevens, Horace 287
Stewart, Nellie 212, 381
Stirling, Maggie 284, 389
Stracciari, Riccardo 235, 383
Stradewitz, Fritzi 68, 69, 75
Strakosch, Karl 147
Strakosch, Maurice 75, 78, 80–81, 147, 364, 365
Stralia, Elsa 389
Strauss, Richard 343, 345, 387
Der Rosenkavalier 343, 345
Salome 246, 383, 384
Streeton, Arthur 285
Sullivan, Arthur 29, 56, 59, 60, 361, 362, 369
Summers, Joseph 14, 41
Sutherland, Duchess of 185
Sutherland, Joan 1, 337, 366, 370, 375, 376, 385, 386, 395
Sydney Liedertafel 51
Sydney Philharmonic Society 51
Szulc, Josef 326, 332, 426

T

Tait, J. & N. 207
Tait, John 215
Tait, Nevin 316, 317, 323, 337
Tallis, Sir George 337
Tamagno, Francesco 157–158, 162, 163, 164, 177, 195, 224, 257, 308, 375
Tanara, Fernando 248

Te Kanawa, Kiri 384
Tempest, Marie 65
Tennyson, Baron 212
Ternina, Milka 186, 198, 378
Terry, Ellen 284
Tertis, Lionel 306, 327, 330, 344
Tetrazzini, Luisa 179, 255-256, 257,
 258, 259, 260, 261, 270, 271, 276, 279,
 302-303, 315, 324, 385, 386, 387, 399
Teyte, Maggie 395
Thill, Georges 326
Thomas, Ambroise 66, 74, 76, 86-87,
 106, 171, 364, 426
   Hamlet 74, 77, 86-87, 93, 94-95, 96,
   97, 98, 103, 106, 112, 131, 147, 150-151,
   152, 165, 170-171, 172, 227, 250, 263,
   364, 366, 367, 369-370, 398, 404, 426
   Mignon 74, 155, 402
Thomas, Arthur Goring 109, 135
   Esmeralda 109, 135, 404
Thornton, Edna 269-270, 277, 430
Tinel, Edgar
   Saint Francis 93, 408
Tolstoy, Leo 118
Tordeus, Jeanne 86
Toronto, Florence 182, 378
Toscanini, Arturo 179, 337, 338
Tosti, Paolo 29, 39, 62, 136-137, 138, 154,
 156, 180, 229, 248, 249, 343, 357, 370,
 406, 427
Trentini, Emma 247, 260
Treweek, Elsie 393
Trowell, Arnold 388
Turner, Charles 33, 36, 358

U
Ulster Hall, Belfast 203
Uttar Pradesh, Maharajah of 312

V
Vaccai, Nicola
   Giulietta e Romeo 139
Valmency, Cyril de 47, 48, 51
Verbrugghen, Henri 308, 310, 366

Verdi, Giuseppe 21, 129-130, 153-154, 191,
 205, 373, 374, 398, 402, 403, 428-430
   Aida 136-138, 180, 181, 277, 281, 314,
   369, 373, 403, 404
   Don Carlos 98
   Falstaff 120, 141
   Il Trovatore 358, 406
   La Traviata 41, 47, 54, 60, 61, 62, 68,
   77, 84-85, 87, 92, 110, 129, 163, 174,
   177, 180, 181, 182, 185, 191, 193, 195,
   200, 201, 208, 213, 214, 221, 227, 228,
   232, 240, 245, 246, 250, 252, 255, 257,
   258, 261, 267, 269-270, 271, 272, 276,
   288, 294, 332, 359, 366, 367, 383, 384,
   403, 404, 428-429
   Otello 120, 130, 136, 138, 141, 154, 157,
   160, 163-164, 195, 241, 257, 259, 261,
   267, 270, 276, 277, 281-282, 321, 322,
   328, 339, 340-341, 385, 398, 403,
   429-430
   Rigoletto 41, 75, 77, 78, 79, 80-82, 84,
   86, 87, 89, 91, 92, 98, 99-100, 101,
   110, 111, 120, 123, 131, 136, 141, 151,
   152, 153, 163, 180, 183, 191, 192, 198,
   205, 208, 214, 216-217, 218, 220, 221,
   227, 240, 246, 248, 252, 256, 257, 259,
   261, 267, 269-270, 271, 276, 279,
   280-281, 321, 322, 359, 366, 367, 368,
   374, 384, 385, 387, 397, 399, 404, 430
   Un Ballo in Maschera 91, 221, 367
Verne, Adèle 302
Veron, Paul 98
Vestey, Pamela, see Armstrong, Pamela
Vestey, Capt. William Howarth 350
Victor Talking Machine Company
 249-250, 261, 271, 280, 288-289,
 409-431
Victoria, Empress of Germany 110
Victoria, Princess 319
Victoria, Queen 59, 79, 109-111, 114, 121,
 133, 177, 202, 355, 370, 372
Vienna Philharmonic Orchestra 343
Vignas, Francesco 144, 149, 152, 164
Vogt, Otto 14, 16, 41
Voluntas-Ranzenberg, Marie 274

W

Wagner, Richard 108, 165, 173–177, 187, 220, 249, 276, 345, 362, 370, 374, 383, 390, 393, 402, 430
   Der Fliegende Holländer 249, 267, 385
   Die Meistersinger von Nürnberg 167, 173, 376, 406
   Lohengrin 108–109, 117, 118, 120, 121, 131, 136, 144, 147, 148, 149, 152, 157, 163, 173, 267, 269, 275, 338, 370, 404, 430
   Parsifal 248–249, 345, 370
   Ring Cycle 133, 209, 345, 370, 376
   Siegfried 174, 175–176, 249, 376, 377, 398, 405
   Tannhäuser 108, 152, 163, 165, 173, 221, 267, 338, 374, 403, 405
   Tristan und Isolde 173, 174, 277, 345, 376, 377, 402
Wagner, Siegfried 345
Wagner, Winifred 345
'Wallabies' rugby league team 386
Wallace, Vincent
   Maritana 358, 359
Walling, Edna 334
Wauters, Emile 85, 366
Weber, Carl Maria von
   Mass in G, Opus 76 46, 408
Wechsberg, Joseph 128
Wedekind, Erika 216
Wedel-Jarlsberg, Baron de 305
Weingartner, Felix 281
Wetzger, Paul 431
White, Maud Valerie 431
Wiedermann-Pinschof, Elise 56, 60, 66, 68, 194, 387, 389
Wigmore Hall (Bechstein Hall) 242–243, 384
Wilhelm II, Kaiser of Germany 110, 121, 192
Wilhelmina, Queen of Holland 191
Williams, Harold 393
Williamson, James Cassius 207, 375
Williamson, J.C. (firm) 267, 274, 275, 323, 337, 393, 394, 400, 401
Wilson, Strella 286, 390
Wood, Henry 63, 144, 218, 273
World War I 282, 283–284, 287, 296, 297, 299, 315, 329, 400, 403
Worth, House of 109, 113, 150, 152, 369

Y

Yorke, Bernard 307, 311

Z

Zelman, Alberto 310
Zenatello, Giovanni 235, 241, 257, 260, 386
Zimbalist, Efram 335–336

Wakefield Press is an independent publishing and
distribution company based in Adelaide, South Australia.
We love good stories and publish beautiful books.
To see our full range of books, please visit our website at
www.wakefieldpress.com.au
where all titles are available for purchase.
To keep up with our latest releases, news and events,
subscribe to our monthly newsletter.

Find us!

Facebook: www.facebook.com/wakefield.press
Twitter: www.twitter.com/wakefieldpress
Instagram: www.instagram.com/wakefieldpress

www.ingramcontent.com/pod-product-compliance
Lightning Source LLC
Chambersburg PA
CBHW040744020526
44114CB00048B/2899